Contents

Part Two: Monarchy Restored and Restrained: Britain, 1649–1702

Introduction

This book on the history of Britain from 1603 to 1702 is written to support AQA's A-level History Breadth Study specification on seventeenth-century Stuart Britain. The seventeenth century is sometimes called England's 'century of troubles', a turbulent century of civil war and political revolution. For some historians this was the most controversial century in English history, and the most fascinating. It includes the English Civil War, the Protectorate of Oliver Cromwell, the Restoration of Charles II and the Glorious Revolution of 1688. During this century England changed from being a relatively weak, peripheral kingdom to a major European power. The relationship between the Crown and Parliament was transformed within four generations, setting England on the road to constitutional monarchy and playing a major part in the making of the United Kingdom.

James I

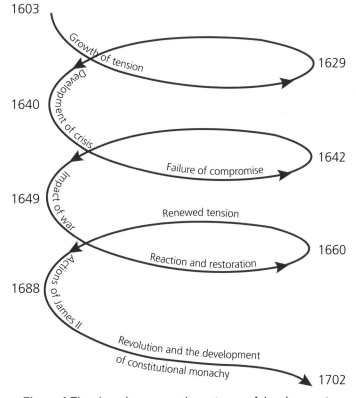

▲ **Figure 1** The changing monarchy – stages of development.

1603

Growth of tension

1629

1640

Development of crisis

Failure of compromise

1642

1649

Impact of war

Renewed tension

Reaction and restoration

1660

1688

Actions of James II

Revolution and the development of constitutional monachy

1702

Queen Anne

The key content

'Stuart Britain and the Crisis of Monarchy, 1603–1702' is one of the breadth studies offered by AQA, and as such covers over 100 years. The content is divided into two parts.

Part 1 (1603–49) is studied by those taking the AS examination.

Parts 1 and 2 (1649–1702) are studied by those taking the full A-level examination.

Each part is subdivided into two sections.

PART 1: ABSOLUTISM CHALLENGED: BRITAIN, 1603–49

This covers developments in Britain from the accession of James I to the execution of his son, Charles I, following the Civil War. It includes the relationship between James I and his parliaments to 1624, and the difficult first years of Charles I's reign until 1629, when he decided to rule without Parliament. After 11 years of Personal Rule, the three kingdoms of England, Scotland and Ireland all fell into civil war, which led to the rise of the New Model Army as a political force in England, the Second Civil War, and the trial and death of the King.

Monarchs and Parliaments, 1603–29

This period focuses on the relationship between the King and Parliament, in which Parliament was asserting its powers by insisting on the redress of grievances before supplying subsidies for the Crown, which was defending its royal prerogative. Growing religious tensions were evident, particularly in the 1620s, a decade during which England went to war with Spain and France, and the Crown was accused of ruling in an arbitrary way. By 1629, the King was ready to rule without Parliament.

Revolution, 1629–49

This period witnessed the most dramatic events of the seventeenth century as the King's Personal Rule was brought down by opposition in England and rebellions in Scotland and Ireland. The nation disintegrated into a civil war between King and Parliament, a conflict which Parliament eventually won, only to find that the search for settlement proved impossible. The breakdown of central government encouraged the growth of radical religious and political ideas which challenged the old assumptions about government and belief. Finally, the relationship between Parliament and the New Model Army broke down over negotiations with the King, leading to a military coup d'etat and the trial of the King on a charge of high treason. The period ended with the execution of King Charles I in front of his own palace of Whitehall.

AQA A-level History

Stuart Britain
and the Crisis of Monarchy, 1603–1702

Angela Anderson

Dale Scarboro

Approval message from AQA

This textbook has been approved by AQA for use with our qualification. This means that we have checked that it broadly covers the specification and we are satisfied with the overall quality. Full details or our approval process can be found on our website.

We approve textbooks because we know how important it is for teachers and students to have the right resources to support their teaching and learning. However, the publisher is ultimately responsible for the editorial control and quality of this book.

Please note that when teaching the **AQA A-level History** course, you must refer to AQA's specification as your definitive source of information. While this book has been written to match the specification, it does not provide complete coverage of every aspect of the course. Please also note that the practice questions in this title are written to reflect the question styles of the AS and A-level papers. They are designed to help students become familiar with question types and practise exam skills. AQA has published specimen papers and mark schemes online and these should be consulted for definitive examples.

A wide range of other useful resources can be found on the relevant subject pages of our website: www.aqa.org.uk.

HODDER
EDUCATION
AN HACHETTE UK COMPANY

for permission to reproduce copyright material:

Photo credit [...] ollection/TopFoto; **p.vi** © Liszt Collection/TopFoto; **p.vii** © Universal Hist [...] Ann Ronan Pictures/Print Collector/Getty Images; **p.14** © Stock Montage/Ge [...] **p.27** © DEA/G. Dagli Orti/De Agostini Picture Library/ Getty Images; **p.36** [...] etty images); **p.48** © FineArt / Alamy; **p.52** Archbishop William Laud (1573–1 [...] Sir Anthony van (1599–1641) / Fitzwilliam Museum, University of Ca [...] © Mary Evans Picture Library / Alamy; **p.61** © FineArt / Alamy; **p.66** © Univ [...] **p.74** © Mary Evans Picture Library / Alamy; **p.76** © Mary Evans Picture Libra [...] ty Images; **p.108** An Eyewitness Representation of the Execution of King Charles I i [...] ohn (d. *c.*1653) / Private Collection / Bridgeman Images; **p.114** © Mary E [...] **p.119** Sir Thomas Fairfax (1612–71) and the General Council of the Parliamentaria [...] sh School, (17th century) / British Library, London, UK / © British Library Board. All Rights Reserved / Bridge [...] mages; **p.126** An Eyewitness Representation of the Execution of King Charles I in 1649 (oil on canvas), W [...] John (d. *c.*1653) / Private Collection / Bridgeman Images; **p.138** © Print Collector / HIP / TopFoto; **p.142** © Mary Evans Picture Library; **p.147** © Universal History Archive / UIG via Getty Images; **p.151** © DEA Picture Library via Getty Images; **p.159** © Print Collector / HIP / TopFoto; **p.165** © The Granger Collection / TopFoto; **p.171** Whitehall Palace and St. James's Park, Danckerts, Hendrick (*c.*1625–80) (attr. to) / Private Collection / © Arthur Ackermann Ltd., London / Bridgeman Images; **p.178** © Universal History Archive / UIG via Getty images; **p.182** Whitehall Palace and St. James's Park, Danckerts, Hendrick (*c.*1625-80) (attr. to) / Private Collection / © Arthur Ackermann Ltd., London / Bridgeman Images; **p.188** © The Print Collector/Corbis; **p.195** © The Print Collector / Alamy; **p.203** © Lebrecht/Lebrecht Music & Arts / Corbis; **p.206** The Duke of Monmouth Pleading for his Life before James II (oil on canvas), Pettie, John (1839–93) / © South African National Gallery, Cape Town, South Africa / Bridgeman Images; **p.212** © The Print Collector / Alamy; **p.218** © Elizabeth Leyden / Alamy; **p.222** © Bryant Coins; **p.224** © Bryant Coins.

Acknowledgements: **p.36**: Conrad Russell: from *The Causes of the English Civil War* (Clarendon Press, 1990); **pp.55–56,107,131,160,183,191,194,221**: Barry Coward: from *The Stuart Age: England 1603–1714* (Longman, 2003); **pp.56,91**: Edward Hyde, Earl of Clarendon: as quoted in *History of the Rebellion and Civil Wars in England Begun in the Year 1641*, ed. G. Huehns (Oxford Paperbacks, 1979); **pp.208,221**: Steve Pincus: from *1688: The First Modern Revolution* (Yale University Press, 2009), reproduced by permission of the publisher; **pp.208,211**: Edward Vallance: from *The Glorious Revolution 1688 - Britain's Fight for Liberty* (Little, Brown Book Group, 2006), reproduced by permission of the publisher.

Every effort has been made to trace or contact all copyright holders, but if any have been inadvertently overlooked the Publishers will be pleased to make the necessary arrangements at the first opportunity.

AQA material is reproduced by permission of AQA.

Every effort has been made to trace all copyright holders, but if any have been inadvertently overlooked the Publishers will be pleased to make the necessary arrangements at the first opportunity.

Although every effort has been made to ensure that website addresses are correct at time of going to press, Hodder Education cannot be held responsible for the content of any website mentioned in this book. It is sometimes possible to find a relocated web page by typing in the address of the home page for a website in the URL window of your browser.

Dale Scarboro's contribution to this work is dedicated to his friend and colleague, Nick Martin.

Hachette UK's policy is to use papers that are natural, renewable and recyclable products and made from wood grown in sustainable forests. The logging and manufacturing processes are expected to conform to the environmental regulations of the country of origin.

Orders: please contact Bookpoint Ltd, 130 Milton Park, Abingdon, Oxon OX14 4SB.
Telephone: +44 (0)1235 827720. Fax: +44(01235) 400454. Lines are open 9.00a.m.–5.00p.m.,
Monday to Saturday, with a 24-hour message answering service. Visit our website at: www.hoddereducation.co.uk

© Angela Anderson and Dale Scarboro

First published in 2015 by

Hodder Education

An Hachette UK Company

Carmelite House

50 Victoria Embankment

London EC4Y 0DZ

Impression number   10 9 8 7 6 5 4 3 2 1

Year   2019 2018 2017 2016 2015

Cover photo: © V & A Images/Alamy

Illustrations by Integra Software Services

Typeset in 10.5/12.5pt ITC Berkeley Oldstyle Std Book by Integra Software Services Pvt. Ltd., Pondicherry, India

Printed in Italy

A catalogue record for this title is available from the British Library

ISBN 978 1 471 837722

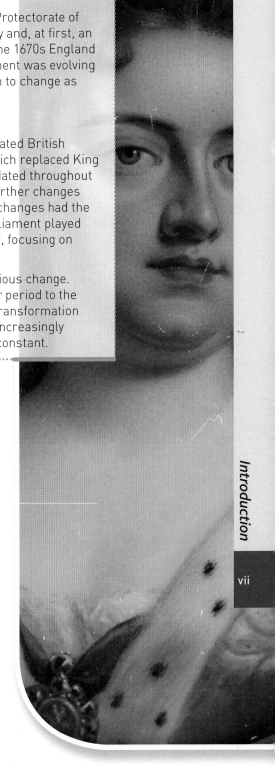

PART 2: MONARCHY RESTORED AND RESTRAINED: BRITAIN, 1649–1702

Part 2 covers further profound changes in British politics and society, including the Interregnum period, when the monarchy and the House of Lords were abolished and England was governed as a republic. The failure of the republican experiment led to the restoration of the monarchy, but in the following decades Britain moved through a series of further crises towards another revolution and an invasion of England by a Dutch army in support of William of Orange. By the end of the century Parliament had placed limits on royal power which, ironically, unleashed the full economic and military possibilities of the British state.

From Republic to Restored and Limited Monarchy, 1649–78

Further important events occurred in this period, dominated at first by the Protectorate of Oliver Cromwell. After his death the Restoration saw the return of monarchy and, at first, an apparent period of stability. This turned out to be illusory, however, and by the 1670s England was in more or less perpetual crisis, even though the machinery of government was evolving to create a more sophisticated state. During this period the monarchy began to change as Parliament became a much more powerful source of wealth and power.

The Establishment of Constitutional Monarchy, 1678–1702

The final section of the book charts the prolonged political crisis that dominated British politics in the late 1670s and 1680s, leading to another revolution in 1688 which replaced King James II with William III and his wife Mary. Once the revolution was consolidated throughout the British Isles, Britain embarked on a major war with France that led to further changes in British government, including a revolution in government finance. These changes had the effect of converting Britain into a constitutional monarchy, one in which Parliament played a permanent role. The book ends with a review of the state of Britain in 1702, focusing on religion, the constitution and changes in the economy.

The seventeenth century is therefore a period of profound political and religious change. It transformed Britain from the religious and political instability of the Tudor period to the stability, prosperity and progress of the eighteenth century. In making this transformation Britain became a more secular society, one in which religious beliefs were increasingly regarded as a private matter, though opposition to Catholicism remained a constant.

Key concepts

But the study of history does not just include narrative – interesting though the stories often are! There are four concepts which steer our thinking and our understanding of the past. These are important in your study and questions may well involve assessing these concepts.

- Change and continuity: To what extent did things change? What are the similarities and differences over time?
- Cause and consequence: What were the factors that led to change? How did the changes affect individuals and groups within society, as well as the country as a whole?

In relation to these concepts, the essay questions you will face will be asking you to assess, for example:

- the extent to which you agree with a statement
- the validity of a statement
- the importance of a particular factor relating to a key question
- how much something changed or to what extent something was achieved.

In addition, you will be learning about different interpretations: how and why events have been portrayed in different ways over time by historians. In the first section of both the AS and A-level examination you will be tested on this skill with a selection of contrasting extracts.

The key questions

The specification lists six key questions around which the study is based. These are wide-ranging in scope and can be considered across the whole period. They reflect the broadly-based questions (covering twenty years or more) that will be set in the examination.

1 How far did the monarchy change?

You will learn about change and continuity in respect of the monarchy over time and whether the abolition of the monarchy between 1649 and 1660 permanently affected its power and prestige. The King of England had an enormous amount of power in 1603 compared to parliament, but to what extent was that still true in 1702?

2 To what extent and why was power more widely shared during this period?

You will discover how and why the monarchy was forced to share more power with Parliament in the course of the century. In 1603 Parliament was called at the King's convenience, but during the civil wars of the mid-century Parliament became a regular aspect of political life. The 'political nation' also expanded as more and more people, whether through their elected representatives or through their own participation in local and national government, became involved in political decisions.

3 Why and with what results were there disputes over religion?

The English Civil War has been called the last of the Wars of Religion. You will discover why religion was such a contentious political issue and how religious radicalism influenced the course of events in the 1640s and 1650s. You will also investigate how the idea of religious toleration was explored by Cromwell and how, by the end of the century, a degree of toleration had been extended to various Protestant churches and denominations.

4 How effective was opposition?

Opposition to what, or to whom? Opposition to the King? Opposition to Cromwell? Opposition to the Church of England? Opposition took various forms during the seventeenth century and although it was not always effective, there is no doubt that, in the course of the seventeenth century, authorities of all types learned that they had to accept challenges to their authority and, to a certain extent, develop more skilful techniques of political management.

5 How important were ideas and ideology?

As you might expect from a century associated with revolution, religion and rebellion, the seventeenth century was rich in ideological thinking and debate. You will learn not only about standard concepts like the 'divine right of kings', but also the politically progressive views of groups like the Levellers, who in 1647 debated concepts of equality and the sovereignty of the people. Two of our greatest political philosophers – Thomas Hobbes and John Locke – lived and wrote in this period, developing theories of government that were almost diametrically opposed, yet based on similar ideas.

6 How important was the role of key individuals and groups and how were they affected by developments?

You will discover that key events and developments were profoundly influenced by key individuals in this period. Oliver Cromwell, for example, with no previous military experience, quickly rose through the ranks to become Lieutenant-General of Horse in the New Model Army. His impact on the key events of the 1640s and 1650s was immeasurable. James I has been described as 'the wisest fool in Christendom'. The personality of King Charles I has mesmerised historians for generations. Charles II was a notorious rake. Everywhere you look in the seventeenth century, you will find individuals like the radical 'Honest John Lilburne', the political philosopher Thomas Hobbes or skilful politicians like Pym, Danby and Shaftesbury.

How this book is designed to help your studies

1 With the facts, concepts and key questions of the specification

At the beginning of each chapter the book flags up the elements of the specification and the key questions that are being covered.

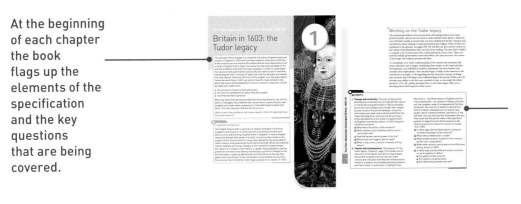

Activities are provided, helping you to create notes, and enabling you to consider the main areas of interpretation throughout the period.

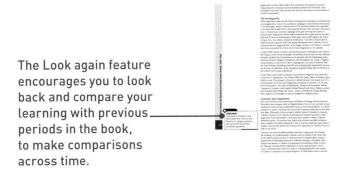

The Look again feature encourages you to look back and compare your learning with previous periods in the book, to make comparisons across time.

Key words and phrases are defined at the first relevant point in the text, and there is a full glossary on pages 251–52.

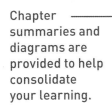

Chapter summaries and diagrams are provided to help consolidate your learning.

Key dates are listed throughout.

2 With the skills needed to answer examination questions

The book provides guidance in answering different types of examination questions in the form of a separate 'skills' section at the end of each chapter.

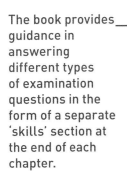

Interpretation skills are developed through the analysis of extended pieces of writing by leading academics.

3 With the skills in reading, understanding and making notes from the book.

Note-making

Good note-making is really important. Your notes are an essential revision resource. What is more, the process of making notes will help you understand and remember what you are reading.

How to make notes

Most note-making styles reflect the distinction between key points and supporting evidence. Below is advice on a variety of different note-making styles. Throughout each section in the book are note-making activities for you to carry out.

The important thing is that you understand your notes. Therefore, you don't have to write everything down, and you don't have to write in full sentences.

While making notes you can use abbreviations:

Full text	Abbreviation
Seventeenth Century	C17
King	Kg
Development	Devt
Catholic	Cath
Protestant	Prot
New Model Army	NMA

You can develop your own abbreviations. Usually it is only yourself who has to understand them!

You can use arrows instead of words:

Full text	Arrow
Increased	↑
Decreased	↓

You can use mathematical notation:

Equals	=
plus, and	+
Because	∵
Therefore	∴

Note-making styles

There are a large number of note-making styles. However you prefer to make notes – by hand or on a laptop or tablet – the principles are the same. You can find examples of three popular styles below. All of them have their strengths and it is a good idea to try them all and work out which style suits you.

Style 1: Bullet points

Bullet points can be a useful method of making notes because:

- they encourage you to write in note form, rather than in full sentences
- they help you to organise your ideas in a systematic fashion
- they are easy to skim read later
- you can show relative importance visually by indenting less important, or supporting points.

Usually it is easier to write notes with bullet points after you have skim-read a section or a paragraph first in order to get the overall sense in your head.

Style 2: The 1–2 method

The 1–2 method is a variation on bullet points. The method is based on dividing your page into two columns: the first for the main point, the second for supporting detail. This allows you to see the structure of the information clearly. To do this, you can create a chart to complete, as follows:

Main point	Supporting detail

Style 3: Spider diagrams

Spider diagrams or mind maps can be a useful method of making notes because:

- they will help you to categorise factors: each of the main branches coming from the centre should be a new category
- they can help you see what is most important: often the most important factors will be close to the centre of the diagram
- they can help you see connections between different aspects of what you are studying. It is useful to draw lines between different parts of your diagram to show links
- they can also help you with essay planning: you can use them to quickly get down the main points and develop a clear structure in response to an essay question.
- you can set out the spider diagram in any wish that seems appropriate for the task, but usually, as with a spider's web, you would start with the title or central issue in the middle with connecting lines radiating outwards.

Britain in 1603: the Tudor legacy

The purpose of this chapter is to establish the nature of government and society in England in 1603 and how they related to other parts of Britain. In the process you will explore the responsibilities and expectations that a King of England had to meet, the resources that were available to him and the problems with which he had to grapple. In order to understand the nature of both government and society you need to look at how they had developed over a century of Tudor rule, and the attitudes and beliefs that they shared. Because the focus of the chapter is on the years before James became King in 1603, you will not need to make detailed notes about the events and developments that are covered. Instead you should be seeking to understand:

- the structure of government and society
- the theories and beliefs on which they were based
- how they worked in practice.

When you have familiarised yourself with these key features, you will be able to investigate the problems that James faced in governing his new kingdom and make some assessment of how effectively he dealt with them. The main question that we will focus on is:

How far were the problems that James faced in 1603–25 inherited from his predecessors?

CHAPTER OVERVIEW

The chapter begins with a summary of relations between the British kingdoms and moves on to three sections concerned primarily with the structure and working of government in England. In theory English monarchs derived their power from God. In practice they relied on the support of the Church and of a ruling class defined by the ownership of land to ensure that government functioned effectively. While the sixteenth century saw few structural changes in the machinery of government, the impact of a religious reformation, a rapidly rising population and the growth of commerce and literacy had brought significant changes to the political nation, requiring adjustments and alterations in the way that government functioned. It was the benefits and problems arising from this process that formed the Tudor legacy passed on to James I in 1603.

1 The British Kingdoms

The accession of James I as King of England in 1603 brought all the regions of the British Isles under a single ruler, but not as a single, united kingdom. There were, and remained, significant political, religious and cultural differences within the British Isles. This would cause problems to any monarch who sought to establish power across the different regions, unless he was willing and able to permit his subjects in some areas to use laws and practices that he denied to others.

England, Wales and Ireland

What did James I inherit?

Wales had been conquered by the English before 1500 and was incorporated into the English kingdom by three Acts of Union passed during the reign of Henry VIII. These had introduced English law and the system of county government based on Justices of the Peace, so that Wales was governed as an integral part of England. Henry had also extended the traditional claim of English kings to be 'Lord of Ireland' into a claim of kingship. By assuming the title of King he not only extended his power in temporal (non-religious) matters, but also claimed to be Head of the Church in Ireland, as confirmed by the Irish Parliament in 1540.

While these claims proved difficult to enforce in practice, strategic needs made them essential. The Protestant Reformation had divided Europe, and after Henry rejected the authority of the Pope and seized control of the English Church in 1534, there was a serious danger of Catholic reprisal. Since the majority of native Irishmen and Old English settlers remained Catholic, Ireland offered a potentially convenient base for an invasion, and it was therefore necessary to assert English control there. English influence, which had been limited to the area around Dublin known as the Pale, gradually increased through the sixteenth century. Irish chieftains were persuaded to accept English titles of nobility. Successive rebellions provoked by the arrogance of some English administrators provided the excuse for extending English military control. In the 1590s a major rebellion led by Hugh O'Neill, Earl of Tyrone, was defeated by Elizabeth's generals, and after a period of uneasy peace, the Earls of Tyrone and Tyrconnel, the last great chieftains of Ulster, fled to Spain in 1605, leaving the English in control of the whole island. However, Ireland remained a separate kingdom, with its own parliament under the control of an English governor.

Anglo-Scottish relations

What difficulties did James face in reconciling his different kingdoms?

There had been similar problems between England and Scotland ever since the failure of English attempts to conquer Scotland in the thirteenth and fourteenth centuries. By securing a marriage between his daughter Margaret and James IV of Scotland in 1502, Henry VII had hoped to bring the two kingdoms together, but the more aggressive policies of Henry VIII had ensured that traditional hostilities lingered, and had encouraged the Scots to maintain an alliance with France. However, a Protestant Reformation in Scotland led by John Knox in 1560 had benefited from English support and therefore to some improvement in relations between London and Edinburgh. Knox was a follower of John

Calvin (see page 14) who had established a Reformed Church in Geneva that gave significant powers to individual ministers, and the Kirk (Church) that he founded was organised in a similar way. By 1603 this clerical independence was a strong feature of the Scottish Kirk, although Catholic influence lingered in the west and parts of the highlands. Both factors would pose problems for a monarch who sought to create religious uniformity.

The accession of James to the throne of England in 1603 brought an end to hostilities between the English and Scottish kingdoms, but left the matter of the relationship between the English and Scottish peoples in doubt. While James and his heirs had a natural desire to create greater uniformity of government and perhaps even to unite the two kingdoms, there were deep-seated cultural differences both within Scotland itself and between the Scots and English. Like Ireland, Scotland had its own parliament as well as a Council of State, and the Scottish Kirk differed significantly from the Church of England. There was also a bitter legacy of hostility and warfare. The English feared an invasion of Scots seeking wealth and opportunity, while the Scots feared the loss of independence and resented English assumptions of superiority. In these circumstances, the problem of ruling multiple kingdoms and of regulating relationships between them became one of the most significant issues facing the Stuart monarchy. In the early years of James's reign there existed a level of hostility between a King with Scottish friends and the English ruling elite who regarded the pickings of power as their own.

2 The English monarchy in 1603

The monarchy that James inherited in 1603 was the product of long-term developments dating back to the Norman Conquest, but many of its most significant features had been shaped or reshaped by the events of the sixteenth century, and above all, by two very separate developments. The first was a steady rise in population dating from around 1500 and reaching a peak in the mid-seventeenth century before gradually levelling off. The second was the emergence of religious divisions across Europe, which enabled Henry VIII to seize control of the Church in England in the early 1530s. Although separate, the impact of these changes gradually intertwined to create significant developments in English government and society, shaping both the responsibilities that James inherited and the means with which he had to manage them. If the seventeenth century was a period of crisis and change in the government of Britain, the causes and outcomes of the crisis were both rooted in the Tudor legacy of social and economic development and religious conflict.

The structure of government

What were the main features of the English system of government?

In broad terms, the structure of English government in 1603 would have been recognisable to the first of the Tudor kings, Henry VII – government by a monarch with the help of a Council drawn from the nobility and Church, and a parliament of two houses drawn from the nobility, gentry and clergy across the kingdom. Parliaments were not a permanent part of government, but assembled as and when the monarch deemed it necessary. The legal system rested on the Common Law, a mixture of custom and precedent backed by Statute Law, which was made by the King-in-Parliament and interpreted by judges appointed by the King. The central courts of the Exchequer, King's Bench and

King-in-Parliament – The term 'King-in-Parliament' needs to be fully understood to avoid confusion. It does not mean the same as King *and* Parliament, which implies two separate powerful institutions. King-in-Parliament refers to government by the King, but implies that some of his functions, in particular the making of law, are carried out in Parliament rather than by the King alone. Through Parliament, the King could make statute law, the highest form of law: a statute (Act of Parliament) that had been agreed by both houses and signed by the King took precedence over any earlier law or custom, and could only be changed by another statute.

Common Pleas were based in London, but their authority at local levels was in the hands of justices of the peace (JPs). These were backed by the County Assizes, where judges sent out on circuit dealt with the more serious cases referred to them by the local JPs. At every level these officials were appointed by the king and supervised by his council, while there were also a number of prerogative courts which represented direct royal authority and were manned by councillors of the king's choice.

Theoretically, therefore, the king, appointed and approved by God, was the source of all power and authority, but in practice he needed to maintain the support of a majority of the nobility and clergy in order to govern effectively. This was achieved through a mixture of loyalty and self-interest known as **patronage**, by which a powerful leader granted wealth, office and status to chosen inferiors and received their loyalty and support in return. Through this relationship the king secured the loyalty of the greater nobility, and they, in turn, used their royal connections to advance the careers of friends and family both at Court and in the regions where they wielded influence. Its impact was therefore felt across the country as a whole, but its centre lay in the royal Court and its ultimate source was the monarch. For Henry VII, as for James I, the skilful manipulation of patronage was essential for the security of the monarch and the peace of the kingdom.

> **Patronage** – A system of influence in which a patron, usually rich and/or powerful, uses their position to help individuals in an inferior position in return for their respect or support.

The role of the nobility

What part did the greater nobility play in making government effective?

Nevertheless, a century of Tudor rule had brought a number of significant changes by 1603, primarily aimed at extending royal authority and ensuring its acceptance throughout the kingdom. Some developments, such as restrictions on **retaining** and the creation of the prerogative councils for Wales and the North, were deliberately aimed at reducing the power of the nobility in the regions and depriving them of the means of rebellion. While the greater nobility, who wielded a powerful influence in the regions through their possession of land and military resources, expected positions at Court and a seat on the council, both their loyalty and their skills were variable. To increase royal authority and ensure the quality of government, the Tudors sought to advance talented individuals of humbler origins on whom they could rely in both areas, rewarding them with appropriate grants of land and titles to maintain their new position. The introduction of new blood with a direct dependency on the Crown helped to dilute local loyalties and enhance royal control, but it also encouraged the emergence of an inner circle of influence at Court where loyalty and professionalism could be rewarded. Over time this inner circle developed into the Privy Council, a group of advisers and office-holders, chosen and trusted by the monarch, who met regularly to help the monarch make decisions and oversee the working of government. The benefits of this development were demonstrated when Tudor government and control survived through fifty years of rule by a child and two women.

> **Retaining** – The practice, common among the medieval nobility, of keeping servants and supporters who were trained in military skills. In effect this created a private army which could be used to keep the peace or to overawe rivals and even rebel against the Crown.

Combined with the increased use of the prerogative courts, an enhanced role for JPs and a system of regional Lieutenancies to manage local defence against invasion, the period of Tudor government saw a significant reduction in the power of the regional nobility and a growing link between their status and their service to the Crown. This was felt throughout the political nation, as the growth of royal power also entailed an increasing number of administrative posts, encouraging greater awareness of the significance of written law and the need for literacy. When they forgot this fact of life, as the northern Earls did in 1536 and 1568, they learned a bitter lesson on the consequences of rebellion that both demonstrated and enhanced royal power. The failure of the Pilgrimage of Grace in 1536 allowed royal nominees to be placed in important positions, and when the Earls rebelled against Elizabeth in 1568 they were unable to raise a credible army. The result was that they were driven into exile and their ally, the Duke of Norfolk, was executed for treason. One unforeseen consequence, however, was that as the power of the nobility declined in the regions and at Court, it found a new channel in the growing frequency and impact of parliaments, where attempts to influence royal policy could be organised and executed in an entirely legal way.

The role of parliaments

How had the role and functions of parliaments developed?

As with other parts of government, the sixteenth century saw little structural change in the functions of parliaments. They existed to enable the King to make new laws that would override existing arrangements and to sanction extra taxation when the monarch was unable to provide for all the functions of government from his own resources. However, the power and importance of parliaments, and especially of the House of Commons, increased significantly across the century, for a number of reasons arising from the social, economic and religious changes explained in more detail below. Three key features need to be explored:

● The rise in population encouraged the growth of trade and commerce, but it also brought rising prices and placed new burdens on the resources of the Crown. The result was a greater need for parliamentary taxation.
● The religious Reformation of the 1530s was enacted in and through a parliament, involving parliamentary influence in key areas of government such as the Church, foreign relations and the succession to the throne. This gave the changes greater legal and moral authority, but it meant that future amendments would also need the approval of a parliament.
● The combined impact of these events and the expanding machinery of government was to give the political nation as a whole more experience and awareness of law and government, and to influence its attitudes and expectations. The main channel for expressing this was the meeting of the political nation with the monarch and his advisers in Parliament.

Boroughs – Towns that had been granted a royal charter giving them some particular rights and privileges, for example, the right to hold a market. In some cases they also had the right to send two MPs to parliaments. The number of these increased significantly in the later sixteenth century.

Yeomen – Independent farmers who usually owned at least some of the land they farmed and were able to achieve a reasonable level of prosperity. They were distinguished from the minor gentry by the fact that they worked their land themselves rather than renting it out.

Using the information on this page and Figure 1 on page 7, in the context of your knowledge of the system of government, explain:

1 Whose help and support the King needed to ensure that government was carried out effectively.

2 How the King could obtain and maintain that support.

The political nation

Political nation is a term used to describe the part of any nation (the people living within a particular state) that is able to exercise political power. In a modern democracy the political nation is all of the citizens old enough to vote. In Tudor and Stuart England this was not the case. Political power and influence was limited to those who had the particular skills and status that enabled them to support the monarch in the tasks of government and whose advice and approval was therefore necessary. At the highest level were the nobility who had a place at Court with the King, or held land in areas where they were needed to maintain order or defend against foreign invasion. Below them came the gentry and in towns some merchants, who often acted as JPs or local officials and could, if they were talented, eventually be promoted to higher offices of state.

In general terms this governing class came from those who owned land and whose income from it enabled them to live without physical labour, but there were other groups who also contributed. Merchants played a significant role in the management of towns and **boroughs**. The Church played a role in providing educated administrators and in teaching the importance of morality and obedience to higher authority, and with the development of the Poor Laws (see page 9) the churchwardens took on wider responsibilities. These were often drawn from the **yeomen** or minor gentry and sometimes from skilled craftsmen. As the diagram of the structure of government and governing class on page 7 shows, those who were active in central and local government formed a governing class on whose support and participation the monarch had to rely, and whose members were able to express their views and concerns at Court or in parliaments. As individuals their influence was limited, but the political nation as a whole, or at least the majority part of it, was a necessary partner to any effective monarch.

Source A From *De Republica Anglorum* by Sir Thomas Smith, 1583.

The king distributes his authority and power in the fashion of five things [in five ways]: in the making of laws and ordinances; in the making of battle and peace with foreign nations; in providing of money for the maintenance of himself and defence against his enemies; in choosing and election of the chief officers and magistrates; and fifthly, in the administration of justice. The first and third are done by the prince [king] in Parliament. The second and fourth by the prince [king] himself. The fifth is by the great assize [law courts].

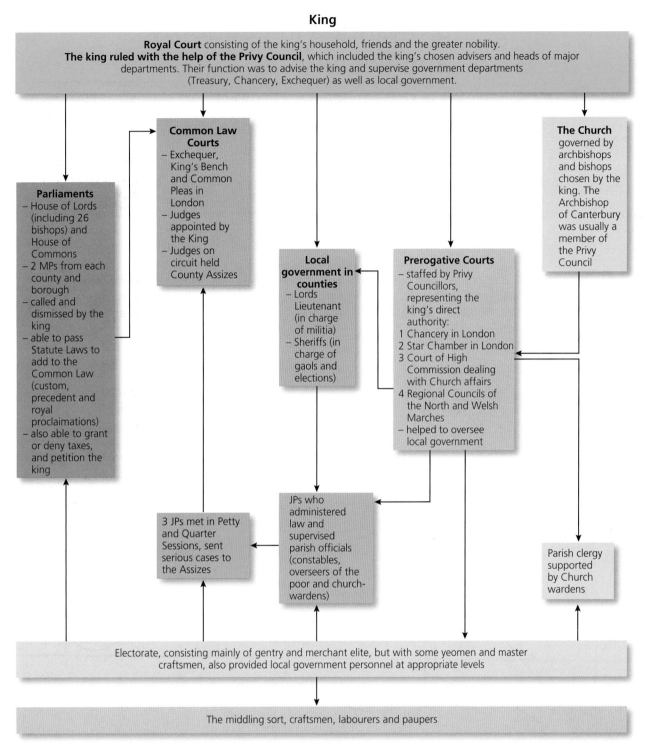

King

Royal Court consisting of the king's household, friends and the greater nobility.
The king ruled with the help of the Privy Council, which included the king's chosen advisers and heads of major departments. Their function was to advise the king and supervise government departments (Treasury, Chancery, Exchequer) as well as local government.

Common Law Courts
– Exchequer, King's Bench and Common Pleas in London
– Judges appointed by the King
– Judges on circuit held County Assizes

The Church
governed by archbishops and bishops chosen by the king. The Archbishop of Canterbury was usually a member of the Privy Council

Parliaments
– House of Lords (including 26 bishops) and House of Commons
– 2 MPs from each county and borough
– called and dismissed by the king
– able to pass Statute Laws to add to the Common Law (custom, precedent and royal proclaimations)
– also able to grant or deny taxes, and petition the king

Local government in counties
– Lords Lieutenant (in charge of militia)
– Sheriffs (in charge of gaols and elections)

Prerogative Courts
– staffed by Privy Councillors, representing the king's direct authority:
1 Chancery in London
2 Star Chamber in London
3 Court of High Commission dealing with Church affairs
4 Regional Councils of the North and Welsh Marches
– helped to oversee local government

3 JPs met in Petty and Quarter Sessions, sent serious cases to the Assizes

JPs who administered law and supervised parish officials (constables, overseers of the poor and church-wardens)

Parish clergy supported by Church wardens

Electorate, consisting mainly of gentry and merchant elite, but with some yeomen and master craftsmen, also provided local government personnel at appropriate levels

The middling sort, craftsmen, labourers and paupers

▲ **Figure 1** The structure of government and the governing class.

3 Changes in economy and society

Developments in the system of government were enhanced by a number of social changes, arising mainly from an underlying growth of population across the Tudor century. A rising population placed pressure on resources, increased unemployment and caused prices to rise as the demand for food and other necessities outstripped supply. While limited and unreliable records mean that it is notoriously difficult to provide accurate estimates of population in this period, the graphs provided below indicate the broad scope of changes. Even allowing for some inaccuracy, the trend of rising prices (inflation) and a resulting fall in real wages (the amount that could be purchased) indicates a level of social upheaval that would inevitably pose problems for government.

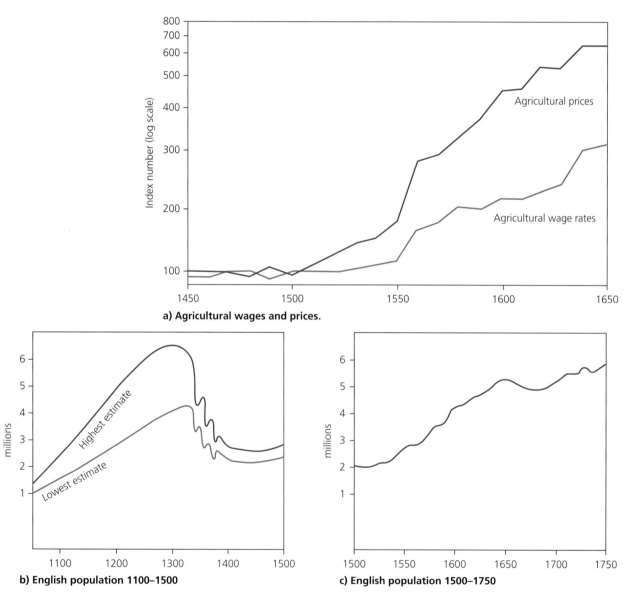

a) Agricultural wages and prices.

b) English population 1100–1500

c) English population 1500–1750

▲ **Figure 2** Population patterns and the effects on wages and prices.

The impact of inflation

How did economic developments bring changes in the social structure?

The impact of inflation on a predominantly agricultural economy was enormous. While there were some industrial activities, mainly mining and the production of woollen cloth, and a few ports such as London, Bristol and Hull, the vast majority of the population at all levels of society earned their living from some form of farming. As a result of the Black Death in 1349 and recurrent plagues thereafter, the fifteenth century had been a period of declining population, labour shortages and relative prosperity for many ordinary people. High wages and low rents had allowed some to purchase their own land and establish themselves as independent yeomen. A rising population reversed this situation, bringing price inflation and lower wage levels and wage labourers and cottagers suffered severely. However, the great landlords and aristocracy were also affected, as was the monarchy itself, as traditionally they leased out land for rent, often on long leases, rather than involving themselves directly in agricultural management, and so they were dependent on the fixed rents that resulted. Like the Crown, they also had a tradition of paternalism and often a significant number of dependents to manage as part of the system of patronage. The maintenance of their power and status could be costly.

However, for those who owned their land freehold or were able to limit their costs, population and price rises presented an opportunity. Food production and profits increased, new land was taken into cultivation and the growing trade in woollen cloth, stimulated by the need to clothe the population across Europe, encouraged the development of sheep farming as a highly profitable enterprise. Yeomen and merchants were able to grow rich enough to purchase landed estates and move into the ranks of the minor gentry. The minor gentry, who also managed their estates themselves rather than renting out their lands, were then able to increase their wealth and status within the governing class. These developments were further encouraged as the Crown's financial problems led to a proportion of the land seized by Henry VIII from the Church being sold or granted as a reward for service. At the same time, some of the independent peasantry, who had previously leased or rented land to farm, slipped into the class of wage labourers, while unemployment reduced a growing section of the labour force to the status of paupers. Ultimately, the rise in population produced a growing gap between rich and poor and associated problems of vagrancy and popular unrest.

Society and government

What were the political effects of social and economic change?

By 1603, when James became king, the worst problems of vagrancy and unemployment had been brought under control by the Poor Laws, brought together in the Elizabethan Poor Law Act of 1601, but within the higher levels of society these changes had some political impact. While the traditional aristocracy and the Crown itself faced financial stress, the wider elite of lesser nobles and gentry were becoming increasingly wealthy, educated and confident. The effects of this were seen where they were directly represented – in parliament. Parliaments were not a permanent part of government. The meeting of parliament was an event entirely within the monarch's control, but the growing cost of government led to a greater need for parliamentary taxation and hence more frequent meetings. This allowed the lesser nobility to express their views and concerns, to gain experience and to become more assertive, and in turn, encouraged monarchs to seek alternative ways of raising money in

The Poor Laws

As a result of the rise in population and growing unemployment, the Tudors were faced with widespread discontent and unrest, including bands of 'sturdy beggars' who roamed the countryside in search of work or some other source of income. A series of laws had been passed to punish vagrants and make provision for the needy within their own parish. Those who left their local area were subject to harsh punishments such as whipping, branding and ultimately death by hanging, while those who stayed within their parish could be given food and money from poor rates distributed by the churchwardens. These laws were eventually drawn together in the Great Poor Law of 1601. This helped to restore control over population movements, but unemployment continued to encourage some mobility and helped to swell the population, criminal and otherwise, of that magnet for migrants, London.

order to reduce their dependence on parliaments. One method, the selling of monopoly patents that included the exclusive right to make or import and sell certain goods, increased the problem of rising prices and led to a parliamentary backlash. Another, the sale of Crown lands, led to a further reduction in royal income. Essentially, the result of the economic and social changes that occurred across the Tudor period was to weaken the finances of the Crown and enhance the importance of parliaments – a problem that was increasingly compounded by the impact of religious changes and divisions arising from the Protestant Reformation and its development across Europe.

4 Impact of the Reformation

The effects of the Protestant Reformation were felt across all parts of government, and as an additional problem for James, the task of ruling separate kingdoms was made more difficult and complex by religious divisions that cut across national borders. The Protestant Reformation had shattered the religious unity of Europe and resulted in reform taking its own course in different areas. While there is no need to discuss the Reformation in detail here, it is necessary to understand some of its main features and effects, because they influenced the political and cultural development of the British kingdoms in important ways.

The European Reformation

How did religious disputes create conflict across Europe?

Christianity in Western Europe had developed under the control of the Catholic Church, centred in Rome and led by the Pope, who claimed to have inherited the power given by Christ himself to the disciple Peter. In different countries the Church was administered by bishops who were often chosen by the monarch, although they received their spiritual power from the Pope. The key features of Catholic belief are described below.

● Jesus Christ, the Son of God, sacrificed himself on the cross to atone for sins.
● Humans could avoid the punishments of Hell and reach Heaven once they died by believing in Christ and following his word in their daily life.
● The knowledge of Christ's word and the power to help human souls had been passed to Peter, and from him to those whom the Church ordained as priests.
● This power was exercised by the priests in the **ceremonies** and **sacraments** ordered by the Church. The most important of these were the ceremony of the Mass and the sacrament of the Eucharist, which re-enacted the Last Supper of Christ and his disciples, and the Confession, in which the priest could forgive the sins of those who truly regretted them.
● It was the duty of the Church to enforce its rules, to bring souls to God.

The implications of these beliefs were that Christians could only reach God through the Church and that the clergy were a special order, separated from the laity (non-clergy) and superior to them. Over the years the Church had become increasingly wealthy and powerful and, like many powerful institutions, appeared to some to have lost some of the spiritual purpose that had justified its position. In the fifteenth century criticism of the Church and the desire of conscientious churchmen for reform had been spread by the growth of literacy and printing. By 1500, there were many complaints from reformers that religion was mechanical, faith had degenerated into superstition and the leaders of the Church were embroiled in politics and luxurious self-indulgence. In time the Church would reform itself, but in the early sixteenth century there were few signs of change.

Ceremonies and Sacraments

Sacraments are sacred acts or ceremonies. The key point about sacramental religion is that taking part in the ceremony is considered to be a sacred act in itself, which could not be replaced by private prayer or meditation. This gave great power to the Church that provided the sacraments, because it made the Church a necessary part of the individual's relationship with God. This was particularly the case with the *Eucharist*, which was preceded by the ceremony of the *Mass* in which the priest's blessing of the bread and wine was believed to transform it into the actual body and blood of Christ. Only a priest properly ordained by the Church could receive and exercise the power to perform this *Transubstantiation*, which made his presence essential within the sacrament. While this strengthened religion as a communal activity, it could also encourage mechanical or superstitious acts by the congregation, which reformers found unacceptable. The Eucharist itself, under the name of Communion or Holy Communion, remained part of worship in most reformed churches, but as an act of remembrance rather than a sign of divine presence. Similarly, the ceremony of *Confession* required the presence of a priest, whereas the reformed churches emphasised private prayer and seeking God's forgiveness as the means of demonstrating repentance.

The Protestant challenge

These criticisms of the Church became the background to the protest mounted by Martin Luther, a German monk who challenged the authorities and demanded reforms. Unlike many contemporary critics of the Church, Luther challenged its ideas as well as certain practices. The core of his argument is described below.

- Salvation – in which the human soul gained a place in heaven with God – could not be guaranteed by the Church or by good works, but only by individual faith.
- God offered salvation as a free gift to those who believed in Him and followed Christ.
- Belief came from private prayer and study of the Bible – the Word of God. It should therefore be accessible to individual Christians, not just the scholars and clergy who could read it in Latin.
- Church ceremonies and sacraments only symbolised internal faith and too many encouraged ignorance and superstition.
- In God's eyes, priests and laity were equal, meaning that priests had no special powers.
- While the Church remained important as a source of guidance, teaching and preaching, there was no justification for the wide-ranging authority claimed by the Catholic Church.

The Pope responded by declaring Luther a **heretic**. He was not the first reformer to suffer this, but the rulers of Saxony, where Luther lived, protected him from the Church and its allies. This allowed him to develop and publish his views and to inspire other reformers such as Ulrich Zwingli and John Calvin. Those who took up Luther's ideas became known as Protestants and by 1550 there were Reformed churches in much of Germany and Scandinavia as well as the Netherlands and England. In response, some of those who remained loyal to the Catholic Church accepted some of his criticisms and set about strengthening the Church by dealing with abuses and clarifying its doctrines.

Heretic/heresy – The name given by the Catholic Church to those who challenged its teachings and the denial of its beliefs. Heretics could be 'excommunicated' (expelled from the Church) or imprisoned. Ultimately, if they refused to give up their views, they were handed over to the civil authorities to be burned alive.

This process of internal reform, known as the Counter-Reformation, began with the Council of Trent which met in several sessions between 1545 and 1563. The authority of the Pope was reinforced, administration was improved and many of the scandals that had provoked Luther's protests were eradicated.

The resulting renewal of faith and of papal authority strengthened the loyalty of Catholics and the fears of Protestants and led to war in Europe. It also contributed to Catholic plots against Queen Elizabeth and James I, and to the anti-Catholic paranoia that affected many English Protestants in the seventeenth century. By the end of the sixteenth century Europe was divided between a militant Protestantism, which rejected the authority of the past and looked for its rules and inspiration to the Bible, and a militant Catholicism determined to recover its control and destroy heresy.

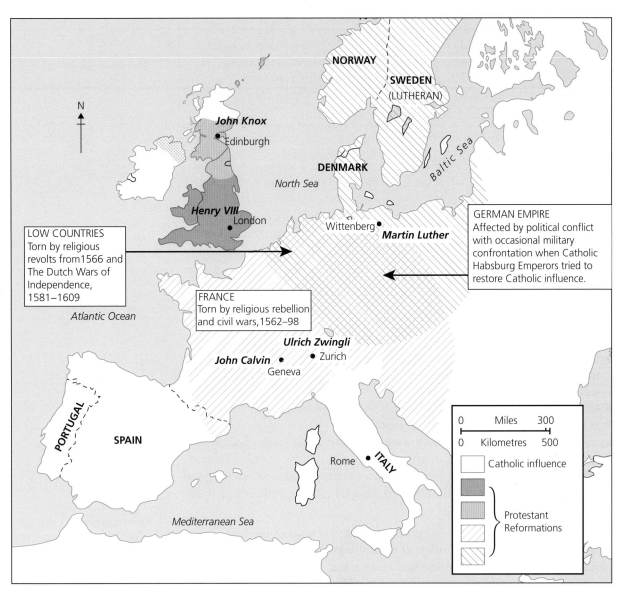

▲ **Figure 3** The religious map of Europe showing major wars and civil wars. By 1603 much of Europe remained Catholic, but Scandinavia and Northern Germany were predominantly Lutheran. Switzerland was dominated by Calvinist Churches, which were also influential in parts of Germany and Holland. France had a Catholic establishment, but with a legally tolerated Protestant minority known as Huguenots. England and Scotland were predominantly Protestant, but the population of Ireland was mainly Catholic.

Britain and the effects of the Reformation

Why did religious conflicts develop across Britain?

In England, a Reformation was carried out on the instructions and in the interests of Henry VIII. Henry was no Protestant and his seizure of the Church and its property was motivated by a desire for power and wealth, as well as the need for a divorce in order to marry Anne Boleyn and, hopefully, to produce a male heir. In 1534 the Act of Supremacy declared the King to be Head of the Church and this was followed by the seizure of Church property, including the monasteries, and laws to enforce royal control and regulate the succession to the throne. By rejecting the authority of the Pope he placed himself in the Protestant camp and was forced to grant positions of influence in the Church to men with Protestant ideas. Equally significant, the chosen method of establishing and enforcing his new powers was the use of statute law, made, and only reversible, in parliament.

Hence, when a genuinely Protestant Reformation was carried out during the short reign (1547–53) of his son, Edward, which his Catholic daughter Mary could not entirely reverse during her even shorter reign (1553–58), both settlements required the co-operation of the political elite in parliament once more. As a result, when Elizabeth sought to create reconciliation and a moderate compromise in the Church of England, not only did she have to establish it by parliamentary statute, she was also faced by parliamentary efforts to modify and change the arrangements that she put in place. The effect of Henry's actions was to enhance both the status and power of parliaments, at a time when religious ideas and conflicts made its members more concerned and more willing to exercise their influence.

Conflict of ideas

Mary's persecution of Protestants and her links with Spain (she married the heir to the Spanish crown) created a backlash against Catholicism across all social classes. Perhaps equally important, her persecution drove some Protestants into exile in Europe, where they came into contact with other Protestant groups. The development of Protestant ideas posed a number of problems for government. Luther argued that the rules for Church government, as well as salvation, could be found in the Bible, and that the Christian monarch, or godly ruler, had the power and responsibility of interpreting and enforcing them. However, the Bible – part history, part mythology, part poetry – was often unclear and contradictory, and men and women who believed that their salvation depended on it were inclined to interpret it for themselves. The result was that Protestant ideas soon began to develop in different ways, and the varied and piecemeal nature of reform in different areas reinforced these differences.

By the time of Mary's death, there was considerable variation of opinion on what constituted a 'true' Church. The model favoured by many was that established by the French reformer, John Calvin. Calvin had extended Luther's ideas about salvation to establish the doctrine that some people were predestined to be saved, because they were able to accept the gift of salvation and the disciplined Christianity that went with it. The sign of such **predestination** was the ability to live a godly life and accept the rules of a godly Church. The idea that God would exclude some souls from a gift that He granted freely was in some ways illogical and would be rejected by later religious leaders, but such assurance of salvation did encourage great dedication and commitment among Calvin's followers. The result was that many exiles

> **Predestination** – The belief held by Calvin and his followers that God chooses beforehand those to whom he will grant salvation.

> **Presbyterianism** – A system of church organisation in which the individual congregations were governed by a minister with the help of lay Elders (senior members) under the supervision of an elected assembly known as a Synod.

returned after Mary's death, determined to reform the Church along Calvinist lines. This meant getting rid of all traces of Catholic ceremonies and rituals and allowing ministers to concentrate on preaching the Word of God and ensuring that their parishioners lived godly lives (whether or not they wanted to!). In Scotland the reformer John Knox was able to establish a Calvinist system known as **Presbyterianism**, but in England the reformers came up against a Queen who was more interested in political control and religious peace than in their cherished schemes of reform.

John Calvin (1509–64)

John Calvin was the most influential Protestant reformer after Luther. He established his own church in the city of Geneva. His doctrine became dominant among Protestants in France, Switzerland, Scotland and the Netherlands and to an extent within the early Church of England. Its core was the idea of predestination, which claimed that God divided humanity into 'saints', who were predestined to follow the path of true religion and escape sin, and sinners, the 'unregenerate' who were condemned to hell. The sign of sainthood lay in a daily struggle to avoid sin and to carry out God's will in daily life, a struggle that required the discipline and support of a Calvinist Church. These gave great authority to the minister and certain senior members of the congregation (known as elders or presbyters) to control the behaviour and lives of their followers, and came to be known as Presbyterian. Only those who were able to accept the restrictions entailed by this discipline could be sure of salvation.

The harshness of this doctrine led it to be first softened (by an implied expansion of the number of possible saints and reduction of the number of irredeemable sinners) and later challenged by other reformers. It also came to be abused by some known as Antinomians, who argued that since they were predestined to heaven by God, they need not fear to sin in their daily life. For most Calvinists, however, the belief that, as long as they genuinely sought a godly life, they could be sure of ultimate victory over sin, was a powerful inspiration. They could serve God in whatever capacity they had – as a merchant or labourer as well as a minister – and any success was evidence of God's approval, as well as enhancing the reputation of God's people. The task was not easy and it was important that the Church to which they had access should support them with good preaching and instruction and not hinder them by unnecessary and possibly corrupting ceremonies and sacraments. Hence Calvinist enthusiasts required the correct forms and organisation within their Church, to reflect doctrine in practice as well as in words.

The Elizabethan settlement

As the daughter of Anne Boleyn, whose marriage to Henry had never been recognised by the Catholic Church, Queen Elizabeth was bound to establish a broadly Protestant form of worship when she came to the throne in 1558. But as a skilful politician she recognised the need for healing and reconciliation in the religion of England. The result was the Elizabethan settlement and the establishment of an Anglican Church which sought to provide a compromise – a 'middle way' between the Catholic and Protestant extremes. Undeniably Protestant in doctrine, it retained many of the familiar ceremonies and services inherited from the Catholic Church, as well as bishops, whom Elizabeth appointed and controlled and who therefore maintained her authority. It was able to satisfy the needs of most of her subjects but, like most compromises, it left dissatisfied minorities at both ends of the spectrum (see Figure 4, below).

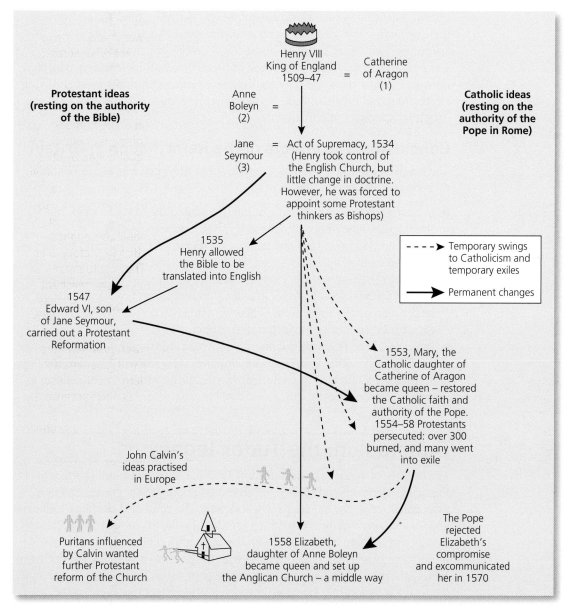

▲ **Figure 4** The Tudor pendulum. Why would the developments shown in the diagram encourage religious confusion and division in England?

A minority of English Catholics gave primary loyalty to the Pope; their treason in attempting to replace Elizabeth with the Catholic Mary, Queen of Scots in the Northern Rebellion of 1568–69 led to a Papal Bull (declaration) issued in 1570, which excommunicated Elizabeth and enjoined a duty on Catholics to remove her from the throne. This, and their links with Spain, did much to create anti-Catholic feeling in England. A minority of Protestants was dissatisfied with a half-reformed Church and sought to persuade or pressurise the Queen into further change. Their desire for further purification of the Church led them to be nicknamed 'Puritans'. In the 1570s attempts were made to introduce reforms through Parliament, prompting the angry Queen to forbid such discussions and raise political conflict over MPs' rights to free speech. Having lost this battle, Puritan preachers attempted to change the Church from within. Elizabeth, who was determined to maintain the system of bishops as the best method of ensuring her own, royal control, suppressed their meetings and muted their protests, but she could not silence them entirely. By 1603 they had been denied the fulfilment of their plans for reform, but were nevertheless able to preach, convert, stimulate and spread their influence and ideas. The impact of Protestant ideas as a whole was to encourage individual faith and teach the necessity of private study of the word of God, resulting in the spread of literacy and an increasingly educated laity. In Puritan ideas and practice this development found its most enduring expression, and nowhere was this demonstrated more effectively than in the debating chambers of parliament.

Conclusion: the effects of the Reformation in Britain

The result of such Reformation was that James inherited a legacy of religious divisions across three kingdoms:

- In Scotland the Presbyterian Church dominated the lowland areas, but a sizeable Catholic minority remained in the Gaelic highlands.
- In Ireland the majority of the population remained Catholic, and the loss of traditional chieftains encouraged the people to look to Catholic priests as leaders in the community. English control, however, led to the imposition of an Anglican Church as the official Church of Ireland, while Protestant settlers, especially those from Scotland, who settled in Ulster, brought an extreme Protestant or Presbyterian tradition.
- In England the established Church was Anglican, based on Elizabeth's 'middle way', with a small Catholic minority who remained loyal to the Pope. Within the Church, however, there was a significant movement seeking to achieve further reform.

Conclusion: the Tudor legacy

The century of Tudor rule that ended in 1603 had seen significant changes in English government and society, which brought both greater powers and new responsibilities to the monarchs who followed. The combined effects of Tudor rule and the extension of royal power in a century of religious conflict and economic development placed new demands on the monarch's skills and increased the importance of an effective partnership with the political nation. On the one hand James inherited a stable system of government in which royal power was accepted across the kingdom and exercised through a legal system that drew on the Common Law and tradition, while also enshrining areas of direct power through the exercise of the royal prerogative. Alongside this he inherited a relatively prosperous and well-ordered society, with increasingly educated and able administrators and systems of social control in the Poor Laws and a state Church.

At the same time, however, as head of the Church of England he inherited responsibility for hugely contentious issues that could affect key individuals at every level of society. In addition he faced significant financial problems, made worse by an ongoing war against Catholic Spain and a rebellion in Catholic Ireland, which affected the power of the Crown to carry out decisions and policies at home and abroad. Perhaps most significantly, the essential forum for dealing with these matters was no longer simply the royal Court and Privy Council, but included an increasingly necessary, but increasingly independent and articulate, section of the wider political elite under the form and name of a Parliament. If James was to manage his legacy effectively, as Elizabeth had already discovered, his handling of this institution would be crucial.

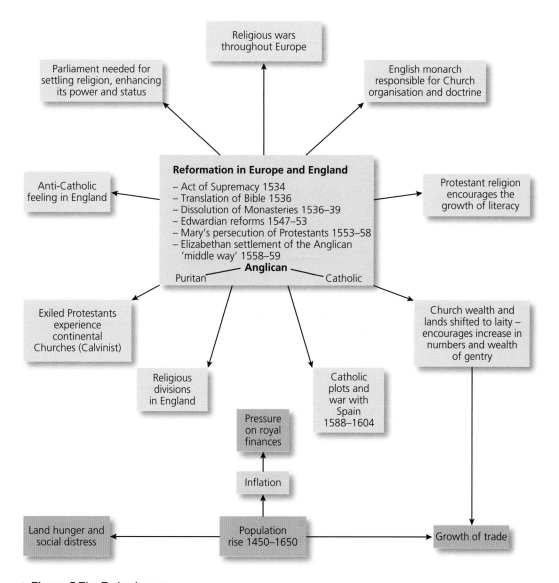

▲ **Figure 5** The Tudor legacy.

Working on the Tudor legacy

The material provided in this section forms the background to your main period of study, and you do not need to make detailed notes about it. However, you will find it useful to ensure that you have understood the key concepts and clarified key terms relating to both government and religion. Many of these are explained in the glossary on pages 256–58, but they are also used in context in the outline of developments that you have been reading. You may find it helpful to compile a list of terms and write a short definition of your own. These can usefully include government courts and offices, the class structure, the system of patronage and religious groups and ideas.

To consolidate your wider understanding of the systems and situations that James inherited, and to begin considering their impact on his reign and later developments, you will find it useful to summarise the main features and consider their implications. You can also begin to build on the material in the Introduction on pages v–viii regarding the key historical concepts of *change* and *causation* that will shape your understanding of the period. While you will develop your ability to do this over a period of time, as you study the whole period to 1702, the outline provided here on the Tudor legacy offers you a starting point in both aspects of the course.

ACTIVITY

1 **Change and continuity**: This part of the activity will help you to familiarise yourself with the nature of monarchy and government in 1603 and enable you to pick out changes and consider their impact as your study of the period develops. Using the information you have read and extracted from the maps and diagrams, write out a brief summary of the key features of the system of government of England inherited by James I in 1603 using the following questions:
   a) What were the duties of the monarch?
   b) What methods and machinery did he use to carry them out?
   c) How did he exercise his power to do this?
   d) Whose help and support did he need?
   e) What, if any, limits could be imposed, and by whom?

2 **Causes and consequences**: The diagram of 'the Tudor legacy' (Figure 5, page 17) provides a brief summary of the events and factors that shaped the system of government across the Tudor century and indicates how they both enhanced the monarch's powers and created potential problems and restrictions. In particular, it highlights two key factors – the Reformation in England and the rise in population – as causes of change, and sets out the complex range of consequences that they produced. You may find it helpful to decide first which of these consequences increased royal power, which created problems, and which, if any, did both. You can then use the information that you have read and the points made in the population graphs on page 8 to write brief answers to the following questions about the causes of change, 1534–1603:
   a) In what ways did the Reformation in England increase the power of the monarch?
   b) What new problems did it create?
   c) What problems were created for the monarch by the rise in population?
   d) What other factors contributed to the difficulties facing James in 1603?
   e) In what ways did the different factors combine or work together to affect:
      ● the powers of the monarch
      ● the influence of parliaments
      ● the relationship between the two?

Kings and Parliaments, 1603–29

This chapter covers the reign of James I and the early years of Charles I's reign, ending with the breakdown of his relationship with Parliament in 1629. It deals with a number of areas:

- James I and Charles I (their character, attitudes and Courts)
- the financial weakness of the Crown and attempts at reform
- religious issues and divisions
- relations and disputes with Parliaments
- the parliamentary crisis of 1629.

When you have worked through the chapter and the related activities, you should have detailed knowledge of all those areas. You should be able to relate this knowledge to the key breadth issues defined as part of your study, in particular the changing powers of King and Parliament, and the relationship between them.

For the period covered in this chapter the main focus can be phrased as a question:

Why did tensions develop between King and Parliament to the point where they were in open conflict by 1629?

The focus of the question is on the development of tensions and the range of causal factors that contributed to that development, as set out briefly in the chapter overview below.

CHAPTER OVERVIEW

In 1603 James VI of Scotland inherited the throne of England in the traditional way, as the nearest relative of the preceding monarch. His accession to the throne was therefore both expected and widely welcomed in England, as it was by no means unusual for one monarch to rule over different and separate states and peoples, as James was now to do. Nevertheless, in 1625 when James died, his relationship with his English subjects was marred by disagreements and tensions in Parliament, and a level of mutual suspicion that would pose problems for his successors.

However, his immediate successor, Charles I, was already playing an active role in government, and it was in his reign that the difficulties of 1625 turned into the conflict of 1629. The material set out in this chapter addresses a range of factors that contributed to this situation – the underlying structural problems facing the monarchy in 1603, the role of key individuals in dealing with them, and the impact of events elsewhere, for example in Europe. By considering the impact of each factor, and the way in which the different parts of the situation combined and interacted, you can begin to explain the causes of tension and the extent to which they suggest that the way England was governed had to change.

19

1 The reign of James I, 1603–25

This section examines James' religious policies, his relations with Parliament, government and finance and his foreign policy. In all of these areas of government James had to begin with the conditions that he inherited from his predecessors – a mixed inheritance. As a monarch and Head of the Church of England, he could claim the loyalty of his subjects as a religious duty, but he was also responsible for the safety of their souls at a time when the true path to God and salvation was the subject of intense debate and bitter disagreement. This was further complicated because he was the ruler of three separate kingdoms, each with its own religious culture. In secular (non-religious) matters government depended on the strength of royal finances and the workings of patronage – and therefore on an effective relationship with the political nation in parliament.

To maintain this relationship, James would need to exercise his power with care and a concern for unity – no easy task when the political nation was, itself, divided by opinion and interest. This success or failure in this would do much to shape the development of the monarchy that he had inherited.

Religious policies

How well did James handle religious problems?

Asserting royal authority

The accession of James I was greeted with relief by most of Elizabeth's subjects – a male Protestant king with several children offered the prospect of security and a stable succession. There were many who expected his accession to be to their advantage. Catholics hoped that respect for his dead mother, Mary, Queen of Scots, would encourage the King to ease the persecution that they suffered, while Puritans hoped that his upbringing in the Presbyterian Church of Scotland would lead him to favour their plans for reform. In the event, both were disappointed. James did suspend the collection of fines for **recusancy**, but when faced with complaints in Parliament, and perhaps regretting the loss of income, he had reimposed them by 1604. This encouraged an extremist minority to look for help from Spain, and led to the Gunpowder Plot of 1605, in which Catholic conspirators attempted to blow up Parliament while the King was present.

The initial hopes of the Puritans, expressed in the **Millenary Petition**, were also short-lived. James agreed to meet them at a conference held at Hampton Court in 1604, but at the meeting he rejected their ideas and warned them that if they would not conform to the rules laid down in the Prayer Book he would 'harry them out of the Kingdom'. Like Elizabeth, James saw the Church primarily in political terms (as an institution that upheld royal power) and was determined to maintain his control through bishops appointed by, and dependent on, him. He followed up his uncompromising stand by appointing the authoritarian Richard Bancroft as the new Archbishop of Canterbury. Bancroft enforced rules contained in the Anglican prayer book on the use of ceremonies and ceremonial dress, and some ministers lost their livings because of their refusal to conform. A few hardy souls left the country in order to set up their own independent churches, emigrating first to Holland and later to

---

NOTE-MAKING

Use the headings in this section to make brief notes as you work through it. Set these notes out clearly using a main heading, sub-headings and sub-points. For example:

Main heading: Religious policies

Sub-heading 1: Asserting royal authority
- Treatment of Catholics
- The Puritan Challenge

Sub-heading 2: Compromise and coexistence.

Conclusion: How well did James handle religious problems?

When you have completed your notes on the first few pages, review the process, and then devise your own sub-headings and points for the remainder of the section, using the headings and questions in the text to help you.

Recusancy – A refusal to attend Anglican services on a regular basis, which had been made compulsory in the reign of Elizabeth. Absentees (usually Catholics) were required to pay a fine. The fines provided a useful source of revenue for the Crown.

Millenary Petition – A list of requests given to James I by Puritans in 1603 when he was travelling to London in order to claim the English throne. It is claimed, but not proven, that this petition had 1,000 signatures of Puritan ministers. This carefully worded document expressed Puritan distaste regarding the state of the Anglican Church, and took into consideration James's religious views as well as his liking for a debate.

the New World to establish Puritan colonies in North America. Most, however, remained within the Anglican Church and tried their best to conform while hoping for better things.

Compromise and coexistence

Within a few years, however, James had softened his stance considerably. Having asserted his authority, he was wise enough to see that political harmony could best be achieved by avoiding unnecessary provocation. Although recusancy fines continued to be levied, the policy was intermittently applied, and discreet Catholics could often worship undisturbed for long periods. Similarly, Puritan ministers who conformed to the Prayer Book occasionally, in recognition of the King's authority, could often ignore unpalatable rules and ceremonies for much of the time. In 1611, when Bancroft died, he was replaced by the more sympathetic George Abbot, who treated Puritan sensitivities with tact. Puritan ministers were expected to demonstrate their obedience to the King by occasional use of signs and ceremonies that they disliked. In return, they were left largely undisturbed.

In addition, James did recognise the need to improve the numbers and quality of the clergy, and shared the Puritan enthusiasm for good preaching. He had no objection to the widespread practice of lay impropriation, which enabled gentry with Puritan sympathies to ensure that Puritan preachers were appointed to many parish livings. Supporters also endowed weekday lectures, often to be held in market towns, which enabled Puritan ministers to preach for a living without undertaking the ceremonial duties required of a parish minister. While the arrangements may have lacked neat logic, they did provide a measure of peace in the Anglican Church, and allowed Puritan reformers to coexist with others as one faction within it.

Meanwhile, in Scotland, James took cautious steps to bring Presbyterian practice into line with English arrangements. By 1621 he had persuaded the Scots to accept bishops, albeit with limited powers. An attempt to establish a Prayer Book similar to that used in England aroused great opposition, and James withdrew it until a more favourable opportunity arose. By such cautious and tactful measures he hoped gradually to bring the two Churches together and to create uniformity across the two kingdoms.

Conclusion – an area of achievement

The success of James's approach to the religious problem can be seen from the relatively few complaints voiced in Parliament. These were mainly limited to grumbles that recusancy fines were not levied rigorously enough, or that the King's foreign policy was insufficiently 'Protestant'. Shortly after his accession he brought Elizabeth's long, expensive war with Spain to an end. While some of the 'hotter sort' of Protestants and Puritans might have reservations about this, the peace was wise and financially necessary. In general terms, religion was not a major cause of tension in Parliament, until the outbreak of the Thirty Years War in 1618 (see pages 29–30) created new conflicts across Europe.

> **Impropriation** – The practice of taking over (impropriating) the collection of tithes (a 10 per cent tax on all households in a parish levied as income for the parish priest). This allowed the impropriator to play a part in choosing the minister. Many parishes had come under the control of the local gentry in this way. Another way of controlling the choice of minister was to buy up the advowson for the parish, which gave the holder the right to nominate a particular minister. Many advowsons were held by the King and the bishops, but a significant number were acquired by the gentry and by borough corporations.

KEY DATES: RELIGION

1603 Millenary Petition presented to James by Puritans.

1604 Hampton Court conference; appointment of Bancroft as Archbishop of Canterbury marks attack on Puritan ministers.

1611 Appointment of Abbot as Archbishop introduces a more moderate approach.

Relations with Parliaments

All experience shows that the prerogatives of princes may easily, and do daily, grow [but] the privileges of the subject are for the most part, at an everlasting stand. They may be by good providence and care preserved, but once being lost are not recovered but with much disquiet.

1 Does the wording of the Commons *Apology* in Source A suggest that MPs distrusted James I?

2 What 'experience' are they referring to?

Why did James clash with Parliaments in the first years of his reign?
Despite the success of James's religious policies, in the first few years of his reign, the political atmosphere soured, with both King and Parliament showing signs of irritation. In 1604 there was a disputed election in Buckinghamshire and a clumsy attempt by the Privy Council to reverse the result in favour of the Court candidate, Sir John Fortescue, produced an angry protest from the House of Commons. Although entitled as a Commons Apology, it was in fact an assertion of their rights (see Source A).

The House of Commons was already sensitive on the matter of its rights and privileges, after its difficulties with Elizabeth (see page 13). MPs may also have been concerned about the King's extravagant claims to divine power and status. James had always regarded himself as something of a political philosopher. In 1598 he had published a learned work entitled *The True Law of Free Monarchies*, in which he had claimed that:

'Kings are justly called gods for that they exercise a manner or resemblance of divine power on earth'

and that:

'they make and unmake their subjects, they have power of raising and casting down, of life and death.'

He also claimed that while 'a just monarch would delight in conforming to his laws' a king was, in fact, above the law, because he made it. To James this was simply a logical argument, but it is likely that such rhetoric gave many MPs cause for concern.

Whatever the reason, the House reacted sharply in asserting the right of the Commons to determine their own membership. James reminded MPs that their privileges had been granted by monarchs, and, by implication, suggested that they might be removed in the same way. In practice, however, he applied his theories with a measure of tact. Faced with the Apology, he defused the crisis by suspending the parliamentary session, and quietly allowing the Buckinghamshire issue to be dropped.

Union with Scotland

When Parliament reassembled in 1605–06, a mood of Protestant unity, created by the Gunpowder Plot, led to reconciliation and a parliamentary grant to settle the King's debts. However, problems were already emerging in relation to the King's Scottish background and the role of his Scottish friends, and now came to a head over his desire for an Anglo-Scottish constitutional union. Wales and Ireland were effectively conquered territories, and could be treated as subordinate to England, but Scotland was an independent kingdom. Either James must continue to rule it separately, or a new relationship with England must be established.

James desired a 'perfect' union, which would amalgamate the best Scottish and English institutions, seeing the possibility for reform and improvement of the governing system in both kingdoms. However, many Englishmen were deeply anti-Scottish – a legacy of past hostilities that had been aggravated by the new King's numerous gifts of titles and pensions to his Scottish friends and courtiers. MPs refused to countenance the idea that English institutions could be improved by importing any Scottish ideas. One of them, Sir Edwin Sandys, suggested that the 'perfect' union could be achieved by abolishing Scottish law and replacing it with the law of England, but even this was unacceptable to some MPs, who saw the Scots as penniless adventurers seeking to swallow up the resources of England. 'If one man owns two pastures', declared one MP, 'with one hedge to divide them; the one pasture bare, the other fertile and good; a wise owner will not pull down the hedge, but make gates to let them in and out, otherwise the cattle will rush in and not want to return.' To refer to the Scots as cattle was deeply insulting to the King, but James's generosity to his Scottish companions was deeply resented, and wider problems regarding the King's finances were already mounting. It was this issue of finance that was to cause the most serious damage to the relationship between King and Parliament.

KEY DATES: KING AND PARLIAMENT

1603 James becomes King; Buckinghamshire election leads to quarrel in Parliament and Commons *Apology* presented in **1604** Gunpowder plot.

1605–07 Debates over constitutional links with Scotland lead to tension and failure of James' plan for Anglo-Scottish union.

Government and finance, 1603–24

Why did James I face financial problems?

By 1607 James had been forced to abandon any ideas of a constitutional union between England and Scotland, in part because it was already becoming clear that a far more serious cause of conflict would arise from the financial problems facing the Crown, and the failure of James to recognise this and act consistently in dealing with it. His generosity to his Scottish courtiers may have been particularly resented, but was, in fact, only part of a far wider extravagance that led to quarrels over taxation and revenue throughout his reign. Contemporaries, and some historians, were deeply critical of his financial management, and with some justification. However, Elizabeth had also faced financial problems, and further consideration of Crown finances, both before and after 1603, suggests that in both cases the difficulties arose from more fundamental weaknesses.

Revenue and resources

The financial problems faced by the Crown arose from two factors. The first was that years of rising prices had left royal income increasingly inadequate for the expenses of government. The second was that James's handling of money and some aspects of his lifestyle amounted to financial irresponsibility, and made a difficult problem far worse. Figure 1 on page 24 shows the nature and sources of royal revenue. According to the political conventions of the time, the King was expected to 'live of his own' in peacetime, that is, to finance government and maintain his household out of ordinary revenue and the customs duties that he was granted at the beginning of his reign. By 1603, that had become impossible, for a number of reasons:

● Before 1600, a combination of price inflation and Elizabeth's sales of Crown land to finance the war with Spain had made ordinary revenue inadequate. James inherited a debt of approximately £100,000.
● As a family man, James's expenses were bound to be greater than those of Elizabeth – he had to maintain a wife and children, including a separate establishment for the heir to the throne, the Prince of Wales.
● In addition, Elizabeth had failed to update tax assessments in line with inflation. Combined with an inefficient system of collection, this meant that even when Parliament did grant extra taxes, the King received much less than was intended.

▼ **Figure 1** Income and revenue, 1603.

Income source	Type of revenue
'Ordinary Revenue' – Crown lands, feudal rights and prerogative	**Crown lands** – leased out for rent, but often on long leases that did not keep up with inflation. Income had also declined because of sales of land by Elizabeth.
	Wardship – the King's right to act as guardian to the children of tenants who died before the child was old enough to inherit. Profits could be made from administering the estate and from profitable marriages and dowries.
	Marriage – the King's right to arrange marriages for the female heirs of tenants or the remarriage of widows.
	Livery – the King's right to receive a gift of money (set by him) from those who inherited land held from him in feudal tenancy.
	Purveyance – the King's right to buy food and supplies for the Court at reduced prices.
	Monopolies – the King's right to grant exclusive rights to make and sell goods of particular kinds.
	Justice – fines, court fees, etc.
Customs duties	**Tunnage and Poundage** – customs duties on wine and wool, normally granted to the King for life by his first Parliament.
	New impositions – new import duties which the King was entitled to raise to protect English trade and industry.
Occasional sources	**Benevolences/forced loans** – gifts and loans from individuals.
	Loans on credit
	Sales of assets
Direct taxes – granted by Parliament	**Tenths and Fifteenths** – a tax on movable goods (except personal clothing) paid by all.
	Subsidies – a tax on income for landowners, office-holders and wage-earners, or movable property for merchants, craftsmen and tenant-farmers. It was not levied on the poor.
	Poll Tax – a tax paid by individuals (rare).
	Ship Money – a tax levied in wartime from coastal areas for building ships.

Strategies for reform

Faced with these difficulties, James's chief financial adviser, Robert Cecil (created Earl of Salisbury in 1605) tried a variety of strategies. A legal ruling given in 1606, when a merchant named Bates challenged the King's right to impose new customs duties, was used to issue a new Book of Rates in 1608. This imposed new duties on some goods and increased the rate of payment on others. These 'impositions' were deeply resented, and complaints were raised in Parliament in 1610 and again in 1614. The issue was not only financial, but had significant implications for royal powers and the legal rights of both Parliaments and individual taxpayers, as Source B illustrates.

Source B From *The Judgement of Chief Baron Fleming in Bates' Case*, 1606. The judgement was given when a merchant named Bates refused to pay new customs duties imposed by the King.

The King's power is double [two-fold], [and consists of the] ordinary and [the] absolute ... That of the ordinary is for ... particular subjects, for the execution of civil justice, and this is exercised by equity and justice in ordinary courts, and is known as common law, and these laws cannot be changed without Parliament. The absolute power of the king is ... that which is applied to the general benefit of the people, and this power is most properly named policy and government. This absolute power varies according to the wisdom of the king for the common good; and these being general ... all things done within these rules are lawful.

1 In what ways would the judgement in Source B enhance the power of the monarchy?

2 How does it undermine the legal rights of citizens?

3 In what ways did it threaten the status and influence of Parliaments?

There was further indignation among MPs when the sale of monopolies was renewed (most had been abandoned by Elizabeth amidst great public rejoicing). While the complaints were significant in themselves, they also contributed to the failure of Cecil's more fundamental reform, the Great Contract. This was a plan whereby the King would give up some of the more irritating feudal dues that he could still levy from his subjects and tenants, in return for a regular parliamentary income of £200,000 a year. Had it been successful, the plan would have placed royal finances on a sound basis. As it was, both sides had reservations which caused them to withdraw. While the King was aware that he would lose a useful means of controlling his more powerful subjects, the House of Commons were wary of providing an income that might give the King financial independence. As the lawyer, James Whitelocke (who was an MP between 1610 and 1622), pointed out, 'Considering the greatest use they make of assembling Parliaments, which is the supply of money', there was reason to believe that Parliament would be giving up their most valuable weapon in obtaining redress for any grievances.

Barriers to reform

While most of these difficulties were unavoidable, and caused as much by the reluctance of MPs to face reality as by government errors, they were compounded by the behaviour of James himself. He significantly overestimated the wealth of his new kingdom, and was consistently overgenerous towards his friends and favourites, to the extent of being financially irresponsible. Complaints that he exclusively favoured his Scottish cronies were not entirely fair, but he was particularly generous to some of his Scottish friends. In 1606, when Parliament granted three subsidies to settle his debts, James promptly gave £44,000 to three Scottish friends. In 1611 he gave away £90,688, with £67,498 of it going to eleven Scotsmen. This, however, was only part of a wider problem relating to the King's lifestyle and the behaviour of many of his courtiers. James's love of hunting, his preference for the company of handsome young men, and his excessive eating and drinking set a tone which degenerated into corruption and scandal. Even efficient ministers like Cecil (Earl of Salisbury) lined their own pockets from the proceeds of government, and the behaviour of Thomas Howard, Earl of Suffolk, who eventually became Lord Treasurer after Cecil's death in 1612, amounted to embezzlement.

Problems increased in 1614 with the fiasco of the Addled Parliament – a term used by James himself when he dissolved the 1614 parliament after the Commons failed to vote taxes and became embroiled in a bitter dispute with the Lords. In an attempt by the powerful Court faction led by Thomas Howard to discredit possible rivals, rumours had been spread of government interference in elections, raising serious concerns among MPs about their rights and privileges. This was followed by complaints about extravagance at Court and the increased use of impositions to pay for it. The rival factions focused mainly on blaming each other and the result was their total failure to manage the Commons, leading eventually to conflict between the two Houses and procedural paralysis. James ended the session and dissolved Parliament in disgust, but the fault lay mainly with his own management of his courtiers and councillors.

Finance and administration: the fundamental problems

James's homosexual relationships and the Overbury scandal (see box on page 26) showed a Court guilty of sexual licence and murder – and the wider political nation found it doubly insulting when the King asked them to pay for it. In part the problems reflect the personality and character of the King, but it was also the result of fundamental weaknesses within the system of government itself.

> **Feudal dues** – Payments made by the nobility and gentry, a relic of the feudal system when they were seen as holding their land as tenants of the King.

KEY DATES: FINANCE

1606 Bates Case – judges approve the 'imposition' of new duties.

1608 New Book of Rates published.

1610 Complaints in Parliament about 'impositions'; failure of the Great Contract.

1612 Death of Robert Cecil.

The court of King James: corruption and scandal

The more self-respecting of the Lords preferred the retirement of their mansions … to Court masques [plays] in which ladies were too drunk to perform their parts, divorce cases and adulteries, and the whisper, scarcely hushed, of scandals yet more vile.

G. M. Trevelyan, *England under the Stuarts*, 1904

There were numerous complaints about the general tone of James's Court, and the drunkenness and gluttony practised by the King and many courtiers. The King was addicted to hunting and this gave him the occasion to enjoy young male company, of which he was equally fond. His open affection towards certain favourites raised questions as to whether he was actively homosexual. Despite a marriage and large family, he clearly had homosexual tendencies, although it is less clear that he indulged them physically. The more established nobility particularly resented the power and wealth given to the favourites, who were placed above them in influence and status.

The first of these favourites was Robert Carr, a young Scot whom James created Earl of Somerset. In 1613 Carr fell in love with Thomas Howard's daughter, Frances, then Countess of Essex, and a divorce was hastily arranged on the grounds that the Earl of Essex was impotent. This was probably untrue, but the Howards were anxious to secure a marriage with the King's favourite. The marriage led to a huge scandal in 1616, when Carr and his wife were found guilty of involvement in the murder of his secretary, Sir Thomas Overbury, and imprisoned in the Tower. They were later pardoned by James, but were banished from Court.

Carr was replaced in James's affections by the young George Villiers (later to become the Duke of Buckingham), who had been introduced to the Court by a rival faction in 1613. By 1618 he had taken control of royal patronage. The Howards therefore introduced a handsome rival, William Monson, to the King's circle, provoking Buckingham to destroy them. With plentiful evidence collected by his protégé, Lionel Cranfield, he brought charges of corruption against Suffolk and his uncle, the Earl of Nottingham, securing their dismissal from office and Suffolk's trial in 1619. Buckingham was, and remained, supreme.

Impeachment – Impeachment had been developed by medieval Parliaments as a means of bringing royal advisers and members of the nobility to justice. They were called to trial before the House of Lords by a petition from the Commons. The device had been unused since 1459, but was revived in 1621 to impeach the monopolists, Mitchell and Mompesson, and Lord Chancellor Bacon for bribery. Thereafter the Commons began to apply it as a political weapon against unpopular ministers and advisers.

The basic problem lay in the system of patronage by which the King was expected to reward those who served him. Most offices in government were unpaid and it was normal for ministers and advisers to be rewarded by the grant of pensions or, for example, the right to collect fines and payments related to particular government courts and departments. Hence there was little distinction between a valid payment for work carried out, and a simple gift to a friend or favourite. The system also encouraged courtiers to take gifts and bribes for providing access to the King or pleading an individual's case – and there was a fine distinction between such customary practices and outright corruption. While Cecil grew rich by staying just on the right side of it, Lord Chancellor Bacon threw away an equally promising career by straying over it. In 1621 he was impeached by the Commons for taking bribes, and although pardoned by the King, he was dismissed from office, fined £40,000, and banned from sitting in Parliament.

Cranfield's attempts at reform

The nature of these problems can be demonstrated by considering the attempts to reform the King's finances undertaken by Lionel Cranfield. In 1618 he became Master of the Court of Wards, and later Lord Treasurer and Chancellor of the Exchequer. He established a series of interlocking commissions to examine royal finances, and by 1620 he had reduced the King's household expenses by over 50 per cent. By 1621 it seemed that King, courtiers and MPs were at last co-operating to deal with the government's problems.

However, this was an illusion. Cranfield did make some difference, but he had risen to power through the influence of Buckingham, the King's personal favourite and a product of the very factional rivalry and corruption that lay at the heart of the problems. At least part of Buckingham's enthusiasm for reform lay in the fact that he could use it to bring about the downfall of his rivals, the

George Villiers, Duke Of Buckingham (1592–1628)

George Villiers, Duke of Buckingham, was born in 1592, and educated at Billesdon School, Leicestershire. His father, Sir George Villiers, was a member of the minor gentry of the county, but the family fortunes were transformed by his son's charm and good looks. He was introduced to the King in 1613, in an attempt to undermine the influence of Robert Carr and the Howards. In 1614 he was appointed Cup-bearer to the King, and knighted and made a Gentleman of the Bedchamber, one of the Monarch's personal servants, in 1615. There is little doubt that his relationship with the King had homosexual elements, the full extent of which are impossible to gauge. Buckingham undoubtedly exploited the King's sexual preferences but private letters written to James by his 'Steenie'

reveal genuine affection. Certainly, Buckingham was charming and affable, no more ambitious and somewhat less vicious than other royal favourites.

From 1615 his rise in status was swift. He became Viscount Villiers in 1616, Earl of Buckingham in 1617, Marquess in 1618 and Duke of Buckingham in 1623. His rapid rise and the manner of his influence incensed the more established nobility, and his control of offices, selling of titles and creation of monopolies caused bitter resentment. Attempts to undermine him, however, were unsuccessful, as Cranfield discovered. He was skilled in the factional politics of the Court, and although he relieved the King of some of the burdens of government, he personified much that was wrong with the political system. Essentially, he was able to manipulate royal patronage in the interests of himself and a large number of needy relatives. Nevertheless, his influence on affairs of state was limited, and James remained in control of key policies.

It was not until he became chief adviser to Charles I that his political influence proved disastrous. Initially disliked by the reserved and pious Charles, he was able to win his friendship during the visit to Spain in 1623 (see page 32), and thereafter his political influence and significance increased. With a young and uncertain monarch, Buckingham was able to indulge his own pride and ambition, and embark on an aggressive foreign policy that England could ill afford. While he was capable, and even gifted, in controlling and manipulating Court rivalries and factions, he lacked statesmanship and had no political vision to pursue. The wars against Spain and France in which he embroiled England from 1624–27 had no clear purpose and were inefficiently managed. In 1628 he was described by MPs as the 'cause of all our miseries', but it has to be said that Buckingham's responsibility for England's troubles was shared with a monarch who identified totally with his favourite's decisions and protected him at the cost of his own relationship with Parliament. When Buckingham was assassinated at Portsmouth in 1628, by an ex-army officer named John Felton, Charles wept alone while his people celebrated.

Howards. By 1620 he had taken control of the whole system of royal patronage, relieving James of the burden of making appointments, and using it to reinforce his own power as well as to line the pockets of his large and needy family. While he encouraged Cranfield's efforts, he never allowed the new financial restraints to extend to himself, and the prosecution of Bacon in 1621 was partly managed by Buckingham to deflect attacks on his own power.

Even worse, Cranfield himself proved to be no different. In 1624, now Earl of Middlesex, he tried to extend his own influence at Buckingham's expense by introducing the King to his handsome nephew. Buckingham arranged his fall by encouraging members of Parliament and resentful courtiers to impeach him for bribery. Cranfield had certainly taken bribes as Master of the Wards, and he now paid the price.

Cranfield's failure illustrates the complexity of the Crown's financial problems, and the difficulty of reforming the system from within. It also indicates that the difficulties faced by James were more deep-seated than personal extravagance. It was not only that income was inadequate, it was also badly managed. Essentially, the English monarchy lacked both resources and the means to manage them effectively. Without a professional, salaried civil service, the King had to rely on patronage and pensions to reward his servants; unless carefully monitored and controlled, this invited corruption.

The effects of financial weakness

In these circumstances, the King had little choice but to ask Parliament for grants of taxation to supplement his income, and members were often ready to grant such aid. However, problems arose for two reasons. The first was that MPs were likely to be aggravated if they felt that the Crown's financial difficulties arose from the King's extravagance or the greed of courtiers. The second was that the King was also driven to apply other financial strategies, such as impositions and monopolies, which caused further friction. While these were offensive in themselves, driving up prices and restricting trade, they also raised constitutional issues. Friction between King and Parliament over finance led to quarrels over rights and privileges. Between 1606 and 1614 the issue of impositions raised concerns in Parliament about whether its right to control taxation was being eroded. This worry remained strong for many years and it certainly contributed to Parliament's refusal to grant Tunnage and Poundage to Charles for life in 1625. In 1621 the desire to pursue the monopolists led Parliament to revive the medieval procedure of impeachment (see page 26) as a means of calling the King's advisers to account.

The significance of financial problems was therefore threefold: they revealed serious problems within the structure of government; they caused a deterioration of the relationship between James and the political nation; and they raised constitutional issues concerning the rights and prerogatives of Parliament and of the King. In isolation, these problems could be dealt with by negotiation and compromise, but by 1621 political tension was increasing dangerously as a result of other problems relating to religion, foreign policy and war. In the parliamentary sessions of 1621 and 1624, these separate problems became interwoven in a way that made them much more difficult to handle, and created serious tensions between the rights and privileges claimed by Parliament and the King's exercise of his power and prerogatives.

KEY DATES: GOVERNMENT AND FINANCE

1618 Lionel Cranfield becomes Master of the Court of Wards and begins to reorganise royal finances.

1620 Expenses reduced by 50 per cent.

1621 Impeachment of monopolists and of Lord Chancellor (Francis Bacon) for bribery.

1624 Fall of Cranfield; Parliament passes an act to restrict the sale of monopolies.

Foreign policy and war, 1618–23

How did events in Europe create problems for James and his Parliaments?

Since 1604, when he had ended Elizabeth's war with Spain, James had kept England at peace. This was partly a matter of necessity, since he could not afford to finance military action, but it was also a matter of preference. James hoped that by standing aside from the religious struggles enveloping Europe he could maintain contact with both Catholic and Protestant powers, and act as peacemaker. Hence he married his daughter Elizabeth to a German Protestant prince, the Elector Palatine, and sought a Spanish Catholic wife for his son Charles.

His friendship with the Spanish ambassador, Gondomar, was regarded with suspicion by many of his subjects, whose fear of Catholic influence was exceeded only by their bitter memories of Spanish plots and Spanish threats against Elizabeth. Nevertheless, James hoped to cultivate contacts with the Habsburg rulers of Spain by marrying his son Charles to the King of Spain's daughter, the Infanta Isabella. Problems arose, however, with the outbreak of the Thirty Years War in Europe, which created serious difficulties for James and for England.

The Thirty Years War

The Thirty Years War began in 1618 when a German prince, the Elector Palatine, was invited to take the throne of Protestant Bohemia, in place of Archduke Ferdinand of Styria, the Habsburg candidate who had been presented in 1617. The Elector was a Protestant, and the son-in-law of James I, who advised him not to accept. When the Elector ignored this advice, he was attacked and driven out of Bohemia by Ferdinand, who had become Holy Roman Emperor in 1619. Ferdinand then sought to punish him by seizing his hereditary lands in the Palatinate. This aroused the other German princes, especially the Protestants in northern Germany, who feared the same treatment. The war therefore escalated – the Protestants of the Dutch Republic and Scandinavia entered in support of the Princes, while the Spanish Habsburgs supported their Austrian cousins. Although nominally Catholic, France took the opportunity to challenge Habsburg power by helping the Protestants.

Germany was ravaged by atrocities on both sides but, to the English, the war was portrayed as a struggle against Catholic tyranny. It finally ended in 1648, although the war between France and Spain continued until 1659, when French victory laid the foundations for the dominance of Europe by Louis XIV and introduced a new threat to English power.

> **Holy Roman Emperor** – The head of the Holy Roman Empire, which was established in Germany in the early Middle Ages, bringing 329 small German states together under a single leader. By the late fifteenth century the Austrian family of Habsburg had established a right to be 'elected' to the position, giving them effective control of modern Germany, Austria and much of central Europe.

War, religion and parliaments

As the largest Protestant power in Europe, England could hardly stand aside in the face of Catholic aggression, but could not finance a prolonged war. As a Protestant King and the father-in-law of the victim, James needed to act, but lacked the means to do so effectively. Initially, he sought to use his contacts with Spain, but tried to increase his impact, and his value as an ally, by making preparations for war as an alternative strategy. In 1621 he summoned a Parliament and asked for money to finance intervention in Europe. Aware of the dangers of inflaming an already volatile fear of Catholicism, he stressed the need to prepare for war to secure peace, and redoubled his diplomatic efforts. At first it appeared that his strategy might be successful. Faced with a depression in trade caused by war in Europe, MPs had no wish to incur unnecessary expense. Nevertheless, they voted two subsidies, and then turned their attention to waste, extravagance and corruption at Court.

Europe during the Thirty Years War

Figure 2 shows the complicated arrangement of states in central Europe that led to the eruption of war in 1618. The Thirty Years War was the final stage of the two great rivalries that dominated Europe throughout the sixteenth century – between Catholic and Protestant, and between French and Habsburg monarchies. The Habsburg family controlled Spain and the Spanish Netherlands and lands along the eastern borders of France, as well as parts of Italy and Austria. Their possessions therefore encircled France and had for some time posed a threat to its independence and security. They had also established a tradition of electing Habsburgs to be Holy Roman Emperor, with nominal lordship over the many petty princes who ruled Germany, and, as a separate title, to be King of Bohemia (now the Czech Republic). The Habsburgs were devoutly Catholic, and supported the aggressive Catholicism of the Counter-Reformation.

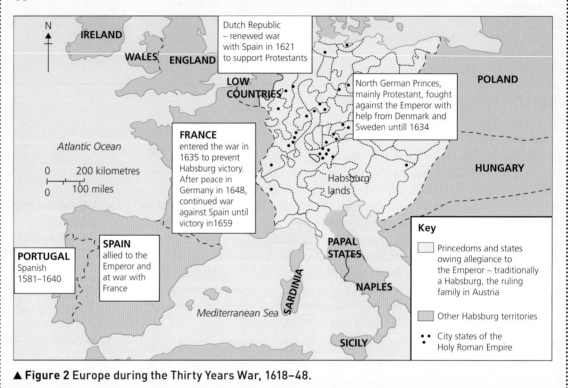

▲ Figure 2 Europe during the Thirty Years War, 1618–48.

These complaints were not directed at the King – in fact many of the attacks were orchestrated by courtiers and Court factions anxious to weaken rivals, especially the Duke of Buckingham. By allowing the Commons to impeach the Lord Chancellor, Sir Francis Bacon, for taking bribes, the Duke survived, and the session ended quietly. In November 1621, when members reassembled, they were directed once again to consider the need for war finance; many MPs did have strong Protestant views and in December they petitioned the King to enter the war against the Habsburgs. At this point, several MPs raised the issue of what kind of war should be fought. The relief of James's daughter and the reconquest of the Palatinate would require a land war and the equipping of an army. Many members were aware of the expense involved, and were equally aware that Spanish strength came from her possessions in South America and the flow of silver from her colonies. To them, it made more sense to consider a naval war, with its echoes of Elizabethan glory and possible financial windfalls from Spanish treasure, and they said so in a Commons debate.

Protestation and dissolution

From James's point of view, this debate over the nature of the war to be fought overstepped the bounds of parliamentary privilege, and strayed into the formulation of policy, which was the prerogative of the King. Angrily, he reminded members of the limits of their privilege of free speech – to freely discuss issues raised by the monarch, not to raise issues of their own – and that it came by the will of the sovereign. Provoked in their turn, the Commons set out a Protestation (see Source C), asserting that the rights of Parliament and the liberties of the subject 'are the ancient and undoubted birthright and inheritance of the subjects of England' – which James tore out of the Commons Journal.

Source C From the Commons Protestation of 18 December, 1621.

That the liberties, franchises, privileges and jurisdictions of Parliament are the ancient and undoubted birthright and inheritance of the subjects of England; and that the arduous and urgent affairs concerning the King, State and defence of the realm and of the Church of England, are proper subjects and matter of counsel and debate in Parliament; and that in the handling and proceeding of those businesses every member of the House of Parliament hath, and of right ought to have, freedom of speech to propound, treat, reason and bring to conclusion the same...

> What does Source C suggest about the relationship between James and Parliament in 1621? If you compare Source C with Source B on page 24, is there any indication that the relationship had changed?

In essence, the quarrel was the same as that of 1604 (see page 22), turning on the issue of whether Parliament's privileges existed by right or by gift of the monarch. In this case, however, MPs were claiming the right to debate royal policy on foreign affairs and religion. Whatever the rights of free speech, these areas of policy came within the King's recognised prerogatives, and the Commons were encroaching on royal powers. James had every right to object, although whether his reaction was politically wise is more debatable. To have allowed the debate would have set a dangerous precedent, but once the issue moved on to parliamentary privileges, there was little chance of agreement. It was clear to James that there would be no grant of taxes, and there had been some attacks on both his policy and his favourite, the Duke of Buckingham. Accordingly, he dissolved the Parliament and continued his diplomatic pursuit of Spanish friendship and a Spanish marriage for his son.

The legacy of the 1621 Parliament

The legacy of the Parliament of 1621 was complex. While his foreign policy had made little progress, the King had defended his prerogative with some success. Nevertheless, there were some worrying signs and precedents. The Commons had been able to bring some government office-holders to account, using the mechanism of impeachment. These proceedings had arisen from rivalries among government factions, but there was no guarantee that the Court or the Lords would always be able to orchestrate their use. The quarrel over privilege and prerogative had sharpened existing fears. Above all, the airing of concerns about foreign policy had alerted Protestant opinion to the Catholic threat and raised concerns about the King's attitude towards Spain. Members had expressed concern about a Catholic marriage, and the concessions that would be required by Spain. The Parliament of 1621 had not precipitated a crisis, but the monarch might well find that it had increased the capacity of later assemblies to do so.

Charles and Buckingham

The likelihood of crisis was also increased by the fact that control of affairs was slipping from James to Buckingham and Prince Charles. As the King grew older, and his health deteriorated, he was more content to leave the running of government to his favourite, although he retained control of political strategy. In 1623, however, his strategy was wrecked by the actions of Charles and Buckingham in undertaking a secret visit to Spain to try to secure the proposed marriage. Their motives are not entirely clear – for Charles it was probably a romantic gesture prompted by naivety and youth, for Buckingham the chance to win the favour of the next King. Whatever their reasons, their secret departure and unannounced arrival in Spain wrecked James's plans. His grand diplomatic strategy was reduced to a need to ensure the safety of his son. For Charles and Buckingham, it was a humiliation; the Spanish stalled on marriage negotiations, and then rejected the match. By 1624 they had returned to England, determined on revenge.

Under pressure from Charles and Buckingham, James summoned Parliament to ask for money to finance a war with Spain. His reservations were set aside by an anti-Catholic Parliament in alliance with his favourite and his heir. The King, who was weakened by age and ill-health, was powerless to resist. In order to secure their war, Charles and Buckingham agreed to the naval strategy favoured by MPs but, nevertheless, paid an army to serve in the Palatinate under the command of German mercenary, Count Mansfeld. This deception and the disastrous failure of the expedition infuriated Parliament when it reassembled in 1625, but it was Charles who reaped the bitter harvest, since James had died in March.

> **KEY DATES: FOREIGN POLICY AND WAR**
>
> **1618** Outbreak of the Thirty Years War.
>
> **1620** Defeat and exile of the Elector Palatine.
>
> **1621** James calls Parliament and debates on foreign policy lead to the Commons Protestation and an early dissolution.
>
> **1623** Charles and Buckingham visit Spain, causing the collapse of James' diplomatic strategy.

Interpretations: James I – the Wisest Fool in Christendom?

It was the contemporary King of France, Henry IV who is reputed to have made this unflattering comment on James I and his skills as a monarch, probably in reference to the publication of his work, *The True Law of Free Monarchies,* in 1598, and the apparent contrast between his philosophical wisdom and his practical management of the role of monarch. This was reinforced by the style of his court and the sometimes personally motivated attacks that are summarised in Trevelyan's claims on page 26. However, the remark has also been interpreted as suggesting that, despite his high-flown claims and rhetoric regarding the Divine Right of Kings, James demonstrated a great deal of common sense and realism in dealing with tensions both in Britain and Europe. For whatever reason, many historians' judgements of James have been deeply unflattering, but others have argued that he managed a difficult legacy well and that it was not until the accession of his son Charles that tensions within the system of government degenerated into open conflict.

ACTIVITY

Sources D–F on pages 33–34 offer three different interpretations of James I's character, court and his government for you to consider and evaluate in the light of your own study of his reign. You should begin by reading each one and listing the main points made and the evidence used to support them. Do not simply read the words – consider the implications as well. You may find it useful to list the points in two columns (headed 'wisest' and 'fool'). You can then compare the arguments from each source and consider:

1 In what ways do the sources agree and disagree?
2 Are they looking at the same aspects of James' character and government or emphasising different areas?
3 Does this help to explain their conflicting views?
4 Does this mean that the conflicts can be reconciled?
5 What other reasons can you suggest for the different interpretations of James and his effectiveness as a monarch?

Finally, you should use the material from the sources to present two conflicting views of James I, and then use your own knowledge in addition to construct a balanced judgement.

Source D From *Stuart Monarchy and Political Culture*, by Kevin Sharpe in John Morrill (ed.) *The Oxford Illustrated History of Tudor and Stuart Britain*, (Clarendon Press) 1996.

For all his considerable intelligence and intellectualism, James was a practical, down-to-earth character, with little sympathy for rituals and florid formalities, let alone entertainments presenting the monarch as a god of love and nature. The Scottish King could be insensitive, blunt and grossly indecorous. Though his detractors exaggerated his personal failings and contributed to this bad press, James himself showed little concern with public relations. He presided over evenings of drunken debauchery and was personally slovenly and unkempt. Such lack of decorum, compounded by James's own homosexual relations and the sexual scandals of his reign, both sharpened the criticisms of the Court and diminished the authority of majesty which depended as much on style and image as on the talents and policies of the ruler.

[Yet] James's personal style in some ways reorientated the Court for the better. During the last years of her reign the isolation and difficulty of access to Elizabeth had dangerous repercussions ... [and she] glossed over problems that needed to be confronted. James, in complete contrast, was willing to acknowledge and ready to tackle problems; and he remained open to a wide variety of influences. No figure or faction during the early years of the reign needed to despair of persuading the king to advance their persons or policies; the Court functioned, as it was meant to, as the centre of all political positions and groups.

Source E From *Politics in an Age of Peace and War*, by Christopher Haigh in John Morrill (ed.) *The Oxford Illustrated History of Tudor and Stuart Britain*, (Clarendon Press) 1996.

James self-selected task in life had been to become King of England and that had been achieved. He had worked hard to survive in Scotland and to succeed to England. He had tried and failed to achieve political Union, and he had tried with more success to reduce religious tensions. He liked to strut as an international statesman and a European scholar, but neither role was, for him, a full-time occupation. There seemed little more for even a conscientious King to do – and James was not very conscientious. So he was free to hunt at Royston or Newmarket with his friends, Hay, Carr, and Villiers. Government was easy once again, with peace, good order, low mortality and religious unity, spoiled only by poor harvests in 1612, 1613 and 1615. He could take time off from England for a trip to Scotland in 1617. But his carelessness allowed royal finances to deteriorate still further, while links between central government and the country gentry were weakened.

Source F From *The Causes of the English Civil War* by Conrad Russell, (Clarendon Press) 1990.

There is no news in stressing the financial difficulties of the early Stuarts. It is conventional to blame the Stuarts themselves for their financial misfortunes, and their reigns, especially that of James, give plenty of material to justify blaming them. However, to say that the Stuarts mishandled their financial system is not to say that it would have worked if they had handled it well, and it is the central contention of this chapter that the Stuarts inherited a financial system which was already close to the point of breakdown. In any country that believes in taxation by consent, the financial and political systems must be very closely related, and the English political system, although it still enjoyed almost universal support and affection, was becoming obsolete because it was no longer capable of successfully financing war. The system the Stuarts inherited was, in essentials, that of the fourteenth century.

All this should be borne in mind when assessing the Stuarts' difficulties in getting adequate supply out of their parliaments. A great deal of the trouble seems to have come from plain incomprehension of the sums needed ... The Crown never seems to have reached a final decision about whether it was more impossible to finance itself with Parliaments or without Parliaments. The fact that Parliaments continued when the crown found that they were no longer fulfilling the function for which they had been created should alone be enough to acquit the crown of any conscious and deliberate absolutist programme.

WORKING TOGETHER

Evaluating the different interpretations of James I is essentially an individual task, but you could also develop your ideas more fully by working with a partner or as part of a group. When you have read and interpreted the sources to define the different views of the historians, work together to prepare a short presentation that puts forward one view of James. By producing four presentations from different pairings or groups, two on each side, you can explore the ideas more fully and demonstrate how arguments will vary, before individually writing your own balanced judgement.

2 The early reign of Charles I, 1625–29

This section will look at Charles's early reign, in particular his deteriorating relationship with parliament and the religious tensions underpinning this period. However, to understand some of the difficulties that arose, it is necessary to begin by investigating his upbringing and personality, which played a significant part in the way that events unfolded from 1625–29.

Charles I: the role of the individual

How did Charles' personal qualities affect his exercise of royal power?

The new King, portrayed on page 36 by Van Dyck, was the second son of James, a fact that had considerable influence on the events of his reign. Until the age of twelve he had lived in the shadow of his older and more confident brother, Henry. Henry had been physically strong, outgoing and aggressively Protestant – exactly the kind of heir to the throne that England desired. Until he died of a fever in 1612, little attention had been paid to the small, sickly and reticent Charles. He had therefore grown up to be shy and unable to communicate easily, as well as sensitive and lacking confidence in his own abilities. In fact, he was intelligent and perceptive in certain matters – he became, for example, a generous and discerning patron of artists and architects, and acquired a considerable collection of fine work, which was housed in Whitehall and at Windsor.

His early childhood left its mark on Charles's behaviour as King. He tended to maintain a protective reserve and to place great emphasis on orderly formality. This was reflected in the procedures and rules that he adopted for his Court – immorality was frowned upon, rank and nobility were carefully preserved, and the royal family's privacy respected. Charles had been greatly impressed by the formality of the Spanish Court during his visit in 1623, and sought to emulate its dignity. The same preferences may have influenced his religious views. A devout and conscientious Anglican, he was undoubtedly Protestant in his beliefs, but his appreciation of the 'beauty of holiness' represented in rich decoration and elaborate rituals encouraged his sympathy for the High Church party and even respect for Catholic views. Unfortunately, none of these qualities were likely to endear him to his subjects.

His lack of confidence was also a problem. His response to opposition was to take refuge in the appearance of certainty and to view those who disagreed as motivated by malice. To a degree, his conscientious attention to duty made it more difficult to accept criticism. Perhaps most seriously, it also created a lifelong tendency to rely on the advice of those close to him. In the words of Edward Hyde, who became chief adviser to both Charles I and his son, Charles II:

'he will be found not only a prince of admirable virtue and piety, but of great knowledge, wisdom and judgement; and that the most signal parts of his misfortunes proceeded chiefly from the modesty of his nature, which kept him from trusting himself enough, and made him believe that others discerned better, who were much inferior to him in those faculties; and so to depart from his own reason, to follow the opinions of more unskilful men, whose affections he believed to be unquestionable to his service…'

Unfortunately the first of these was the Duke of Buckingham, closely followed by the equally determined and equally ill-informed Henrietta Maria.

NOTE-MAKING

1 Make a list of what you consider to be the main features of Charles I's character and attitudes and retain it for future reference.

2 As you read through the material that follows, make notes on 'The early reign of Charles I, 1625–29'. Use the headings and questions to help you create sub-headings and select material. When you have completed your notes, cross-reference with your list and highlight any events and situations where you think that Charles's character and attitudes played a part.

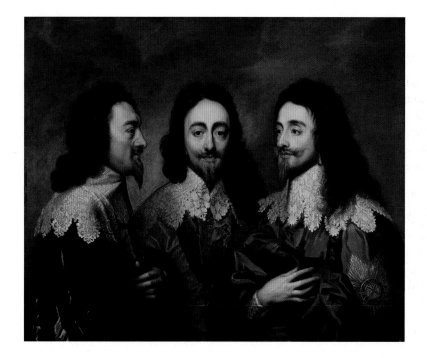

Three Faces of Charles I, painted ▶ by Van Dyke in 1635. What image of kingship does this portrait project?

Charles, Buckingham and war, 1625–27

Why did relations between King and Parliament deteriorate so quickly?

The brief alliance of Charles, Buckingham and the House of Commons collapsed with a refusal by MPs to vote the new King Tunnage and Poundage (customs duties, see page 24) for more than one year. Apart from the effect on his finances, the denial of the traditional lifetime grant was a considerable insult, but it came as a direct result of his actions during James's last year of life. By agreeing to conduct a naval war and using the resulting subsidies to fund a (disastrous) land expedition, Charles had given MPs every reason to distrust him, even without the widely recognised problem of Buckingham's influence. Granting the right for the King to levy customs duties for one year only was a means of ensuring that a Parliament would have to meet at the end of that time. Unfortunately, it was also a direct challenge to the new monarch.

The new reign therefore got off to a bad start, and it rapidly continued downhill. Unlike James, Charles lacked confidence and experience in diplomacy, and relied upon the advice of Buckingham. Freed from the restraints imposed by James, the Duke embarked on an adventurous foreign policy designed to glorify himself and his King. Unfortunately his lack of planning, failure to attend to detail and unrealistic expectations ensured that it was a disaster. An unsuccessful naval expedition to Cadiz was followed by demands for Buckingham to be impeached, and in 1626, in order to save his friend, Charles dissolved Parliament without receiving any financial supply.

Worse was to follow. In 1624 Buckingham had negotiated a marriage for Charles to Henrietta Maria, the sister of the French King, promising that she would be permitted to practise her own Catholic religion, and that English ships would help to suppress a French Protestant rebellion in La Rochelle. MPs were furious, and became even more so when in 1626 Buckingham's inept diplomacy led to war with France, and an expedition sent in 1627 to help the Protestants in La Rochelle failed miserably because of inadequate planning. By the end of 1627 the influence of Buckingham and Charles's stubborn refusal to contain it was directly threatening his ability to govern his kingdom.

Charles, Parliament, and the rule of law

How did tensions develop into a parliamentary crisis?

As complaints about Buckingham mounted, Charles recognised that he would obtain no money from Parliament without sacrificing his friend but, on this, he would make no concession. It was not only a matter of personal loyalty; Charles was also infuriated by the attempt to call his chosen adviser to account in Parliament. Convinced of the need to govern according to his own views, he moved to obtain money by alternative measures.

Forced loans

Not only did he continue to collect Tunnage and Poundage without parliamentary approval, Charles also demanded a forced loan to be collected by JPs, and threatened that any who refused to lend the King money would be imprisoned or conscripted into the army. He was not the first monarch to demand such a loan, but he was the first to carry out his threats against those who refused. In 1627, five gentlemen, who came to be known as the Five Knights, challenged his right to imprison them. After a good deal of pressure from the King, the judges reluctantly found in his favour. Charles then sought to have their judgement entered as a precedent for the future. While he believed that he was merely asserting his right to govern effectively, in practice he was denying the rule of law and laying a foundation for tyranny. It was inconceivable that a Parliament, if one was called, would not attempt to challenge his actions in some way.

> **Forced loan** – A relic of feudalism in which the king had the right to ask his wealthier subjects to lead him money in an emergency. In fact, they were rarely paid back, so it was a form of taxation outside parliament.

The Petition of Right

By 1628, therefore, Charles had provoked a constitutional crisis, which he lacked the means to handle. Still at war, and in desperate need of money, he was forced to call a new Parliament to ask for supply. Led by the experienced lawyer, Sir Edward Coke, the Commons put together a Petition of Right, which reversed the judgement in the Five Knights' Case and asked the King to declare that in future there would be no more:

- forced loans
- imprisonment without trial
- use of free lodgings (billeting) for soldiers in civilian households
- use of martial law against civilians.

Five subsidies were voted, but would not proceed to the House of Lords until the King accepted the Petition. He had no choice but to agree.

The term, 'Petition of Right', was carefully chosen to convey the fact that Parliament were asking the King to help them – in this case to define the law – and also asserting a *right* rather than making a request. Hence it maintained an outward respect for the King while also avoiding any implication that such rights were dependent on his good will. By claiming that the rights already existed, and that the King was merely redefining the law to correct a mistake by the judges, the Petition avoided asking the King to admit a mistake while also ensuring that, since he was not granting the right to refuse a forced loan, he could not take it away. Once he accepted the Petition, its contents had the force of law.

> **KEY DATES: THE RULE OF LAW**
>
> **1624** Parliament assembles and grants money – intended for a naval war but used for the Mansfeld expedition.
>
> **1624** Marriage of Charles to the French Catholic princess, Henrietta Maria.
>
> **1625** Parliament reassembled after failure of Mansfeld; death of James I.
>
> **1625** Accession of Charles I.
>
> **1626** Parliament dissolved to prevent impeachment of Buckingham.
>
> **1626–27** Forced Loan levied.
>
> **1627** Five Knights Case.
>
> **1628** Petition of Right presented. Buckingham assassinated.

At this point it was possible that the Petition of Right and the grant of money could provide the opportunity for reconciliation between King and Parliament, and the chances of this improved in August 1628, when Buckingham was assassinated (see page 27). However, mistakes by both the King and the more volatile MPs destroyed this opportunity. When Parliament reassembled in 1629 there were open celebrations of Buckingham's death, which angered the grief-stricken King. In turn, when Parliament began to prepare a bill to extend the King's right to collect Tunnage and Poundage, Charles denied that it was necessary, undermining Parliament's control of taxation. The most serious rift, however, was caused by growing concern about the King's religious views and his policies regarding the Church.

Religion and the Church

Why did religious fears increase after the death of James I?

The caution and tact used by James in making changes to the Church had resulted in years of relative harmony over its organisation and the role of bishops. While the Puritan ministers and their sympathisers had not given up hope of further reform, and had preached their message with enthusiasm, they had been able to accept the existing rules to the extent of at least partial conformity. Under the leadership of Archbishop Abbot, the majority of bishops used their powers of enforcement with care. Above all, the Calvinist beliefs held by the King and the majority of bishops reassured Puritan minds and established an Anglican identity which most could accept.

The Arminian group

This tactful approach came to an end with the accession of Charles I. Unlike his father, Charles placed order and uniformity above tact, and he was not prepared to proceed slowly. His personal beliefs were closest to those of the Arminian group (see Figure 3, page 39), who had recently emerged within the Anglican Church. Their name is derived from a Dutch reformer, Jacob Arminius, who had challenged the influence of Calvinism among Protestant thinkers, and rejected the doctrine of predestination (see page 13). However, the chief characteristic of the English Arminians was their emphasis on ritual and sacraments in place of preaching, and the enhanced role and status that they gave to the Church and the clergy in the individual's search for salvation. Because they regarded the Roman Catholic Church as misguided rather than evil, and respected the common heritage derived from the medieval Church, they traced the power and authority of the clergy back to Christ himself. They hoped that the next thing to happen would be for the King to use his power and authority to establish order, decency, and uniform practice throughout the Church of England.

To a man with Charles's love of beauty and sense of order, Arminian ideas held great appeal. Unfortunately, to many of his subjects both in and out of Parliament, they were uncomfortably close to Catholicism. Oblivious of the fears that he was generating, Charles embarked on a campaign to reform the Church according to his own vision. Where James had promoted and favoured men from all religious factions, Charles exclusively advanced the Arminians, who responded by supporting a heightened royal power.

When they defended the King's behaviour over the Forced Loan of 1627, and argued that subjects had a duty to obey even an unjust King, they reinforced the fears of all those who believed that Catholicism, **absolute monarchy** and tyranny went hand in hand. In 1628 the Arminian leader, William Laud,

---

KEY DATES: RELIGION AND THE CHURCH

1627 Arminians defend King's right to raise forced loans.

1628 William Laud (Arminian) appointed Bishop of London.

Absolute monarchy – A monarchy in which the king is responsible only to God and thereby has absolute, unchallenged, power and his will and decisions alone make the law. Fear of absolutism was increasing at this time, because the French and Spanish monarchies were moving in this direction by destroying the independence and in some cases even the existence of local assemblies and Parliaments. Because these were Catholic monarchs, and the Catholic Church was also organised in this way, the association of Catholicism, absolutism and tyranny in English minds was deeply entrenched.

became Bishop of London. By 1629 there were many who feared that Charles intended to restore Catholicism and establish an absolute monarchy in England; or that if he did not, he was being led in that direction by his advisers and his Catholic Queen.

The result was another stormy session of Parliament in 1629, which the frustrated King decided to prorogue (suspend). Fearing that they would have little opportunity to protest in future, a group of MPs ignored the summons to disperse, held the Speaker in his chair to keep the House of Commons in session, and passed Three Resolutions against the growth of Arminianism, the levying of Tunnage and Poundage, and the actions of those who paid it. Angered by such open defiance, Charles dissolved Parliament, and declared that he would not call another until his subjects should 'see more clearly into our intentions and actions' and have 'a better understanding of us and themselves'. What this represented was an open breach between King and Parliament, and a significant breakdown within the system of government.

▼ **Figure 3** The religious spectrum.

	Puritan view	Anglican view	Arminian view	Catholic view
Faith and salvation	Salvation gained as a gift from God to those who were predestined to be saved. Evidence of predestination was the willingness to accept discipline and seek a godly life.	Salvation by faith alone.	The gift of salvation was open to all who would seek it through a true Church. God offers salvation to all – mankind is free to accept or reject it.	Salvation for all but only through the Catholic Church.
Role of the Church and priesthood	To guide and educate according to the rules laid down in the Bible. The chief function of the minister is to preach God's Word, to allow souls to find their way to Him. Ministers also apply discipline to support the saints and control the sinners.	The Church has authority to guide people to salvation.	The Church guides through a priesthood which has special powers and status. Their authority is symbolised by robes and ceremonies. There is a place for preaching, but teaching through set prayers and rituals is as important.	The Catholic Church and its rituals provide the path to God. Taking part offers salvation.
Ritual and preaching	Preaching and private prayer, Bible study and reading are the key to salvation. Sacraments like communion are symbolic only. Ritual distracts the ignorant from true religion and creates superstition and idolatry.	There is a place for some ritual to symbolise aspects of faith – for example, Holy Communion.	Ritual creates reverence and brings the ignorant to God. If it is beautiful in itself, it is a form of worship. Ritual is essential to promote order and decency.	Ritual is part of salvation – we are saved by our actions and works, such as taking part in a ritual.
Role and power of bishops	Bishops have no special power. The parish minister is the true leader of the congregation, and the best organisation would be with committees of ministers, advised by bishops if desired.	Bishops have authority to rule the Church and represent the King.	Bishops have a special place and authority, passed down from Christ himself through St Peter and the medieval Church. They receive power to enforce rules from the King.	Bishops have special authority from Christ passed through the Pope.
Attitude to Catholicism	Catholicism is evil: the devil seeking to corrupt true faith. The Pope is the Anti-Christ, the devil himself.	Catholics threaten true faith; but many of their errors are not a threat to salvation.	Catholicism represents the early Church, misled by error. It is a sister Church, like those set up by Calvin and Luther, and should be treated as such. There need be no Protestant identity which shuts out Catholics.	The true Church.
Obedience to authority	Obedience should be given to those in authority unless they threaten God's cause and true religion.	Obedience should be given to higher authority except on a few matters vital to salvation.	Obedience to authority in Church and State should be total. If, on rare occasions, conscience makes it necessary to disobey, the subject should surrender to authority and accept punishment.	The authority of the Pope is from God – the Pope is therefore speaking for God and obedience is essential.

WORKING TOGETHER

- Firstly, compare the notes that you have made on this section. Add anything that you have missed and check anything that you have disagreed on.
- Next, one of you should identify how Charles as an individual contributed to the difficulties he faced in his relationship with Parliament. The other should note the other factors that caused these difficulties.
- After you have finished, discuss your findings. Overall, how would you assess Charles's role in contributing to his difficulties?
- Find examples of situations where Charles was under pressure because of other issues, and consider how this influenced his actions.
- Similarly, consider areas where Charles made existing problems worse.

By doing this you will be developing a sense of how different factors combined and interacted to cause problems. For example, Buckingham was a very bad political adviser and administrator, who created big problems for Charles. However, Charles allowed him to make decisions of a kind that James never did, probably because of his lack of confidence. Therefore the *interaction* of their particular personalities could be said to be the real problem, rather than the individual actions of either man.

- To complete the process, you should each write a summary to explain how the different factors worked together – for example, how older problems became worse, or how the personalities of Charles and Buckingham interacted, which will help you to come to a conclusion about Charles's role and responsibility.

Chapter summary

- From 1603 to 1620 there were occasional tensions between the King and parliaments, mainly over finance and the extravagance of the Court.
- However, James's handling of religious issues was reasonably effective, especially after the appointment of Archbishop Abbot to Canterbury in 1611.
- From around 1620, and certainly by 1621, that tension had increased because financial problems were compounded by the outbreak of the Thirty Years War and the Commons Protestation of 1621.
- From 1621–24 relations were complex, and made more difficult by the actions of Prince Charles and Buckingham.
- In 1625 the death of James and the accession of Charles I brought a rapid deterioration in relations, leading to the Petition of Right in 1628 and eventually to an open breach in 1629.
- By 1628–29 there were serious problems, arising from the interaction of the personalities of Charles and Buckingham with a growing opposition in Parliament.
- In 1628 the Petition of Right highlighted fears that Charles's autocratic behavior threatened basic liberties and the rule of law, but offered a carefully worded and face-saving opportunity for the King to find a way around the problem and begin to repair the damage.
- However, Charles was unwilling to compromise and the assassination of Buckingham made the situation much worse.
- In addition, Charles's continued promotion of Arminians in the Church raised fears of a Catholic, absolutist conspiracy.
- In 1629 the opportunity to settle the fears and conflicts had passed, and after the defiant behaviour of MPs in delaying their departure to pass the Three Resolutions, Charles issued a Proclamation in which he made it clear that he intended to govern without Parliaments for the foreseeable future.

▼ Figure 4 This thematic summary of events traces the development of tensions and the growth of conflict between King and Parliament from 1603–29.

Date	Political and economic developments	Religion and foreign policy
1603	James becomes King.	Millenary Petition presented to James by Puritans.
1604	Peace with Spain. Disputed election leads to quarrel in Parliament and Commons 'Apology'.	Hampton Court conference. Appointment of Bancroft as Archbishop of Canterbury marks attack on Puritan ministers.
1605	Debates over union with Scotland lead to tension and failure of James's plan in 1607.	Gunpowder Plot.
1606	Bates Case – judges approve the 'imposition' of new duties.	
1608	New Book of Rates published.	
1610	Complaints in Parliament about 'impositions'. Failure of Great Contract.	
1611		Appointment of Abbot as Archbishop introduces a more moderate approach to Puritan concerns within the Church.
1612	Death of Robert Cecil.	
1614	Impositions help to cause chaos in the 'Addled Parliament'.	
1618	Lionel Cranfield becomes Master of the Court of Wards and begins to reorganise royal finances.	Elector Palatine becomes King of Bohemia.
1620	Expenses reduced by 50 per cent.	
1621	Impeachment of monopolists and of Lord Chancellor (Francis Bacon) for bribery.	Elector Palatine defeated by Emperor Ferdinand and driven from his lands. English Parliament votes subsidies for war but the quarrel over Parliament's right to discuss foreign policy leads to Commons Protestation.
1623		Charles and Buckingham visit Spain.
1624	Fall of Cranfield. Parliament passes an act to restrict the sale of monopolies.	War with Spain and marriage of Charles and Henrietta Maria.
1625	Accession of Charles I.	
1626	Parliament dissolved to prevent impeachment of Buckingham. Forced Loan levied.	Failure at Cadiz. War with France. King's right to imprison those who refused the forced loan defended by Arminian writers.
1627	Five Knights Case.	Failure at La Rochelle.
1628	Petition of Right presented. Buckingham assassinated.	William Laud (Arminian) appointed Bishop of London.
1629	King and Parliament quarrel over Arminian appointments and Tunnage and Poundage. This leads to the Three Resolutions and dissolution of Parliament.	Peace negotiations bring wars to an end.

Working on essay technique

Whether you are doing the AS or the A-level, Section B in the examination presents you with essay titles. If you are doing the AS exam you answer one (from a choice of two). If you are doing the full A-level exam you answer two (from a choice of three). Each question is marked out of 25.

Several question stems are possible as alternatives, but they all have the same basic requirement. They all require you to analyse and reach a conclusion, based on the evidence you provide. For example:

- 'Assess the validity [of a quotation]'
- 'To what extent…'
- 'How successful…'
- 'How far…'

Each question will reflect, directly or indirectly, one of the breadth issues in your study. The questions will have a fairly broad focus.

Over the following chapters, you will practise these type of questions, but the first stage is to consider basic essay technique and to develop your awareness of the historical concepts involved – the concepts of *causation* and *change*. Because you cannot really begin to address change until you have covered a long enough period for changes to take effect, this section will focus on the concept of causation.

You should also be aware that this section is not intended to provide examination practice – that will come later. The main purpose here is to introduce essay planning and show you how to explain the causes of an event, i.e. a basic causal explanation.

How to plan your essays

You will already have experience of writing essays from previous study. Some of this will be really useful to build on.

Effective essays are planned essays and, in exam conditions, planned quickly. To achieve this you need to develop and practice a method of planning, so that it comes quickly and easily when you need it. The suggestions below offer you a method that can be adapted to suit different individuals and circumstances, and you will find out what suits you best by practising it over a period of time.

Basic method: a good essay will have:

- an *introduction* (no more than a paragraph long) that sets out the issues to be discussed

- a *main essay* which works through points in order to set out an explanation
- a *conclusion* that summarises the explanation as an answer to the question.

Before you start writing it you need to plan all these things together. Let's take, for example, the question posed at the beginning of this chapter:

Why did tensions develop between King and Parliament to the point where they were in open conflict by 1629?

This is not the kind of question that you will meet in an examination, but it is a good one to consider how to plan a causal explanation. Once you know how to do that, you will be able to adapt it to a range of more complex questions.

Taking the following steps will help you to write an effective answer to this question.

Step 1: Analyse the question

Analyse the question to decide what it is asking you to do – what are the key issues that is raises? A summary of these issues will often make a good *introduction*, which enables you to focus on the question from the start and sets out where your explanation is going.

This is a question about *causes*, so you will need to start by looking into what happened to identify the *causal factors* that created and built up the tension. Notice:

- The question refers to 'King and Parliament' rather than individual kings and parliaments. You know that the king in 1629 was Charles I, but until 1625 the king was his father, James, so the question requires you to consider events involving both.
- In addition it refers to tensions 'developing' to 'a point where', implying a process by which they built up and gradually got worse.

Both these things indicate that this is a 'breadth' question. To answer it, you will need to take a broad view and look for causes across the whole period that you have covered in this chapter. Throughout the essay it is important to remember that you are not discussing the causes of tension generally, but specifically why they affected the relationship between King and Parliament to the point of an open conflict. This open conflict is your main focus. What you are looking for across the period are the long-term and short-term factors that brought it about.

Step 2: List your main points

A clear structure makes for an effective essay and is crucial in an exam. Write down the *main points* of your explanation in the order you intend to make them. Numbering will help.

Step 3: Write your conclusion

Write out a paragraph that *answers the question, to serve as your conclusion.* You may well find that you adapt it slightly when you come to use it at the end of the essay, but it will serve as a guide while you are getting there.

Some people find that they prefer to reverse the order of steps 2 and 3. Once they have analysed the question they write their answer in a paragraph, then underline the main points. Once you have tried it a few times you will know what works best for you. Remember, you are developing skills that you can apply to a range of essay questions.

EXAMPLE

In an essay dealing with causation, you must break down 'what happened' into causal factors. In this case you will find them by looking at what the kings and parliaments quarrelled about, to see if there were similar issues that appeared over the period. This would give you three key factors:

- The powers of the monarch and claims to Divine Right.
- Religious conflicts and fear.
- Finance, extravagance and the impact of war.

These factors apply right across the period, but given that it involves two kings, it makes sense to divide the period into two, and see if the individuals made a difference. This would give you five factors to cover:

- The exercise of powers by Charles I, 1625–28.
- The impact of Arminianism, 1625–29.

At this point you could write these out as a numbered list, in the order that you intend to deal with them. However, you need to think about the links between them if you are going to turn them into an *answer to the question.* A better way may therefore be to write out a paragraph that *links them together* into an answer – in other words, a potential *conclusion.*

For example:

When James became King of England he found that the monarchy was facing problems caused by religious conflicts, a lack of money, and an expensive war with Spain. James ended the war, and eventually created a fairly tolerant Church, which helped to calm religious conflicts. But his high-flown claims to Divine Right and his financial extravagance caused a number of arguments with Parliaments. The situation became much worse after the Thirty Years War broke out, because it heightened religious fears and raised issues in Parliament about the costs of a war and what kind of war to fight. However, it was not until Charles I became King that relations began to break down. His reliance on Buckingham, his attempts to raise money without Parliament and his promotion of Arminians in the Church created fears that he intended to establish an absolute monarchy, and possibly a Catholic one. It was the combination of these underlying fears and problems with the particular personality of Charles I that brought open conflict in 1629.

ACTIVITY

The concluding paragraph in the example above sets out how tensions built up in three stages:

- The first covers the underlying problems/factors.
- The second brings in the impact of the Thirty Years War.
- The third adds the extra factor of Charles I.

Using this structure you should now write an answer to the question by taking each sentence in the conclusion separately as the beginning of a paragraph and developing it with detailed examples and support. To do this you will need to add relevant detail to back up the claims made in the sentence and finish each paragraph with a specific link to the question, showing how the events you have covered helped to build up tension. There is advice to help you deploy detail and keep focused on the question on page 42.

Some sentences may well give you two or three paragraphs if they contain reference to different factors. When you have completed each paragraph you will have the main body of your essay, and will only need to add a focused introduction (see page 44), and an amended conclusion in the light of your further research.

How to use detail effectively

As well as focus and structure your essay will be judged on the extent to which it includes relevant and accurate detail. Detailed essays are more likely to do well than essays which are vague or generalised.

What is detail?

There are several different kinds of evidence you could use that might be described as detail. This includes correct dates, names of relevant people, statistics and events. If you look back through Chapter 2 you will find profiles and names, key dates and definitions to help. Many of the events have particular titles, like the Great Contract, the Addled Parliament, the Petition of Right and the Three Resolutions, which provide specific points of reference. You can also make your essays more detailed by using the correct technical vocabulary. The glossary terms will help you here.

How to use detail

You should use detailed evidence to support the points that you are making. For example, the first sentence refers to 'religious conflicts'. To develop this you could refer to anti-Catholic feeling, the war with Spain (and memories of the Armada), the Puritan demand for further reform, the Hampton Court conference and the appointment of Archbishop Bancroft.

Later, when the second sentence mentions James's successes, you can use his support for a preaching ministry and his appointment of Archbishop Abbot in 1611. The purpose of detail is to show that the claims made in the sentence are accurate and to give examples to illustrate them.

How to stay focused

Throughout your answer it is the specific links that you make to the question that maintain the focus of your essay and show why you have included that material in it. The advantage of writing a 'conclusion' as part of your planning lies in establishing such links in your own mind. In a similar way, a focused introduction helps to set out where your essay is going and how it will answer the question. It should not be the same as a conclusion, but it should set out the direction of your argument.

How to write a focused introduction

One way to do this is to use the wording of the question to help write your argument. The first sentence of the answer to the question 'Why did tensions develop between King and Parliament to the point where they were in open conflict by 1629?' could read, for example:

The open conflict that developed between King and Parliament in 1629 arose from a series of clashes that had begun when Charles I succeeded to the throne in 1625, but its roots lay much deeper, in tensions that had existed since 1603.

This could be followed by reference to long- and short-term problems, and the need to explain why they built up over the period.

Throughout the essay

You can then move into the main body of your essay, using the structure that you have set out in your list of factors and your brief conclusion. To maintain this throughout the essay you can again use the wording of the question, by ensuring that you refer to it at both the beginning and end of each paragraph. Thus each paragraph will explicitly show how a particular factor helped to develop tension, either directly or in combination with other factors, until you can pull it all together in your final conclusion.

SUMMARY

When writing causal explanations:
- Work out the main focus of the question.
- Plan your essay with a series of factors focusing on the question.
- Use the factors to construct a conclusion that brings them together to answer the question.
- Use the conclusion to create the main sections of your answer.
- Use the words in the question to formulate an introduction.
- Return to the primary focus of the question at the beginning of every paragraph and make explicit links to the question at the end of it.

What next?

When you have completed this task you will have considered how causation works through a combination of factors *interacting* to bring about a particular result. In this case the question simply asked you to explain *why* something happened and to construct an answer by defining and linking a range of factors. However, causation can be explored at more complex levels involving the role and significance of different factors, in essays that require you to construct arguments and counter-arguments before coming to a judgement. These issues will be considered in later chapters.

Working on interpretation skills

Section A of the exam paper is different from Section B. Unlike Section B, it contains extracts from the work of historians and is compulsory with no choice of question. Significantly, this section tests different skills. In essence, Section A tests your ability to evaluate different historical interpretations to assess how convincing they are. Therefore, you must focus on the interpretations outlined in the extracts. The advice given in this chapter on interpretations is for both the AS and the A-level exams.

- For the **AS exam**, there are two extracts and you are asked which is the more convincing interpretation of a specific topic (25 marks).
- For the **A-level exam**, there are three extracts and you are asked how convincing the arguments are in relation to a specified topic (30 marks).

An interpretation is a particular view on a topic of history held by a particular author or authors. Interpretations of a development can vary, for example, depending on how much weight an historian gives to a particular factor and whether they largely ignore another factor. Interpretations can also be heavily conditioned by events and situations that influence the writer.

The interpretations that you will be given will be largely from recent or fairly recent historians.

Interpretations and evidence

The extracts given in the exam will contain a mixture of interpretations and evidence. The mark scheme rewards answers that focus on the *interpretations* offered by the extracts much more highly than answers that focus on the *information or evidence* mentioned in the extracts. Therefore, it is important to identify the interpretations.

- *Interpretations* offer a specific argument about the topic under discussion. They tend to make claims such as 'James I was responsible for the growth of tensions with Parliament'.
- *Information or evidence* tends to consist of specific details, usually offered in support of such claims. For example: 'James's extravagance provoked a great deal of opposition, especially in parliaments when they were asked to grant taxes'.

Analysis of an interpretation

We start by looking at an individual extract and seeing how we can build up skills. This is the essential starting-point for both the AS and the A-level style of question on interpretations.

The AS mark scheme shows a very clear progression of thought processes:

Level 5	Answers will display a good understanding of the interpretations given in the extracts. They will evaluate the extracts thoroughly in order to provide a well-substantiated judgement on which offers the more convincing interpretation. The response demonstrates a very good understanding of context. *21–25 marks*
Level 4	Answers will display a good understanding of the interpretations given in the extracts. There will be sufficient comment to provide a supported conclusion as to which offers the more convincing interpretation. However, not all comments will be well-substantiated and judgements may be limited. The response demonstrates a good understanding of context. *16–20 marks*
Level 3	The answer will show a reasonable understanding of the interpretations given in the extracts. Comments as to which offers the more convincing interpretation will be partial and/or thinly supported. The response demonstrates an understanding of context. *11–15 marks*
Level 2	The answer will show some partial understanding of the interpretations given in the extracts. There will be some undeveloped comment in relation to the question. The response demonstrates some understanding of context. *6–10 marks*
Level 1	The answer will show a little understanding of the interpretations given in the extracts. There will be only unsupported, vague or generalist comment in relation to the question. The response demonstrates limited understanding of context. *1–5 marks*

Now study Extract A on page 46, which is about the Duke of Buckingham and his role in the growth of tensions between King and Parliament before 1629.

Extract A

Buckingham was, of all things, a political pragmatist [and he] was not incapable as an administrator ... A dazzling figure, immensely charming, an eloquent if sometimes incoherent orator, he was also an impetuous lightweight, and the conjunction of his rashness with Charles's fixed idea of royal honour brought English foreign policy to disaster ... To judge by contemporary comments his rapaciousness [greed for more] brought the Court into further disrepute. His goodwill had to be bought in all appointments and his influence over the King as his only close friend distorted the operation of patronage and added to the instability of early Stuart politics. In 1628 when Coke named Buckingham as 'the grievance of grievances', members exploded, crying 'It is he, it is he!'.

Adapted from *Authority and Conflict: England, 1603-1658* by Derek Hirst, (Arnold), 1987, pp.155–56.

ACTIVITY

Look at Extract A and then answer the following questions:

1 What argument does Extract A put forward about the causes of political conflict in 1628–29?
2 What evidence can you find in the Extract to support the argument?
3 What do you know about the first four years of Charles I's reign that supports these claims?
4 What contextual knowledge do you have to contradict these claims?
5 Using your judgement, do you consider that the evidence in the Extract and your own contextual knowledge provide convincing support for this interpretation of the causes of political conflict in 1628–29?

Comparing two interpretations

As part of the building up of skills, we move on to comparing two interpretations. This is the format of the AS question, but will also be useful in establishing a foundation for A-level students. The process by which you will answer questions in the exam, and the skills you will need, will all be explored here, but in the actual exam the question will cover a longer period of time of at least 20 years.

In the question below you are offered two different interpretations of what caused the political conflicts between King and Parliament in 1628–29. The interpretations focus on two different factors and may both be valid in themselves. What creates the conflict between them is the question that is asked:

With reference to Extract A and Extract B (page 47) and your understanding of the historical context, which of these two extracts offers the more convincing interpretation of what caused the political conflict between King and Parliament that came to a head in 1628–29?

Extract B

An authoritarian personality, Charles was incapable of making concessions at a time when compromises were desperately demanded from the English monarchy. He was full of that outward self-certainty (seen in such doctrines as divine right) that only intense inner doubt can create. ... Closely associated with an authoritarian personality is the inability to compromise. Charles found friendships hard to make because they demanded give and take between equals ... Charles saw his kingly role as a judge to whom issues were taken for decision ... not that of a bargainer who settled disputes between rival branches of his government and negotiated settlements with other powerful interest groups. No wonder Charles' parliaments all ended in discord ... Charles was psychologically incapable of dealing with a parliament that was anything more than a rubber stamp ...

From 'Three British Revolutions and the Personality of Kingship' by C. Carlton, in *Three British Revolutions, 1641, 1688, 1776*, J. G. A. Pocock ed., (Princeton University Press), 1980.

ACTIVITY

6 Follow the same five steps for Extract B as you did for Extract A in the activity on page 46, then compare the results of the two and come to a conclusion about which extract provides the more convincing interpretation of the causes of the political conflict in 1628–29.

Make sure that you apply your contextual knowledge, not only of the events and actions to which the extracts refer, but also to the ways in which the political system operated and the impact of the two individuals on the situation.

This should give you the direction of your overall conclusion and judgement about which of the extracts is more convincing.

The top two levels of the mark scheme refer to 'supported conclusion' (Level 4) and 'well-substantiated conclusion' (Level 5). For Level 4 'supported conclusion' means finishing your answer with a judgement that is backed up with some accurate evidence drawn from the source(s) and your knowledge. For Level 5 'well-substantiated conclusion' means finishing your answer with a judgement which is very well supported with evidence and, where relevant, reaches a complex conclusion that reflects a wide variety of evidence. In this case, therefore, you could argue that both factors played a part in the conflict, but that one was more important than the other.

There is no one correct way to write the answer! However, the principles are clear. In particular, contextual knowledge should be used *only* to back up an argument. None of your knowledge should be 'free-standing' – it should all be linked to the judgement of how convincing each of the interpretations is.

ACTIVITY

7 For each extract (A and B) in turn:

- Explain how far the evidence in the extract, backed up with your own contextual knowledge, makes the argument convincing.
- Then write a conclusion that reaches a judgement on which is more convincing as an interpretation.

Charles I: Personal Rule and political breakdown, 1629–40

This chapter covers the years of Charles I's reign between 1629 and 1640, when Charles established a Personal Rule without calling a Parliament, known in later years by many who disapproved of his actions as the 'Eleven Years Tyranny'. It deals with a number of key areas:

- Personal Rule – the reaction of the political nation
- Charles I – government and Court
- divisions over religion – Arminians, Puritans and others
- political divisions and their impact
- the failure of the Personal Rule and the calling of the Long Parliament.

As in Chapter 2, the areas of content are presented as part of a developmental analysis that addresses the issues which contributed to the growth of political tensions. While the breadth question formulated in Chapter 2 can be extended to the material in this chapter, and in particular to the calling of the Long Parliament, the issues addressed are more clearly indicated by two further questions:

Why did the attempt by Charles I to govern without the aid of Parliament end in failure?

How did this contribute to a developing crisis for the monarchy?

As with Chapter 2, you will be analysing what happened in order to identify changing situations and attitudes, and more extensively, exploring the causes of opposition, the reasons for its growing intensity and for the ultimate failure of the Personal Rule.

CHAPTER OVERVIEW

For Charles I, the necessity of calling a Parliament in 1640 represented the defeat of his efforts to govern according to his cherished ideas of kingship, and, to that extent, it can be considered a crisis for the monarchy. The nature of government between 1629 and 1640 provides important clues about how to interpret the crisis that faced the monarch in 1640 and about how to understand its causes. The key issue debated by historians in recent years has been whether the crisis arose from deep-seated causes that made it likely, if not inevitable, or whether it was created by individual personalities and specific errors. How far did it arise from the Tudor legacy, the rule of James I, the wider problems created by war and religious conflict in Europe, and how far was it the work of Charles I, his allies and advisers?

However, you should remember that these explanations are not mutually exclusive. It is possible to define problems that created the possibility of a crisis, while arguing that individuals and their errors influenced its shape and timing. Whichever approach you consider, you will first need to work out what Charles was trying to do in the situation that faced him and why his attempts to deal with it led to confrontation rather than agreed remedies.

1 The Personal Rule of Charles I, 1629–37

The years of Personal Rule provide one of the most contentious areas of seventeenth-century historiography, and the subject of intense and ongoing debate. This is partly because the political parties that emerged later in the century had their roots within this period and therefore developed and maintained their own conflicting interpretations of what happened. Hence there is a need to consider the nature of historical interpretation before addressing the issues and events to which they relate.

Interpretations: absolutism and the Personal Rule

The activity to the right is focused on historical interpretations and how they are influenced by the context in which they are created. However, it also requires you to define your view of this particular issue – the aims and actions of Charles I – on the basis of what you already know about him, and then to review it later after working through this chapter.

Some of the reasons for historical events being explained and interpreted in different ways have already been addressed in preceding sections of this book, but the Personal Rule of Charles I provides a particularly clear example. Debates about the causes of the Civil Wars have been long and fierce, and the role of Charles I as an individual has been central to them. By the early twentieth century the prevailing view was based on the writings of Whig historians, who saw Charles as a tyrant seeking to establish absolute monarchy, and saw Parliament as engaged in a conscious struggle for liberty. This was challenged by a number of Marxist historians who argued that economic factors and class rivalries were more important. More recently, some historians have produced a revised explanation and argued that the collapse of authority in the mid-seventeenth century was not caused by long-term problems, but by a clash of personalities and errors of judgement by the King and many others, and could well have been avoided. These differing views of Charles can be summarised in three statements:

1 Charles I was an authoritarian who believed that kings were appointed by God and should rule alone, according to their conscience. He tried to create effective government in these terms and believed that it was the duty of subjects to obey.
2 Charles I represented a feudal ruling class of King, nobility and Church, which was facing an increasing challenge from the middle order of gentry, merchants and yeomen. They believed that their growing wealth and importance entitled them to a greater share of power and a greater role in making decisions and saw Parliaments, and particularly the House of Commons, as the means of achieving it.
3 Charles I was well-meaning but naïve and lacking in confidence, which made him defensive in the face of any opposition. In many ways he governed effectively, but relied too much on advisers, whom he did not always choose wisely and therefore made serious mistakes that could have been avoided.

The period of Personal Rule falls into two main sections, divided by the outbreak of rebellion in Scotland in 1637. Although there was opposition to many of the measures adopted by Charles and his advisers in 1629–36, the lack of a parliament and the difficulty of organising resistance meant that it went largely unheard. In 1637 the Ship Money case and the treatment of Burton,

---

NOTE-MAKING

The information in the chapter can be set out in two parts covering the nature and effectiveness of the Personal Rule (1629–37) and the reasons for its failure and collapse (1637–40). Within each section you can use the headings provided to create a structure that you can fill out with numbered points of your own devising. It is also useful to include comments and summaries of your own, which will bring out the implications of the material as you read it and help to develop your own thinking about the issues covered. Note-making should be more than simply copying facts – it should be the result of an interaction between the material you read and your own understanding of the issues.

ACTIVITY

1 On the basis of what you have already learnt about Charles in the years to 1629, make a list of points to support and challenge statements 1–3. Which statement do you consider to be most accurate?
2 How far do you consider these judgements to be conflicting? Is it possible to reconcile any or all of them into an overall assessment of Charles's character and aims?

Keep what you have done so that you can revisit your interpretation in the light of further knowledge as you work through this chapter.

Bastwick and Prynne brought it closer to the surface, but it was the decision to extend religious reform to Scotland in the form of a Scottish Prayer Book that transformed the situation, sparking open rebellion and a different kind of challenge to royal authority. By considering the effectiveness of the Personal Rule in the first half of the decade you can begin to assess the significance of that decision and the events that followed.

The dissolution of Parliament, 1629–30

What did the dissolution of Parliament in 1629 mean for Charles and for those who opposed his plans?

The dissolution of Parliament in 1629 initiated a period in which Charles governed without reference to Parliament. This was not, in itself, significant, but 1629 to 1640 was also a period of personal government in that it appears to have reflected Charles's particular view of what good government should be. The Proclamation of 1629 declared that he would summon no more parliaments until his subjects had a better understanding of what he sought to do. This suggests that, in the years that followed, he sought to put his ideas into practice. For the Whig historians, this was part of a conscious attempt to establish absolute monarchy in England. If this was the case, then he was remarkably unsuccessful, but his failure should not be presumed inevitable. Recent research by the revisionist historians, who challenged the Whig interpretation, emphasises how effectively Charles governed until 1637, when he tried to extend his reforms to his more remote kingdom of Scotland. However, if he was not acting like a tyrant, if he only sought to reform and improve his government, why should his plans have created such opposition? The answers to these questions may lie in the nature and effectiveness of government in the years of Personal Rule.

In 1629 there was very little reaction or resistance to the dissolution of Parliament. A brief refusal by merchants to pay Tunnage and Poundage collapsed when one of them, Richard Chambers, was imprisoned. Nine MPs were arrested for their part in forcing the Speaker to sit after the King had ended the session, but five were quickly released. The three ringleaders, Denzil Holles, Benjamin Valentine and Sir John Eliot, were held in prison and brought to trial in 1630. There was a measure of vindictiveness in Charles's determination to keep them under lock and key; in 1629–30 they were shifted from prison to prison in order to evade writs of *Habeas Corpus* that would have secured their release until trial. Thereafter, they were imprisoned in the Tower of London, but Holles and Valentine were released within weeks when they apologised to the King. Only Eliot, who refused to do likewise, remained in prison, to die two years later of a fever. His death later provided Parliament's propagandists with a martyr for the cause of liberty, but at the time few remarked upon it.

At the time, the dissolution of 1629 was considered less significant than it later appeared. Although the events that led up to it, and Charles's declaration that he would call no more parliaments until his subjects had a better understanding of him, indicated that the circumstances were exceptional, it was not unusual for long periods to elapse between parliaments. James had allowed seven years between the parliaments of 1614 and 1621. Parliaments were not an essential part of daily government, and it was mainly the financial problems experienced by the Crown in this period that had led to more frequent sittings. If Charles could finance his government by other means, then he had no need of Parliament.

This was the consideration that worried those who disliked Charles's ideas about reform and about what constituted good government. If he could collect customs duties and other dues without hindrance and govern without recourse to Parliament, they had no means of preventing the changes that he wished

Habeas Corpus – A Latin phrase, meaning 'to have the body'. A writ of *Habeas Corpus* issued by a court was the standard way of preventing someone from being held in prison indefinitely, without being properly charged and brought to trial. It was regarded as a vital safeguard for personal liberty against the abuse of power by the monarch or those acting in his name.

to make. The King's prerogatives gave him the right, and the power, to mould government in both Church and State according to his own preferences. In 1629 there was no doubt that those who disliked his preferences had gone too far in openly defying his wishes. Now they could do little but watch and wait.

Organisation and administration

How was England governed in the early years of the Personal Rule?

The centre of administration was the Privy Council, which included key officials and the King's chosen advisers. As well as providing central administration, the Privy Council controlled local government through the choice of Lords Lieutenant in the counties and Justices of the Peace in each locality. In addition, individual privy councillors staffed the prerogative courts of Star Chamber and Chancery, and the regional Councils of the North and the Welsh Marches (see Figure 1, page 7). The effectiveness of administration and the extent of royal control depended entirely on how this structure was used, how much attention the King and his councillors gave to it, and how determinedly they used their powers to obtain local co-operation.

In this area, Charles was generally conscientious. Unlike his father, who had tended to leave business to his advisers, he attended meetings regularly, checked that his decisions were understood and ensured that they were put into effect. When he chose to delegate, he was ably supported by two key figures – Sir Thomas Wentworth (see page 66) and William Laud, Bishop of London and, from 1633, Archbishop of Canterbury (see page 52). Both were conscientious and able administrators, whose concern for detail gave their policies the nickname of 'Thorough'. The work of Wentworth in the Council of the North and in Ireland ensured that royal authority was maintained in these outlying areas, while Laud controlled the Church and rapidly became the dominant figure on the Privy Council. His influence in secular, as well as religious affairs, is symbolised by the Books of Orders that were issued to local government from 1631.

It would appear, therefore, that as far as administration is concerned, Charles's government was highly effective, as Source A suggests. It was also, undeniably, Charles's government. After the death of Buckingham he never allowed any adviser to occupy the same place in his affections, moving closer instead to his wife, Henrietta Maria. Their marriage, after Buckingham's death, was remarkably stable and happy and Charles enjoyed a close family life. In political terms, the Queen's influence was something of a liability, since she understood little of English government and society and constantly reinforced Charles's tendency to be stubborn and high-handed (see page 35). Even so, her influence was never as great or as dangerous as that of Buckingham. Other key advisers, like Wentworth and Laud, were kept at arm's length. They were servants and political advisers to the King rather than friends; the architect of the Personal Rule was undoubtedly Charles himself and it was his attitudes and personality that it reflected.

Impact and opposition

Charles was therefore responsible for both the strengths and weaknesses of administration in this period. The effectiveness of supervision was impressive, but it was also demanding and occasionally unpopular. After 1635, when JPs were also involved in the collection of Ship Money, the efficiency with which the Books of Orders were administered began to decline. After 1637, when preparations for suppressing the Scottish rebellion were added to their burdens, complaints from harassed justices increased sharply. Similarly, the Council itself was unable to maintain such close supervision. While much could be achieved by attention to detail, there were limits to the time and energy of even

Source A From 'County government in Caroline England, 1625–40' by L. M. Hill, in *The Origins of the English Civil War* by Conrad Russell (ed.).

The poor were better treated and better cared for than ever before. Grain stocks were better administered and waste was curtailed. The quality of local government was markedly improved and little doubt lingered as to the Council's ability to cause the King's writ to run into local parts with considerable authority.

Books of Orders – These consisted of 314 books of instructions to JPs, detailing their duties in the collection of Poor Law rates, treatment of beggars, law enforcement, storage of grain, control of local markets, movement of goods and upkeep of roads and bridges. Under Laud's supervision, the issue of instructions was followed up to ensure that they were carried out.

William Laud (1573–1645)

Born in 1573, the son of a Reading clothier, Laud was educated at a Free School in Reading and later at Oxford University – a path which emphasises both his humble origins and his intellectual abilities. By entering the Church he was treading a well-worn route to advancement, but there is no reason to doubt the strength of his faith and commitment. Ordained as a priest in 1601, he served as chaplain to the Earl of Devonshire and Vicar of Stanford (Northants) before a sermon preached before King James in 1608 led to his appointment as a royal chaplain. Thereafter he rose through royal service to become Bishop of St David's (Wales) in 1621, and his close friendship with the Duke of Buckingham ensured him a measure of influence at Court.

Access to real power came in 1625 with the accession of Charles I, for whom Laud's ideas of order, dignity and authority in the Church had great appeal. Although Laud has been called an Arminian, he was less concerned with the details of doctrine than with Church organisation and respect for the appearance and form of worship. His famous phrase 'the beauty of holiness' expressed a desire to see churches that created an atmosphere of reverence and appealed to the emotions rather than the intellect. In pursuit of this he encouraged Charles to promote only Arminians, at the expense of Puritan thinkers, and his own career also flourished. He became Bishop of Bath and Wells in 1626, a Privy Councillor in 1627, Bishop of London (the largest diocese in England) in 1628, Chancellor of Oxford University in 1630 and Archbishop of Canterbury in 1633. In fact he had been acting as Charles's chief religious adviser for some time before this, since George Abbot, the existing Archbishop had found it necessary to live privately after he accidentally killed a gamekeeper while out hunting in 1624.

Throughout the 1630s Laud dominated the Privy Council through his access to the King, his personal attention to administrative matters and the increasing number of his protégés who were given appointments and offices. Although he was genuinely concerned to establish good order in both Church and State, his fussy attention to detail sometimes destroyed the shape of a strategy. In addition, his power was greatly resented by the traditional nobility. His humble origins, his use of the High Commission and the Star Chamber to enforce rules and silence opposition and his interference in secular (non-religious) affairs made him a natural target for their frustrations and a popular target when Parliament reassembled in 1640. He was impeached in December 1640 and held in the Tower of London until his execution as a traitor to liberty and the Protestant religion in January 1645. In many ways he paid the price for serving his King too well.

the most dedicated of councillors. While Charles had brought determination and energy to the business of government, he made few structural changes and did little to alter the basic methods applied. As long as the system was reliant on unpaid amateurs at a local level, its scope and effectiveness would be limited.

It would also need to be managed with a measure of political sensitivity, to take account of the concerns and interests of the ruling class whose support was essential. Government attempts to regulate wages and prices to help the poor, for example, were largely unsuccessful when the JPs who were required to set wage levels were also the employers who would have to pay them. While the prerogative courts and councils were respected for their speed and efficiency, they were also resented when they overrode local interests for the benefit of the King or his advisers. The Star Chamber was instructed to uphold the rights of the nobility, for example, and in 1632 awarded huge damages to the Earl of Suffolk because he had been forced to endure 'undeferential behaviour'. There was significant resentment in Yorkshire when Wentworth used his power as President of the Council of the North to further the interests of his family against a neighbour and rival, Sir John Savile. A number of Savile's friends and supporters would eventually support Parliament in the Civil War. It is no coincidence that the prerogative courts were abolished in 1641 and were not restored with the monarchy in 1660.

Role of the bishops

Resentments were further fuelled by the presence on the Privy Council of a number of bishops and protégés of Laud. While it was normal for the Archbishop to be a member, there was considerable vexation at his dominant role. In 1632 he was able to make his candidate, Francis Windebanke, Secretary of State, and in 1634 he persuaded the King to dismiss the Lord Chief Justice, Sir Robert Heath, because of his Puritan views. In 1635, when Lord Treasurer Weston died, he was replaced by the Bishop of London, William Juxon. The presence of a cleric in an important office of state was bitterly resented for two reasons. In the first place, the bishops were appointed by and dependent on the King, and tended to carry out his wishes without reservation. Lord Brooke expressed the views of many in 1642 when he pointed out that, unlike the landed nobility, bishops had no way of securing the future of their families except by retaining the King's favour and therefore had no independence in their exercise of power. Second, since the Reformation it had become customary for the secular nobility and gentry to manage secular affairs and the extension of clerical influence carried unfortunate associations with Catholic tradition.

Conclusion

It could therefore be argued that the administration of government in the period of the Personal Rule was in many ways highly effective, but that its effectiveness relied on personalities and a level of central supervision that irritated the political nation. The level of irritation was variable and in itself would not have created a crisis, but it did add to other concerns. Perhaps most importantly, it did nothing to secure royal power in the long run. When the attention of the King and Council was distracted by more pressing problems after 1637, their control of the machinery of government proved fragile.

Finance and taxation

What problems arose from the need to finance government without parliamentary subsidies?

The King's ability to govern without Parliament depended on securing an adequate income from his 'ordinary' revenue. This meant that he had to address the financial problems that had weakened his father and given Parliament a grip on affairs in the early years of his own reign. A series of financial measures were undertaken (see page 54) in order to increase revenue, which succeeded in balancing the current budget by 1637, although nothing had been done to settle debts arising from past difficulties. For the most part these gains were made by increasing the efficiency with which finances were managed, rather than by developing new strategies. Only Ship Money could be called a new tax, and even that was based upon a traditional right to aid naval defence.

> **KEY DATES:**
> **ORGANISATION AND ADMINISTRATION**
>
> **1631** Books of Orders issued as instructions for local government.
>
> **1632** Laud's nominee, Francis Windebanke, appointed as Secretary of State and member of the Privy Council.
>
> **1635** Bishop Juxon became Lord Treasurer, an office that had normally been held by one of the lay nobility.

The financial measures of the Personal Rule

The 'Ordinary Revenue'

● *Crown lands*
1630: Commission for Defective Titles set up to examine the titles and leases of Crown tenants. New rents imposed on those unable to prove a reason why they should not pay more and fines levied for illegal enclosures of waste or common land or for any encroachment on royal forests.
   – 1634: Special judicial enquiry set up to detect and fine for any encroachment by farmers/landowners on royal forests.
   – 1635: Second Commission for Defective Titles.

● *Feudal Duties* – in feudal law all men owning freehold land worth £40 a year had to take a title of knighthood (for which they had to pay). In 1630 a commission was set up to contact all who had failed to do so and arrange for compliance or a fine. This raised £165,000 by 1635. Other duties continued to be levied, for example the Court of Wards and Liveries produced £53,866 per year from 1631–35 and £75,088 per year from 1636–41.

● *Monopolies* – the sale of monopolies renewed through loopholes in the 1624 Act against them. This was exploited by courtiers as well as the King. Charles also sold the same monopolies to different groups, for example, a licence to the East India Company resold to a rival group led by Sir William Courten. The worst example of fraudulent monopolies was the 'Popish Soap' scandal, in which a group of Catholic courtiers obtained a monopoly on soap by rigged demonstrations to prove that it washed whiter!

● *Justice* – fines and court fees, increased by new offences such as proclamations restricting building around London. Buildings were allowed to stand on payment of fines from owners and fees from tradesmen.

Customs duties

● *Tunnage and Poundage* – a declaration issued in 1630 of the King's right to levy customs duties despite parliamentary refusal of grant. Duties continued to be levied throughout the Personal Rule and their value rose significantly with increased trade.

● *New impositions* – introduced by Elizabeth and James I, these were also levied as usual, producing £53,091 per year from 1631–35 and £119,583 per year from 1636–41.

Direct Taxes – normally granted by Parliament so not applicable

● Tenths and Fifteenths – not applicable (N/A)
● Subsidies – N/A
● Poll Tax – N/A
● Ship Money – levied from coastal areas in 1634, extended to inland areas in 1635; levied each year thereafter yielding an average of £107,000 per year from 1635–40. All this was done without consulting Parliament.

Nevertheless, Ship Money was significant for several reasons. In the first place it did establish a new style of taxation. Where parliamentary subsidies were levied as a proportion of income and depended on individual assessments which were cumbersome to administer, Ship Money targets were set by the government as a global sum to be levied from the county as a whole. This placed the burden of collection on local justices and cost the government little or nothing. Second, in combination with rising customs revenues derived from growing trade, Ship Money offered a long-term prospect of real financial independence for the monarchy. Third, and perhaps for that very reason, it does seem to have created serious and deep-seated opposition.

Opposition to Ship Money

The extent of the opposition to Ship Money has been the subject of considerable debate among historians. The traditional Whig interpretation of the period portrayed Ship Money as an attempt by Charles to finance absolutism, which was recognised and resisted by the political elite in the country. Recent revisionists have challenged these claims, in relation both to the purposes of the tax, and the opposition that it created. According to the historian J. P. Kenyon:

'We are assured by Whig historians … that this aroused the most furious opposition in the provinces and this 'fact' is generally accepted. [In reality] there is scarcely any hard evidence for this, and what there is, is associated with predictable individuals like the Earl of Warwick and Lord Saye and Sele [the leaders of the Puritan faction].

There is certainly some truth in this point – John Hampden, whose refusal to pay the tax in 1636 led to the famous test case of 1637, was a close friend and associate of both Lord Saye and Sele and the Earl of Bedford. His contacts extended through them to John Pym and his family links covered many of the opposition leaders of 1640–42. Kenyon also points out that the tax was used to build up the navy and that it was efficiently and successfully collected until the outbreak of rebellion in Scotland distracted the attention of the Privy Council and many local officials. In 1635 the government received all but £5,000 of the £199,000 demanded, in 1636 all but £7,000 and in 1637, all but £18,000. Only in 1638, when the assessment had been reduced to £70,000 by the government, was there a serious shortfall.

Interpretations: How significant was opposition to Ship Money?

Some historians, such as John Morrill, have supported some of the arguments put forward by Kenyon, at least in relation to how successfully the tax was imposed. It would appear, therefore, that the Whig argument is fatally undermined or at least shown to be significantly overstated. With regard to Charles's intentions, this may well be the case. There is no doubt that Ship Money was initially used for naval defence and its extension to the inland areas was not unreasonable. As with other aspects of Charles's financial policies, it can be seen as a natural and logical desire to maximise the Crown's resources. With regard to the nature and extent of opposition, however, the revisionists' case is less convincing.

Source B From *The Early Stuarts, 1603–40* by Katherine Brice, (Hodder and Stoughton), 1994, pp.122–23.

The most profitable of the new ways of raising money was Ship Money. Initially the tax was extremely successful. It raised £190,000 a year and the rate of non-payment was very low – 2.5% in the first three years. However, the methods of assessing and collecting the tax gave rise to much opposition. The sheriff, who was the chief agent of royal authority in each of the shires, was made personally responsible for collecting the sum decided for his county, and this placed a heavy burden on him, both financially and in terms of time. The unpleasantness of collecting the tax weakened support for the government among the gentry, upon whom it was heavily dependent. In order to spread the burden of taxation, new rating systems were introduced in many areas ... which was much more equitable, but spreading the net of taxation wider meant that more people were affected by it and this led to a greater degree of political awareness, which would be significant when parliament reassembled. Nevertheless, despite the grumbles and dissatisfaction, up to 1637 Ship Money was the most profitable tax ever recorded in peace time.

Source C From *The Stuart Age: England, 1603–1714* by Barry Coward (Longman), 1997, pp.89–90.

During the Personal Rule the king's annual income rose from £600,000 to nearly £900,000 per annum. However, the relative success of the measures in financial terms was achieved at a great political cost. The evidence for this statement is unfortunately not conclusive. Yet it is reasonable to assume that the constitutional disquiet at impositions, voiced earlier in the century, did not evaporate in the 1630s ... What is more certain is that forest fines and Ship Money caused much opposition among wealthy and powerful people. Some were fined huge sums in the

ACTIVITY

1 Sources B and C put forward arguments which are clearly different, but are they conflicting? To what extent do Sources B and C agree or differ about:
   a) the extent of opposition to Ship Money
   b) the reasons for it?
2 Now use the contemporary sources (Sources D–G) on page 56 in the context of your own wider knowledge to evaluate Sources B and C. Decide how far the conflicts can be resolved to incorporate the different views into an overall judgement about the opposition to Ship Money.

forest courts (the Earl of Salisbury was fined £20,000 for encroaching on Rockingham Forest) and even though some fines were reduced, they were a great grievance. The clearest evidence that such grievances were caused by constitutional fears relates to Ship Money. In the Ship Money case of 1637–8, even some of the judges showed that they doubted the legality of the levy. The most convincing evidence of the depth of opposition to Ship Money is in the petitions to and speeches in the parliaments of 1640. Surely these reflected sentiments that it had not been possible to voice earlier?

Source D From *History of the Rebellion and Civil Wars in England Begun in the Year 1641* by Edward Hyde, Earl of Clarendon. Edited by G. Huehns, (Oxford Paperbacks), 1979.

Lastly, for a spring and magazine that should have no bottom, and for an everlasting supply of all occasions, a writ is framed in a form of law, and directed to the sheriff of every county of England, to provide a ship of war for the King's service ... and with that writ were sent to each sheriff instructions that, instead of a ship, he should levy upon his county such a sum of money, and return the same to the Treasurer of the Navy for his majesty's use, and from hence that tax had the denomination of Ship-Money, a word of lasting sound in the memory of this Kingdom.

Source E From 'The Judgement of Sir Robert Berkeley', one of the majority who found for the King in Hampden's Case.

Where Mr Holborne [one of Hampden's lawyers] supposed that in case the monarch of England should be inclined to exact from his subjects at his pleasure, he should be restrained, for that he could have nothing from them, but upon a common consent in Parliament. He is utterly mistaken herein ... The law knows no such Kingyoking policy. The law is, of itself, an old and trusty servant of the King's; it is his instrument or means which he useth to govern his people by ...

Source F From an account of the reaction of JPs in Kent to the news that the judges had found against Hampden, in a memorandum in the papers of Sir Roger Twysden.

When [Judge Weston] came to speak of ship-money, the audience which had before hearkened but with ordinary attention did then ... listen with great diligence, and after the declaration made I did, in my conceit [belief] see a kind of dejection in their very looks ... Some held ... that the declaration the judges had made was fully to the point and by that the King had full right to impose it, and all concluded that if a Kingdom were in jeopardy it ought not [to] be lost for want of money ... Others argued far differingly ... that in a judgement that not may, but doth, touch every man in so high a point, every man ought to be heard ...

Source G From *History of the Rebellion and Civil Wars in England Begun in the Year 1641* by Edward Hyde, Earl of Clarendon. Edited by G. Huehns, (Oxford Paperbacks), 1979.

It is notoriously known that pressure was borne with much more cheerfulness before the judgement for the King than ever it was after; men before pleasing themselves with doing somewhat for the King's service, as a testimony of their affection, which they were not bound to do. But when they heard this demanded in a court of law, as a right . . . and instead of giving were required to pay, and by a logic that left no man anything which he might call his own; they no more looked upon it as the case of one man but the case of the Kingdom ...

Religion and the Church

Why did religious conflicts intensify during the Personal Rule?

Whatever resentments may have arisen from Ship Money, there was little scope for them to be expressed in the absence of Parliament. The same can be said of the changes that Charles was introducing in the Church.

The Laudian reforms

In 1633 Laud became Archbishop of Canterbury and issued new instructions, which the bishops were to enforce in each diocese. Preaching was to be limited to Sunday mornings and evenings, and replaced by teaching of the **Catechism** in afternoon services. The substitution of catechising for preaching symbolised the Laudian emphasis on ritual, authority and communal worship in place of the intensely personal, Bible-based faith encouraged by Puritan thinkers. Weekday lectures were to be banned, removing a favourite Puritan device that provided preaching opportunities for ministers who objected to the ceremonies and sacraments required by the Prayer Book. A legal challenge was launched against the **Feoffees** and the parishes that they had controlled were taken into the gift of the King, ensuring that men of orthodox Anglican or Arminian views would be appointed to them. Churches were to be decorated, music was encouraged, and in Hull, for example, the Church bells were restored to Holy Trinity Church despite the objections of the Mayor and Corporation. Most obvious of all, the plain communion tables that occupied the centre of many churches were removed to the east end and covered with richly embroidered cloth, reminiscent of the Catholic High Altar, railed off from the ordinary lay members of the congregation.

Intentions and reactions

From the point of view of Charles and Laud, these changes established order and beauty in the Church. Replacing preaching with set prayers and ceremonies reduced the scope for individuals to express their views and avoided controversy. Music, decoration and ritual encouraged reverence for God and joyful worship, a celebration that appealed to the emotions rather than the intellect. Catechisms and the public recitation of official confessions of faith expressed the unity of a harmonious Christian community. The protection of the altar from abuse by placing it behind rails was a mark of respect. The King and Archbishop were fulfilling their duty in caring for the Church and ensuring that others did the same. The policy was described by Laud himself:

'The inward worship of the heart is the great service of God ... but the external worship of God in his Church is the great witness to the world, that our heart stands right in that service ... Now, no external action in the world can be uniform without some ceremonies; and these in religion, the ancienter they be the better, so [as long as] they may fit the time and place ... And scarce anything hath hurt religion more in these broken times than an opinion in too many men, that because Rome had thrust some unnecessary and many superstitious ceremonies upon the Church, therefore the Reformation must have none at all; not considering therewhile, that ceremonies are the hedge that fence the substance of religion from all the indignities which profaneness and sacrilege too commonly put upon it.'

Unfortunately, Laud's instructions were interpreted in very different ways by many of the ministers and laity upon whom they were imposed. They thought that restrictions on preaching did the devil's work by leaving people in ignorance and darkness, and that rituals and ceremonies encouraged a mechanical and superstitious emphasis on appearances at the expense of inner

Catechism – The Catechism provided an outline of the key doctrines and creeds of the Anglican Church, as set out in the Prayer Book. It was taught as a set of questions and learned responses, some of which appeared as set prayers in certain services. It therefore supported uniformity of belief, unlike preaching, and was reminiscent of traditional, Catholic practices.

The Feoffees – A group of Puritan trustees who were empowered to raise money and buy up impropriated parishes (see Chapter 2, page 21) in order to provide good preaching ministers for them. Established in 1626, they had acquired a little over thirty parishes and were looking to extend their work to the purchase of advowsons (see Chapter 2, page 21) when Laud banned them and took over the parishes that they had bought. Although they shared his objective of improving the quality of the ministry, their preference for Puritans and emphasis on preaching earned them his disapproval. His action offended Puritans on religious grounds and many others as an attack on property.

faith. They also believed that decorations and statues encouraged the worship of symbols, and that the new placing of the altar recalled the Catholic Mass in which, it was claimed, the communion bread and wine were miraculously transformed into the actual body and blood of Christ (Transubstantiation). For many people, not only of the Puritan faction, this was a return to superstition and idol-worship, attacking the heart of the Protestant faith. It was particularly controversial and also particularly obvious to the ordinary layman, who saw the physical evidence of the change in his own parish church.

There were also other associations. If the altar was railed off and approached only by the clergy, then this emphasised the status of the clergy as a separate order, above the laity. What was, for Charles and Laud, an attempt to improve the quality of religious provision by creating uniform standards and raising the quality and status of the clergy, appeared to many laymen to be a renewal of the clerical pretensions associated with the Catholic Church. In this context, the presence of bishops on the Privy Council, the claims that they derived their authority from Christ himself, handed down through the Catholic Christian tradition, the emphasis on authority and the special status of the clergy all came together to create fear of absolutism and Catholicism.

The Catholic threat

The growing evidence that Catholic influence was tolerated at Court increased these fears. The Queen could worship as a Catholic according to her marriage terms, and her priests and confessors sought to gain converts where possible. Catholicism became fashionable in Court circles, and several Privy Councillors, such as Lord Treasurer Weston, were Catholics. In 1637 Charles welcomed an ambassador from the Pope, George Con, and their shared appreciation of art encouraged a growing friendship. Many suspected the King of Catholic sympathies, and even those who accepted that neither he, nor Laud, held Catholic beliefs, feared that by indulging High Church attitudes they were allowing secret Catholics to enter and undermine the Anglican faith. In an era when the Pope was identified as the Anti-Christ, the head of a vast international conspiracy supported by Spain and dedicated to the destruction of true religion, such fears and suspicions isolated the King from many of his subjects.

As with other areas of government, there was little that could be done to prevent the changes being made. Ministers who refused to accept the new rules risked losing their livings and Laud ensured that the bishops carried out regular visitations to enforce the King's will. Serious acts of defiance were brought before the prerogative court of High Commission, which also imposed censorship through the licensing of books and pamphlets. In more extreme cases, those who defied the law could be brought before the Star Chamber. In 1637 three Puritans named Burton, Bastwick and Prynne, who had published a series of pamphlets attacking Laud and the Queen, were brought to the Star Chamber accused of sedition (encouraging unrest). Burton was a physician, Bastwick was a preacher, and Prynne was a lawyer – all university men of gentry status. Despite this, they were sentenced to be placed in the pillory, branded on the cheeks and to have their ears cropped. Such mutilation was rarely inflicted on men of their status, and the sentence was carried out before a shocked and horrified crowd, who sympathised with both their views and their sufferings.

Growth of opposition

Faced with this kind of action, those who opposed Charles and Laud on religious grounds reacted in one of two ways. Within the lower ranks of society there were already a few more radical Puritans who had come to believe that a state Church was, in itself unacceptable, and that a true Church consisted of a

Emerging religious groups

The term *Separatist* covers a number of religious groups who had developed ideas of their own within the broad category labelled 'Puritan'. Although there were variations, the common factor was their desire for the right to establish independent and self-governing religious groups, organised according to their own reading of the Bible. The *Baptists*, for example, practised adult baptism by total immersion as a symbol of membership, based on the story of Jesus being baptised by John the Baptist at the start of his ministry. Others, known as *Independents* or *Congregationalists*, simply emphasised the need for voluntary membership and self-government.

Within these groups some members also adopted *Millenarian* ideas, based on the Book of Revelations, and argued that in time all earthly monarchies would be swept away to allow for the return of Jesus himself, to inaugurate a thousand years of rule by the Saints.

The events of the 1640s would bring about a significant upsurge of all these ideas, and in time the intense individualism of the radical Puritans and their belief in spiritual equality would convert into new and highly subversive political ideas.

▲ 'Honest John Lilburne' would not be regarded as a radical thinker today, but from the 1630s to the 1650s he spent a lot of time in prison for believing in things like equality before the law, religious toleration and universal suffrage.

body of believers joining in a voluntary association and governing its members by its own rules. The persecution carried out by Archbishop Bancroft in the early years of James's reign (see Chapter 2) had led to small congregations taking refuge in Holland, where some of them came into contact with Baptist and Millenarian ideas. In 1616 the first English Baptist church was established by an exiled minister named John Smyth. A few years later, another such group, later termed the Pilgrim Fathers, set off to sail to the colony of Virginia in search of religious freedom, and being blown off course, established the first English colony in New England. There they were joined by others whose separatist views made life in England dangerous and by the mid-1630s there were a number of such colonies.

Little is known of the separatists within England at this time, since they were, of necessity, scattered and secretive, but there was a brief glimpse of their potential in the actions of John Lilburne, a protégé of Dr Bastwick, who was arrested in 1638 for attempting to smuggle copies of Bastwick's sermons into England from Holland, where they had been printed without licence. Brought to trial and sentenced to be pilloried, Lilburne used his public moment to harangue the populace of London on the evils of bishops and was promptly imprisoned. He remained in prison until after the calling of the Long Parliament, when a sympathetic intervention by the MP for Cambridge, Oliver Cromwell, secured his release.

Both Lilburne and Cromwell would play a more significant role in the growing crisis in later years, but during the 1630s the radicals and separatists remained a small and isolated minority. In the short term a far more significant reaction came from the more moderate Puritans who were, and wished to remain, within the Anglican Church. Nevertheless, they were deeply resentful of the Laudian bishops and feared that both the religious and political aims of Charles and his advisers posed a threat to England as they knew it. Fear of Catholicism, resentment at the pretensions of the Laudian clergy and a sense that the King was willing to override both law and Parliaments in pursuit of his perception of royal government, combined to convince some that he was seeking to create an absolute monarchy. In 1637, faced with Hampden's failure to challenge

KEY DATES: RELIGION AND THE CHURCH

1633 Laud appointed Archbishop of Canterbury; new injunctions issued laying down rules and changes in the Church.

1635 William Juxon, Bishop of London, appointed as Lord Treasurer.

1637 George Con, Ambassador from the Pope, welcomed at Court and took up residence; Star Chamber trial and punishment of Bastwick, Burton and Prynne.

Ship Money, the prospect that financial independence would enable Charles to dispense with parliaments completely (and the example of Burton, Bastwick and Prynne to show what could happen to those who resisted), leaders of the Puritan interest like the Earl of Bedford considered emigration to New England as a way out. This proved unnecessary because neither Charles's intentions nor his effectiveness were quite what they seemed.

Assessment: the nature of the Personal Rule

How successful was the Personal Rule of 1629–37?

In 1629 Charles declared that he would call no more parliaments until his subjects understood him better. By 1637 his financial and religious policies had convinced some of them, at least, that his aim was absolute power, and some historians have agreed. In 1649, on the eve of his execution at the hands of a parliamentary faction, Charles wrote to his son urging him to 'be not out of love' with parliaments, which 'in their right constitution' were mainstays of monarchy. Given that he had already chosen to die a martyr and that this was his last advice to the man whom he regarded as his successor, it seems unlikely that Charles would deliberately lie. Yet this view of parliaments seems to contradict any absolutist ambitions or any plan to destroy Parliament as an institution.

If Charles planned to establish absolute monarchy, he made surprisingly few changes to the structure of government in this period. The key features of continental absolutism were the concentration of legal powers in the hands of the king, the reduction of local independence in favour of central authority and the establishment of a professional bureaucracy paid by a financially independent king. On one level, Charles appeared to be pursuing these objectives – he called no parliaments, exercised power over local interests through the prerogative courts and councils and raised unparliamentary taxes to finance his government. Only in the last of these, however, did he try to exercise new powers or greatly extend the old, and even there it could be argued that his extension of Ship Money was no more revolutionary than James's use of 'impositions' to extend customs duties in 1606–08 (see page 24). The hallmark of Charles's government was attention to detail in order to make the existing system more effective, or to exploit existing sources of revenue more completely. While it could be argued that he had little time to bring in extensive changes before 1637, the time and energy devoted to making the existing system work was considerable. If there had been a coherent plan to destroy parliaments and make monarchy absolute, such time would have been better given to establishing a standing army and a system of salaried officials.

If Charles did not therefore plan to create absolutism, what were his aims? Some clues can be found by looking at the nature of his Court and the image of monarchy that he sought to establish there. The royal Court was the heart of government, the centre of society and the pinnacle of the social hierarchy on which government was based. The style and behaviour of the Court reflected the personality and aims of the monarch who shaped it. Where Elizabeth and her father had created public magnificence, and James permitted licence and indulgence, Charles sought dignified formality. Access to the monarch was limited and strictly according to rank. Ceremonies were carefully staged and often conducted at Windsor, away from the public gaze. A strict code of behaviour was enforced and entertainments took the form of plays and masques, in which the King and Queen sometimes appeared in a symbolic role to restore order and end confusion. This indicates the kind of king that Charles tried to be. Reserved, dignified, aloof and personally chaste, he tried to shape the monarchy and the kingdom in his own image. Even his critics, like the fiercely Puritan Lucy Hutchinson, recognised some of his virtues:

'King Charles was temperate, chaste and serious; so that the fools and bawds … of the former court grew out of fashion … Men of learning and ingenuity in all the arts were in esteem and receiving encouragement from the King, who was a most excellent judge and a great lover of paintings.'

This image reveals Charles's view of monarchy and symbolises what he tried to achieve across all aspects of government. Administration was to be efficient and well-ordered and the Church was to be beautified and dignified by ceremony. Hierarchy was to be upheld by insisting on respect for rank – of bishops in the Church and nobility in the State. At the head of both was the King, his authority accepted and exercised for the benefit of his people. The results would be peace and harmony, a well-oiled machine with all parts working in their place.

1 What image of Charles does this portrait attempt to promote?
2 How does it disguise the fact that he was under five feet tall?

▲ Charles I on horseback, by Van Dyke, 1638.

Causes of opposition

If this is the case, then it is necessary to explain why such a vision would give rise to significant opposition within a governing class that shared the King's belief in hierarchy and order. The reasons seem to lie partly in the nature of Charles's beliefs and partly in the methods by which he sought to pursue his aims. In relation to religion and the Church, his beliefs raised fears that he does not seem to have understood. The changes that he introduced into the Church offended Puritans at every level, but Puritans never constituted a majority among his subjects. What offended a far wider number was the fear and suspicion raised by the respect shown to Catholics. Charles never understood that for many Protestants, not only those with Puritan sympathies, the Pope was Anti-Christ, the servant of the devil. To allow Catholics into positions of power and to make it easier for them to be accommodated within the Church was to undermine the defences of true religion and liberty. Against the background of militant Catholicism and war in Europe, Charles appeared to be furthering the cause of an international Catholic conspiracy by giving a foothold in Protestant England to its most dangerous enemies.

Dramatic though these images may be, they reflected the anti-Catholic prejudice in English thinking, which encompassed political as well as religious fears. Catholic monarchs were thought of as absolutists and destroyers of parliaments. Catholic bishops were seen as enforcing the Pope's will, persecuting other faiths and interfering in the affairs of governments. The architect of absolutism in France was a cleric, Cardinal Richelieu – and rumour had it that Laud had been offered a cardinal's hat by the Pope himself. Laud claimed that bishops in the Anglican Church inherited their power from Christ himself, encouraged the pride and pretensions of the clergy, dominated the Privy Council and gained appointments for his protégés, both clergy and laymen. The similarities were too close to ignore.

In this context, Charles's Personal Rule took on a more sinister appearance than he could imagine. Historians who suggest that there was little reaction to the dissolution of 1629 are probably correct; opposition grew with the development of Charles's policies and the apparent hardening of his intentions after that date. To some extent this was a matter of the cumulative effect of his policies in different areas, but it was also the result of his personality. Charles was no more autocratic in his political beliefs than his father, but he lacked James's grasp of political reality and suffered from a dangerous combination of naïvety and determination. Because he had no plans to destroy Parliament he was incapable of understanding the fears that he generated. Faced with opposition for which he could see no justification, he assumed that it was maliciously intended. Feeling himself under attack, he responded with a determination to assert his authority that included vindictive punishments of those who opposed him. While Charles was not an autocrat by belief, he was certainly autocratic in temperament; for many of his subjects, the effect was much the same.

2 The failure of Personal Rule, 1637–40

By 1637 a combination of political and religious grievances had created opposition among a far wider spectrum of public opinion than the 'Puritan faction'. That opposition, however, had few opportunities to express itself in the absence of a parliament. If Charles could maintain his control of the situation, there was no reason why he could not continue to impose his will. A combination of growing trade and Ship Money offered the prospect of financial independence and if that were the case, then even if he chose to call a parliament, it would have little prospect of influencing the King's decisions. Without a need for parliamentary taxes, Charles could dissolve any parliament that obstructed him as and when he chose. The apparent growth of parliamentary influence and independence that had occurred since the Reformation could be rapidly reversed by a King whose administrative grip and financial position were secure. In these circumstances, Charles's decision to extend his programme of reform into his outlying kingdoms highlights his fatal lack of political awareness.

The Scottish Rebellion and the First Bishops' War, 1637–39

Why was Charles faced by a rebellion in Scotland?

In Ireland Charles had already withdrawn the royal proclamations known as the Graces, which had given Irish Catholics a measure of religious freedom, and Strafford's iron grip as governor appeared to have suppressed any resistance. In Scotland, however, the independence and strength of the Presbyterian **Kirk** created difficulties for the monarchy, as well as an encouragement to English Puritans. James I had already taken some cautious steps towards greater uniformity, but Charles lacked his father's understanding of Scottish politics and culture and he made little effort to acquire it. He had visited Scotland only once and tended to rely on advice from a small group of Scots living in London rather than from the Scottish Privy Council in Edinburgh. James had attempted to create stronger links between the English and Scottish Churches, persuading the Scots to restore the office of bishop, although their role was to advise rather than to enforce conformity as in England. In 1621 he had proposed the establishment of a formal order of service, similar to the English Prayer Book. The fierce opposition that it aroused convinced him to withdraw the plan. Charles, however, was not only less aware of Scottish concerns than his father, but also considerably less tactful.

In 1637, Charles ordered that a new prayer book, based on the one used in England, should be formally adopted and read in Edinburgh churches. The order was imposed by proclamation and without reference to either the Scottish Parliament or the Assembly of the Kirk. When the book was read in St Giles's Cathedral in Edinburgh, a woman named Jenny Geddes was so incensed that she threw her stool at the bishop who was reading it. The service erupted into a riot, which rapidly sparked off riots elsewhere among a people who were infuriated by both the book and the manner in which it was imposed. The Scottish Council withdrew the book but Charles insisted that his orders were carried out. The Scottish clergy and nobility united in anger

Kirk – The Scottish Kirk was a Presbyterian Church, founded by John Knox in 1560. When Mary, Queen of Scots, returned to Scotland from France in 1560 she found a Protestant Reformation already completed. The result was that the Kirk, run by committees of ministers and elders rather than bishops, was in many ways independent of the monarchy. Worship was based on preaching and improvised prayers, both provided by ministers who had little hesitation in speaking their minds. From the point of view of the monarch, this independence needed to be curbed, but for many Scots, the Kirk was a symbol of both their religious and cultural identity.

Covenant – A contract or agreement in which the parties bind themselves to carry out certain obligations. The Scottish Covenant was a national treaty in which those who signed it agreed to come together to defend the existing Kirk, if necessary by force of arms, and to remain together until its safety was assured. It was therefore an act of rebellion, which Charles could not ignore.

Enclosures – Fences used to designate private land, often taken from land that had previously been for communal use, and hence much resented by the poorer members of the community.

at such arbitrary English domination and early in 1638 they met to draw up a declaration for supporters to sign, hence known as the Covenant, to defend the Kirk. Predictably, Charles was outraged by their defiance, especially as the Covenanters claimed to be acting in God's name.

The First Bishops' War

It was not surprising that Charles responded to this defiance by raising an army. He regarded the Covenanters as rebels and had no hesitation in using military force to put down such a rebellion. Unfortunately, he was in no position to do so. Lacking the money to employ mercenaries, he had to rely on English support. Many of the nobility had no wish to fight and the JPs were half-hearted in their preparations, perhaps alienated from the King or preoccupied with the need to collect Ship Money. The militia was locally based and men were reluctant to move from their home areas. When they did, the number who became involved in attacking Church ornaments or joining local rioters in pulling down enclosures demonstrates their lack of enthusiasm for the cause for which they were asked to fight.

The Scots, on the other hand, were committed to their cause. The Covenanters saw the Kirk as the embodiment of both their religion and culture and regarded the King as unwittingly serving the cause of the Anti-Christ by restoring devilish ceremonies in the Church. They would fight to defend their religion and felt justified in resisting their sovereign in the name of God. Even Charles realised that he did not have the strength to win, and signed the Treaty of Berwick in 1639. This allowed the Scots to decide on their own religious settlement and they immediately exercised their freedom by abolishing both the Scottish Prayer Book and the Scottish bishops.

If Charles had ever intended to respect the treaty, this action ensured that he would not do so. His political isolation was clear. The London merchants refused to lend him money to raise a new army, and some of the English nobility among the Puritan faction, such as Lord Saye and Sele and his son Nathaniel Fiennes, were already in contact with the Scots to encourage them to intervene in England. Charles, however, was unaware of the depth of resentment that he faced and determined to reassert his authority. To do so, he recalled Sir Thomas Wentworth, now Lord Strafford, from Ireland.

Defeat and collapse, 1640

Why was Charles unable to reassert his authority in 1640?

Strafford advised Charles to call Parliament, hoping that traditional anti-Scottish feeling would enable him to rally support. This was a dangerous strategy, but there was probably little alternative. The Bishops' War had forced the government to borrow money and the financial gains of the Personal Rule had already been wiped out. Generous concessions on grievances might have enabled the King to win over his critics, although the number of petitions listing grievances sent to Westminster to greet the MPs who assembled in April 1640 suggests that it may already have been too late.

The Short Parliament

In any case, Charles's handling of the situation destroyed any chance of success. Without offering any concessions, or even perhaps realising that they were needed, he demanded money to defend the kingdom from a crisis that he had created.

The result was a chaotic session in which the 'opposition' began to assume shape and structure. The key figures in the Lords were the Earl of Bedford, Lord Saye and Sele and Lord Montague, later Earl of Manchester. In the Commons the dominant figure was John Pym, Bedford's legal adviser. Nathaniel Fiennes was already in touch with the Scottish army and awareness of these contacts may have encouraged Charles to dissolve Parliament quickly; had he had proof of these activities, it is likely that Fiennes would have faced a treason charge. As it was, the April Parliament, which became known as the Short Parliament, achieved nothing for the King.

The Second Bishops' War and the calling of the Long Parliament

In spite of everything, Charles was determined to restore his authority. His actions in this period highlight the best and worst aspects of his character – courageous and determined, stubborn and high-handed, and – most dangerous in political terms – seriously out of touch. His lack of political awareness is revealed by his willingness to borrow from Catholics and use Catholic officers, while the rank and file busied themselves in burning altar rails and other Catholic symbols. Not surprisingly, the under-equipped and unenthusiastic English army proved unable to match the Scots, who had by now entered England. After a brief battle at Newburn-on-Tyne, the army disintegrated, leaving the Scots in control of Newcastle and able to force their terms on the King once more in October 1640, in the Treaty of Ripon. Their conditions – a further truce, payment by Charles of their expenses at £850 a day and the postponement of further negotiations to end the war until a Parliament met – were designed to give that Parliament the advantage. In fact, Charles had already accepted the need to call a new Parliament and had concluded, somewhat late in the day, that some concessions would be needed to gain support. He had little idea of just how many!

> ### KEY DATES: DEFEAT AND COLLAPSE
>
> **1637** At Charles's insistence a new Prayer Book is imposed on the Scottish Church.
>
> **1638** Scottish nobility and leaders of the Church sign the Covenant.
>
> **1639** First Bishops' War ends in Treaty of Berwick.
>
> **1639–40** Scottish Assembly votes to abolish both Prayer Book and bishops.
>
> **1640** Charles recalls Strafford who advises calling Parliament.
>
> **April–May:** The Short Parliament
>
> **June–October:** Second Bishops' War, ending in the Treaty of Ripon.
>
> **November:** The Long Parliament meets.

Thomas Wentworth, Earl of Strafford (1593–1641)

Sir Thomas Wentworth was a gentleman of south Yorkshire with wide connections of blood and marriage. Knighted in 1611, he became MP for Yorkshire in 1614. His election as a county MP (rather than a borough representative) indicates his influence and status within the county. As an MP he was initially associated with the defence of parliamentary rights against royal encroachments, being imprisoned in 1627 for refusing to pay the forced loan, and playing an important role in the presentation of the Petition of Right. Much of his opposition, however, was directed at the influence and inefficiency of George Villiers, the Duke of Buckingham, and when the King offered Strafford the post of President of the Council of the North after Buckingham's assassination in 1628, he accepted. This decision was regarded as a betrayal by some MPs, a perception that increased with his active role in the Personal Rule of Charles I. In 1629 he was appointed to the Privy Council, where he shared with Laud the responsibility for the administration of 'Thorough' (see page 51). In 1632, however, he was appointed Lord Deputy of Ireland and was absent from England for the next eight years.

Strafford was an able and energetic governor, a good administrator and a man of iron determination. In Ireland he promoted trade, reformed the administration and built up the army, but he was resented for his harsh control and dictatorial methods. This led Charles to recall him in his time of need and promote him to an earldom and the role of chief adviser. It was Strafford who recommended Charles to call Parliament, believing that he could manage it by exploiting anti-Scottish sentiment. This was a mistake, arising possibly from his long absence or possibly from his dislike of Puritan ideas. Whatever the reason, he soon paid the price. When Parliament reassembled in November 1640, he was a primary target for the opposition, who may have desired revenge for his betrayal and certainly feared his abilities. Strafford was aware that the opposition leaders were in contact with the Scots and planned to impeach them for treason, but was himself accused of having plotted to bring over an Irish army to use against Parliament. While he may have been willing to do this, there was little evidence to support the claim. He defended himself brilliantly against impeachment proceedings in the House of Lords and his accusers were forced to introduce an Act of Attainder in April 1641, by which he was simply declared to be guilty. He was executed on 12 May 1641.

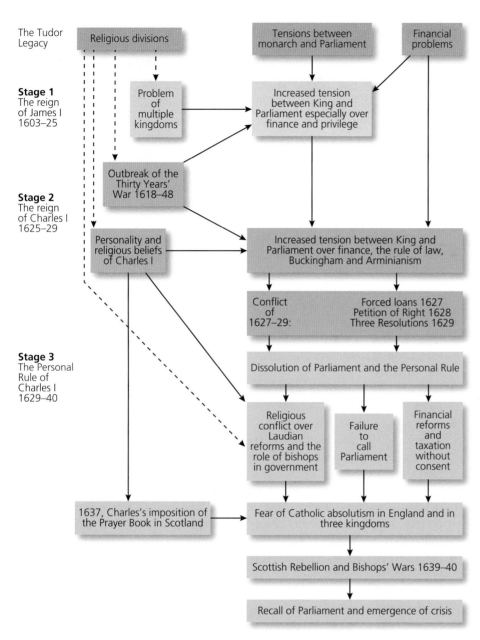

The Tudor Legacy

Stage 1
The reign of James I 1603–25

Stage 2
The reign of Charles I 1625–29

Stage 3
The Personal Rule of Charles I 1629–40

Religious divisions

Tensions between monarch and Parliament

Financial problems

Problem of multiple kingdoms

Increased tension between King and Parliament especially over finance and privilege

Outbreak of the Thirty Years' War 1618–48

Personality and religious beliefs of Charles I

Increased tension between King and Parliament over finance, the rule of law, Buckingham and Arminianism

Conflict of 1627–29:

Forced loans 1627
Petition of Right 1628
Three Resolutions 1629

Dissolution of Parliament and the Personal Rule

Religious conflict over Laudian reforms and the role of bishops in government

Failure to call Parliament

Financial reforms and taxation without consent

1637, Charles's imposition of the Prayer Book in Scotland

Fear of Catholic absolutism in England and in three kingdoms

Scottish Rebellion and Bishops' Wars 1639–40

Recall of Parliament and emergence of crisis

▲ **Figure 1** Summary of the development of crisis, 1603–40.

ACTIVITY

Using the diagram to help you and referring to your notes for detailed information you should now consolidate your learning by carrying out the following tasks:

1 Take each of the six factors listed on page 69 in turn and write a summary of how it contributed to growing tensions.

2 In 1621, 1628 and 1629 there were open confrontations between King and Parliament. Write a brief explanation of what combination of factors caused each of these and describe how it made tensions worse.

3 Summarise the part played by each factor in bringing the crisis to a head in 1640.

4 Review your analysis of the actions of Charles I. Did he cause the crisis of 1640? Was he simply grappling with problems already created by others or did he make existing problems worse? Write a list of arguments for and against the claim that he was the main cause of the crisis, and a conclusion to explain which arguments you find most convincing.

Chapter summary

- The reaction of the political nation to the dissolution of Parliament in 1629 was not particularly hostile, even though Charles's proclamation had made it clear that he did not intend to call another for some time.
- He was able to punish the MPs he considered responsible and force an apology from all but one of them. That MP died in prison within two years.
- Government and administration in the early years of the Personal Rule were characterised by efficiency and given the name of 'Thorough'.
  - Taxes, including an extended Ship Money from 1635, were paid and collected without difficulty until problems began in Scotland in 1637.
  - New orders were imposed in the Church, against considerable hostility, but those who opposed the changes had no way to prevent them.
- However, by 1637 it had become apparent that many of the ruling elite were concerned by recent developments. Charles was establishing an open-ended system for raising taxes without going through Parliament, which deprived them of the right to consent.
- At the same time, the changes in the Church, the role of Laud in both religious and secular affairs and the influence of Catholics at Court, raised fears about Catholicism and absolute monarchy, well beyond the ranks of the Puritans.
- Nevertheless, those who protested were silenced – for example Burton, Bastwick and Prynne, and opposition leaders like Bedford were in despair.
- Only when Charles tried to impose his reforms on Scotland did he meet an opposition that was both strong and capable of organising resistance. His Scottish opponents had institutions like the Kirk where they could meet and plan their response.
- In 1638–40 the Bishops' Wars revealed significant problems in the system of administration in England and a lack of support for Charles within the political nation, which increasingly took the form of calls for a parliament to meet.
- Despite this, Charles had several opportunities to achieve a compromise in both Scotland and England, which he refused to consider.
- As a result, in 1640 he faced total defeat. The calling of parliament in November was forced upon him by the Treaty of Ripon and the opposition knew it. For Charles, and for the monarchy, 1640 was a year of crisis.

Working on the failure of the Personal Rule

The main focus of Chapter 3 has been the Personal Rule and the reasons for its failure, with an emphasis on causation rather than change. Although there were changes in the way government worked and the attitudes of the political nation which became apparent in 1640, there had been few changes in the structure of government and the expectation of all those who assembled with the Long Parliament in 1640 was that adjustment and compromise, not wholesale change, would be required to deal with the problems. This is reflected in the essay advice set out below, and the focus of the questions remains causation and the role of different factors in bringing about a crisis.

However, as indicated in the Interpretations set out at the beginning of the chapter, this crisis can be viewed in different ways – as a short-term conflict created by Charles I and those who opposed his ideas of monarchy, or as part of a more fundamental crisis that had built up from underlying problems across several stages. In Chapters 1, 2 and 3 you have covered a substantial body of material which traces these developments and in 1640 you have reached a good point at which to review and consolidate what you have learnt. An apparent attempt to create absolutism in Church and State had led to a growing challenge in response, which the misjudgements of Charles I brought to a head in 1640. Using the knowledge and understanding that you have accrued so far and recorded in your linear notes, you can begin to investigate the development of a crisis that would eventually transform government across three kingdoms.

Understanding the development of the crisis is derived from two key questions – *how* did it develop and *why* did it happen. These questions are different, but there are links between them. If you understand how the crisis occurred, it helps you to explain why. *How* asks you to examine a process, to look at what happened and organise it into stages of development. When you do this, you will see that certain *factors* seem to cause problems in each of the stages, although perhaps in different ways at different times. These factors enable you to explain *why* the crisis developed.

You have already looked at factors and how they worked together in the tasks at the end of Chapter 2. Once you are to be able to explain the crisis as a whole, you then need to widen your perspective and look at the factors that were present across the whole period 1603–40. It could be said that the factors provide the building blocks of your explanation and the stages of development define the pattern in which you lay them out. For example, the explanation in Chapter 1 of what James inherited and experienced in Chapter 2 defined four key areas where problems existed. This gives you four factors that help to explain why there was a crisis:

- religious divisions
- financial problems
- relations between King and Parliament
- the problem of governing three kingdoms.

You also know from your study of Chapter 2 that these problems were made worse in the 1620s by the addition of two new factors:

- the Thirty Years War in Europe
- the personality of Charles I.

The interaction of these six factors created a breach between King and Parliament in 1629, which increased tensions during the Personal Rule. Hence we can see that problems were building up during three stages of development, given focus by confrontations between King and Parliament in 1621, 1629 and 1640. It finally came to a head when the Scottish rebellion brought together the problem of religion in different kingdoms and the King's financial weakness. This combination forced him to recall Parliament and address their accumulated grievances.

One of the best ways to express this process is to set it out in a diagram. While linear notes are good for recording detailed information about each factor, diagrams and flow charts can be more effective in expressing the links between them and how they worked together. Figure 1 sets out the process that we have just described, to provide you with a basic explanation of how and why the crisis of 1640 developed. It shows what factors were involved and how they worked together in different stages.

Working on essay technique: investigating issues and planning essays

The activities at the end of Chapter 2 emphasised three key skills needed for planning effective essays – analysis, explanation and focus. Having *analysed* the question to establish its *focus*, you wrote out a list of key points and set out an *explanation* of each one, which included supporting evidence, development of the implications and specific links to the question, and drew it together at the end in a conclusion that was *focused* as an answer to the question. However, the best essays do more than this.

In an essay dealing with *causation*, for example, the purpose is *to explain why* something happened, and that is what your conclusion should focus on. However, it is not simply a matter of covering all the causal factors, but of showing how they combined and *interacted* to bring about a particular outcome, and that can be quite complicated. Are all causes of equal significance? Do they all interact in the same way? The best essays will look at these issues in presenting an overall judgement, and therefore they are planned with that in mind. The work that you have done on investigating the development of the crisis should also help with this. You have already explored the causal factors that provide the building blocks for your answer, and you have already looked at how they interacted at certain times.

Whether you are taking the AS exam or the full A-level exam, Section B presents you with essay titles. Each question is marked out of 25.

AS examination	The full A level examination
Section B – Answer ONE essay (from a choice of two).	Section B – Answer TWO essays (from a choice of three).

Several question stems are possible as alternatives, but they all have the same basic requirement. They all require you to analyse and reach a conclusion, based on the evidence you provide.

For example: 'Assess the validity (of a quotation)', 'To what extent…', 'How successful…', 'How far…', etc.

The AS titles will give a quotation and then: Explain why you agree or disagree with this view. Almost inevitably, your answer will be a mixture of both. In essence, it is the same task as for the full A level – just more basic wording.

Each question will reflect, directly or indirectly, one of the breadth issues in your study. The questions will have a fairly broad focus.

Although the questions will differ, both require a planned response and they are addressed together below. The basic approach in terms of planning is relevant to both. In both cases the starting place for causation essays is *the analysis of events to define causal factors*, the use of supporting detail and links to explain *how each one helped to cause a particular event*, and the exploration of *how they combined and interacted* to bring it about.

Planning and writing essays on the development of the crisis

Once you have your building blocks in place, writing essays is a matter of applying them to different questions you are asked. Before you ever attempt to write an essay, it has to be planned so that you know what you want to include, and it is your building blocks of factors which enable you to plan it. There are many different ways to plan essays, but what is suggested in the example on page 71 provides a method that you can practice and apply to the questions that follow the example.

EXAMPLE

Begin with a straightforward question such as:

'Why did Charles I face a crisis in government in November 1640?'

This is not the kind of question that you would be asked in an exam, but it is very useful for assembling the building blocks and practising a method of planning that you can apply to a whole range of exam questions. Since this is a breadth paper the exam questions will cover at least 20 years within the period studied, and although the question here focuses on the end point in 1640, your response will need to address events and developments from the reign of James I as well as that of Charles.

Using the diagram on page 67 to help you, write out a summary that answers the question. This would probably provide the conclusion to your essay. For example:

Charles inherited financial weakness as well as some tensions with parliaments from his father. Both of these problems were made worse by the adventurous foreign policy and inefficiency of his favourite and adviser, the Duke of Buckingham. In a sense he had also inherited Buckingham, but allowed him far greater influence on policy than James had ever done. This caused friction with Parliament and led to an open breach in 1629. Relations were made worse by his religious policies, which involved promoting Arminians in the Church and raised fears of Catholic influence. The resulting grievances grew during his Personal Rule, but it was his attempt to extend these reforms to Scotland that brought the crisis to a head in 1640 and brought him face to face with a Parliament that was determined to restrict his powers for the future. Although all of these factors played a part in the crisis, it was Charles himself who brought them together in this way.

Review your summary, and set out the key factors that you will have to explain. These will provide the main sections of your essay. These six sections will give you a coherent essay, which you can draw into a final conclusion.

You will see that the starting point for this plan was the question that was asked. The building blocks that you have can provide you with the material that you need to answer a variety of questions, but you will need to arrange them differently and explain the links between them in a different way.

EXAMPLE

Look at the following question:

To what extent did religious issues cause the crisis that Charles faced in 1640?

To answer this type of question, you need to focus on the impact of religious divisions and then set them against other factors that played a part. This is known as establishing an *argument* and a *counter-argument*, in order to come to a final judgement. Hence you would rearrange your building blocks to respond to the particular question, but you would still use them all.

ACTIVITY

● Using the diagram on page 67 to help you, write out a summary/conclusion to the question:

'Religious fears, increased by the impact of war after 1618, were the main cause of the crisis that faced Charles I in 1640.' Assess the validity of this view.

● Divide the summary into key factors required for the essay.
● Write out a plan using the factors, the effect of each one and the important links between them. Once you are used to the method, you will probably not need to write out a separate plan – your subdivided conclusion will serve the purpose.

Once you have completed the process, you can practise the method on the question below. While the wording may differ slightly from those you will meet in an exam, the requirement for a broad view and the ability to explain developments over a period of time provide good preparation.

ACTIVITY

'Greedy courtiers and evil counsellors were to blame for the problems faced by the monarchy in the years 1618–40.' Explain why you agree or disagree with this view.

Working on interpretation skills: extended reading

Why was there a crisis of the monarchy in 1640?

Simon Healy discusses the varying reasons for the crisis point reached by 1640.

In the autumn of 1640 the Scottish Covenanters inflicted a minor defeat on Charles I's English army and occupied Newcastle. The royal army should have counter-attacked, but instead Charles faced criticism from many of the English nobility, who negotiated a truce with the Scots and compelled him to summon a Parliament. The Long Parliament swiftly dismantled the legal, financial and administrative apparatus which had sustained the 'Personal Rule' of the 1630s, impeached many royal advisers and paid off the Scots army on generous terms. This radical agenda was widely supported, even by future Royalists, but disagreements over further reforms propelled Ireland and then England into civil war in 1641–42. *(5 ... 10)*

Many contemporaries and some historians have laid the blame for this crisis upon the King. Charles was not an easy man to work with, but his father and sons all struggled to cope with a broadly similar situation. It is perhaps fairer to say that the Stuarts had a difficult inheritance, to which Charles applied radical measures, which left many of his critics suspicious of his motives and made the negotiation of a settlement difficult. *(15)*

The Stuarts' chief problem was religion. Ecclesiastical organisation was different in each of their three realms: the Scottish Kirk was governed by a decentralised Presbyterian system, on which James VI and I had superimposed bishops; the Church of England was centralised around the Crown and an authoritarian group of senior Protestant clergymen; while in Ireland the Protestant Church was dominated by English- and Scottish-born settlers and administrators. Most Irish were Roman Catholic, as were a small proportion of the English and Scottish population, and while they all faced severe legal penalties for practising their religion, enforcement varied considerably according to political, geographical and diplomatic circumstances. The exception to this rule was at Court, where Charles's French wife, Henrietta Maria, acted as a focus for Catholic patronage from 1625. Also at Court, the favour shown to Protestant clerics prepared to concede some degree of engagement with Catholic traditions – those often, though not always accurately, termed 'Arminians' or 'Laudians' – became a serious point of contention from the early 1620s. *(20 ... 25 ... 30)*

Finance was another problem: the English Crown raised far lower taxes per head of population than its rivals in France, Castile or the United Provinces; and while Scotland was self-sufficient after the royal Court departed for England in 1603, in Ireland, the cost of a standing army required English subsidies until the 1630s. The Crown's financial position should have been much stronger in 1603, as the Tudors had seized vast amounts of English and Irish church property, but this was used to buy political support rather than increase Crown revenues. English customs tariffs also increased sharply in 1558 and again in 1608, but the latter increases caused a political controversy resolved only in 1641. Excises, a major component of Continental tax revenues, were politically taboo in England and were only seriously exploited from the later 1630s. *(35 ... 40)*

As well as studying the facts of an event in history, historians also use these facts in order to reach conclusions on, for example, why something happened. In other words, they have to interpret the facts in order to reach their conclusions. Often the evidence does not just point in one direction. There is scope for historians to reach different conclusions and produce different interpretations.

In this chapter, as well as Chapters 6 and 9, there is one, longer interpretation to read, followed by some questions that are designed to help you build up your skills as well as helping you to consolidate your knowledge of each chapter.

The political consequences of fiscal stagnation were high: English taxpayers were happy to have an under-funded Crown beg for assistance in Parliament, where supply could be offered in return for political concessions. This high-risk strategy led to angry dissolutions of Parliament in autumn 1610, 1614, autumn 1621, 1625 and 1626, but, as King James discovered in 1611–20, the Crown could not dispense with parliamentary taxation under the existing financial system. Charles inaugurated such a policy in 1626, raising peacetime revenues by at least 60 per cent over the next 14 years. He achieved this partly by maximising income regardless of the political controversy this incurred and partly by raising short-term credit from private entrepreneurs who farmed the collection of revenues. Similar reforms took place in Ireland in the 1630s, while in both realms, Catholics were allowed to purchase a degree of religious toleration.

The Stuarts' third problem was geopolitical. The circumstances of Queen Elizabeth's birth committed her to an anti-Spanish policy, but the Stuarts had no such constraints and James remained at peace throughout his reign, despite growing tensions on the Continent from 1618. Charles overturned his father's pro-Spanish policy – to widespread applause – in 1624–25, but by 1629–30, military failure abroad and political strife at home led him to withdraw support from the embattled Protestant cause in Europe and to dispense with parliaments, which had failed to fund his war effort. This alarmed many in his three kingdoms, but his critics could exercise little leverage so long as his regime remained at peace and solvent.

The Stuarts' final problem was that of coping with a rapidly evolving situation in multiple kingdoms with divergent interests – any alteration in the political or religious balance of one realm had serious consequences for the others. Thus when the Scots rebelled in 1637, Charles's English critics did their best to stiffen the Covenanters' resolve and exploited the King's military reverses in order to recover the political initiative they had lost over the previous decade. Charles, aware of their intentions, distrusted their assurances of good faith and appealed to those who stood to lose most in the event of a Covenanter victory: Scottish and Irish Catholic peers and the Spanish Crown. Rumours of Charles's plotting fuelled his critics' deepest fear, that he intended to establish a Catholic absolutist state, and while civil war was one of the less likely outcomes of the crisis his realms faced in the autumn of 1640, the growing spiral of mutual distrust, plot and counter-plot made it difficult to negotiate a permanent settlement.

Simon Healy works at the History of Parliament Trust, London.

ACTIVITY

Having read the essay, answer the following questions.

Evidence
The writer describes a range of problems that caused difficulty for all the Stuart kings and supports his description with some detailed reference. Are there any points of information that you feel have not been given due consideration?

1 Write out a list of the main points of supporting evidence that the writer has included.
2 Use your own knowledge to add any extra points that you think should be included.

Interpretation
3 The author suggests in paragraph two that some historians have blamed Charles I for the crisis of 1640. How does he challenge this interpretation? Does he acknowledge any way in which Charles contributed to the emergence of a crisis?
4 What does the author consider to have been the main causes of the crisis? Summarise his argument in a paragraph.

Evaluation
The author clearly considers that Charles is not the primary cause of the crisis, but he does mention his use of 'radical measures'.

5 Using your own knowledge, write a paragraph to explain what these measures were and how they contributed to the crisis.
6 Write a concluding paragraph that explains the crisis by linking both.

4

Division and conflict, 1640–46

This chapter covers the years of political crisis and the drift to war, as the divisions within the Long Parliament became increasingly apparent and enabled the formation of two 'sides' necessary for military conflict. It traces the process by which war broke out, despite widespread neutralism, and explains why, in 1646, Parliament emerged victorious. The specified areas covered are:

- the Long Parliament and the role of John Pym
- Parliamentary divisions and the drift to war
- the Civil Wars: England, Scotland and Ireland
- the New Model Army and the emergence of radicalism
- the victory of Parliament.

In this case the specified areas follow a broadly chronological sequence, although the analysis of how different factors interacted requires some overlap in reviewing their significance. This analysis will also address the specified breadth issues, in which this short period of six years produced some key developments. Although the powers of the monarchy were not changed on a permanent basis, the experience of organising an effective opposition and conducting a war created the potential for very significant changes in the role and powers of parliaments. The emergence of religious radicalism and the creation of the New Model Army brought important developments in disputes over religion, the significance of key individuals and the development of ideas and ideology.

The main question focused on in this chapter is:

How did the experience of war affect attitudes towards the monarchy, society, and the structure of government?

CHAPTER OVERVIEW

In 1640, those who assembled in the Long Parliament expected to achieve a settlement with the King. At that point, war was not possible because the King had neither the money nor the support to create an army. However, in the year that followed, the unity of the Commons crumbled and Charles was able to rally enough support to make a military solution to his problems a possible option. It is therefore necessary first to consider why this happened. However, the fact that war was possible does not make it inevitable and the reluctant drift to military action that occurred in the early months of 1642 suggests that it was unwanted. It is therefore necessary to consider how war broke out, to what extent it came about through mistakes and misjudgements and why men were prepared to fight in those circumstances. Finally, given the apparent superiority of the King's forces, why was it that the balance of strength changed and that the war resulted in the victory of Parliament?

1 From crisis to war, 1640–42

Expectations and attitudes, November 1640

What kind of opposition did Charles face when the Long Parliament met?

When Parliament assembled in November 1640 it was clear that the King had summoned it because he had no choice. The terms of the Treaty of Ripon placed him in urgent need of money, and he knew that he would have to make some concessions in order to obtain it. Nevertheless, he hoped that traditional loyalty and anti-Scottish feeling would enable him to rally support and limit any concessions to those he found acceptable. Certainly, once the Scottish emergency was over and his freedom of action restored, there would be some possibility of limiting the effects. In short, Charles was unprepared for the kind of opposition he now faced – determined, wary and above all, organised.

Pym's junto

Explanations of how the crisis of 1640 became a civil war in 1642 can most easily be made intelligible to a modern audience by the use of terms such as 'opposition', 'sides' and 'parties', although they do not actually match the reality of what was happening in seventeenth-century parliaments. While factions among the nobility and rivalry between ministers were normal, the idea of opposition to the King was close to treason. Yet it is undeniable that Charles did face a coherently organised group of MPs, linked to certain members of the Lords, with a planned strategy for defeating his most cherished plans and imposing their own. This group has been described by the historian Conrad Russell as 'Pym's junto', reflecting the leadership of John Pym and the somewhat conspiratorial nature of the group. Its activities in opposing Charles and his 'evil counsellors' encouraged some historians to accept the contemporary Royalist view that its members plotted and schemed to manipulate Parliament in pursuit of their own ambitions. This is supported by the evidence that they were in touch with the Scots in the spring and summer of 1640 and that part of their strategy was to replace Charles's advisers with their own men. In May 1641 a scheme to appoint the Earl of Bedford as chief adviser to the King, with Pym as Chancellor of the Exchequer, was aborted by the death of Bedford from a fever.

Against these claims it can be argued that there was nothing unusual or underhand in planning to replace bad advisers with good ones and that a willingness to contribute to the King's government was perfectly natural among those who wished to influence it. This was precisely what Strafford had done in 1628. It can also be argued that the manipulation of Parliament was a necessary strategy – long employed by monarchs through the presence of Privy Councillors in both Houses – if the King was to be pressurised into redressing grievances and abandoning his plans for government in Church and State. The majority of members came to Westminster with a desire for change but little understanding of how to achieve it. What requires explaining in relation to 'Pym's junto' and its associates is not the willingness of its members to use political tactics in pursuit of their cause, but their ability to do so.

NOTE-MAKING

As always, you will need to make linear notes throughout the chapter, as you have for Chapters 2 and 3. As the events of 1641–42 are quite complex, you will find it helpful to create your own timeline to help you structure your notes on the period. You should colour code your timeline to identify different areas and issues:

- Any events that have significance regarding religious issues should be circled in red.
- Any events that have significance relating to constitutional issues and the distribution of power should be circled in blue.
- Any events that have significance in creating mistrust should be circled in green.
- Any event can be circled in more than one colour if it has significance for more than one set of issues.

The main purpose is to create a visual record of how different developments interacted to produce mistrust and divisions within Parliament and between Parliament and King.

Pym's junto – The term 'junto' refers to a small, organised group who work together to gain or maintain power.

John Pym (1583–1643)

Born in Somerset, Pym was the son of a wealthy landowner and was educated at Oxford. He spent his early manhood managing his estates in Somerset and was first elected to Parliament in 1621. Pym sat in every Parliament thereafter until his death from cancer in 1643.

By 1640 he was an experienced parliamentarian, an able speaker and a clever tactician, enabling him to lead and manage the opposition campaign in the Commons. The group associated with Pym in 1640–42 was not formally organised and it is difficult to draw a distinction between members and associates, but it is clear that Pym had a number of trusted allies. Their experience in the 'Short' Parliament of April 1640, which had been quickly dissolved by Charles, enabled them to be better prepared when they re-assembled in November in the 'Long' Parliament, so-called because it lasted nearly twenty years.

Organisation and tactics

Three factors seem to have been important in this – the junto's previous experience of Charles I, their personal and political links and the outstanding political skills of John Pym. Most of the opposition leaders had been MPs in the 1620s, many of them being supporters and protégés of Sir Edward Coke, who had formulated the Petition of Right in 1628. Pym, in particular, learned a great deal from Coke's management of parliamentary opinion over the Commons Protestation of 1621 (see Chapter 2, page 31) and the Petition of Right (see Chapter 2, page 37). After the dissolution of Parliament in 1629, some contacts had been maintained through business and family links. Pym was employed as a lawyer and agent by the Earl of Bedford. In 1629 Bedford, Lord Saye and Sele, Lord Brooke and the Earl of Warwick founded a trading company named the Providence Island Company, to trade with the colonies in America and to attack Spanish ships and property in the West Indies. Both Pym and John Hampden were included as co-directors. There is little doubt that these men helped to organise the Ship Money case (see Chapter 3, page 49), in which Hampden employed as his counsel another of Bedford's agents, Oliver St John. Hampden himself had wide contacts of blood and inter-marriage in Buckinghamshire and East Anglia, including the MP for Cambridge in 1640, Oliver Cromwell.

While these contacts provided a core that contributed to the coherence of the group, they are not sufficient to explain its effectiveness or its impact. The adherence of others such as Sir Arthur Haselrig, whose family home was in Durham, Sir Henry Vane and Denzil Holles, son of the Earl of Clare, was based upon political and religious conviction. It is significant that all of the central group and most of their associates held Puritan views in religion. The brief calling and dissolution of parliament in April 1640 gave them occasion to meet and an awareness of the tactics that would be needed to avoid a repetition of its failure, as well as useful contacts with the Scots brought by Nathaniel Fiennes, MP, son of Lord Saye and Sele, who had been in touch with the Covenanters since 1639. It is probably fair to say that the opposition group, as such, took shape at this time and that its planned strategy for the Long Parliament was based on the experience of its predecessor of April. When Parliament assembled in November, Pym launched an attack on existing grievances and established the group in positions of influence by proposing various committees with his associates as members and chairmen. From that base, they were able to put forward proposals and influence debates.

The need for parliamentary unity

It is important to consider the relationship of this group to other members of the Long Parliament. It is difficult to support the Royalist perception that they tricked and manipulated an assembly of innocents into supporting strategies that they did not understand. Nevertheless, it is clear that there was a difference in political perception between men like Pym and the average country member. According to Clarendon, he met Pym in Westminster 'some days before the Parliament' and was told by Pym that:

'[T]hey must now be of another temper than they were the last Parliament [the Short Parliament of April 1640] … that they now had an opportunity to make their country happy, by removing all grievances and pulling up the causes of them by the roots, if all men would do their duties.'

This suggests more radical measures than those envisaged by the Yorkshire MP, Sir Henry Slingsby, who left home on 2 November commenting that:

'Great expectance there is of a happy Parliament, where the subject may have a total redress of all his grievances.'

While the two men shared a concern for the redress of grievances, there was a significant difference in their political awareness of what it would take to achieve it.

It could be argued, therefore, that the opposition leaders differed from the majority of MPs in their political experience, the depth and intensity of their opposition and possibly the importance of religion in their concerns. But it should be remembered that it is difficult to make effective generalisations because the Long Parliament was, above all, an assembly of individuals and local factions rather than a coherent political body. The county petitions (traditionally sent from each county at the beginning of a parliament) that arrived at Westminster on this occasion show that there was a widespread concern with grievances and a demand for the reversal of Charles's policies in Church and State. To this extent the opposition leaders were a part of, and in tune with, the electorate that they represented. In terms of strategies for achieving their aims, however, they were far more advanced and radical in their thinking than the majority of members on whose support they had to rely. They would therefore need to proceed carefully, at a pace and in a direction that they could make acceptable to the varied and often cautious representatives of the political nation around them.

Redress of grievances

How successful were the opposition leaders in the first year of the parliament in obtaining the reforms that they desired?

Politics and the constitution

When MPs assembled for the meeting of what was to become the Long Parliament in November 1640, they did so in a mood of optimistic expectation. The obvious weakness of the King's position and his desperate need for financial support seemed to guarantee the opportunity to gain redress for the accumulated grievances of the Personal Rule and to ensure that it could not be repeated. The list of events in the box on page 79 indicates the extent to which they were successful. By the summer of 1641, the future of parliaments had been secured by the Triennial Act, the 'evil counsellors' had been replaced and punished and the machinery (such as Ship Money and the prerogative courts) by which Charles had raised money and silenced opposition, had been dismantled and abolished.

This record of success, however, disguised a number of problems. While the King had given his assent to the Triennial Act, the obvious reluctance and resentment with which he did so raised fears that he might later seek to reverse the decision and possibly punish those whom he regarded as responsible. In a speech made to Parliament on 16 February 1641, the day on which he gave his assent, he complained that Parliament had,

'hitherto done what concerns yourselves'

rather than attended to the needs of the kingdom (and King). He concluded:

'You have taken the government almost to pieces, and, I may say, it is almost off the hinges'.

These concerns were greatly increased by the execution of Strafford, which followed in May. The dangers of openly criticising the King had led the opposition leaders to place the blame for the events of the Personal Rule on the shoulders of the King's 'evil counsellors', especially Strafford and Laud. Proceedings for the impeachment of both had begun in November 1640, but those against Strafford ran into difficulty. Since he had, in fact, been carrying out the wishes of the King there was little evidence to support a charge of treason and it soon became apparent that he had every chance of successfully defending himself in the Lords. The MP Sir John Coke wrote in April 1641:

'Without question they will acquit him'.

However, to many MPs the removal of Strafford was a political necessity rather than a judicial matter. The opposition leaders therefore introduced an Act of Attainder, a parliamentary law by which Strafford was simply declared to be guilty and condemned to death. It passed the House of Commons by 204 votes to 59. To ensure its passage through the Lords, Pym stirred up fears by revealing a plot to dissolve the House of Commons and release Strafford by force. Concocted in March–April by a group of army officers, it had all the ingredients required to induce panic. Some of the participants were Catholics and although there was no evidence to implicate the King, his refusal to dismiss those involved raised serious questions. To protect the Parliament, Charles was forced to agree to an Act declaring that this Parliament could not be dissolved without its own consent. When the Bill of Attainder moved to the House of Lords, the London mobs appeared in Westminster and threatened any who opposed it. Many who opposed the bill chose to stay away and those who attended voted in favour. However, the attainder required the King's assent and Charles had promised Strafford that he would never agree, but faced by angry demonstrations in London and fearing for the safety of his family, Charles gave in. Strafford was executed before a jubilant crowd of several thousand on Tower Hill on 12 May 1641.

The Constitutional Reforms of the Long Parliament, 1640–41

The events and reforms listed below are those which were successfully established by the Long Parliament in 1640–42 and, for the most part, not reversed in the Restoration of 1660.

- November 1640 – Impeachment proceedings begun against Laud and Strafford in order to remove the King's 'evil counsellors'; this was not a new procedure, but an extension of the use made of this device in the 1620s.
- February 1641 – The Triennial Act passed through Parliament and received the King's assent. It ensured that Parliament would be called at least every three years and made provision for a Parliament to assemble even if the King had not called it. The Act survived the Restoration, but in 1664 it was replaced with a weakened version, which lacked this provision.
- May 1641 – An Act of Attainder declared Strafford to be guilty of treason and he was executed on 12 May. This use of Parliament's legislative powers to punish a minister without trial was doubtful on grounds of justice and equity, but did provide an alternative means of calling the King's advisers to account.
- July 1641 – The abolition of the prerogative courts of Star Chamber and High Commission removed the King's capacity to deal with legal cases directly through his prerogative powers. They were important steps in dismantling the machinery of Personal Rule, but did not remove the possibility of such courts being re-established in future under a different name. However, the prerogative courts were not revived with the Restoration.
- August 1641 – An Act was passed declaring Ship Money to be illegal. Again, this removed an important element of government during the Personal Rule, but did not guarantee that a future king might not try to establish a similar tax. In practice, however, none did.

The growth of mistrust

The measures used to destroy Strafford had a number of effects. Such devices undoubtedly disturbed a few MPs who had previously supported the opposition campaign, but the main impact was on the King. Having lost the capacity to dissolve this Parliament, he was more likely than ever to consider other strategies, including force. More immediately, he was angry and humiliated; a King who had been intimidated into breaking his word and betraying his chief adviser was unlikely to feel obliged to deal gently with those who had forced him into this position. As long as the opposition leaders had the support of a united Parliament, he was in no position to punish them, but if they should lose that support, they would not only endanger the rights and liberties of Parliament, but their own liberty and lives as well.

By the summer of 1641, therefore, the opposition had attained many of their initial objectives, but at the price of alienating the King and placing themselves at risk. It was no longer enough to dismantle the machinery of the Personal Rule and remove those responsible for it; there was also a need to ensure security for the future. Hence these developments forced the opposition leaders to formulate new demands and place further restrictions on the King. The first example of this came with the Ten Propositions of June 1641. In the aftermath of Strafford's execution, Charles had announced his intention to visit Scotland and finalise the treaties that had ended the Scottish rebellion. For the opposition leaders, understandably suspicious of his intentions, this posed problems. If Charles could escape the financial burdens imposed by the Treaty of Ripon (see Chapter 3, page 65), he would gain much greater freedom to manoeuvre with Parliament. Worse still, if he could conclude a different agreement with the Scots and build up his support there, he might well be able to use an experienced Scottish army to impose his will in England. To prevent this, the opposition put forward a list of ten points, including parliamentary control of the King's choice of advisers, and asked the King to delay his visit until after he had considered and agreed to them.

Such demands were a clear encroachment on the King's existing powers and there was little chance that Charles would agree to them. More importantly, many MPs also had reservations about such demands. The majority were not professional politicians, but country gentlemen who regarded the King's authority as their guarantee of order and the main pillar of the social hierarchy upon which they themselves depended. They had come to Westminster in November with a conviction that the King had overstepped his powers and infringed both law and the rights of parliaments. They were therefore united in demanding the removal of such abuses and securing parliaments for the future. To go further and make significant changes that would alter the balance of the constitution was something that they had not considered. To make matters worse, many were already concerned about other changes that had been put forward to deal with religious grievances and the difficult issue of reforming the Church.

Religion and the Church

As with other grievances, the changes introduced by Charles and Archbishop Laud in the Church had created widespread and apparently united opposition. In December 1640 the Commons had accepted a petition from London and the surrounding counties, which called for the reversal of Laud's reforms and the abolition of episcopacy (government of the Church by bishops). When the petition was debated, it became clear that many MPs were reluctant to go so far, but the issue was laid aside to deal with more urgent matters and caused little damage to the unity of Parliament. By May 1641, however, those other matters had been dealt with and MPs turned their attention to the matter of the Church.

It was quickly apparent that the widespread unpopularity of the Laudian bishops disguised a variety of different ideas about the future of the Church. While the majority of MPs disliked the pretensions of the clergy, the inquisitions of the Church courts and the interference of bishops in affairs of state, this fell far short of the Puritan schemes for wholesale reform of the Church. While most were willing to see the removal of the rituals imposed by Laud and restore a distinctively Protestant identity based on a preaching ministry, few were committed to any Presbyterian model, and even fewer to the complete abolition of bishops. While Laud was in power and the threat of Catholic influence immediate, Protestants of many shades of opinion could agree on the need to remove him. When it came to deciding on how to replace him, such unity quickly dissolved and the underlying divisions were revealed.

These problems were illustrated by the varying success of the religious measures introduced in 1640–41. By January 1641 the King had agreed to remove the bishops from his Privy Council, reducing their role in administration and government. In May the opposition introduced a bill to exclude bishops from the House of Lords, which rapidly passed the Commons only to be defeated in the Lords by a combination of the bishops themselves and the King's influence. In June, the Puritan faction attempted to bring in a Root and Branch Bill, to abolish the office of bishop completely and reform the Church along Presbyterian lines. Although this was now the only means of removing their political influence, it was clear that it would fail and its supporters laid it aside.

The attitude of many moderate members was expressed by the Yorkshire MP, Sir Henry Slingsby of Scriven, as recorded in his diary:

'I went with the Bill for their taking of [the Bishops'] votes in the House of Peers and for meddling with temporal [non-religious] affairs, but I was against the Bill for taking away the function and calling of Bishops ... I could never be of that opinion that the government of the Church, as it is now established by Bishops and Archbishops to be of absolute necessity, so that the taking of them away should quite overturn the state and essence of the Christian church; but I am of the opinion that the taking of them out of the Church ... may be of dangerous consequence to the peace of the Church ... considering that this government hath continued from the Apostles ... it were not safe to make alteration from so ancient a beginning.'

For men like Slingsby, the issue of Church government was not simply a matter of religious belief, but also of social order. While some MPs, particularly among the opposition leaders and their supporters, were deeply committed to reform of the Church along Puritan lines, there were many who regarded this as dangerous innovation, threatening the vital role of the Church in teaching the lower orders to obey and defer to those in authority. Others, like Edward Hyde, later Lord Clarendon, had a genuine affection for the traditional Anglican services practised since the time of Elizabeth. Others again, like Lord George Digby, disliked any clerical pretensions to power over the laity. Hence, while they opposed the activities of the Laudian Church courts and clergy, they had no intention of replacing them with a Presbyterian clergy who would claim similar powers. It is no coincidence that all the men mentioned here ultimately fought on the side of the King. More than any other issue, the religious divide of June 1641 foreshadowed the eventual divisions of the civil war itself.

KEY DATES: THE REDRESS OF GRIEVANCES 1640–41

1640 December: 'Root and Branch' debates reveal religious divisions.

1641

January: Removal of bishops from the Privy Council.

February: King's response to the Triennial Act shows reluctance to make real concessions.

April–May: Trial and execution of Strafford shows opposition use of intimidation and popular support; first Army Plot raises fears that the King will use force; Act against the dissolution of the Long Parliament raises fears of Catholic plots and reduces Charles's non-military options.

May: Bill to exclude bishops from the House of Lords passed the Commons, but was defeated in the Lords by a combination of the bishops' votes and pressure from the King.

June: King's visit to Scotland raises fear that he intends a new agreement with the Scots and an attack on Parliament; Ten Propositions raises fears that opposition seeks further power; Introduction of the Root and Branch Bill to abolish the office of bishops leads to divisions in the Commons and fears for stability among 'moderates,' alongside fears of failure and retribution within the opposition group.

NOTE-MAKING

In 1640 a civil war was impossible because the King faced a virtually united Parliament and both believed in the possibility of a compromise settlement. In the year that followed, this possibility grew fainter, largely because of the attitude of the King, while the growing extremism of the opposition in response undermined the trust that would be required for it to work. Nevertheless, war would have remained impossible had Parliament remained united. Your linear notes for this section need to trace the process by which these two developments – the growth of mistrust and the division of Parliament – took place, and Figure 1 on page 85 will allow you to review them and add conclusions about the interaction between them.

The shaping of the conflict

How did gathering mistrust become open conflict between 1641 and 1642?

By the late summer of 1641 the situation between the King and his critics had reached something of a stalemate. Charles's initial strategy of regaining control through limited concessions had clearly failed and his alternative of building a separate power base in Scotland had achieved little. Although he had brought the rebellion to an end, he had neither weakened the power of the Covenanters nor built up a Royalist party among the nobility. At the same time, the opposition in England had lost much of the momentum of 1640. While able to maintain parliamentary unity in redressing the grievances of the past – the prerogative courts were finally abolished in July 1641 – they were aware of concerns about further encroachments on the King's power, and had failed to find an agreed way forward in reforming the Church. While neither party, therefore, had a clear strategy for progress, there was still no reason to expect anything other than further compromises of some kind.

The Irish rebellion

What changed this situation was the outbreak of rebellion in Ireland. In October, when MPs returned to Westminster after the summer recess, they were met by rumours of a rising among the Irish Catholics and attacks on Protestant settlers. Wildly exaggerated stories circulated, claiming that as many as 200,000 had been murdered, many of them tortured before death. There were reports that an Irish army had landed in England and that the English Catholics would rise to join them. The reality was much less dramatic, but the rebellion was real enough and there were undoubtedly atrocities committed. Most terrifying of all, the leaders of the rebellion claimed to have the King's approval and support.

Nothing could have been more effective in stirring up panic among MPs and people alike than the conjunction of Irish influence, Catholicism and a King who was already mistrusted. According to the Puritan minister, Richard Baxter, *'there was nothing that with the people wrought so much [had such an effect] as the Irish massacre and rebellion. This filled all England with a fear both of the Irish and of the Papists [Catholics] at home ... And when they saw the English Papists join with the King against the Parliament, it was the greatest thing that ever alienated them from the King'.*

To make matters worse, Charles seems to have reacted remarkably slowly. He remained in Scotland until late November, returning to a sumptuous welcome from the corporation of the City of London on 25 November. By that time, steps had already been taken in Parliament that proved both divisive and dangerous.

The rebellion posed a difficult problem for the opposition leaders. On the one hand, they wanted to take action to deal with the rebellion and rescue their fellow Protestants. They were ready to supply the King with the money necessary to raise an army to go to Ireland. On the other hand, they were unwilling to entrust such an army to a King whom they feared might be in league with the rebels and who might even use it against Parliament instead. The suggestion that Parliament should maintain control of the army itself was an infringement of the King's powers and a considerable insult to him, infuriating a growing number of MPs who believed that the opposition had gone too far. Since the Ten Propositions and the religious debates of June 1641, a number of moderate MPs led by Edward Hyde and Sir John Culpepper, with the aid of Lord Falkland, had been arguing the case for the King. Any attempt to make further inroads into the royal prerogative would undoubtedly create the kind of divisions in Parliament that the opposition most feared.

Reaction and remonstrance

Under pressure and deprived of time to manoeuvre, Pym devised a strategy that he hoped would reunite the Commons. On 22 November 1641 he introduced a Grand Remonstrance to be forwarded to the King, which reviewed the events of the previous year and reminded the House what had been achieved by their united efforts, before setting out the challenges that remained. This was presented to the King on 1 December. Six days later a Militia Bill providing an army for Ireland was introduced, with an amendment from Sir Arthur Haselrig proposing that Parliament should be given the right to approve the King's choice of commander. The result was uproar and many of the uncommitted MPs rallied to the King. The division in Parliament had been revealed by the Grand Remonstrance, which passed the Commons by only 11 votes, and the Militia Bill was an additional offence. For the first time in a year, Charles was able to watch opinion in Parliament moving in his favour.

The response of the opposition was to take an even more radical step and appeal to public opinion. On 15 December the decision was taken to publish the Grand Remonstrance, to the fury of Royalist MPs. In the words of Sir Edward Dering:

'[W]hen I first heard of a Remonstrance ... I did not dream that we should remonstrate downward, tell stories to the people and talk of the King as of a third person'.

In London, however, the strategy was effective. The elections to the City's corporation on 20 December produced a large majority for the friends of the opposition and new demonstrations against the bishops. Charles responded by appointing a new Warden to the Tower of London, in the person of a brutal and aggressive soldier, Colonel Thomas Lunsford. When this provoked further demonstrations, Lunsford had the demonstrators beaten and arrested.

Confrontation and conflict

By late December, therefore, the Irish rebellion and the reaction of the opposition leaders had destroyed the parliamentary unity on which the opposition relied. There were now, quite clearly, two opposing sides, and a military solution to the King's problems was a growing possibility. Had Charles waited and allowed the tide of opinion to flow more strongly in his favour, he might even have gained the upper hand through purely legal means. At this point, however, a number of factors led him into rash action. In late December a quarrel erupted between the bishops and the lay nobility about the validity of business transacted in the Lords when demonstrations in London had prevented the bishops from attending. Such a reminder of the arrogance of the Laudian bishops was likely to provoke MPs as well as the Lords. At the same time, rumours reached the King that Pym was planning to impeach the Queen – the rumours had possibly been started by Pym himself to provoke the King. If this was the case, the strategy worked. On 3 January 1642 the King ordered the House of Lords to begin impeachment proceedings against Viscount Mandeville (later Earl of Manchester) and five MPs, including Pym and Hampden. Still angry at the behaviour of the bishops, the Lords failed to act. On 4 January Charles appeared in the House of Commons, bearing a warrant for the arrest of the MPs and accompanied by 300 armed guards, whose presence was a clear threat to the members involved and a gross breach of parliamentary rights. To complete the King's embarrassment, the members were absent, having been warned in advance and taken refuge in London.

Charles's action undid much of the good work carried out by Hyde and Culpepper, and turned moderate opinion against him. Had he succeeded in arresting the opposition leaders, his gamble might have paid off, but to have been seen to use force and fail was disastrous. Fury erupted in and outside Parliament, and on 10 January the King left London for Hampton Court, claiming that he feared for the safety of his family. Despite hasty concessions over the militia and the exclusion of bishops from the Lords, Charles was unable to recover support and in February he moved the Court to his northern capital of York. By now, effective communication with Parliament had ceased, and as increasing numbers of those loyal to Charles joined him in York, control of the Commons passed ever more securely to the opposition. The existence of two sides, both aware of the threat and possibility of using force, could no longer be doubted.

NOTE-MAKING

The growth of mistrust and the division of Parliament, 1640–42

Using the material that you have read and the summary provided in Figure 1 on page 85:
● Construct a brief explanation of how civil war became the most likely outcome of the crisis.
● Explain the significance within this process of the execution of Strafford, the Irish rebellion, the Grand Remonstrance and the attempted arrest of the Five Members.

KEY DATES: SHAPING OF THE CONFLICT, 1641–42

1641

October: Outbreak of rebellion in Ireland; Pym revealed a second army plot in England.

November: King slow to return to London fuelling fears; triumphal welcome in city of London; Pym introduces the Grand Remonstrance; rejected by Charles.

December: Decision taken to publish Grand Remonstrance; Militia Bill introduced giving choice of commander to Parliament; London council elections favour opposition; public demonstrations for Parliament and attacks on bishops; King appoints Lunsford to Tower of London.

1642

January: Attempt to arrest MPs; riots and demonstrations; King leaves London.

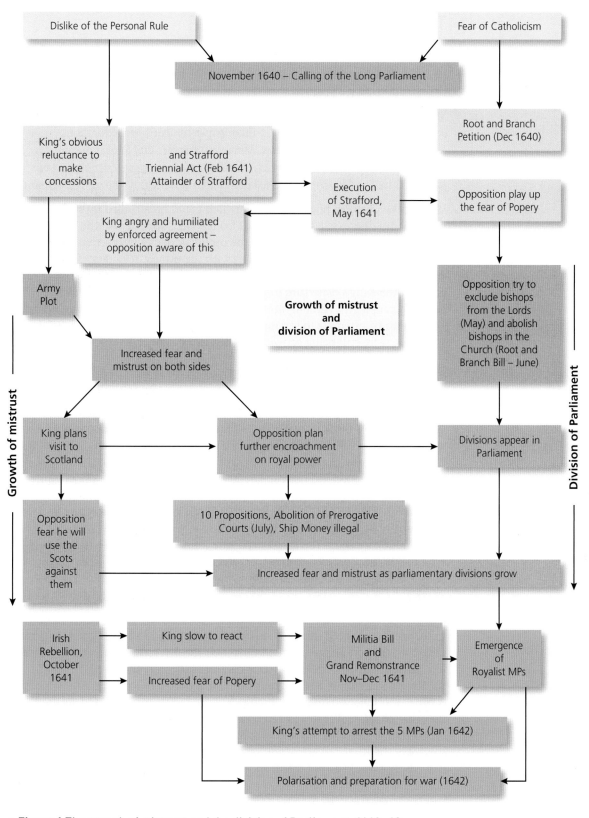

▲ **Figure 1** The growth of mistrust and the division of Parliament, 1640–42.

The drift to war, 1642–43

How did the military conflict begin?

In a speech to the Commons in the summer of 1642, Bulstrode Whitelocke, the Parliamentarian lawyer, declared:

'It is strange to note how we have slid into the beginnings of a civil war by one unexpected accident after another ... From paper combats, by Declarations, Remonstrances, Protestations, Votes, Messages, Answers and Replies, we are now come to the question of raising forces ... Yet I am not for a tame resignation of our Religion, Lives and Liberties into the hands of our adversaries who seek to devour us.'

Whitelocke's view of how war began, which could be matched by similarly puzzled and distressed commentaries from some supporters of the King, reveals three important elements in the outbreak of civil war – that it was unintended, unwanted and engaged in with the utmost reluctance. The development of military action and the taking of sides occupied almost a year between the King's departure from London and the beginning of effective military campaigns. Although the first major battle took place at Edgehill in October 1642, attempts to secure treaties of neutrality and prevent the war from spreading were still being actively pursued in December 1642.

The first steps to war

The point is illustrated by the box on the outbreak of war, opposite, which sets out the major steps taken in pursuit of war and peace in 1642 and 1643. What is also significant is the defensive nature of many of the military measures that were taken – the acquisition of arms, the securing and fortification of strong points and houses – rather than any positive deployment of troops or planning of strategy. The fear of military action had been apparent, especially on Parliament's side, before the end of 1641. Reactions to the Irish rebellion were increased by the revelation of a second Army Plot in October, and one reason for the anger provoked by the appointment of Lunsford to the Tower of London was the fear that it was the first step in a military coup. The King's departure from Whitehall was hastened by the action of the citizens in taking up arms and closing the gates of the city. On both sides, thinking and action in the early months of 1642 were dominated by fear of attack and the need to take precautions – and each precaution helped to convince the other that a military strategy was being planned.

In the meantime, both sides embarked on a propaganda war, designed to increase their own support and to discredit the other side. In April, when Sir John Hotham forestalled the King's attempt to seize control of the port and arsenal of Hull, the King declared him a traitor and Hotham appealed to Parliament for support. A paper war followed, in which each side defended their actions and accused the other of acting illegally. In June, Parliament followed this up with Nineteen Propositions offering terms for negotiation. Since they included parliamentary control of the King's choice of advisers and of the militia, there was little chance that Charles would accept them, and they are more appropriately regarded as a declaration of Parliament's aims. Similarly, the King's reply, drafted by Hyde and Falkland, was a statement of his legal rights and a defence of mixed monarchy. It was also a claim to stand for order, justice and the rule of law.

▼ Figure 2 Steps leading to the outbreak of war, 1642–43.

1642	
January	Parliament reorganised the London Militia to defend Parliament and the City after the King left London.
	Charles sent the Earl of Newcastle to secure the port and arsenal of Hull, but the Mayor refused to accept an external governor.
	Charles accepted Parliament's choice of Sir John Hotham as Governor to avoid open confrontation.
	The King accepted the exclusion of bishops from the House of Lords.
February	Henrietta Maria sailed for France to seek help and raise forces.
	Charles set up Court in York.
March	Parliament issued a 'Declaration of fears and jealousies' and took control of the Militia.
April	The King attempted to seize control of Hull and declared Hotham a traitor for denying him entry.
	Hotham's appeal to Parliament sparked a propaganda war, which continued throughout May.
May	Henry Parker issued his *Observations*, a pamphlet in which he justified Parliament's right to preserve itself against the King's authority, effectively claiming a right to take arms against the King.
June	Parliament issued the Nineteen Propositions as an attempt to negotiate a settlement; however, since it included parliamentary control of the militia, the right to approve the King's advisers and reform of the Church with Parliament's advice, it was a declaration of Parliament's aims rather than a serious attempt at negotiation.
	The King's reply, drafted by Hyde and Falkland was a similar statement, staking his claim to represent legal power and order.
	The King also issued Commissions of Array to all counties.
	Parliament responded by sending out Militia Commissioners.
	The King and the Earl of Lindsay tried to seize Hull after a token siege.
	Cromwell secured Cambridge Castle for Parliament.
July	The navy declared for Parliament.
	Both King and Parliament appointed commanders.
August	22 August: The King raised his standard at Nottingham and called for volunteers.
	Staffordshire JPs declared the county to be a neutral zone.
	Gentry in Yorkshire agreed a treaty of neutrality.
September	Parliament appointed Lord Fairfax commander in the north.
	At first he did not act, but under pressure from Parliament he began to raise forces in Yorkshire.
October	Battle of Edgehill – the first major battle of the war.
November	King's march on London halted by London Trained Bands (militia) at Turnham Green.
December	County Associations set up to coordinate defence in groups of counties.
	Cheshire JPs concluded a neutrality treaty at Bunbury.
1643	
January–May	Failed peace negotiations at Oxford marked a new phase of war.

The failure of neutrality

These arguments were met with widespread fear and confusion. According to the historian Derek Hirst, the summer of 1642 saw desperate attempts in many parts of the country to hold any military action at bay:

'Everywhere men sought escape in neutralism ... Sir John Hotham's fear lest "the necessitous people ... set up for themselves to the utter ruin of all the nobility and gentry" was widely shared. In county after county gentlemen shunned both the militia ordinance and the commission of array ... Towns like Leicester shut their gates ... But zealots could be found everywhere and the neutralists could not build quarantines against them.'

His comments are supported by the number of neutrality pacts that were made by county communities (see Figure 2, page 87) and indicate two reasons for the desire of the political nation to avoid the looming conflict. Not only did many of them find the arguments of both sides persuasive in different areas, making a clear choice exceptionally difficult, but the months leading to military action had seen a growing, and terrifying, tendency for the propaganda war to engage and encourage action from beyond the ruling elite. From the early days of the Long Parliament there had been signs of popular involvement in political action and a willingness among the ruling elite to exploit it. This was particularly, but not only, the case in London. The London mobs had played an active role in the death of Strafford, intimidating the King into signing his death warrant, and were brought into the struggle for power that followed the Irish rebellion. Across the country there was a small but significant minority of the lower orders, especially among the better educated craftsmen and yeomanry, who had strong religious convictions and were easily roused by the fear of Catholic influence and the oratory of the preachers who thundered from the pulpits in support of Parliament.

Following the King's departure from London and the open propaganda war that followed, popular awareness intensified and expanded beyond religious issues to include attacks on property and threats to the established order. It is almost impossible to assess accurately how deeply the lower orders were engaged, or how support for the competing causes was distributed, but the early years of the war saw a significant number of volunteers for Parliament, who fought with both determination and increasing skill. In the meantime, for many provincial gentry the obvious engagement of popular sentiment posed a threat to stability, and they were well aware that the breakdown of order arising from any military conflict could prove disastrous.

The outbreak of war

Why, then, did war start? The answer seems to lie in three main factors. The first is the fear and mistrust that existed on both sides, made worse by military preparations of any kind. Arising from this is the second factor, that there was no mutually trusted arbiter to stop it. While both sides postured and propagated their own interpretations of the situation, they not only weakened the prospects of serious negotiation, but also set in motion a series of developments whose only logical end was war. Despite the efforts of Royalist moderates and a Parliamentarian 'peace party' to renew negotiations into the spring of 1643, the military actions and preparations continued and ultimately took over when alternatives ran out. Mutual mistrust meant that both sides sought to negotiate from a position of strength and that depended on military success. Even more importantly, the reluctance and confusion in which the war began should not be allowed to disguise the third factor, that great issues were at stake. Derek Hirst has described the failure of neutrality pacts at the hands of 'zealots', the determined minorities whose commitment to their cause overpowered their more lukewarm neighbours. The key point about such zealots is that they represented the fact that, for some, the war arose from a clash of ideologies involving political and, especially, religious issues, for which they were prepared to fight and die.

Source A From *The Causes of the English Revolution, 1529–32* by Lawrence Stone, (Routledge), 1972, p.143.

In Yorkshire over a third of the Royalist gentry were Catholics and over half of the Parliamentarians were Puritan. To put it another way, of those who took sides, 90% of all Catholics became Royalists and 72% of Puritans became Parliamentarians. All the Parliamentary leaders in Yorkshire had a previous record of strong Puritan sympathies. There is reason to think those who had opposed the crown on purely constitutional and political grounds in the 1620s and 1630s tended to swing back with Sir Edward Hyde in 1642, while those who had also opposed the crown on religious grounds were far more likely to stick to Pym and fight for the parliamentary cause.

1 What does Lawrence Stone (Source A) see as the main cause of the outbreak of the Civil War?
2 Does this mean that it could not have been 'accidental' as suggested by Whitelocke on page 86?

However, historians such as Christopher Hill, who were influenced by Marxist arguments about the importance of economic trends in shaping political history, saw economic rivalries rather than politics or religion as the major cause of the Civil War. They argued that changes in population and price inflation created economic opportunities for rising gentry, who found the monarchy to be an obstacle to their political and economic development. Hence they explain the war in terms of a class struggle. Recent research has shown that the situation was more complex and that there was little correlation between the economic fortunes of the gentry and their support of either King or Parliament. Nevertheless, some links between economic and political changes can be identified.

In the first place, the overall trend of economic development does suggest that the number of the gentry as a social group increased. The effect of the Reformation and the dissolution of the monasteries was to expand the market in land, allowing more landed estates to be purchased. It also ended the clerical monopoly of education, reducing dependence on clerical administrators and increasing the role of the nobility and gentry as an administrative class – one reason why the role of the Laudian bishops in government had provoked fears of Catholic influence. The Protestant religion encouraged literacy, and the demands of administration and pursuit of office encouraged university and legal education. The result was that the gentry in the early seventeenth century were probably more numerous, more articulate and more confident than ever before.

This produced several results. If there were greater numbers of gentry, then by the early seventeenth century there were more men chasing and competing for a fixed number of posts and offices. This placed greater stress on the working of patronage, at precisely the time that the aristocracy, who formed the vital link between the Court and the localities, were weakened by inflation and fixed rents. As a result, they were unable to satisfy the demand for 'places' in the Court and administration and less able to provide leadership and management in Parliament, to act as a bridge between the central government of King and Court and the political nation in the localities and parliament. For this reason, as Goldstone suggests in Source B, the gentry who made up the bulk of the ruling elite were caught between an authoritarian monarch and a restless nation, forcing them to choose between the defence of their rights and the desire for stability.

What aspects of the drift to war can be explained by social and economic pressures?

Source B From *Revolution and Rebellion in the Early Modern World* by J. Goldstone, (University of California), 1991, pp.35–36, 80–81.

The causes of revolutions need not be sought solely among sudden events. Such events can be considered as 'triggers' or 'releasers' of pent-up social forces, but they are not the fundamental causes. Indeed, such 'releasing' events are, themselves, generally the result of cumulative social pressures ... From 1600–1640 England grew by 25% in population. London doubled in size and grain prices rose until, in the 1630s, they reached double the level of the 1580s. Charles I's real income rose by about 10% [compared to Elizabeth's in the 1560s] to rule over a nation whose population had risen by two-thirds and whose gentry, always hungry for patronage, had tripled in number. State finances, the stability of the elite hierarchy and popular employment were all adversely affected by population growth and consequent inflation.

[In the outbreak of war] three factors stand out as crucial. First there is the fiscal distress of the state – a shortage of money led the Crown into policies and projects that created opposition. Second, there are multiple conflicts within classes ... generating fears for stability [so that] the unity of the upper classes against the Crown rapidly dissolved with the outbreak of popular uprisings in London, Ireland and elsewhere. Third was the growth of popular disorders among the lower classes [as the elite conflict unfolded] ... The English Revolution became a revolution, not merely an effort by Parliament to restrict the Crown, when popular disorders in London and the countryside presented an extraordinary dilemma to the elite: should authority be returned to the King in order to put down the disorders, or should Parliament itself take authority and attempt to profit from popular opposition to the King?

Interpretations: taking sides

The extracts from the work of Stone and Goldstone (Sources A and B) offer different explanations of why war broke out – the one emphasising religious motives, the other social and economic pressures. While you can evaluate their arguments by reference to your own knowledge of events, another way is to consider the evidence given by contemporaries. Sources C–F set out below offer an overview of the complex process by which war broke out in different areas of the country and some indications of the overall distribution of support that resulted from it. Using the questions opposite to help you, you should interpret the sources in the context of your own knowledge and then consider how far they support or challenge the points made by Stone and Goldstone in Sources A and B.

Source C From *Memoirs of the Life of Colonel John Hutchinson* by Lucy Hutchinson, 1660.

Before the flame of the war broke out in the top of the chimneys, the smoke ascended in every country. The King had sent forth commissions of array, and the Parliament had given out commissions for their militia ... Between these, in many places, there were fierce contests and disputes ... for in the progress every county had the civil war (more or less) within itself. Some counties were in the beginning so wholly for the Parliament that the King's interest appeared not in them; some so wholly for the King that the godly (for those generally were the Parliament's friends) were forced to forsake their habitations and seek other shelters.

[In the county of Nottingham] The greatest family was the Earl of Newcastle's [commander of the King's northern armies]. He had indeed, through his great estate, his liberal hospitality and constant residence in his country, so endeared [the gentry and their dependents] to him that no man was a greater prince in all that northern quarter ... Most of the gentry ... were disaffected to the Parliament. Most of the middle sort – the able substantial freeholders and the other commons who had not their dependence upon the malignant nobility and gentry – adhered to the Parliament ... Mr Henry Ireton ... was the chief promoter of the Parliament's interest in the county. But finding it generally disaffected, all he could do when the King approached it was to gather a troop of those godly people which the cavaliers drove out, and with them to go into the army of my lord of Essex.

Source D From the *Apology of John Weare* (1642) – a Devonshire Parliamentarian.

I undertook not this service for private interest, revenge or pay. I had an estate left by my ancestors; the office of a justice of peace I long had executed in my country; and I wanted not [did not lack] solicitations to adhere to the King's party ... But upon assembly of the gentry that were that way affected, hearing some discourse that tended both to the dishonour of God and the overthrow of the common liberty, I ... fully resolved with my utmost to promote the purity of religion and the public [by raising a regiment for Parliament].

Source E From *Reliquae Baxterianae* by Richard Baxter, 1696.

A great part of the Lords forsook the Parliament and so did many of the House of Commons, and came to the King; but that was after Edgehill fight, when the King was at Oxford. A very great part of the knights and gentlemen ... adhered to the King; except in Middlesex, Essex, Suffolk, Norfolk, Cambridgeshire, etc., where the King with his army never came. And could he have got footing there, it is like that it would have been there as it was in other places. And most of the tenants of these gentlemen, and also most of the poorest of the people, whom the other called 'the rabble' did follow the gentry and were for the King. On the Parliament's side were (besides themselves) some of the gentry in most of the counties, and the greatest part of the tradesmen and freeholders, and the middle sort of men, especially in those corporations and countries which depend on clothing and such manufactures.

Source F From *History of the Rebellion and Civil Wars in England Begun in the Year 1641* by Edward Hyde, Earl of Clarendon, edited by G. Huehns, (Oxford Paperbacks), 1979.

The people generally (except in great towns and corporations where, the factious lecturers and emissaries from Parliament had poisoned the affections) were loyally inclined ... [In the west] most of the gentry were engaged [against the Parliament] as they were in truth throughout the Kingdom; yet the common people, especially in parts of Somerset, were generally too much inclined to them ... [Their leaders were] for the most part clothiers [who] had gotten very great fortunes; and by degrees getting themselves into gentlemen's estates, were angry that they found not themselves in the same esteem and reputation with those whose estates they had ... Those, from the beginning were fast friends to the Parliament ... [In Gloucestershire] the yeomanry [have] been most forward and seditious, being very wealthy ... [In Lancashire] men of no name .. and the town of Manchester opposed the King ... [In Yorkshire] besides the Lord Fairfax ... few of good reputation and fortune ran that way ... Leeds, Halifax and Bradford [three very populous and rich towns which, depending wholly upon clothiers naturally maligned the gentry] were wholly at their disposition.

ACTIVITY

Study Sources C–F and answer the questions that follow.

1 What evidence suggests that the process of taking sides was confused and influenced by external pressures?

2 What evidence suggests that issues of principle, especially religion, played a significant part?

3 What evidence suggests that the choice of side was influenced by class and social status?

4 Given the range of sources you have considered, how reliable is the evidence and the conclusions that you can draw from it?

The interpretations considered in Sources A and B both emphasise long-term 'conditional' causes of the war – so-called because they create conditions in which some kind of conflict becomes likely. Although they appear conflicting, in that one focuses on religion and the other on social and economic causes, there is no reason why both cannot be correct in that different individuals may well have been influenced by different factors. Given an event of such magnitude as the outbreak of a civil war, that is likely. In addition, some of the sources above seem to hint that religious and social attitudes were linked, and since both Baxter and Clarendon (who were on opposing sides in the conflict) make such claims, they seem to have some substance. It is therefore quite possible that the apparent conflicts can be reconciled into an overall judgement that accommodates both.

However, Source G below takes a different approach to the issue and suggests that conditional factors do not offer a full explanation of the war. Although underlying conditions can create the likelihood of a conflict of some kind, the outbreak of a war, especially at the time and in the way that it happened, requires some consideration of short-term factors – what Goldstone described as 'triggers' or 'releasing' events, often also labelled 'contingencies' or 'contingent' events. In a large and detailed study of the events of 1640–42, Antony Fletcher examined the evidence and drew different conclusions.

Source G From *The Outbreak of the English Civil War* by A. Fletcher, (Arnold), 1981, pp.407–09, 413, 415.

Great events do not necessarily have great causes, although it is natural for historians to seek them ... Most of those who rode up to Westminster in November 1640 had no concept of a parliamentary cause in their minds. Reconciliation and settlement were seen as the purposes of parliaments and the reforms that most MPs envisaged seemed perfectly compatible with such an end. Only Pym and a few close friends saw the matter in totally different terms: for them the parliamentary cause was the rooting out of a conspiracy that struck at the core of the nation's life. Their fundamental misconception of the political situation ... must surely be the starting point for an explanation of how war came about ... External events and contingencies contributed to this process, bringing home to MPs the apparent substance of Pym's story – Parliament's propaganda related every royal action between January and November 1642 to the papist conspiracy.

All this, though, is only one side of the picture. Charles I had a jaundiced view of parliaments and a strong sense of distrust of certain individuals, who he believed were ready to challenge his monarchy for private and selfish ends ... The king's misunderstanding of his opponents' aims and motives would have been less serious if his character had been different. He was a man who magnified distrust even in the most loyal hearts...

What happened in 1641 and 1642 was that two groups of men became the prisoners of competing myths that fed on one another, so that events seemed to confirm two opposing interpretations of the political crisis that were both originally misconceived and erroneous.

ACTIVITY

1 To complete your investigation of the outbreak of war, use the arguments put forward by Stone, Goldstone and Fletcher (Sources A, B and G) on pages 89–92 to write your own summary of why war broke out. If you use the factors of religious and social conflict as conditional causes, making a conflict of some kind likely, and the growth of mistrust because of competing myths as the contingent factor making a settlement impossible, you can construct an effective explanation of why war broke out.
2 How far is the interpretation given in Source G supported by Whitelocke's description of an 'accidental' war on page 86?

2 The military struggle, 1643–46

The campaigns and main battles of the First Civil War in England are outlined on the maps on pages 94–95. Although the Civil Wars involved three kingdoms, and events in England were mirrored by conflicts elsewhere, it was in England that the centres of power lay, and it was in England that both sides focused their main efforts. In Ireland the Duke of Ormonde was able to bring the rebellion to an end on the King's behalf and secure the support of both native Irish and English settlers for the King's cause. Some volunteers were dispatched to fight in England, proving to be a mixed blessing. In Scotland the control of the Kirk and the Edinburgh-based leadership was eventually challenged in the west by the Earl of Montrose, but his successful campaign there was too distant to directly affect the situation in England. Hence the Scots and Irish would have an impact on events up to and including the collapse of the monarchy in 1649, but the crucial military confrontation, especially in the First Civil War of 1642–46 would take place within England and Wales.

The development of the conflict, 1643–46
Why did Parliament win the First Civil War?

Broadly speaking, in 1642 the King held the north and west, while Parliament controlled the south-east, and the campaigns of 1642–43 focused on the Royalist effort to attack and take London. At the end of 1643, the entry of the Scots on the side of Parliament tipped the balance in the north, but weaknesses within the Parliamentarian command strengthened the Royalist hold on the west and led to the restructuring of Parliament's armies in the winter of 1644–45. In 1645, after a decisive battle at Naseby, near Leicester, the Royalists began to weaken, and Parliament's New Model Army was able to mop up resistance in the final year of war.

Various reasons have been put forward to explain Parliament's victory, including criticisms of the King's leadership, the indiscipline of Royalist troops and the weakness of Royalist administration. In fact, recent studies suggest that the two sides were remarkably similar in their methods and approach until late 1644. Both relied at first on locally-based forces, run by county committees, and both experienced difficulty in persuading them to release forces for duty elsewhere. Both experienced internal divisions and rivalries. The King's advisers disagreed over war aims and there was considerable rivalry among his military commanders, while Parliament was divided between a 'peace' party who wanted a negotiated settlement and a 'war' party who sought outright victory first.

Ultimately, the Parliamentarian victory was based on three main factors: the failure of the Royalists to capitalise on their early advantage, the superior resources enjoyed by Parliament and the military and political restructuring in 1644–45 that enabled those resources to be effectively exploited.

The failure of the Royalists
Why were the Royalist forces unable to capitalise on their initial advantages?

In the early stages of the war, the advantage lay with the King. Although the gentry divided between the two sides, the greater number joined the King, bringing with them their tenants, horses and military expertise, at least in terms of the ability to ride and fight. Many were quick to donate money and plate. The King was also able to call on the professional soldiers, mainly officers, who had been fighting abroad in the Thirty Years War, and in his nephews, Rupert and Maurice of Nassau, he had two experienced and battle-hardened commanders. Some of these advantages were revealed in the battle of Edgehill in October 1642, where Parliament's forces, led by the Earl of Essex, were driven back into London. The day ended in a stalemate that left the road to London open, and the King's forces were only prevented from reaching the capital by the London Trained Bands (volunteers from the city) under the command of Philip Skippon and by the approach of winter. At the same time, the determination with which these volunteers supported the remnants of Essex's forces at Turnham Green in November could be seen as an indication of their commitment to Parliament's cause.

After wintering at Oxford the Royalists planned a three-pronged attack. The northern army, under the Earl of Newcastle, extended its control from a secure base in York, and succeeded in defeating Parliament's Yorkshire army at Adwalton Moor in June 1643. The southwestern army, under Sir Ralph Hopton, had secured Cornwall and much of Devon and was ready to march east. In July, Prince Rupert took Bristol while his brother, Maurice, defeated the Parliamentarian forces at Roundway Down in Wiltshire and captured Dorchester to gain control of Dorset. There seemed to be little to prevent the King's armies from approaching London from Newbury, Oxford and the north. With a Peace Party in Parliament demanding negotiation, they would probably not need to attack the city, but could rely on internal pressures to force the Parliamentarian leaders to sue for peace.

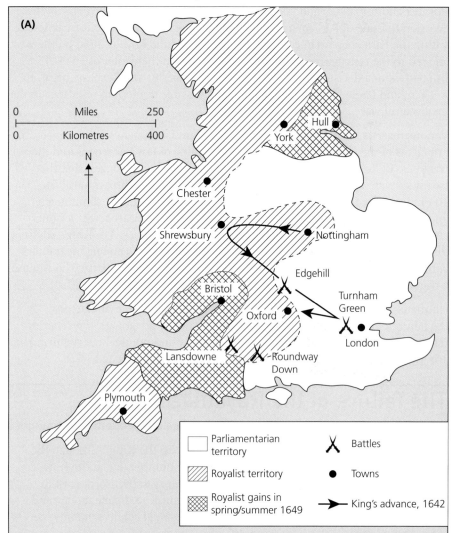

Figure 3 The Civil War campaigns, 1642–46. Map A shows the Parliamentarian campaign at its weakest point in 1643. Map B shows the King's planned attack on London in 1643 and the vital importance of the Parliamentarian strongholds of Hull, Gloucester and Plymouth. The threat of attack from these garrisons in the rear of the advancing Royalist armies prevented his strategy from being successfully carried out.

Peace Party

One of three groups within Parliament with clear but conflicting war aims. About half of the MPs who continued to support Parliament were essentially backbenchers, but the remaining ninety or so members had coalesced into three groups, described by Derek Hirst as 'loose clusters of friends and allies associated for limited political ends'. They were:

- A 'War Party' led by Henry Marten, Sir Arthur Haselrig and Sir Henry Vane, who were of the opinion that Charles must be defeated utterly in order to secure safety for their lives and liberties.
- The 'Peace Party', however, led by Denzil Holles in the Commons and closely associated with most of the minority of Lords who had remained at Westminster, sought to conduct a defensive war in the hope that a demonstration of force or a stalemate would persuade the King to negotiate.
- Straddling these extremes was a 'Middle Party', led by John Pym with support from John Hampden and Oliver St John in the Commons and aided by the Earl of Warwick and Lord Saye and Sele. Also included in the Middle Party was the relatively obscure MP for Cambridge, a cousin of Hampden, named Oliver Cromwell.

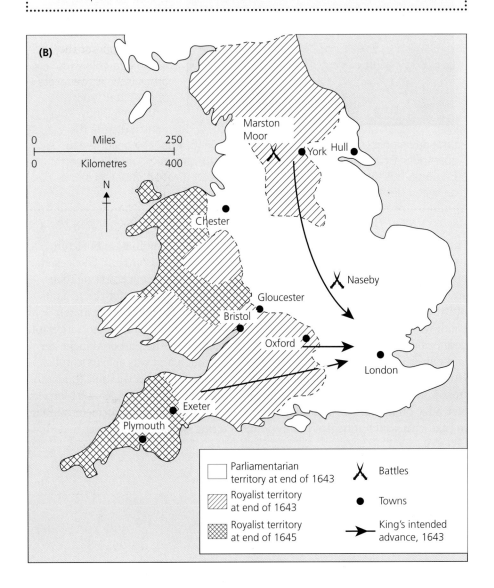

Prince Rupert of the Rhine (1619–82)

Prince Rupert, one of the leading Royalist generals, was the son of Charles's sister Elizabeth and the Elector Palatine (see Chapter 2, page 29). Already experienced through service in the Thirty Years War, he and his brother Maurice joined Charles at Nottingham in 1642. Both served him well as military commanders and Rupert was justly famed for his skill and courage as a leader of cavalry, but his abrasive personality led to quarrels with other Royalist generals and a bitter feud with Lord Digby. This contributed to the fatal decision to attack at Naseby. Later, in 1645, Rupert was forced to surrender Bristol, for which the King never forgave him. In 1646 he left England, but returned with Charles II and served with distinction in the navy and became First Lord of the Admiralty (1673–79).

Parliament was saved from the Royalist advance by a combination of factors. Its control of the navy helped Parliamentarian strongholds at Hull, Gloucester and Plymouth to hold out, preventing the Royalists from concentrating their strength on London. In particular, Hull provided a safe refuge for the remains of Parliament's Yorkshire army, and the Earl of Newcastle refused to march south with hostile forces at his back. In East Anglia, the Eastern Association (of counties) had developed a strong force commanded by the Earl of Manchester and Oliver Cromwell, which captured Gainsborough and was able to support Hull from the south. Finally, in September, the Earl of Essex was able to march from London to relieve Gloucester and succeeded in defeating a Royalist force at Newbury on his return. In military terms the year ended in a stalemate, similar to that with which it began, but in political terms, significant changes had taken place.

The turning tide, 1643–44

How did the Parliamentary leaders consolidate their strength and ability to resist the Royalist forces?

The shift in the fortunes of the Parliamentarians was the work of John Pym. In the early part of the year he concentrated his efforts on building up an effective system of taxation and administration in Parliamentarian areas, introducing an excise tax in May 1643 which gave Parliament a sound financial base. With great skill he maintained a balance between peace and war parties, securing a precarious unity among MPs. Finally, in the autumn of 1643 he persuaded Parliament to sign a Solemn League and Covenant with the Scots, by which Parliament would receive the help of the Scottish Covenanters' army. This was no mean achievement. The price demanded by the Scots was the introduction of a Presbyterian system into the Church of England. While many MPs held Puritan views and wanted to see further reform in the Church, few were committed to a full Presbyterian system and certainly not the rigid version used in the Scottish Kirk. Pym's tactics were to avoid divisions and satisfy the Scots by calling an Assembly of Divines (clergy) to discuss and devise a suitable model for England. The Assembly met in December 1643, the same month in which Pym died.

> **Excise tax** – This was placed on home-produced beer and cider and on a range of imported goods. It was easy to collect and, in principle, no different to customs duties. But it was unprecedented in England and was highly unpopular.

The agreement with the Scots would prove to be of considerable significance. In military terms it secured Scottish aid at the time of Parliament's greatest need and posed a serious threat to Royalist control of the north. The parliamentary forces there, led by Sir Thomas Fairfax, had regrouped after taking refuge in Hull and in January 1644 had been able to destroy and disperse forces sent to aid the King from Ireland at Nantwich in Cheshire. Meanwhile an advance by Newcastle's army into Lincolnshire led to the reorganisation of Parliament's forces in the east under the leadership of the Earl of Manchester, with Oliver Cromwell in command of the cavalry. By April these forces had succeeded, with the aid of the Scots, in bottling up Newcastle's army in York and the King was forced to send a relieving force under Prince Rupert. The Prince succeeded in drawing off Parliament's forces and relieving York, but made the serious error of accepting battle against them at Marston Moor in June.

Even when supported by Newcastle's troops the Royalists numbered no more than 18,000 men, while the parliamentary forces were nearer 28,000, and the acknowledged quality of Rupert's cavalry and Newcastle's Whitecoats was more than matched by the experienced Scottish contingent led by David Leslie and the disciplined troopers known thereafter as 'Cromwell's Ironsides'. The result was a major defeat, the loss of York, which surrendered a fortnight later, and the effective withdrawal of Royalist forces to the west. In military terms, Marston Moor was significant; politically, it was a turning point, described by Cromwell as 'an absolute victory obtained by the Lord's blessing upon the godly party'. The battle did not guarantee the military superiority of Parliament, but the confidence in their cause given to some, at least, of Parliament's supporters was to prove a significant step towards it.

This mattered a great deal, because the Scottish alliance had also brought disadvantages and complications. After the death of Pym the management of Parliament's cause passed into the hands of a Committee of Both Kingdoms, making Scottish pressure for religious uniformity a significant problem and bringing into the open the various conflicting views on religious reform that existed among Parliament's supporters. The Assembly of Divines, the gathering of clergy who met at Westminster in 1644 to discuss reform of the Church, was dominated by ministers who favoured some form of Presbyterianism, but there were already some among MPs and in Parliament's armies who were unwilling to accept any national establishment. In early 1644 five members of the Assembly issued a public appeal for a limited measure of religious toleration, and when this was denied, sought to prolong debates and delay reform. As a result, the Assembly was unable to complete its scheme, the Directory of Worship, until 1646. In the meantime, religious separatists of all kinds had mounted a campaign for toleration that changed the whole political situation (see page 99), and the Directory was never fully implemented.

In addition, what might have been a decisive victory for Parliament's forces was largely negated by the Earl of Essex in the south. Determined to assert his importance as Parliament's senior general, he set off in pursuit of a similarly prestigious victory in the west. Marching from Lyme Regis, where he had lifted a Royalist siege, he sought to relieve Plymouth and then to march into the Royalist stronghold of Cornwall. Hopton simply parted his forces to allow the Parliamentarian army through, then closed again behind them. The result was a serious defeat for Essex at Lostwithiel in Cornwall, followed by an even more disastrous surrender of 6,000 men with all their cannon and supplies. While Essex took a ship back to London, what was left of his army was forced to walk, devoid of weapons, through hostile country. Fewer than 600 men reached London alive. To make matters worse, Waller, Manchester and Cromwell allowed the King to return safely to Oxford after an indecisive battle at Newbury.

This disaster, combined with successes for the Royalists under Montrose in Scotland, did much to restore the military balance but it was the political effects that were most important. The humiliation of Essex brought into the open a simmering dispute between the Peace and War Parties in Parliament over how the war should be fought. Complaints were partly based on military considerations – Sir William Waller, for example, had been arguing for a mobile, professional army to replace the locally-based forces – but there were deeper concerns about the attitudes and aims of Parliament's commanders. Men like Essex and Manchester had, in the normal seventeenth-century manner, been appointed to command because of their noble status rather than their military talent, and both their social position and political outlook made them cautious. They were accused of seeing the war only in defensive terms and of seeking to avoid defeat while hoping for negotiations, rather than pursuing victory. The issue had already led to open conflict between Manchester and his commander of cavalry, Oliver Cromwell, and the conflict was complicated by political and religious rivalries. By December 1644 it was clear that a way had to be found to resolve the differences and avoid disaster.

The victory of Parliament

How did the measures taken in response to Parliament's military failures by 1644, secure their victory?

The solution adopted to the military problems facing Parliament by 1644 became known as the **Self-Denying Ordinance**, in which all members of Parliament agreed to give up their military commands. By separating the military and political commands, it allowed the failed commanders, who were members of the House of Lords, to be removed without losing face.

The Ordinance was proposed by a member of the War Party, Zouch Tate, and supported by Cromwell. The military failures of late 1644 led to recriminations among Parliament's generals, revealing their political and religious differences. While Cromwell accused Manchester and Essex of preferring negotiations to victory, Manchester and the Scots accused Cromwell of favouring political and religious radicals. The Self-Denying Ordinance resolved these issues and permitted a reorganisation of Parliament's forces and the creation of a single, mobile and professional army of 22,000 men – a New Model – to fight the war more effectively. Its commander was to be Sir Thomas Fairfax, a man of proven military talent with little awareness of politics, whose aim was to achieve military success and to leave the politics to others. An unexpected bonus for the War Party was that, unable to agree on a new commander of cavalry, MPs appointed Cromwell to fulfil the role until a replacement could be found – he was to continue in this position on a series of temporary commissions until after the war ended.

Self-Denying Ordinance – An agreement to separate military and political functions which allowed failed commanders, who were members of the House of Lords, to give up their military commands. The Ordinance allowed political and religious divisions to be set aside while a new and more effective army was created: the New Model Army.

Source H From *Reliquae Baxterianae* by Richard Baxter, 1696.

When I came to the Army among Cromwell's soldiers I found a new face of things, which I never dreamt of: I heard plotting heads very hot upon that which intimated their intention to subvert both Church and State … I found that many honest men of weak judgements and little acquaintance with such matters, had been seduced into a disputing vein, and made it too much of their religion to talk for this opinion and for that; sometimes for State democracy, and sometimes for Church democracy.

The New Model Army – soldiers or saints?

Officially formed on 4 April 1645, under the command of the Lord General, Sir Thomas Fairfax of Nun Appleton, near Tadcaster, the New Model Army consisted of:

- Twelve regiments of Foot (14,000 men) under the command of Major-General Philip Skippon, previously commander of the London Trained Bands under service with the Earl of Essex.
- Eleven regiments of Horse (6,600 men) under the command of Lieutenant-General Oliver Cromwell, previously Lieutenant-General to the Earl of Manchester in the army (see Source H, page 99) of the Eastern Association.
- One regiment of dragoons (1,000 men) armed with muskets.

The character of the New Model Army has been the subject of much debate. There is no doubt that it became a highly effective fighting unit, contributing significantly to Parliament's victory. Opinions differ, however, as to the reasons for its effectiveness.

- Historians like Sir Charles Firth who published a study of 'Cromwell's Army' in 1904 explored the religious radicalism of the army (see Source H, page 99), described in more hostile terms by critics like the Presbyterian minister, Thomas Edwards. Firth argued that the religious separatists recruited and protected by officers like Oliver Cromwell dominated the army. Its effectiveness came from their discipline and dedication in pursuit of what they regarded as God's cause, which also explains the political role of the army after 1647.
- More recent research has challenged this view and argued that the effectiveness of the army came from thorough training, regular pay and professional discipline rather than religious fervour. The 'Army of Saints' was, in fact, an army of well-trained soldiers.
- The likelihood is that both factors played a part. The army was not made up of religiously motivated volunteers, but there were a number of them, especially among the cavalry regiments. Such men set a tone of restraint and good discipline which enabled these standards to be more easily enforced. They also made egalitarian policies such as promotion by merit more effective, and this contributed to the spirit of comradeship that held the army together. Regular pay, effective training and a habit of victory helped to maintain this spirit and establish mutual respect and loyalty between officers and men. In addition, many of their officers, including Cromwell, shared their attitudes to some degree and encouraged the sense of dedication to a cause. The result was a formidable fighting unit, and a potential political force.

In many ways the creation of the New Model Army in the early months of 1645 was a military revolution, but its full effects were not felt immediately. It took time to train and prepare the force and time for its unity and identity to become established. Nevertheless, it was to play a crucial role in Parliament's victory. Its first success, at Naseby in June 1645, was helped by rivalries and misjudgments among the Royalist commanders, but thereafter it proved its value in the speed with which Fairfax could move around the country to mop up the remaining Royalist forces. In June he defeated Goring's army in Somerset, in September Rupert was forced to surrender Bristol, and by the end of the year the Royalists had been driven back into Wales and the south-west. In early 1646 the New Model Army took control of Devon and Cornwall and in May the King accepted defeat, surrendering to the Scots at Southwell in Nottinghamshire on 5 May. From there he was taken to Newcastle, before being handed over (with considerable relief) by the Scots to their Parliamentary allies as they withdrew across the border.

In fact, Naseby had proved decisive. Not only had it destroyed the main Royalist army, but the capture of the King's baggage-train had provided Parliament with a significant political victory. The baggage-train contained the King's correspondence and when this was published it revealed his determination to secure victory on his terms, the lack of good faith with which he had approached peace negotiations since 1642 and his willingness to take help from any source, including the Irish Catholics and the Pope.

Royalist support was further weakened by the increasing demands laid on Royalist areas for taxes, men and provisions. Resentment at the impact of civil war and the demands made by competing armies had been rising steadily. The result was the outbreak of Clubmen risings in many counties, where local forces and residents combined to oppose all military activity in an attempt to defend what was left of their property and livelihoods. Although this resurgence of neutralism was not confined to Royalist areas, the strongest Clubmen organisations were in the west and west Midlands where the Royalist armies had been based. In Somerset the Clubmen joined with Fairfax to drive out Goring's army, which was notorious for its lack of discipline and brutality towards civilians. But most Clubmen groups were strictly neutral. Their effect on the Royalist war effort was greater because the King's armies were more dependent on provisions seized from the land, and because their crumbling effectiveness and morale made them more vulnerable to such external pressures.

Conclusion: the impact of war

By 1646, therefore, Parliament had secured the victory that MPs hoped would force the King to accept a settlement on their terms. The Nineteen Propositions of 1642 were quickly revived and presented to the King with some amendments while he was still with the Scottish army at Newcastle. Nevertheless, the situation in which MPs began the task of finding peace was already very different from that of 1642. The process of war and the steps taken to secure victory had altered attitudes and expectations in a way that could not have been foreseen at its outset. On the one hand, there was an overwhelming desire for peace, which acted to the benefit of the King. The country had endured levels of taxation that dwarfed Charles's demands before 1640 and a dislocation of trade, physical

KEY DATES: PARLIAMENT'S VICTORY

1642 Battle of Edgehill, followed by victory of the London Militia at Turnham Green, prevented the King from entering London.

1643 Sieges of Hull and Gloucester prevented Royalist march on London; Scottish alliance with Parliament.

1644 Battle of Marston Moor secured the north for Parliament.

1644–45 The Self-Denying Ordinance and establishment of the New Model Army transformed Parliament's military organisation.

1645 Battle of Naseby destroyed the King's main army.

1646 Charles surrendered to the Scots.

damage and personal suffering that translated into a desire for the return of pre-war normality. In Parliament this was reflected in a resurgence of support for the Peace Party. On the other hand, the war effort and the propaganda required to maintain it had encouraged the development of new ideas and new expectations among some who had fought most enthusiastically for Parliament. It was this effect – the emergence of new and radical ideas – which caused most immediate concern to those involved in the search for peace. In this they were probably misled. Whatever had changed as a result of war, they were to discover that it did not include the aims, beliefs and character of Charles I.

The causes of the English Civil War

Before attempting any exercises or essays on this chapter, you should ensure that you have accurate linear notes that record the information that you need. If you have not already done this, reread the chapter and make notes using the headings and issue boxes to help you.

The material in this chapter has been divided into two key issues – the outbreak of military conflict and the outcome of that conflict in a victory for Parliament. In terms of assessment and examination questions, these are unlikely to be addressed together. Therefore, while the summary of events set out below addresses both, the exercises and activities that follow treat the areas separately and focus on the particular issues to which each has relevance.

The focus of this chapter has been the process by which a crisis – studied in Chapters 1, 2 and 3 – became a war that, most historians would agree, was neither expected nor planned when the Long Parliament assembled in 1640. The material has therefore focused on *how* the war came about, requiring detailed analysis of the interaction between those involved. In order to explain *why* it happened, however, it is necessary to consider the wider range of factors that shaped that interaction, which you addressed in considering the different interpretations offered by historians on pages 89–92. These focused on both conditional and contingent factors, using a broad perspective to explain them and consider the interaction between them. Since these provide the foundation for explaining the causes of war, you will find it useful to consider the summary set out below and ensure that you have understood all the factors listed and their impact in causing the crisis of 1640 and the war that broke out in 1642. For example, the interpretation offered by Fletcher in Source G on page 92 focused on the immediate causes of the war and the role of 'competing myths' – but the explanation of those myths and their impact in 1640–42 relies on a contextual understanding of how they had developed across a century of change and conflict.

This outline will give you a broad picture of the causes of the First Civil War. However, when you come to deal with essay questions and construct an explanation that focuses on the question, you will need to adapt this broad picture and select material that relates to the way that the question is phrased. Consider the research questions on the next page.

ACTIVITY

1 Working with your partner, analyse each question on this page and define its key focus.

2 Use your notes and knowledge of the period to construct an essay plan. This should list the factors involved in the order in which you will explain them, establish links between them and summarise their part in causing the war.

3 Using Figure 4 and your notes, work with a partner to decide:

  a Which factors created conditions in which a conflict of some kind was possible?

  b Which factors caused these conditions to build up and make conflict probable?

  c Which factors dictated the nature and timing of the conflict as a war beginning in 1642?

'Why did civil war break out in England in 1642?'

This question has a largely neutral focus. You can select factors and determine the emphasis of your response, but you do need to ensure that you cover all those that played a significant part and you will have to create a structure for your argument.

'A conflict of some kind between King and Parliament was always likely in the seventeenth century, but it was the personality of Charles I that brought it to civil war.' How far do you agree with this statement?

This question directs you towards a conditional/contingent approach. The use of 'how far do you agree?' also gives you a structure, because it encourages you to set out conflicting arguments and then choose between them or bring them together in an overall judgement.

'In 1640 most MPs wanted and expected to redress grievances and settle the problems created by the Personal Rule of Charles I. Why, then, did they find themselves at war in 1642?'

This question directs the focus of your argument towards the immediate situation and the contingent causes of war. However, you know from the explanations that you have considered and the range of factors that you have studied that this is not a sufficient explanation. In addition to the events of 1640–42, you need to explain the underlying problems and show how they influenced the attitudes and events that occurred within that period.

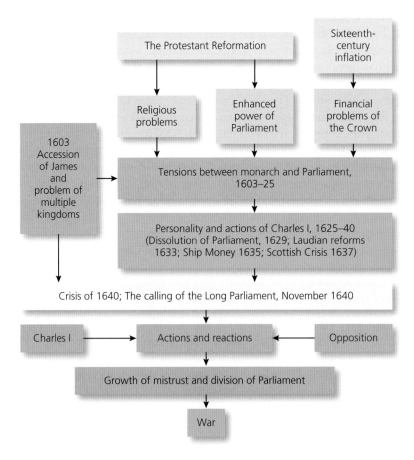

▲ **Figure 4** Summary of the causes of the Civil War.

Chapter summary

- The apparent unity of the Long Parliament over the 'redress of grievances' in 1640 concealed serious differences. In particular, MPs disagreed about what to put in place of the Laudian bishops in the Church and the extent to which the King's powers should be restricted.

- Although Pym and his allies sought to preserve unity and find a compromise, their efforts were undermined by the obvious hostility felt by the King towards any significant limits on his power. They were aware that if he was able to rally support and regain the initiative then both their desired reforms and their own safety were at risk.

- Throughout 1641 divisions and mistrust intensified, especially over reform of the Church, but it was the Irish rebellion that brought them to a head because it involved the raising of an army and required an immediate response. The resulting misjudgements by both King and opposition leaders led to an open breach and the emergence of two 'sides' in the quarrel.

- The early months of 1642 saw both sides take up arms in their own defence, but the outbreak of war was complex and piecemeal because both sides were aware of its significance. In August, the King raised his standard at Nottingham, effectively declaring war, but the process of taking sides across the nation lasted well into 1643.

- Across the country there was widespread neutralism and a reluctance to take action. However, on both sides there were committed minorities who forced others to make a choice. The overall pattern of loyalties appears to have been based on social class as well as political and religious belief – perhaps because there was a link between them.

- Initially the military advantage lay with the Royalists and this was compounded by the reluctance of some parliamentary leaders to fight anything but a defensive war and to wait for further negotiation.

- However, the determination of others, the political and administrative skills of John Pym, the support of the Scottish Covenanters and rivalry among the Royalist commanders enabled Parliament to survive the initial phase of the war and begin to develop its assets.

- In the longer term the control of the more prosperous south-east and of the navy, as well as weaknesses in Royalist organisation gave Parliament an advantage.

- This was negated, however, by the attitudes of the parliamentary generals, leading to a crisis and military reorganisation – the establishment of the New Model Army. In contrast, the King's military leadership and failure to control the rivalries around him led to military failure and declining support in the areas still under Royalist control.

- The result in 1645–46 was a successful campaign beginning with the battle of Naseby, in which the new Model Army destroyed the Royalist forces and gained control of the country, thereby delivering the victory of Parliament and forcing the King to accept defeat.

Working on essay technique: argument, counter-argument and evaluation

Essays that develop a good argument are more likely to reach the higher levels. This is because argumentative essays are much more likely to develop sustained analysis. As you know, your essays are judged on the extent to which they analyse. The mark scheme shown is for the full A-level but it is virtually the same for AS level. Both stress the need to analyse and evaluate the key features related to the periods studied. It distinguishes between five different levels of analysis (as well as other relevant skills that are the ingredients of good essays).

As with the activities at the end of Chapters 2 and 3, the main focus of work here has been to develop a broad view of the issues involved and an understanding of causation. Hence the questions asked are not necessarily of the type that you will meet in an examination, which usually require the construction of an argument, a counter-argument and a final judgment. One reason for this is that they give you the opportunity to demonstrate a range of high level skills and understanding in a relatively short time.

Arguments and counter-arguments

Good essays are based on sustained analysis, in which points are linked into an *argument*, which brings factors together to offer an explanation as you would in a concluding paragraph. However, where a concluding paragraph seeks to collect points into an overall explanation, an argument is intended to lay out and explain *part* of an explanation – for example the importance of factors in making a particular outcome likely. A full explanation will then require a *counter-argument*, such as the role of contingent factors, and the final judgement will emerge from weighing and balancing the two, either by showing that one is stronger than the other, or more often, showing that some of the apparent conflicts can be reconciled and a balanced judgement based on elements of both.

You have already utilised this approach in dealing with the arguments put forward by Stone, Goldstone and Fletcher earlier in this chapter (pages 89–90, 92), although the 'arguments' there were short extracts that simplified the task. You can now practice a more developed response. The essential ingredient is a question that sets up two conflicting arguments, normally by using a question stem involving 'how far', 'to what extent' or defining a 'main factor'.

Level 5	Answers will display a very good understanding of the full demands of the question. They will be well organised and effectively delivered. The supporting information will be well selected, specific and precise. It will show a very good understanding of key features, issues and concepts. The answer will be fully analytical with a balanced argument and well substantiated judgement. *21–25 marks*
Level 4	Answers will display a good understanding of the demands of the question. It will be well organised and effectively communicated. There will be a range of clear and specific supporting information showing a good understanding of key features and issues, together with some conceptual awareness. The answer will be analytical in style with a range of direct comment relating to the question. The answer will be well balanced with some judgement, which may, however, be only partially substantiated. *16–20 marks*
Level 3	Answers will show an understanding of the question and will supply a range of largely accurate information, which will show an awareness of some of the key issues and features, but may, however, be unspecific or lack precision of detail. The answer will be effectively organised and show adequate communication skills. There will be a good deal of comment in relation to the question and the answer will display some balance, but a number of statements may be inadequately supported and generalist. *11–15 marks*
Level 2	The answer is descriptive or partial, showing some awareness of the question but a failure to grasp its full demands. There will be some attempt to convey material in an organised way, although communication skills may be limited. There will be some appropriate information showing understanding of some key features and/or issues, but the answer may be very limited in scope and/or contain inaccuracy and irrelevance. There will be some, but limited, comment in relation to the question and statements will, for the most part, be unsupported and generalist. *6–10 marks*
Level 1	The question has not been properly understood and the response shows limited organisational and communication skills. The information conveyed is irrelevant or extremely limited. There may be some unsupported, vague or generalist comment. *1–5 marks*

EXAMPLE

Consider the following practice question.

'The years from 1621–42 saw a series of clashes between King and Parliament that divided the political nation in England, but it was the personality of Charles I that brought them to war.' Assess the validity of this view.

When faced with this kind of question the first step is to analyse it, because there is quite a lot that needs to be dealt with. The first statement is focused on the growth of tension, which relates to the conditional factors and the context in which war broke out. The main assertion is that the outbreak of war was caused by the personality of Charles I and that is where your initial argument and counter-argument lie. Was the war caused by the personality of the King (shown in the actions that he took) or were other factors more significant? In particular, did the earlier clashes and the divisions they created make a war likely (if not inevitable) or did they merely provide the context in which Charles's personality made an impact?

To construct your arguments with this type of question, you need to already have knowledge of what actions Charles took, and of the attitudes and beliefs that led him to act in this way. You also need knowledge of other factors – such as events and views in Parliament and the country and in Ireland. You now need to list your factors and decide which ones will form your argument and which will form your counter-argument.

When a particular factor is stipulated in the question, it is often a good idea to address that first, to ensure that you cover it fully. However, it can also be a good idea to put the weaker argument first, so that your counter-argument can consist of both elements that challenge it and positive points to take your essay into a strong conclusion. In this case, as in many questions where a single factor is singled out from a range of others, both of these considerations suggest that you should start with the role of Charles and use the wider range of factors for your counter-argument.

Once you have selected your factors, you need to link them into a summary that focuses on the question and sets out one side of the answer – an argument. As in your earlier activities, use the wording of the question to help. For example:

There is no doubt that the personality of Charles played a significant part in the outbreak of war in 1642. His political inexperience, his refusal to compromise his beliefs, and his inability (or unwillingness) to explain his actions had already contributed to the crisis that built up throughout his reign, forcing him to call a parliament in November 1640. In the months that followed, the reluctance with which he granted concessions did much to weaken any beneficial impact and build up the suspicion that he would take them away as soon as possible. The result was a growth of mistrust that drove the parliamentary leaders to demand more, until real compromise became impossible.

This summarises the part played by the stipulated factor – Charles – with a brief summary of his attitudes and clear links as to how they contributed to war. You now need to do the same for the other factors, to create a counter-argument. For example:

However, Charles was not acting in isolation. Throughout his reign he was faced by real problems created the system of government in England and the impact of events elsewhere, for example in Europe. The attitudes and actions of the parliamentary leaders also created mistrust, causing divisions within parliament that added to their fears. There were important political and religious differences that obstructed a settlement and enabled Charles to rally support. Perhaps most importantly, these divisions within the ruling elite allowed popular unrest to develop, in England and more seriously in Ireland, depriving both parties of time to resolve their differences.. The role of Charles and the significance of his personality must be assessed in the context of other factors.

Once you have established your two arguments, you can use them in this summary form as an introduction, which sets out where you are going. The main body of the essay will take each argument in turn and provide supporting examples as well as extending and explaining the links that bind the argument. In the process you will be exploring the interaction of the different factors so that you can come to a final conclusion, in which you *evaluate* both arguments.

Evaluation

Evaluation means that you support and challenge an argument to assess its strength and quality. By setting out the arguments in your introduction and using the essay to support and challenge both, you are laying the foundations of a final evaluation. Hence your conclusion will flow naturally from the main body of the essay. You will need to summarise the strengths and weaknesses of both arguments and in some cases you will make a choice as to which is stronger. More often, however, you will find that both arguments are valid and that the final outcome resulted from the interaction of factors within both.

ACTIVITY

To complete your work on the outbreak of war you should now re-read the first section of Chapter 4 (or review your notes) to refresh your memory and write out a more developed evaluation and conclusion of your own. You can then construct a plan for the following practice question and then write your own answer.

'The main cause of conflict between King and Parliament in the years 1603–49 was disputes over religion.' Explain how far you agree or disagree with this view.

Working on interpretation skills

Here is a practice question:

Why did Parliament win the First Civil War?

This is a fairly wide-ranging question, involving a number of different factors and a huge range of specific actions and events that were capable of influencing the outcome of the struggle. It is therefore not surprising that historians have different views about why Parliament emerged victorious in 1646,

but there is also a significant area of agreement. In general terms, the list of factors involved does not vary greatly between different historical accounts. What creates debate is usually the significance attributed to particular factors and the issue of their relative importance. The extracts set out and page 107 below attempt to illustrate this and allow you to utilise your own knowledge to evaluate and extend the arguments that have been presented.

Extract A

Charles did have some initial assets – a dashing cavalry force at his disposal and his own unquestioned leadership of the royalist cause, but he listened to too many different voices in his council of war. His inability to win a decisive victory in 1642 or 1643, when he held the military initiative, gave his opponents the opportunity to begin to organise their superior material assets. He was rarely able to achieve a firm administrative grip over the regions that he theoretically controlled and was never able to match the revenue which the parliamentarians enjoyed from 1643 onwards, as a result of the introduction [by John Pym] of an entirely new fiscal system founded on a productive excise tax. Parliament was able in the same year to exploit Scottish desires to see a Presbyterian Church in England to conclude a Solemn League and Covenant which brought military aid and played an important part in the notable parliamentary victory at Marston Moor in 1644 – a battle which gave Parliament control of the north of England. The following year Parliament refashioned its own forces by the creation of a 'New Model' army, a national force under the command of men who were prepared to press Parliament's military campaigns with new vigour. The King was defeated at Naseby in 1645, and the following year, realising that further resistance was useless, he surrendered to the Scots. He had been overcome by the superior material strength at Parliament's disposal.

From *The Emergence of a Nation State: The Commonwealth of England, 1529–1660* by A. G. R. Smith, (Pearson Education), 1997, p.310.

Extract B

Rather than being a major reason for parliament's victory in the civil war (which is how it is often portrayed) the Scottish alliance nearly helped parliament to lose it. The Scottish army did help to extinguish the military threat posed by Newcastle's army in the first half of 1644, but thereafter the Scottish contribution to the war was slight, and its impact was to weaken the parliamentary cause. The Covenanter army was unable to commit itself wholeheartedly to its task in England because of the threat from the royalist forces of Montrose in Scotland. They had also lost their enthusiasm for the war in England because huge divisions on religion appeared between themselves and their English allies. Furthermore, this brought about deep religious/political rifts in the ranks of the English parliamentarians. By the end of 1644 it would have taken amazing powers of foresight for anyone to have prophesied that the parliamentarians would have won the Civil War within less than two years. Neither side had achieved military superiority and both sides were being torn apart by internal squabbles. But within a few months of the eruption of the serious quarrels among the king's opponents, the military deadlock of 1644 was ended, as the battle of Naseby proved to be a major turning-point, followed by a series of parliamentary victories.

From *The Stuart Age: England, 1603–1714* by Barry Coward, (Longman), 1997, p.133.

Extract C

In the early stages of the war Cromwell observed a 'spirit' among the cavaliers that he felt was lacking in Parliament's troops. But when Cromwell raised his 'men of a spirit' in East Anglia, who knew what they wanted and were prepared to fight for what they knew, he was forging an army with a spirit that was even more pervasive and more durable than that of the cavaliers. And when, with the new modelling of their army, they were also subject to efficient control and direction, they became virtually invincible. Cromwell himself, besides being essentially professional, was also a brilliant soldier. There were missed opportunities on the part of the royalists, but basically Parliament had more resources and a wider base of support. The disparate nature of this support would prove to be a weakness, but it helped to win the war. Even so, Parliament had to call on the assistance of the Scots, and its victory was no foregone conclusion.

From *King Charles I* by Pauline Gregg, (Phoenix Press), 1981, p.402.

ACTIVITY

1 Read Extracts A, B and C and write down a list of all the factors that are put forward as influencing the outcome of the war. Bear in mind that some may be mentioned only briefly, and that there will be both positive and negative factors to consider.

2 Use your own knowledge to add any factors that you think need to be taken into consideration.

3 Taking each source in turn, write a summary of the argument put forward. In the light of the list of factors that you have compiled, how convincing is the explanation that it provides of parliament's victory?

4 Where the sources appear to be in conflict, use your own knowledge to decide how far the conflicts can be reconciled.

5 Now write your own answer to the following practice question. The questions you will face in the exam will be in the same format, but will cover a period of at least 20 years in their scope. Answering questions, such as the following practice question, however, will enable you to develop the skills you need to answer essay questions in your exam.

Using your understanding of the historical context, assess how convincing the arguments in these three extracts are in explaining why Parliament won the First Civil War.

5

Radicalism and regicide, 1646–49

The focus of this chapter is the sequence of events that led to the execution of Charles I in 1649, followed by the abolition of the monarchy and establishment of a Republic. The following specified areas are addressed:

● social divisions and the emergence of radicalism, including the Levellers and other groups
● post-war divisions between Army and Parliament
● the failure to secure a post-war settlement
● the regicide and its significance.

The chapter seeks to explain the process by which an intention to establish a limited monarchy changed into a decision to rid the country of the monarchy entirely and create a new form of government in both Church and State. Historians have debated whether this constituted 'an English Revolution' of the kind that later occurred in France and Russia, or whether it was simply a desperate measure taken for lack of any viable alternative. The regicide (the killing of a king) itself was neither planned nor intended until shortly before it took place and did not constitute a lasting change. In relation to regicide and revolution, therefore, the main issues to consider relate to how it came about, why it happened and what it meant for the development of the state. Hence the key breadth issues to be addressed are the continuing disputes over religion, the importance of individuals and the role of ideas and ideology.

The main question focused on in this chapter is:

To what extent did the events of 1649 constitute an English Revolution?

CHAPTER OVERVIEW

The chapter therefore begins by examining the effects of four years of war on the society that endured it, and the ways in which relationships between the participants had changed. King Charles was not the first king to be removed and disposed of, but he was the first to be publicly tried, condemned and executed. Those who carried out the process were convinced that it was justified to 'cut off his head with the crown upon it' in the words of Oliver Cromwell. If this was not a revolution it was sufficiently revolutionary to suggest a change of political culture that requires some explanation. At the same time, the obvious reluctance to take such a step and the fact that it had only minority support suggests that other factors were at work to drive them on and that ultimately the decision to act may well have been taken out of desperation or necessity. This chapter therefore traces the process by which this moment was reached to assess the impact of events in 1646–48 and the actions of individuals, including the King. In the light of this combination of causal factors and events, changing attitudes and ideology and individual actions and motives, it then offers a judgement as to how far these developments constituted an English Revolution.

1 The impact of war, 1642–46

Given the horror of war, it is unlikely that any society would have emerged from these years unchanged. However, the impact of the war relates not only to events within it, but also to the problems that caused it, and the extent to which some changes would have occurred anyway. Historians therefore have to assess the effects of the war in a wider context and make judgements about its significance on that basis.

The emergence of radicalism

Why did radical ideas and attitudes emerge in the years of war?

Throughout the reigns of James I and Charles I the influence and actions of those labelled 'Puritan' had helped to create tensions between King and Parliament, and the role of Puritan convictions in the taking of sides in 1642 was clearly significant. The definition of what constituted a Puritan has proved much more difficult to establish, since their positions ranged from a general emphasis on individual prayer and study of the Bible to the desire for a fully fledged Presbyterian Church along the same lines as the Scottish Kirk. In a major study of 'The Rise of Puritanism' written in 1938, and re-published in revised form in 1957, the American scholar William Haller traced the emergence of a movement that he designates 'Historic Puritanism' (as opposed to a wider puritanical religious devotion that exists in all faiths) which can be seen in the reign of Elizabeth and which flowered throughout the early seventeenth century. The centre of Haller's argument is that the Puritan clergy sought to reform the Church and were denied the power to do so, but were allowed to preach and, more importantly, publish their sermons and opinions to an ever-growing audience of literate men and women who sought to find God through whatever means were available. The preachers had, therefore, the power to inspire, enthuse and direct their audience in this search, but not the means to control its outcomes.

Source A From *The Rise of Puritanism* by W. Haller, (New York), 1957, pp.173–74, 271–72.

The object of the Puritan reformers was the reorganization of English society in the form of a Church governed by Presbyterian principles [see Chapter 2, page 20]. Until they were summoned by Parliament to the Westminster Assembly, they were granted no opportunity to put their ideas into effect, but they were allowed, within limits, to preach to the people and to publish books … The immediate result … was that they spent two generations preaching a doctrine and a way of life which promoted active, individual religious experience and expression, promoted it much faster than means could be found to control or direct it. By such process the propagation of Puritanism passed more and more out of the control of Puritan churchmen, becoming at the same time more and more revolutionary … Having created a reading people, an articulate people and a confident people, the preachers told the people that they must obey conscience. When the Stuart regime collapsed there was, consequently, a host of preachers, but there was also a host of other able, energetic and enthusiastic writers ready with matter to keep the printers busy. One of these was a political journalist of genius, another was a great poet.

In the final part of this source Haller is referring to two Johns, Lilburne and Milton, who would both take an active role in the civil wars and their aftermath and who would both propagate revolutionary ideas based on individual freedom and equality. Nevertheless, both began their journey under the influence

NOTE-MAKING

As always, you will need to make linear notes as you work through this chapter, to record important information in a way that makes it easier to access for later reference and revision. Within each section you can use the headings provided to create a structure that you can fill out with numbered points of your own devising. Remember to include comments and summaries of your own, to help you develop your own thinking about the issues covered.

Providence

Belief in God's *Providence* – the force by which he governed the affairs of men and shaped events on earth – was not simply a radical idea, but part of Protestant thinking. What distinguished radical thinking was the extent to which events tended to be interpreted as acts of divine will, and the courage and faith that could be drawn from them. For John Milton the civil wars indicated that God had chosen the English to undergo an ordeal by fire and to create a truly godly nation as an example to the world. To stand in the way of its success was to reject God's will and those who did so must bear the consequences, even if they were kings.

of respectable Puritan clergy, who were horrified to discover what they had initiated. As Haller indicates, the ferment of ideas that produced 'the founding of New England and the revolutionising of English society' was a feature of the entire period from 1603–42, but for the most part its activities remained hidden. From time to time it emerged in the activities of sectarians who lived, and sometimes died, for their faith, in the unlicensed printing presses of London, in pamphlets smuggled in from Europe, and more openly, in the popular demonstrations and debates that formed a background to the struggles within the political nation in 1640–42. Only with the breakdown of normal controls in 1642 did they fully emerge, to support, and undermine, the parliamentary cause.

The impact of war, 1642–46

It was the impact of war that enabled and encouraged the separatist groups and their allies to emerge, and the experience of war also served to heighten the effect of their ideas. Success against their traditional masters, the King and his allies, encouraged the millenarian and providential aspects of their beliefs, with a certainty that their victories were granted by God as a sign that they were acting according to his will. Their Cause was God's Cause, and in their victories, God had spoken. While it is easy to portray these ideas as eccentric, especially in their most extreme form, they were often combined with a rational, practical approach to the world, as most men saw it in 1642, that produced effective soldiers and confident political leaders. Even more significantly, this radical religious thinking freed some men from the acceptance of a rigid social and political hierarchy, enabling them to think the unthinkable: If men were spiritually equal and equal in the eyes of God, why not in other practical ways on God's earth? If a king was chosen by God but stood in the way of godliness, did his people not have the right to remove him?

The emergence of radicalism

Figure 1 opposite traces the emergence of religious radicalism from its roots in mainstream Protestant thinking. It illustrates a number of important points including the common origins and links between religious and political radicalism:

- Radical ideas and groups had existed in England before 1640, but their illegal status forced them to be secretive and they left little evidence of their existence.
- Their roots and origins lay in the same Protestant ideas as the mainstream reformers, especially the emphasis on private faith, the authority of the Bible and Calvinist predestination.
- The first separatists were therefore only 'radical' in their desire to separate, that is, to set up separate churches outside the Church of England, whose members had voluntarily chosen to join.
- Some had done this because they found the Anglican Church inadequate and despaired of reform; others because they believed that the 'saints', the godly minority whom God had predestined to salvation, should withdraw from contact with sinners and work together to find their way to God.
- This meant that the first separatists were not seeking rights for all, but privileges for the saints; their interests were religious, not political.

- However, separation was in practice a political act, threatening to a government and society that believed religious uniformity to be an essential part of political unity.
- This meant that the separatists had to develop in isolation and secrecy. In those circumstances they tended to become more radical and eccentric, drawing new enthusiasms from the Bible and their own interpretations of it.
- The collapse of authority, especially of the bishops, who were responsible for censorship and control of preachers and the press, in 1640–42, allowed the radicals to emerge from hiding, to debate in public and to develop their ideas in new forms and directions. By 1644 a coherent campaign in favour of religious toleration had developed in London.
- In turn this led to the emergence of political radicals like the Levellers and to an explosion of new ideas. The execution of the King in 1649 convinced many that a new world was opening up, and even that God himself would soon return to earth to rule in person.
- In these conditions, new and even more eccentric groups emerged, arguing for complete freedom and the authority of individual conscience above all else.

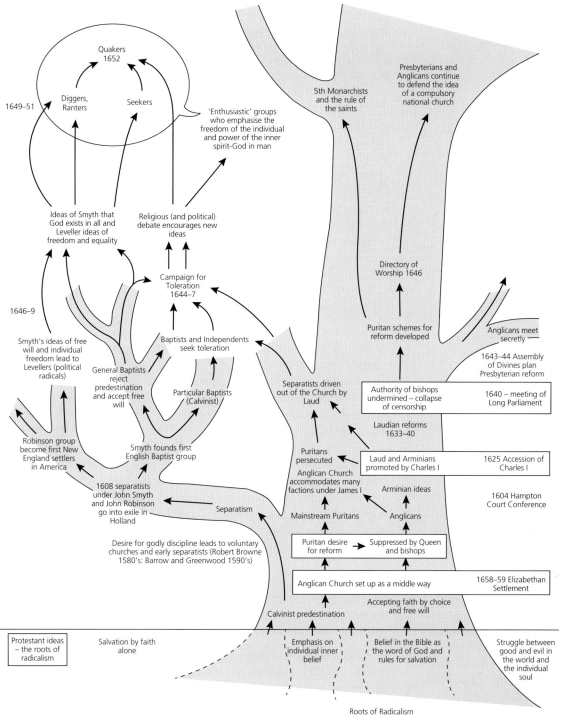

▲ **Figure 1** The development of radical groups and ideas.

The effects of radicalism

What was the political impact of radicalism?

The impact of radicalism was significant in a variety of ways. As early as 1641, the emergence of separatist groups and popular preachers in London frightened many of the more conservative MPs into supporting the King's power as the guarantee of authority, a tendency that increased in 1642 as social disruption and popular unrest followed the breakdown of authority. At the same time, the radicals and their preachers provided many of Parliament's most dedicated supporters and activists. The clearest, but not the only, example of the military effect can be seen in the army of the Eastern Association, where Oliver Cromwell deliberately recruited troopers who 'knew what they fought for and loved what they knew'. The image of his cavalry, and of the New Model Army that they later created, as a disciplined body of psalm-singing saints has been considerably exaggerated (see Chapter 4, page 99), but there is no doubt that men of this kind formed an influential core, which contributed a great deal to the dedication and effectiveness of Parliament's forces. In the House of Commons and on the battlefield the radicals contributed much to the victory of Parliament.

For many of the conservative Parliamentarians who celebrated this victory, however, they constituted a new and disturbing threat to their vision of a reformed monarchy and Church. The first sign of this came in 1643–44, at the time when the Solemn League and Covenant threatened the imposition of a Presbyterian uniformity that would be no more acceptable to some radicals than the Anglican Church and the bishops. In early 1644, five members of the Assembly of Divines published an *Apologetical Narration*, arguing for the right of orthodox Protestant saints to establish their own congregations outside the Church and to exercise discipline over their members. It was a cautious and limited appeal, but it was quickly followed by bolder spirits who began to argue for extensive religious toleration. By the end of 1644 there was an organised campaign for toleration and for freedom of speech and the press, which brought together figures such as Roger Williams, the founder of the American colony of Rhode Island; John Milton, the Puritan poet; and the later leaders of the Leveller movement, John Lilburne, Richard Overton and William Walwyn. These men had begun to argue as a matter of principle, that religious beliefs were private, personal and no concern of governments and magistrates. The Puritan vision of godly uniformity was being threatened from within its own ranks.

By 1645, therefore, a division had become apparent both within and outside Parliament. The majority of MPs and their supporters, the City of London authorities and the Scots remained committed to a single, national Church and a rapid peace to restore the King and his authority. They tended to be labelled Presbyterian, although not all of them were committed to a fully Presbyterian organisation of the Church. A minority of MPs, including influential leaders like Cromwell and Sir Henry Vane, were sympathetic to some of the radical demands and favoured a limited toleration for 'tender consciences' who sought spiritual support in 'independent' congregations of like-minded souls. Labelled Independents, they also wanted to pursue the war vigorously. They were prepared to restore the King, but only from a position of strength, with significant limitations being placed on his powers. They had the support of radical groups and a strong base in the newly created New Model Army.

Presbyterian and Independent

The use of religious labels such as Presbyterian and Independent to describe political attitudes can be confusing, because not all members of either group adhered strictly to the religious beliefs that they implied. It is probably easiest to define the political Presbyterians by their concern with order and hierarchy and hence desire for a reasonably strong monarch to work alongside Parliament and the return of a compulsory national Church. Some preferred a form of Presbyterianism, others would have accepted bishops with reduced powers, but both emphasised compulsion and authority. The Independents are defined by their insistence on allowing a measure of religious freedom, which would also involve restricting the powers of the King.

The conservative reaction

The victories of the New Model Army were therefore a mixed blessing to the conservative MPs. As long as the Royalists were in arms, they depended on its successes throughout the country and could do little but fret about the radical churches that sprang up wherever it went. By 1644 the Baptist groups were already strong in London and in parts of East Anglia, and in that year the first Independent Church was formally constituted in Hull, helped by the presence of the army chaplain, John Canne. By 1646, there were six such churches in Yorkshire alone. Although many were not specifically created by army men, the army's mobility, the contacts created by soldiers drawn from many areas and the protection provided to radical preachers by leading officers like Cromwell, made it a powerful influence in spreading radical ideas. Although the radicals never constituted more than a tiny minority of the population, they were quite sufficient to frighten those who believed that social harmony and their own social position depended on the restoration of authority in Church and State.

The result was a conservative overreaction that widened divisions and drove some radicals to new heights. In 1645 an attack was launched against radical leaders, especially the outspoken and uncompromising John Lilburne. An account of his troubles and how they led to the formation of the Leveller movement is set out on pages 114–15. Meanwhile, conservative complaints about the army increased in volume and intensity. In 1645 the Presbyterian minister, Richard Baxter, complained of the talk of 'church democracy and state democracy' that he heard among soldiers, and in 1646 the less moderate Presbyterian, Thomas Edwards, published a book entitled *Gangraena*, a vitriolic (vicious) account of radical groups and ideas, likening them to a poison in the blood of the body politic. When Parliamentarian victory and the desire for a rapid peace strengthened the influence of the conservatives on the parliamentary committees, they determined to use their position to ensure that the search for peace included the destruction of radical influence.

KEY DATES: SECTARIAN STEPS

1608 John Smyth and John Robinson take their separatist congregations to Holland, where they develop the first Baptist and Congregationalist groups.

1616 First Baptist church in England.

1641 Breakdown of censorship; separatists emerge in London; seven Baptist churches publish joint statement of doctrine.

1644 Assembly of Divines – Independent ministers call for toleration; first Independent (Congregationalist) church established in England, at Hull.

1644–45 Press campaign for toleration brings Leveller leaders together.

1645–46 Emergence of Leveller political movement.

John Lilburne and the emergence of the Levellers

Mr. JOHN LILBORNE.

Lilburne's life story is in many ways the story of Puritan development in this period, from its enthusiastic but ill-defined beginnings to the fragmentation and internal divisions that undermined hopes of godly reform. In the process, the godly reformers created something far more significant and radical in the long term – a demand for fundamental human rights and political influence for the people as a whole. While the Leveller movement, which formulated and published the demand, was short-lived and easily crushed in this period, its ideas were able to survive as a radical tradition and inspiration for later reformers.

Lilburne: the making of a Leveller

John Lilburne was the second son of a gentleman from County Durham, a member of the minor gentry, who was apprenticed at the age of 14 to a cloth merchant in the City of London. It is likely that his family and his master were Puritan in their outlook, and Lilburne regularly attended sermons preached by the ministers of the day. He and a number of other apprentices were in the habit of attending a morning sermon and meeting later to discuss and debate its meaning. Through these activities, Lilburne became

acquainted with John Bastwick (see Chapter 3, page 58) and concocted a scheme to have Bastwick's 'Letany' (an illegal tract written against the bishops) printed in Holland and smuggled back for resale. The likelihood is that he hoped both to serve the Puritan cause and provide himself with enough money to establish his own business on completing his apprenticeship. Instead he was arrested, brought before the Star Chamber in 1638 and sentenced to be whipped and pilloried.

When the sentence was carried out he protested loudly that this was an abuse of his rights as a free-born Englishman, and harangued a gathering crowd so effectively that Laud had him gagged. Removed to the Fleet prison, he was placed in solitary confinement, but continued to petition for release and deny the power of prerogative courts to punish free men (see Chapter 1, page 5 and Chapter 3, page 58). He remained in prison, however, until the meeting of the Long Parliament, when friends persuaded the MP for Cambridge, Oliver Cromwell, to secure his release. This initiated a friendship between the two men. The story of Lilburne's early troubles illustrates the variety of opinion held by 'Puritans' at this stage. Lilburne was already moving towards the General Baptist view that God offered salvation to all, a denial of the Calvinist belief in predestination, held and defended by men like Bastwick, Prynne and Cromwell. Conflicting ideas could be fudged or set aside while there was a common enemy to fight in Laud and the bishops, and ideas did not need to be fully explored and defined until the opportunity existed to put them into practice. That moment did not arrive until 1643–44, in the Solemn League and Covenant with Scotland, and the calling of the Assembly of Divines. By then Lilburne had served in the army under Lord Brooke and later the Earl of Manchester, but in early 1645 he refused to join the New Model because it involved accepting the Covenant, with its commitment to a compulsory Presbyterian Church.

The Levellers: the making of a movement

Returning to London he became engaged in a pamphlet war and campaign for religious freedom that had begun in 1644. It is at this point that he began to work with William Walwyn, a prosperous merchant, and Richard Overton, a shadowy figure who made a living through printing and publishing unlicensed political tracts. In July 1645 his activities led him to be imprisoned in Newgate by the House of Commons, on a charge of slandering the Speaker. Released in October, he continued his campaign for toleration, but now began to extend it by questioning the behaviour of MPs in imprisoning men without proper trial. In 1646 he was campaigning against a similar imprisonment of Overton and his wife, when a combination of Presbyterian enemies from his army days and his London activities succeeded in having him brought before the House of Lords. Lilburne pointedly ignored their warrant, but presented himself at the bar of the House to tell their assembled lordships that they had no right to try him, no power over free men and no valid cause beyond their own interests. Not surprisingly, he found himself in prison in the Tower of London.

The 'Agreement of the People'

Lilburne's clash with the Lords marks the beginning of the Levellers as a coherent political movement. His stand against the Lords raised serious issues regarding individual rights under the law and he had widened that issue to question what Parliament stood for and what the war had been fought to achieve. While Overton (now released) and Walwyn organised petitions and demonstrations calling for his release, Lilburne began to formulate and develop the argument that Parliament's power was derived only from the people and that the people could and should call them to account. Against a background of economic distress, high taxation and the dislocation of trade, the Leveller leaders drew on the support of the 'middling sort' in London, to demand social justice, economic freedom and political rights. Over the two years between Lilburne's imprisonment by the Lords and the beginning of the second civil war, they formulated a democratic constitution in the 'Agreement of the People'. The hierarchical nature of seventeenth-century society (see Chapter 1) and their own errors denied them the opportunity to put it into effect, but in historical terms their failure is far outweighed by the significance of their thinking.

Interpretations: the origins and development of radicalism

The arguments put forward by William Haller in Source A on page 109 stress the importance of puritan ideas and preachers in the origins of the radical ideas that emerged in the 1640s and developed thereafter. Other historians, however, have argued that a wider range of influences were at work, some related to the impact of war, but others rooted in a longer past and a less controlled environment. The sources below set out a range of arguments for you to consider.

Source B Adapted from *Radicalism in the English Revolution* by F. D. Dow, (Blackwell), 1989, pp.58, 60.

Without the conflicts and controversies of mid-seventeenth-century England and the breakdown of the old order in Church and state, it is impossible to imagine such a flowering of radical religious beliefs, but they were not entirely new. At least as far back as Elizabethan times, radical dissent had had a shadowy, underground existence in areas such as the Weald of Kent, the Chiltern Hills and the moorland communities of Yorkshire ... After 1642, the relaxation of censorship allowed the radicals an outlet for their ideas, while social and economic dislocation provided a further stimulus to men to rethink their world. In this period, it is impossible to separate political from religious thinking ... Puritan beliefs played an important part in the parliamentarian cause after 1642 ... [but] it would be wrong to see religious radicalism in the 1640s and 1650s as simply the extension of the type of Puritanism that had attracted a large following before the war. Other streams flowed into it; yet the background to much radical religious thinking is formed by the loose cluster of beliefs, attitudes and assumptions which we call Puritanism.

Source C From *The World Turned Upside Down* by Christopher Hill, (Penguin), 1975, pp.85–86.

I have stressed the social background – the isolation and freedom which permitted radical ideas to develop among some communities in woodland and pasture areas; the mobile society of early capitalism, serviced by itinerant merchants, craftsmen, pedlars; the crowds of masterless men, vagabonds and urban poor who no longer fitted into the categories of a hierarchical agrarian society. The great shake-up of the Civil War suddenly and remarkably increased social and physical mobility. The New Model Army itself can be regarded as a body of masterless men on the move ... It linked up the hitherto obscure radical groups scattered up and down the kingdom, and gave them new confidence, especially in the lonely North and West. It was also, in itself, an outstanding example of social mobility ... The New Model Army was the match that fired the gunpowder ... but once the conflagration started, there was plenty of material lying around, ready to burn.

Source D From *Politics, Religion and Society in Revolutionary England* by H. Tomlinson and D. Gregg, (Macmillan) 1989, pp.85, 88.

In the course of the Civil War an unexpected but not unnatural expansion of political consciousness occurred ... Moreover, the breakdown in effective censorship of the press and pulpit ... enabled 'the lower sort' to participate more fully in political processes, and the focus of political debate gradually extended beyond Westminster, to include Churches, taverns and places of work ... Those participants in the conflict who hoped for more radical change in English society tended to present their arguments in terms of freedom: liberty to express opinions, verbally or in print, liberty to attend whatever form of religious worship they desired, freedom of trade from monopolies and liberty to play an active role in political affairs through the franchise. The quest for liberty was first and foremost an attack on religious uniformity, but rapidly extended beyond the issue of individual conscience in the 1640s ... The desire for toleration in religion naturally led to a campaign for secular liberties ... And when Parliament treated popular petitions with contempt, it caused the radicals finally to advocate political remedies for their grievances.

Source E Adapted from *The Levellers* by H. Shaw, (Longman), 1973, pp.12–13, 16.

The smaller tenant farmer [see Chapter 1, page 6] was frequently ejected from land that his family had farmed for centuries ... The woollen industry, the oldest and most important of English industries had for some time been completely dominated by the capitalist clothier ... The decline of the small operator was taking place all over the country; it was mirrored and magnified in London. Its recent growth in population had been remarkable ... From a figure of about 60,000 in the early sixteenth century, it had risen to something like 350,000 by 1650. It sprawled five miles along the northern bank of the Thames and three miles along the south. Seat of Court and government, centre of trade and law, London exercised a dominance that was, as Christopher Hill said 'unique in Europe'.

The prosperity of the City was not shared by all its inhabitants: the master craftsman was a victim of the new capitalist age. He sold his labour – he was a wage earner ... and bitterly mortified to find himself sliding down the social sale. Between 1646 and 1649 these tensions were brought into high relief by the uncertainties of war and nature. A series of poor harvests had a catastrophic effect on food prices ... and wages failed to rise, while unemployment was widespread. The distress was countrywide, but it was in London that it merged with virulent Puritanism.

ACTIVITY

1 What different reasons are suggested in Sources B–E for the rise of radical ideas and movements in the 1640s?

2 To what extent do the sources suggest that the impact of war was responsible for the growth of radicalism in these years?

3 Why did London emerge as a centre of radical activity?

4 How far do the arguments put forward here challenge Haller's interpretation of radicalism (Source A, page 109) as the natural result of Puritan ideas and influence?

2 The search for peace, 1646–48

The emergence of the radicals was one of a number of factors that would complicate the search for a broadly accepted peace. In surrendering to the Scots rather than parliamentarian forces, Charles had already indicated a reluctance to deal with those he regarded as rebels. More seriously perhaps, those 'rebels' in the Parliament and Army were by no means united in their aims and priorities.

The aims of Parliament

What were the aims of the majority of MPs in 1646–47?

By early 1647 the Presbyterians in Parliament appeared to be close to success. The King had been handed over to their custody by the Scottish army, which had withdrawn to Scotland shortly afterwards. The Scottish commissioners had hoped to work with Charles to ensure a conservative settlement, and would have supported the restoration of most of his powers, but had found him unwilling to compromise on the future of the Church. He was held at Holdenby House in Northamptonshire, where he appeared to be considering his response to Parliament's revised propositions, put to him at Newcastle in 1646. The key demands were:

- that he granted control of the militia to Parliament
- that he sought its approval of his choice of advisers
- that he allowed a reformed Church of England.

The Westminster Assembly had finally produced a scheme for reforming the Church – the Directory of Worship – which was broadly Presbyterian even if the Scots considered it insufficiently rigorous in its discipline. Parliamentary elections held in 1646 to 'recruit' numbers of MPs to a more nationally representative level had strengthened conservative support. With a clear majority in Parliament, the leaders of the political Presbyterians, Denzil Holles and Sir Philip Stapleton, could expect to create a peace settlement that reflected their aims.

In the meantime, they sought to deal with the legacy of war. Popular complaints of high taxation and economic dislocation made it logical to consider disbanding Parliament's forces now that they were no longer needed. Accordingly, MPs voted in February 1647 to disband the New Model Army, retaining only a force of volunteers to go to Ireland, where rebellion still lingered, under the leadership of new officers. The decision was perfectly logical, although there were signs of an ulterior motive in the plan to remove the old, radically-minded officers and replace them with good Presbyterians. Nevertheless, the plan would probably have been accepted if MPs had not, in their haste to get rid of the radical threat, neglected to make provision for either arrears of pay or indemnity for the disbanded troops.

> **Indemnity** – The protection of ex-soldiers from legal proceedings for any action undertaken as part of the war. For example, troopers who had requisitioned horses as part of their wartime duties might find themselves sued or accused of theft if they did not have the protection of a legal indemnity. Given the range and type of actions that they might well have carried out under orders, this was a serious matter for soldiers of all ranks.

The politicisation of the army

How did the army emerge as a political force?

Faced with provision for neither arrears nor indemnity, several regiments petitioned their general, Sir Thomas Fairfax, to intercede on their behalf, while Cromwell and his son-in-law, Henry Ireton, who were both officers and MPs, put the army's case in Parliament. The refusal of the conservatives to reconsider was probably a result of their fear of radical influence in the army, but in fact it opened the way for that radical influence to increase. In March and April the soldiers elected representatives called Agents or Agitators to speak on

Sectarians – Sectarians or 'sectaries' was the word used to describe the Puritan separatists. The forms of organisation and worship used in sectarian meetings tended to encourage open discussion and blur the distinction between the minister and the other members of the congregation. Within the army, the frequent absence of any ordained clergy encouraged talented speakers among the soldiers to lead worship and preach in their place. The whole experience of radical religion helped to produce men of the 'middling sort' who were both willing and able to challenge the assumptions of their social superiors.

their behalf, and many of those elected had radical views and connections. Experience of sectarian worship, with its emphasis on godly debate and lay preaching, encouraged ordinary troopers to become both articulate and confident, and it is not surprising that such men should have been the ones chosen to speak for their companions. While the radical activists were never a majority, especially among the infantry who tended to be less educated than the cavalry, their ability to lead gave them significant influence in shaping the army's protests.

Under their leadership, the complaints about disbandment without arrears and indemnity began to widen into concern about the nature of the settlement that such MPs would establish, encouraged by radicals both within and beyond the army itself. By early 1647 the Levellers in London were despairing of persuading Parliament to reform, and saw the army as a potential power base. Infiltrating the military was not difficult for men who, like Lilburne, had been soldiers, and shared contacts among the sectarian churches. There is little doubt that by May, when the army threatened open mutiny, the Agitators were in touch with, and influenced by, civilian Levellers. There is also little doubt that the existence of religious radicals within the army was a crucial link between the civilian radicals and the majority of soldiers who were concerned first and foremost about their indemnity and arrears. What finally shaped the army into a political force was the decision by certain leading officers to join with their men in a campaign to influence the outcome of any settlement. In April and May 1647, Cromwell and Ireton found their pleas for better treatment of the army ignored in Parliament with the same determination as their desire for a religiously tolerant settlement. By the end of May it was clear that the army would act, with or without them. They were therefore faced with the choice between betraying the Parliament in whose name they had fought, or seeing the army and their religious allies embark on a strategy that could end in chaos.

The Solemn Engagement

On 27 May 1647, Parliament ordered the army to disband without arrears. On 28 May the Agitators informed Fairfax that the regiments would not obey, and on 29 May a council of officers agreed to support them. On the orders of the Agitators, and possibly with Cromwell's knowledge, Cornet (Second Lieutenant) George Joyce and an armed escort left for Holdenby House to secure the King. Joyce visited Cromwell in London, but it is unclear whether this was to gain his support or merely to inform him of the plan. Whatever the purpose, the visit seems to have been decisive, since a few days later both Cromwell and Ireton left London to join the army while Joyce brought the King from Holdenby to the army at Newmarket. On 5 June the army met in a general rendezvous led by Fairfax and Cromwell and agreed on a Solemn Engagement to hold together until a fair settlement was assured. It was agreed to establish a General Council of the Army, made up of the leading officers and the Agitators, to co-ordinate strategy. On 14 June an Army Representation (Declaration), written by Ireton, set out the army's case and its determination to oppose Parliament until its rights were secured in a fair and just settlement. What this meant is analysed in the activity feature on page 119. The army had become a third political force in the English search for settlement, alongside the existing elements of Parliament and King.

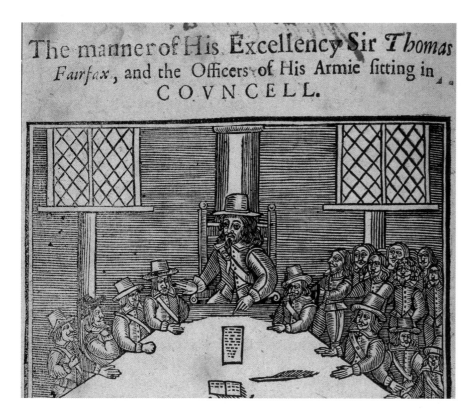

The manner of His Excellency Sir *Thomas Fairfax*, and the Officers of His Armie sitting in COVNCELL.

▲ A meeting of the Army General Council, as shown in contemporary pamphlets. What is the significance of the way that the members are presented, with the officers seated and drawn as larger figures?

The Army General Council

The Army General Council was unusual in that it contained representatives of the rank and file as well as officers. It was a symbol of army unity, but it was used by the Levellers to try to pressurise Fairfax and his leading officers into adopting Leveller policies. They came closest to success in the Putney debates of October/November 1647, but were defeated by the determination of Cromwell and Ireton and the King's escape from custody. With a second war imminent, Fairfax was able to disband the Council in January 1648. After the Second Civil War, the army reverted to a council of officers, although some of these kept radical influence from disappearing completely.

Source F Adapted from *The Representation of the Army*, 14 June 1647.

We were not a mere mercenary army, hired to serve any arbitrary power of a state, but called forth by the several declarations of Parliament to the defence of our own and the people's just rights and liberties. And so we took up arms in judgement and in conscience to those ends … We cannot but wish that such men and such only might be preferred [appointed] to the great power and trust of the commonwealth as are approved at least for moral righteousness, and of such we cannot but in our wishes prefer those that appear acted [motivated] thereunto by a principle of conscience and religion in them … [And by this means] justice and righteousness shall flow down equally to all …

The House of Commons [shall have] the supreme power … of final judgements. [It is] a mere tyranny that the same men should sit during life or at their own pleasure [as in the House of Lords] … The people have a right to regular elections unto that great and supreme trust at certain periods of time … [so that] if they have made an ill choice at one time they may mend it at another …

[There should be a] general act of oblivion … whereby the seeds of future war or feuds, either to the present age or posterity, may be better taken away. We do not seek to overthrow Presbytery or hinder the settlement thereof or to have Independent government set up … We only desire that according to the declarations promising a privilege for tender consciences, [those] who upon conscientious grounds may differ from the established forms may not for that be debarred from the common rights, liberties or benefits belonging equally to all men and members of the commonwealth, while they live soberly, honestly, inoffensively towards others and peacefully and faithfully towards the state.

Use the evidence skills that you have practised in earlier chapters to analyse the *Representation of the Army* (Source F) and explain:
● what the army was seeking to achieve
● how it justified such interference in political matters.

Division, 1647–48

How did the politicisation of the army affect the search for peace?

The result of the politicisation of the army was to greatly complicate the search for a settlement. With Parliament and army divided, the King was encouraged in his belief that he could play for time, widen the conflicts among his enemies and win the peace in spite of losing the war. Believing that there could be no settlement without him, he was determined to hold out for a settlement of his choosing, and that would involve the restoration of his powers as well as the Anglican establishment in the Church. He therefore listened to proposals from both army and Parliament, without any intention of accepting either. In the meantime he maintained contact with the Scots and looked around for other opportunities, such as the Queen's continued efforts to raise forces abroad. Given Charles's stubborn nature, sincere convictions and refusal to accept the reality of his position, the search for settlement would always have been difficult. The divisions in Parliament that developed in 1646–47 and the emergence of the army as a third political force rendered it well-nigh impossible.

To complicate matters still further, the summer of 1647 saw an internal struggle for control of the army between the leading officers who sought moderation and compromise and the Levellers who sought to use the army for revolutionary purposes. In July 1647 the conservative MPs who dominated the Committee of Both Kingdoms encouraged a series of demonstrations in London that led to the expulsion of the Independents from Parliament. When some of them took refuge with the army at Newmarket, Fairfax was persuaded of the necessity to march the army to the City and restore order. While the army was camped at Putney during the summer a group of officers and civilian Levellers sought to persuade the Army General Council to adopt their ideas. A London Leveller, John Wildman, had drafted a political declaration, *The Case of the Army Truly Stated*, which called for a democratically elected Parliament as the centre of political power and guaranteed popular rights to religious toleration and freedom of speech. Although it did not demand the removal of the King, the source of power was unequivocally located in the people, and for the purposes of debate it was summarised as *The Agreement of the People* and presented to the Army Council at Putney Church in October.

Under the chairmanship of a rather bemused Fairfax, the Council debated the Leveller proposals with Wildman, the agitator Edward Sexby, and one of the officers, Colonel Rainsborough, offering impassioned pleas for freedom and justice to extend to all men. The opposing arguments, that while freedoms should be as universal as possible the needs of stability required political power to be restricted to the educated and propertied elite, were presented mainly by Henry Ireton. Cromwell attempted to moderate the arguments in order to maintain unity in the face of threats from parliamentary conservatives and the supporters of the King. What the final outcome might have been is uncertain, because in November 1647 the debates were brought to an abrupt end when the King escaped from his imprisonment at Hampton Court and fled to the Isle of Wight, claiming that he feared for his safety. The effects of this, and the complex events of the summer and autumn, are set out in Figure 2 opposite.

The renewal of war, 1647–48

The army was immediately forced to resume its readiness for further action by calling a general rendezvous (assembly) of the troops, and although a group of London Levellers attempted to stir up a mutiny among those gathered at Ware in Hertfordshire, swift action by Cromwell ensured that it had little effect. Riding into the ranks of the regiments he quickly brought them to order, and the outcome was the execution of only one trooper. There has been considerable debate among historians about some of the relationships and issues involved, although the main developments are clear. Historians of the Levellers, for example, have followed the Leveller leaders themselves in claiming widespread support within the army and a major influence on the army's proposals for peace. Others have challenged the extent of radical influence within the army and emphasised the role of the leading officers (known as the Grandees) in exploiting the army for their own political purposes. What is clear is that the efforts of the four parties to find an acceptable settlement in 1647 were ended by the King's Engagement to (treaty with) the Scots in December and the ensuing outbreak of the Second Civil War.

Figure 2 reveals a number of key points related to the search for a settlement, which help to explain why it failed and why it ended in the execution of the King.

● The army leaders had no intention of removing the King at this stage. The Heads of the Proposals, drawn up by Cromwell and Ireton, were the most flexible plans for settlement ever offered to Charles. Although he would have lost control of the militia and his choice of advisers for ten years, there was considerable emphasis on reconciliation. Only seven Royalists would have been excluded from a pardon (as compared to 58 in Parliament's Newcastle Propositions) and the Proposals included the restoration of bishops in the Church, although with advisory powers only.
● There is also evidence of Leveller influence in the Proposals, for example, in the plans to reform Parliament by redistributing seats according to taxation

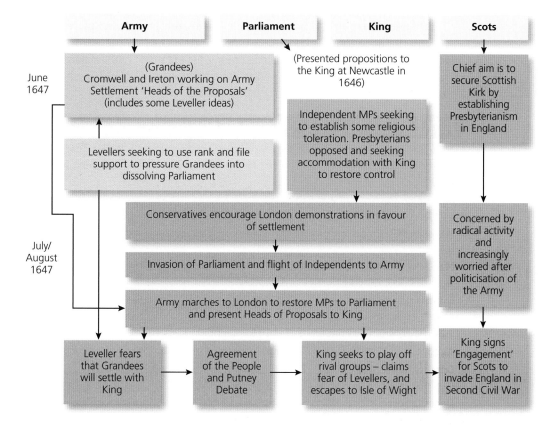

▲ **Figure 2** The search for peace, June–December, 1647.

and holding elections every two years. Legal and economic reforms were proposed, as well as a measure of religious toleration. This undoubtedly reflected Leveller views, but there is no reason to believe that the Grandees objected to them.

● It is also clear that the army leaders were determined to limit Leveller influence and maintain the social and political hierarchy. Their plans were a compromise and they consistently refused to agree to Leveller demands for a dissolution of Parliament. When the army did march to London in July, it was to restore the Independent MPs who had been chased out by conservative supporters and only 11 conservative MPs were named as responsible for the divisions among Parliament's supporters. It was Leveller fears that they were about to be outflanked that led them to propose the Agreement of the People in October.

● Surviving records of the debates suggest that the Levellers may have had the best of the argument. However, in the rapid ending of discussion after the King's escape, the General Council accepted three rendezvous, rather than a single rendezvous of the army as the Levellers wanted. This, and the ease with which Cromwell dealt with the mutiny at Corkbush Field, suggests that Leveller support among the rank and file was never as great as it appeared. The impression of widespread support owed much to the soldiers' grievances over arrears and indemnity and to the outspoken and articulate views of the Agitators. It should also be remembered that the leading officers could call on a loyalty based on shared religious views as well as shared victories and dangers.

● Above all, what is revealed by the events of 1647 is the bad faith with which Charles approached the search for a settlement. On one level, this is understandable. He was a King forced to negotiate with rebels, and few monarchs of this age would have felt any obligation to be honest with them. He was also being asked to compromise his most deeply held convictions. For the most part, he did not lie as such – he merely stalled and played for time in the hope that his situation would improve. Such hopes were greatly encouraged by the obvious divisions among his enemies. Only in secretly negotiating with the Scots and inviting them to invade England can he be accused of serious betrayal.

KEY DATES: THE SEARCH FOR PEACE

1646 Parliament presented terms for peace to the King at Newcastle; Charles delayed a reply, and later rejected the terms.

1647

February: Parliament voted to disband the New Model Army without providing arrears of pay or legal indemnity.

March/April: Election of Agitators to represent the soldiers and obtain better terms.

May: With Leveller influence growing in the ranks, the Agitators organised the seizure of the King by Cornet Joyce.

5 June: Army rendezvous, leading to the Solemn Engagement and establishment of the Army General Council.

July: Army entered London to restore Independent MPs after city riots.

August: Army peace terms – The Heads of the Proposals – presented to the King.

October/November: Putney Debates, ended by the King's escape to the Isle of Wight.

December: King Charles signs an Engagement with the Scots, initiating the Second Civil War.

3 The army revolution, 1648–49

The renewal of military action in 1648, mainly as a result of the King's refusal to negotiate in good faith and his agreement with the Scots, marked the beginning of truly revolutionary action by the army and its leaders. Despite the influence of radical ideas and discussion of significant political changes at Putney and elsewhere, the purpose of both Parliament and army was reform, not revolution, and there was no question of a threat to the King's person, let alone the institution of monarchy. The quarrel between Parliament and army was about the nature of a settlement, not the search for settlement in itself. By renewing the war, however, and inflicting a new phase of death and destruction on his subjects, Charles not only convinced some that a settlement was impossible while he lived – he also appeared to place his own powers and will above that of God and his duty as monarch.

The Second Civil War, 1648

What were the causes and consequences of the Second Civil War?

The main cause of the Second Civil War was the refusal of Charles I to accept the outcome of the first. His refusal to seriously consider proposals for peace reflected his total conviction that, as King, he had the right to use whatever means were necessary to suppress rebellion. Given that many of his supporters remained loyal, Charles used the growing disillusionment felt by the Scots towards their English allies to suggest that the best guarantee for the future of the Kirk was a Royalist alliance. He therefore encouraged a Scottish invasion to create the opportunity for Royalist risings. By January 1648 it was clear that renewed war was imminent, and the army prepared itself. In January 1648 the Agitators apparently ceased to sit in the Army Council and military discipline was restored along with army unity. Parliament voted 'No Further Addresses' to Charles Stuart and in an emotional prayer-meeting of the Council of Officers in April the King was condemned as a 'man of blood'. By then scattered Royalist risings had developed in England and Wales, while the Scots prepared to invade in accordance with their commitment to Charles. While Fairfax besieged Colchester, the centre of royalism in Essex, Cromwell advanced into Wales. Unfortunately for Charles, the Scots invasion was delayed and Cromwell was able to deal with the Welsh risings and then cut off the Scots at Preston, before advancing into Yorkshire to mop up Royalist resistance there. Although the siege of Colchester was long and bitter, dragging on until September, the outcome was never in doubt. By the autumn of 1648, the military crisis was over.

While the Second Civil War was of little significance in military terms, its political impact was enormous. Most of Parliament's supporters viewed the first war as unplanned, and more importantly as a trial of strength between the King's cause and that of Parliament, in which God gave his judgement for Parliament. In neither context was Charles judged to bear all blame. In 1648, however, he deliberately waged war on his people, using a foreign army to do so. Moreover, by taking this action he rejected God's judgement and God's will. Not only was he a man of blood in the providential thinking of many Protestants, he had rejected God – and in the view of the army, he must be brought to account for his crimes.

By November 1648 the army was virtually united in a demand that the King should be brought to trial. The strategist in this case was not Cromwell, who remained in Yorkshire to complete military operations, but his son-in-law, Henry Ireton. On 20 November he published an Army Remonstrance, demanding that the King be brought to justice. Meanwhile, he renewed negotiations with

Providence – Providential beliefs were widespread among seventeenth-century Protestants, although they tended to appear in their most extreme forms among radicals. They were based on the belief that God intervened directly in the affairs of men to ensure that the outcome of events conformed with His will. Matters such as the victories of the New Model Army or Charles's refusal to compromise were therefore interpreted as acts of providence – evidence of God's judgement and purpose. Men like Cromwell sought to read these providential signs in order to know God's purpose before deciding what action to take.

Vote of No Addresses – A vote in the House of Commons on 3 January 1648 that no further addresses (i.e. offers to negotiate) be made to the King. This was in response to his perceived betrayal by signing an Engagement with the Scots, but, above all, it reflected the anger and despair felt by most MPs at his consistent refusal to enter genuine negotiations.

the Levellers to ensure their quiescence, if not their support. The army was now represented by a Council of Officers rather than the old General Council, significantly reducing Leveller influence and support. At the same time, the army's allies in Parliament, the Independent MPs, pressed the case for dealing with the King according to Parliament's Vote of No Addresses.

Pride's purge and the execution of the King

Why did the army leaders feel justified in purging the Parliament in whose name they had waged war?

In Parliament, however, the mood had changed since January. The scattered uprisings in support of the King had not been the work of old Royalists as much as an expression of popular desire for peace and a return to normal government. Aware that a tide was running in favour of a conservative settlement, the majority of MPs supported renewed efforts to negotiate. For most, the concept of a settlement without the King was unthinkable, and many feared their radical allies far more than their Royalist enemies. In September 1648 parliamentary commissioners were sent to the Isle of Wight to renew negotiations with the King. In early December they returned with the King's answers to four key bills which formed the first stage of a treaty. While one, Sir Henry Vane, made it clear to the House that the King remained unwilling to make real concessions, most MPs were now so desperate for negotiations that his views were ignored. On 3 December a bill was passed to give Parliament direct control of the militia (a first step to disbanding the army), and on 5 December the Vote of No Addresses was repealed.

In these circumstances, the army was bound to act. If negotiations followed, the King would be returned to London and a wave of Royalist enthusiasm would leave little scope for extracting the concessions that he was so clearly unwilling to make. At best, the conservatives were giving up the advantages of victory; at worst, they were deliberately working with the King to destroy the army and its allies. There was little doubt that any settlement that emerged would restore most of the King's powers and, above all, a compulsory national Church. It was not only the army's interests that were threatened, but the religious rights and freedoms that civilian and military radicals enjoyed. For many also this was a betrayal of God's cause. The fruits of victory and the interests of a significant minority in and outside Parliament were about to be thrown away. Ironically, the behaviour of the conservative MPs does much to vindicate the King's assumption that peace could not be achieved without his agreement. What he had failed to recognise was that the emergence of the army as a political force had introduced a new, and ultimately revolutionary, element into the equation.

On 6 December the regiment of Colonel Pride surrounded the Houses of Parliament and refused entry to those who were known to support the negotiations with the King. A few of the conservative leaders were arrested and imprisoned, but most (about 186 MPs) were simply excluded. Another hundred or so who heard of what was happening chose to stay away, leaving a minority of around 70 MPs who remained in Parliament to carry out the procedures involved in bringing the King to trial. Although Ireton had originally intended to dissolve Parliament, he had been persuaded by Sir Arthur Haselrig that this 'rump' of MPs would represent legal authority and maintain stability in this crisis period. On 7 December Cromwell returned to London and took his seat in Parliament after expressing his approval of what had been done. Having agonised, prayed and 'waited on the Lord' for a sign as to how to proceed, he interpreted conservative provocation and the actions of the army as the sign that he sought, and thereafter he drove the business forward with his usual energy and determination. The results can be seen in Figure 3.

Timeline of events

1648

5 December

MPs voted to renew addresses to the King on the basis of his answers to the Four Bills presented to him in the Isle of Wight.

6 December

Pride's Purge; that evening, Cromwell returned to London and signified his agreement.

1649

1 January

Ordinance establishing a High Court to try the King was passed by the Rump of the Commons, but rejected by the House of Lords.

4 January

The Rump passed Three Resolutions, claiming sole authority to make law.

20 January

The King's trial began; Charles denied the right of the Court to try him and refused to enter a plea.

27 January

Charles found guilty and sentenced to death.

30 January

The execution of the King.

13 February

A Council of State was appointed to govern in his place.

17 March

Abolition of the monarchy.

19 March

Abolition of the House of Lords.

19 May

England declared a Commonwealth.

Figure 3 The trial and execution of Charles I.

Source G From the charge of treason drawn up by Parliament against the King, 28 December 1648.

That Charles Stuart hath acted contrary to his trust in departing from the Parliament ... making a war against them, and thereby hath been the occasion of much bloodshed and misery to the people whom he was set over for good ... and since was the occasion of a second war, besides what he has done ... tending to the destruction of the fundamental laws and liberties of this Kingdom.

Source H From the King's reply to the charge of treason drawn up by Parliament.

I do stand more for the liberty of my people than any here that come to be my pretended judges. And therefore let me know by what lawful authority I am seated here.

Having refused to plead he remained silent until the sentence was announced. He was then refused permission to speak, replying:

I am not suffered to speak – expect what justice others will have.

4 Was the execution of Charles I an English Revolution?

To paraphrase the words of the historian Barry Coward, if there ever was an English Revolution, then it surely took place on 30 January 1649 with the execution of Charles I. Certainly the King's public trial and execution can be regarded as a revolutionary act. He was placed on trial in the name of his people and charged with treason because he had waged war against them. The crime of treason had always related to an action against the King – the embodiment of the State. It was now being interpreted as action by a King against the people, implicitly claiming that the people, not the King, represented the State. This change in ideas was followed up by publications such as John Milton's *Tenure of Kings and Magistrates* in 1649, which explicitly argued that power belonged originally to the people and was given to kings in a social and political contract in order to provide for government. By this contract the King was obliged to use his powers for the benefit and safety of the people, and if he abused them, the people (or their representatives) had the right to remove him. Although Charles refused to plead and challenged the legality of the proceedings, the fact that he was executed and that it was justified in these terms amounts to a political revolution and the destruction of divine right monarchy.

1 What does the artist of the below image imply about the attitude of contemporary observers to these events?
2 How reliable is this as historical evidence?

▲ The execution of Charles I.

At the same time, however, it is clear that the action was taken by an armed minority, against the wishes of the majority both inside and outside Parliament, and then only as a matter of necessity. The army and its allies were forced to act in defence of the liberties for which they had been fighting, because the parliamentary majority was about to restore an untrustworthy king to a position from which he could destroy them. Even if Charles made promises to protect and respect their rights (and there was no reason to think that he would), he could not be trusted to keep them. In fact, experience suggested that, once restored to power, he would ignore his promises and pursue with vindictive energy those who had defied him. If he could not, therefore, be restored to power, he would have to be killed; alive, he would always be a threat. His beliefs would never permit him to abdicate (resign the throne) and if he did not, there was no possibility of a peaceful replacement. His sons would not be willing to take his place and there were no other viable candidates. If removed from the throne and left alive, Charles would simply try to raise a new army to regain his throne. Those who could not accept Charles as king had little choice but to destroy him. What remains revolutionary, however, was that they chose to do so by public trial and to try him as King. Unlike the medieval depositions in which a king was forced to abdicate and then quietly murdered, leaving the kingly office undiminished, the army leaders and the Rump of Parliament acted publicly in the name of the People and bolstered by their belief in a providential God.

The English Revolution therefore displays a number of contradictions. It was carried out, reluctantly and out of necessity, by a minority whose conscious choice was to act in public. In the name of a Parliament that they had purged by force, they created a political revolution that was largely motivated by religion. The charge against Charles was presented in the name of the people, but those who presented it also saw themselves as the instruments of God's will. The men who made the revolution were members of the social and political elite, while the radical revolutionaries who had called for popular rights and freedoms were left in impotent isolation. Above all, it was unintended. It occurred only because circumstances made it necessary, which explains not only the inherent contradictions of 1649, but also the divisions and uncertainties that emerged thereafter and suggest why it was unlikely to prove permanent and lasting.

The execution of Charles I

As with earlier chapters, you should have completed notes on the material covered in this chapter. The conclusion sections in Chapters 1 to 4 have suggested ways of defining causal factors as the basis of writing essays about causation and a conditional/contingent approach to considering the part that they play in the causation process.

Example

It would be quite possible to use these ideas about causation and a conditional/contingent approach to explain the execution of Charles I. For example, the following argument could be made:

> The personality of Charles I, his belief in divine right kingship, his devotion to the Anglican Church and his past betrayals of those whom he regarded as rebels created conditions in which settlement would be difficult if not impossible. These conditions worsened with the quarrel of army and Parliament, which encouraged Charles to believe that he could

manipulate his enemies, and the emergence of radical groups who appeared to be a threat to the Church in Scotland as well as England. The result was that Charles was able to initiate a second civil war, which combined with the providential beliefs of the army and its leaders, to convince them that the King must be brought to justice for his betrayal of man and God. What dictated the timing of the process was the attempt by conservatives to renew negotiations with Charles in December 1648, which triggered the army into purging Parliament and enforcing the trial and execution of the King.

These factors and the interactions between them are summarised in Figure 4. In this case, however, the conditional factors that created a situation in which the execution was possible, and eventually probable, may be considered less important than the contingent action of MPs in preparing to restore Charles to power without adequate security for the future. In those circumstances the army leaders felt forced to take action to protect their cause and the action they took was enabled by their beliefs. To explain their *actions* you need to assess their *intentions*, which were, in turn, shaped by their *beliefs* about what God willed and the safety of the people necessitated.

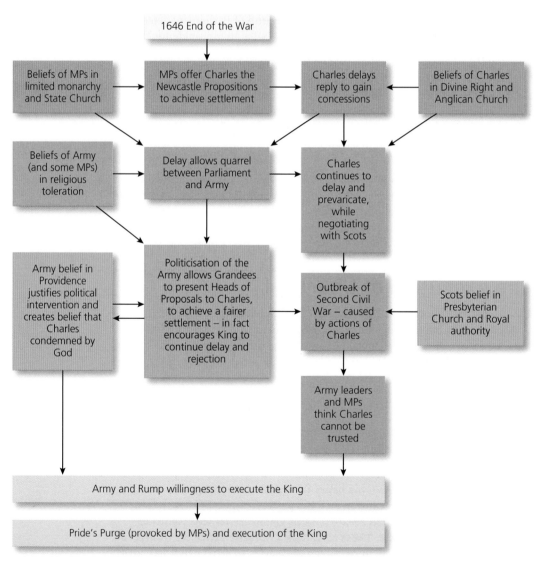

▲ **Figure 4** The execution of Charles I: actions, intentions and beliefs.

Chapter summary

- When the First Civil War ended in 1646, the intentions of Parliament and its supporters were to use their victory to negotiate a peace settlement that would ensure both the stability of government and society and the protection of essential rights and liberties by limiting the powers of the Crown.
- Although more radical ideas had existed in small, isolated pockets for some time, their significance was largely unrecognised at this point.
- The source of radical ideas was religion, which had developed from the essential Protestant belief in individual faith, prayer and study of the Bible as the Word of God.
- The first stage of their development was shaped by Puritan thinkers who were free to stimulate religious enthusiasm, but lacked the authority in Church and state to control the outcomes. The second was the experience of war, in which all forms of traditional authority were weakened and the direct intervention of God's Providence was seen in the outcome of events.
- While most radicals remained focused on religious issues, a persuasive minority began to debate the political and social implications of spiritual equality and develop more radical political ideas. Most significantly these related to individual rights and freedoms and the nature of political authority as a contract between the ruler and the ruled.
- Despite these developments, the main priority for most people, including MPs and the leaders of the army, was peace and settlement. Had negotiations succeeded in 1646–47 as expected, radical ideas would have been quickly contained. In that context, the crucial factor in bringing about a different outcome was the character and beliefs of Charles I. It was Charles who prevented the achievement of a settlement.
- As a result the inherent divisions among the supporters of Parliament rose to the surface, and the fears created by a radical minority provoked the conservatives to attempt their suppression. In the process they alienated the army and its leaders, resulting in its politicisation.
- For Charles this was an opportunity to rally support from both English and Scottish conservatives and renew the war to regain his power. Militarily this was easily defeated, but the political consequences were significant.
- For the army, the radicals and those who shared their providential beliefs, Charles had not only waged a deliberate war on his people, he had also rejected God's verdict on the struggle. He was a man of blood who had forfeited all claims to divine approval, and he could never be trusted. Faced with the determination of conservative parliamentarians to restore his powers and sacrifice all that had been fought for, they felt compelled to act.
- The result was a reluctant revolution, the only alternative left.

Working on interpretation skills

Historians have regarded the events of 1648–49 in a number of different ways. For those who wrote after the return of the monarchy in 1660, it was a seizure of power by a tyrannical minority, the culmination of a Great Rebellion. This view, labelled Tory in the political battles of the late seventeenth and eighteenth centuries, was challenged by the Whig idea of a Puritan Revolution. This was given substance by the more scientific research and writing of the late nineteenth and twentieth centuries, and further developed by 'Marxist' historians who found economic and social motives within the demands for political and religious liberty.

Further research in the last 50 years then challenged some of these assumptions, arguing that the trial and execution of the King was unplanned and forced upon the army leaders and their allies in Parliament by two factors. The first was the absolute refusal by Charles I to compromise on essentials, along with behaviour that demonstrated his willingness to go back on any promises that he did make. The second was that they were faced by a parliamentary majority who appeared willing to sacrifice what they had all been fighting for. In that context the army and its allies undeniably did seize power – but the more important question in terms of the social and political development of England and Britain, is why? Was it a determination to create a different system of government and establish new freedoms, especially in religion? Or was it an unintended outcome created by simple necessity? Could it be both?

ACTIVITY

In earlier chapters of the book you were given the opportunity to develop skills in answering Interpretations questions. It is probably a good idea to re-read the advice given earlier in the book at the end of Chapters 2 and 4 before you answer the following question. The questions you will face in the exam will be in the same format, but will cover a period of at least twenty years in their scope. Answering questions, such as the following question, however, will enable you to develop the skills you need to answer interpretations questions in your exam.

Using your understanding of the historical context, assess how convincing the arguments in these three extracts are in relation to whether the execution of Charles I and the abolition of the monarchy in 1649 constituted an English Revolution.

The extracts are on page 131 and guidance on how to answer this question is on page 132.

Extract A

The English Revolution – the purge of parliament in December 1648 and the trial and execution of the King in January 1649 – was carried out by a tiny clique against the wishes of the vast majority in the country. By October 1648 this clique included Ireton among the 'grandees' (though not yet Cromwell, who was in the north), rank and file supporters of the agitators in the army, civilian republicans like Henry Marten and Edmund Ludlow in parliament, and their militant supporters in the counties ... The fact that these events were carried out by a minority drawn largely from outside the traditional ruling elite in England, and against the wishes of that elite, goes a long way towards explaining the eventual failure of the new English Republic. The history of the Republic confirms that only a limited revolution had taken place in 1648–49, and one that was reversed in 1660. The basic structure of society remained unaffected. Yet it is surely semantic quibbling to deny the unique revolutionary nature of the abolition of episcopacy [bishops], monarchy and the House of Lords, the involvement in politics of masses of people from outside the normal political sphere, and the ventilation of radical ideas.

From *The Stuart Age: England 1603–1714* by Barry Coward, (Longman), 1980, pp.200–01.

Extract B

Why did England ever become a republic at all? ... The army bore a large responsibility for it. Dr Kishlansky has argued that the New Model was not a radical body in origin, but first became politicized in 1647, and it was not until late 1648 that its officers agreed in pressing for capital charges against the King. Among the minority of Englishmen who concurred with them, many did so, not because they rejected monarchy as such, but because they felt that Charles himself had left them nowhere else to go.

Charles took a huge gamble at the end of 1647, and he lost. Since July the Army commanders had been offering him, in the Heads of the Proposals, terms as honourable as he could reasonably expect, and his shrewdest advisers urged him to accept them. Instead he went on trying to play off the army against the parliament, and then jilted both in favour of new proposals from Scotland. The result was to be the Second Civil War ... [This] deepened the political divisions in parliament, and it made the army's politics much more radical ... When parliament voted on 24 May to resume negotiations with Charles if he accepted certain demands in advance ... the army felt that the causes for which it had risked life and limb were being bartered away, especially the cause of liberty of conscience ... On 5 December both Houses voted that the King's answers to the proposed terms were 'a ground to proceed upon' for settling the kingdom. The next day MPs found the parliament-house beset by troops under Colonel Pride ...

From *England without a King* by A. Woolrych, (Methuen), 1983, pp.1–8.

Extract C

Of the 150 or so men listed as Commissioners in the act instituting the High Court of justice to try the King, at least 60 never sat at all. Hesilrige and Lilburne were both conveniently absent in the north of England, and Vane refused to take part, though he remained an active member of the government (which cost him his life after the restoration). In the end 59 men signed the warrant for the King's execution, and another ten, having been present and assenting when sentence was given, may also be counted as regicides. Much has been written about the illegality of the trial and how little it accorded with the popular will. But the great impact which the regicide made on contemporaries, both at home and abroad, was precisely because it did take the form of a public trial and execution. A summary court martial, followed by the shooting of the King, would indeed have been no more unjust, but would have had far less effect. In Thomas Carlyle's words, 'I reckon it perhaps the most daring action any Body of Men to be met with in History ever, with clear consciousness, deliberately set themselves to do'

From *Rebellion or Revolution?* By G.E. Aylmer, (OUP), 1986, pp.98–99.

Possible answer

First, make sure that you have the focus of the question clear – in this case, the nature and significance of the regicide in 1649.

Then you can investigate the three extracts to see how convincing they are.

You need to analyse each of the three extracts in turn. A suggestion is to divide a large page into nine blocks.

Extract's main arguments	Knowledge to corroborate	Knowledge to contradict or modify
A		
B		
C		

- In the first column list the main arguments each uses.
- In the second column list what you know that can corroborate the arguments.
- In the third column list what might contradict or modify the arguments. ('Modify' – you might find that you partly agree, but with reservations.)
- You may find, of course, that some of your knowledge is relevant more than once.

Planning your answer – one approach

Decide how you could best set out a detailed plan for your answer. For example, you could do the following:

- Briefly refer to the focus of the question.
- For each extract in turn set out the arguments, corroborating and contradictory evidence.
- Do this by treating each argument (or group of arguments) in turn.

- Make comparisons between the extracts if this is helpful. The mark scheme does not explicitly give credit for doing this, but a successful comparison may well show the extent of your understanding in your judgement of each extract.
- An overall judgement is not required, but it may be helpful to make a brief summary, or just reinforce what has been said already by emphasising which extract was the most convincing. In some cases your contextual awareness may also allow you to combine the arguments put forward in the Extracts to create a conclusion that encompasses all three.
- Look back to the mark scheme on page 45 to remind yourself of what you need to do to achieve each level.

Remember that in the examination you are allowed an hour for this question. It is the planning stage that is vital in order to write a good answer. You should allow sufficient time to read the extracts and plan an answer. If you start writing too soon, it is likely that you waste time trying to summarise the *content* of each extract. Do this in your planning stage – and then think how you will *use* the content to answer the question by identifying the arguments in each extract and evaluating how convincing they are.

Then the actual writing!

- Think how you can write an answer, dealing with each extract in turn, but making cross-references or comparisons, if this is helpful, to reinforce a point.
- Make sure your answer:
  - shows a very good understanding of the extracts
  - uses knowledge to argue in support or to disagree
  - provides a clear argument which leads to a conclusion about each extract, and which may reach a conclusion about the extracts as a whole.

Working on essay technique: evaluating relative significance

The summary conclusion and diagram provided on page 128 offers an explanation of why Charles I was executed, based on the actions and interactions of different factors and individuals. However, the best judgements will also offer an evaluation of their relative importance within the process of causation. In order to assess relative significance you must first construct your essay plan as you normally would, by considering the nature, role and interaction of your causal factors, because the significance of any factor depends on the role it plays within the wider causal process and in conjunction with others. To make the judgement there are a number of criteria that you can look at, by asking yourself the following questions:

- Is any factor present in many of the situations that build up over the period under consideration?
- Does any factor lead on to, or introduce, other factors, thereby influencing the situation in a wide-ranging way?
- Is there any factor of which you can say that, if it had not happened, the end result/event being explained would not have happened either? This is called 'counter-factual evaluation' and you have to *demonstrate that it would have changed the outcome, not just speculate that it might.*

It is also possible to evaluate relative significance by focusing on a *combination of factors* rather than just one. One way of doing this is to look for a minimum number of factors that are *necessary* to provide a *sufficient* explanation for the event that you are explaining.

As you work through the second part of this book there will be opportunities to utilise a number of these ideas. The best one to use will often depend on the question that is asked, but be aware of two things:

1 A final judgement based on evaluation is often a mark of a good essay, but it must be drawn from the preceding arguments, not simply tacked on the end.
2 Some questions will lead towards a particular approach, such as argument and counter-argument, when a question stipulates a particular factor as 'main' or influential, or when it asks 'how far' or 'to what extent'. Others are more open questions, but you can still use these techniques to ensure that you offer sustained analysis and an overall judgement based on evaluation. Simply set out your factors as two competing arguments in your introduction and show how they address the question, then develop and evaluate both of them as the main body of your essay, before using them to construct a concluding judgement that answers the question.

ACTIVITY

Using the summary conclusion and diagram set out on page 128, compile a list of factors that explain the execution of Charles I. When you have done this, consider the factors that you have defined, and use them to plan responses to the practice question below. Begin, as always, by writing a conclusion that answers the question and use that to set up your arguments and the introduction. Ensure that your conclusion addresses the relative significance of the factors involved as well as the links and interaction between them. Then use your plan to write the essay.

'Despite a history of conflict with parliaments stretching back to 1625, the main factor in the execution of Charles I was the politicisation of the army.' Assess the validity of this view.

Key questions: Britain, 1603–49

The specification on Stuart Britain states that it requires the study in breadth of issues of change, continuity, cause and consequence in the period through six key questions. These have been either featured or mentioned at various points in the chapters you have studied. The various chapters that you study represent stages of development within the overall evolution of government and society in Stuart Britain, and the key questions offer themes that you can use to link the stages and assess the extent and causes of change. It is therefore very useful to pause to consider developments across the whole time period you have studied so far, before extending your perspective to the second half of the period.

The six key questions include three that are focused mainly on change and development and three that look primarily at cause and effect. These different concepts need to be analysed and assessed using different techniques, although for both of them you will need to make judgements about the significance of particular events. It is therefore useful to deal separately with the two conceptual areas and approach the questions as two sets of overlapping issues.

Change, continuity and development

The development of monarchy and government in Stuart Britain can be explained using the three key questions below:

Key Question 1: How far did the monarchy change?

Key Question 2: To what extent and why was power more widely shared during this period?

Key Question 3: How effective was opposition?

Because these questions are designed to explore change and development over the period as a whole, they need to be adapted to consider the first part of the period. For example, in 1649 the monarchy had not merely changed – it had been abolished! However, it returned in 1660 and one of the influences on its development thereafter was the lessons learned as a result of that experience.

It is also clear that the questions overlap – the effectiveness of opposition and the distribution of power played a significant part in changing the monarchy, and were affected in turn by the changes that took place. At this point, therefore, the best way to explore the issues relating to changes and development in 1603–49 is to combine the questions by asking:

'How was power exercised, and by whom, at different points in time?'

Doing so will enable you to identify changes, continuities and the resulting development of monarchy and government in early Stuart Britain.

How was power exercised, and by whom, at different points in time?

How far did the monarchy change?

To what extent and why was power more widely shared during this period?

How effective was opposition? (Did this change across the period?)

In Chapter 1 you considered the structure of government and the ways in which it was made to work by the monarch, with the help of the Church and the political nation (see page 7). To identify changes and continuities in this area you need to look at this structure at different points across the period and draw comparisons, not only in the formal machinery that existed, but also in the practices used to make it work and the responses they produced.

Questions to consider

1 Theory and practice

In theory the power of the monarch was restrained only by law and he was accountable only to God, but in practice he needed adequate finance and a measure of co-operation to make government work.

a) Did the nature of the political nation change between 1603 and 1640?

b) What evidence is there of continuity?

c) What was the overall effect on monarchy and government?

2 The machinery of government

a) Did the ability of the monarch to provide the finance and resources needed to maintain the machinery of government, change over the period?

b) What extra demands made this more difficult at certain times, and could they have been avoided?

c) Did this enable opposition to become more effective, and if so, how?

d) How important were the changes brought about by the Long Parliament in 1640–42?

3 Acceptance of the monarch's rights by the political nation and the Church

a) In what ways did attitudes and values change between 1603 and 1640?

b) How far was the Church able to fulfil its social and political functions?

c) How did this affect the exercise of power by the monarch and the relationship between the monarch and the political nation?

4 Ruling three different kingdoms

a) How significant were the demands generated by ruling three diverse kingdoms, and how did they affect the monarchy in England?

5 The Civil War

a) In what ways did the experience of war affect attitudes and beliefs?

b) How far was the collapse of the monarchy the result of the war?

c) How far do the circumstances in which the monarchy was abolished reflect the significance of particular events as opposed to the changes and developments that had built up over the whole period that you have studied?

WORKING TOGETHER

When you have considered and responded to the questions above you can return to your three key questions and draw some conclusions to discuss with others. By comparing your judgements you can amend and develop them. However, the nature of the period that you have studied may require you to do this in two parts:

● Between 1603 and 1642 when monarchy and government in Britain developed under relatively normal conditions, even if they were difficult and demanding at times.

● And between 1642 and 1649 when civil war and the victory of Parliament dramatically changed the situation.

You should therefore discuss and analyse the developments of the period using four questions:

1 In what ways did the monarchy change in the years 1603–42?

2 Did the means of opposition become more effective in this period?

3 Did the exercise of power become shared more widely over this period?

4 In what ways did the experience of civil war and the victory of Parliament affect the nature of the monarchy and the distribution of power in the years 1642–49?

Cause, effect and significance

The remaining key questions are focused on causation, specifically the causes of change:

Key Question 4: Why, and with what results, were there disputes over religion?

Key Question 5: How important were ideas and ideology?

Key Question 6: How important was the role of key individuals and groups, and how were they affected by developments?

Question 4 asks you to explain why a particular factor existed and to assess its effects, while Questions 5 and 6 ask you to focus on the impact of one factor among others by addressing its importance within the process of change. You have investigated and considered this process of cause and effect across all five chapters that you have worked on so far, although mostly in explaining particular events rather than changes across a period of time. To explain the causes of change you need to apply it across the period and consider a series of events and changes, as set out, for example, in the spiral of stages of development on page v. In addition to looking at causal factors within each stage of development, you need to take into account the outcome of that stage and its effects in causing the next one. In particular, if the outcome was a change in the structure and machinery of government, or in the attitudes and beliefs that shaped the way it worked in practice, then it could go a long way in explaining what came next. This chain of development is particularly significant in explaining how mistrust built up and tensions increased to the point of causing war and revolution.

Religious disputes: investigating a key factor

Questions to consider

1 Why were there anti-Catholic feelings in England, and why did they intensify after 1618?

   a) Consider the political impact of anti-Catholic fears derived from past experience in 1603 and the extent to which the Thirty Years War intensified them. However, in assessing the results you may need to consider the influence of other factors such as the rise of Arminianism and the personality of Charles I, which interacted with existing fears.

2 In what ways did Puritan ideas threaten the influence of the Church, and how did this affect monarchy and government?

   a) Consider the impact of the Puritan emphasis on individual faith and conscience on role and authority of the Church and monarch.

   b) How important were religious convictions in causing a civil war and preventing a settlement?

   c) What part did religious convictions play in making regicide possible in 1649?

Ideology and individuals: interaction and relative importance

Alongside religious disputes the key questions single out the importance of ideas and ideology and the role of particular individuals and groups in causing both particular events and more gradual changes. These are not the only factors that played a role in causing change, but it is suggested that, along with religious disputes, they were of particular importance. You should also be aware of some overlap between these factors – 'ideology' for example covers both religious beliefs and 'political' attitudes and assumptions, such as belief in the rule of law and belief that power was rightfully exercised only by a political and social elite.

One way to assess the role and importance of different factors is to pick out the main events and occasions that you perceive as causing change and analyse the part played by these factors in creating them. Do they appear frequently? Do they seem to have a particular impact? This enables you to judge each factor as 'important', but 'how important' requires more. It is not possible to quantify importance and judgements will vary – the benefit of attempting further analysis is that it leads you to explore the issues more extensively and by constructing an argument to support your judgement you will extend your understanding of the period.

In assessing the importance of one factor you have to look at the part played by others, and you may well find that, rather than a single factor having greatest importance, you are looking at particular combinations and interactions. This is particularly useful in considering change and development over time because they enable you to trace the process across a number of years. Among the specified factors in these questions, for example, how far do ideas relate to particular individuals and groups, such as Charles I or the opposition leaders? How far was it the combination of religion, fear of absolutism and Charles I as an individual that brought existing tensions to a point of crisis and war?

Questions to consider

1 What issues caused conflict between King and Parliament in the years 1603–29?

  a) How many of them involved an element of ideology, other than religion?

2 Is there any evidence that conflicts became more intense over the period, and if so, why?

  b) If you find links between the occasions of conflict to explain growing intensity – for example, the sequence of clashes between Charles and his parliaments in 1625–28 – this may well suggest that conflict in itself brought about change. However, if you find the presence of other factors as conflict intensified, such as the successes of the Catholic powers, or English failures, in the Thirty Years War, this would emphasise the importance of interaction between factors.

3 Did opposition to royal policies and decisions become more effective over the period 1603–42?

  a) To consider this you will need to compare different parliaments, with considerable gaps between them. Does it appear that opposition groups were learning from experience? Or could differences be attributed to different individuals and personalities?

4 How far were events in England affected by events elsewhere in Britain?

  a) Did the need to govern three kingdoms with different religious and political structures create conflict within England? If so, did the problems increase across the period 1603–42?

WORKING TOGETHER

When you have completed your investigation of the various causal factors and the way that they affected the development of monarchy and government in England in these years, work with a partner to apply your ideas to this central question:

Why was the monarchy abolished in 1649?

Some historians have explained the civil wars and regicide of the 1640s by arguing that underlying factors such as religion, ideology and financial weakness made some kind of crisis inevitable. Others have attributed them to particular events and individual mistakes, suggesting that the crisis was avoidable. As always, these conclusions are not 'facts' but judgements based on how much weight is given to particular factors and opinions about how they worked together. Most historians would agree that religious disputes, ideological attitudes and beliefs and the actions of individuals and groups all played an important part, but they differ in their view of exactly how important. This is partly because evidence always has to be interpreted and partly because it also has to be interrogated – and the questions asked, which arise from the particular interests of the historian and the purpose of the investigation, will influence the answers that are produced. This is the benefit of working with a partner (or as part of a group) because, having previously investigated the issues individually, you will bring different perceptions and questions to be considered. By working through them together and resolving your differences, you will be able to develop a more rounded and balanced judgement about this part of your course, which will also influence your understanding of why the monarchy returned and why there were further conflicts within its evolution.

Conclusion

You have now reviewed the first part of your study of Stuart Britain and considered the issues involved in explaining both change and continuity and the causes of change and development. However, the story of monarchy and government in Stuart Britain is by no means complete. The final event of this study, the trial and execution of a reigning monarch in the name of his people, can be considered a Revolution, marking a new and very different stage of development. Its ultimate significance, however, can only be judged in the context of Part 2 of your study, by looking at the different ways that it impacted on monarchy, government and society over a further forty years of development and beyond. Was the regicide of 1649 a revolution, or merely a step within the evolution of government and monarchy in Stuart Britain? By using the longer perspective offered in Part 2 to reassess the judgements that you have made here, you will able to decide which, or argue that it was both.

Oliver Cromwell,
F ENGLAND, SCOTLAND, FRAN
RRITORIES THEREUNTO F
Cha⁵ Turner, from the celebrated

6

Republic and restoration, 1649–60

Chapter 6 covers the years between the regicide of 1649 and the restoration of the monarchy in 1660. It focuses on the failed attempts to find a stable form of government, the reasons for their failure and the extent to which the experience of republican government affected later developments. These are addressed by considering a number of developments:

● the establishment of the Republic
● the Parliament of Saints
● the Protectorate and its problems, 1654–57
● 'King' Oliver – the role of Cromwell, the Humble Petition and Advice and the evolution of government
● death and defeat, 1658–60.

The material relates to a number of the key breadth issues addressed by this course of study, which are:

● to what extent and why was power more widely shared during this period
● how important was the role of key individuals and groups and how were they they affected by developments
● how important were ideas and ideology.

The chapter focuses on two questions, the first on causation and the second on change and development:

Why did republican government fail and lead to the restoration of monarchy in 1660?

In what ways did the legacy of republican government shape the development of monarchy and society from 1660 to 1702?

CHAPTER OVERVIEW

The chapter begins by considering the problems that faced the new regime after the regicide of 1649 and the steps taken to establish a new form of government, a republic known as the Commonwealth. It then considers why, in 1653–54, the Commonwealth collapsed and was replaced with a Protectorate backed by the army, with Oliver Cromwell as Lord Protector. After three years of government he was offered the Crown by a parliament in 1657. While this was in some ways a tribute to his success in providing stability, it was also an indication of the widespread belief that monarchy represented stable and legal government and of a desire to minimise military influence. When Cromwell refused the Crown he was reinstalled as Protector under a revised constitution, which bore more than a passing resemblance to traditional royal government. When he died in 1658, his son Richard lost the support of the army and was forced to resign as Lord Protector in 1659. The drift to anarchy that followed brought about the return of Charles Stuart – King by the invitation of a parliament, but without specific pre-conditions to address the problems that had led to 20 years of conflict.

1 The Interregnum, 1649–60

You have already met the term 'regicide' – the killing of a king – in Chapter 5, and the Latin root of the word, i.e. *rex, regis*, meaning king in Latin, also gives rise to the term 'interregnum' to describe this period when England had no king and was 'between reigns'. Although the Royalists did not accept the idea, and officially dated the reign of Charles II from 1649, they had no power to enforce this in legal terms. The two forms of government experienced within England were a Commonwealth – a term used to describe the people and nation as a whole – and a Protectorate in which the designated Protector took responsibility for the nation's well-being. Both of these were technically 'republican' forms of government, a term also taken from Latin to describe a government that managed public affairs without electing or accepting the need for a monarch.

The revolution and its enemies

What problems did the Commonwealth inherit from the circumstances in which it was created?

The execution of Charles I was greeted with shock and horror across Britain and in Europe, where hostile demonstrations culminated in the murder of English ambassadors in the Netherlands and Spain by Royalist agents. In Scotland, Charles II was immediately proclaimed King, while the Irish rebels were still in arms and claimed allegiance to the Stuarts. The most immediate threats, however, were closer to home. The groan that had echoed from the crowd as the axe fell symbolised the shock and outrage felt by many across the nation, but the first action came, ironically, from the republican radicals, the Levellers. At the time of Pride's Purge they had been sidetracked by Ireton into discussions of a new Agreement of the People, building up their expectations that any action against the King would be part of a wider settlement. In mid-December these negotiations failed and the Levellers were left isolated and angry while the army executed the King and placed the power to govern in the hands of around 70 MPs who supported these actions. Among this group, however, there were differences and divisions that mirrored the external threats to the regime and weakened it from within.

The legacy of regicide

The arrangements adopted to govern England in the aftermath of the King's execution in 1649 emphasise the fact that the regicide was hastily planned and carried out. Ireton had intended to dissolve Parliament and call new elections, but was persuaded that this would merely produce a Royalist majority, and so agreed to purge Parliament instead. Thus government devolved by default to the MPs who remained thereafter, who came to be nicknamed the Rump. When the few remaining Lords refused to co-operate with regicide, the Rump declared itself to be the sole legislative authority. After the King was executed, the same body elected a Council of State to take charge of government, while reserving legislative and supervisory powers to the Rump as a whole. Not until March 1649 were the monarchy and House of Lords abolished, and not until May was England declared a Commonwealth.

NOTE-MAKING

As you work through the chapter you will trace the introduction and development of the new forms of government and will be able to explore the reasons for their failure. You will need to make linear notes using the section headings to help you construct your own headings and sub-headings as you have already learned to do.

When you have completed your notes you should review the key features of each regime and the reasons for its removal, to consider whether each failure was unique, arising from the mistakes of those involved, or whether the pattern of failure indicates more deep-seated problems faced by them all. This will allow you to address the question of whether the restoration of monarchy was inevitable, thereby exploring the first of the questions set out on page 167. You should summarise your conclusions at the end of your notes. You will then be able to move on to address the second question as you work through the remaining chapters from 1660 to 1702.

1 The Commonwealth	
1649	
March	Monarchy and House of Lords abolished.
May	England declared to be a Commonwealth.
August	The Pacification of Ireland began.
1650	
June	Fairfax resigned as Lord General and was replaced by Cromwell.
August	Outbreak of the Third Civil War (between England and Scotland).
1651	
September	Charles II defeated at Worcester.
1653	
April	Cromwell dissolved the Rump and the Council of State; Army Council of State appointed.
July	Nominated Assembly met and declared itself a Parliament; dissolved itself in December.
2 The Protectorate	
1653	
December	Cromwell established as Lord Protector under the Instrument of Government; government by a Single Person, Council of State, and a single-chamber Parliament.
1654	
September	First protectorate Parliament met; MPs forced to sign a 'Recognition' of the Instrument – about 100 refused and were excluded.
1655	
January	First Protectorate Parliament dissolved.
August	Establishment of eleven military districts and governors – the Major-Generals.
1656	
September	Second Protectorate Parliament met.
1657	
January	Sindercombe Plot to assassinate Cromwell; ending of the Decimation Tax and the Major-Generals.
February	Remonstrance (Humble Petition and Advice) introduced in Parliament.
March	Humble Petition and Advice presented to Cromwell with the offer of the Crown.
April	Cromwell refused the Crown.
May	Cromwell accepted the revised Humble Petition and Advice, with a Lord Protector, Council and two-chamber Parliament; installed in June.
1658	
February	Second Protectorate Parliament dissolved.
September	Death of Cromwell: Richard Cromwell proclaimed Lord Protector.
1659	
January	Third Protectorate Parliament met.
April	Army Council began meeting again and forced Richard to dissolve Parliament.
May	Richard Cromwell resigns as Lord Protector; Rump Parliament recalled.
3 The Commonwealth	
1659	
October	The army dissolved the Rump and set up an Army Committee of Safety.
December	Rump restored after intervention by General Monck.
1660	
February	Monck recalled the MPs excluded in 1648, restoring the Long Parliament on condition that it dissolved itself and called new elections.
April	Convention Parliament assembled; voted for government by King, Lords and Commons.
May	Charles Stuart returned as Charles II.

The piecemeal process by which the new regime emerged, and the intense opposition faced in its early years, reveal certain key features which helped to shape the events of the next decade. The first is the lack of prior planning that lay behind the revolutionary act of establishing the Commonwealth. Pride's Purge had been provoked by the determination of conservative MPs to restore a king who would not admit defeat. The army had taken the necessary action to prevent this and to ensure that its interests, particularly the desire for religious toleration, were taken into account. There was little time or scope, however, to plan how to replace the institutions that were damaged or abolished, and the result was that supporters of the new regime often had very different visions of what that Commonwealth should be. While the Rump was concerned to ensure stability and calm conservative fears, the army and its radical supporters visualised a much greater social transformation to accompany the political changes.

This problem was increased by the fact that the regime could only command the support of a minority of the population. Within weeks of the execution it faced threats from enemies at home and abroad, and the first two years of its existence were primarily occupied by a struggle for survival. While this process kept the army from interfering directly in politics, it also demonstrated that the regime could not survive without military support. The regimes of the Interregnum therefore faced a circle of problems. In order to widen support and ensure stability, they had to gain the confidence of the political nation, whose participation in local government and social leadership in the counties made them essential allies. Until this occurred, an army was necessary for security, but it was expensive to maintain and radical in politics. It therefore offended public opinion on both counts and alienated potential supporters from the regime. While this problem was to grow in significance throughout the Interregnum, the events of 1649 quickly revealed that for the moment the new government had little choice.

The Leveller Challenge, 1649

Furious at being outmanoeuvred and denied influence at such a time, the Leveller leaders launched a bitter attack on Cromwell and Ireton, accusing them of ambition and deceit. More dangerously, they sought once more to use the army as a power base, encouraging the rank and file to petition against martial law now that the war was over. By March 1649 this had become an attempt to incite mutiny in the army and it was undoubtedly this that motivated Cromwell to act against them. At his instigation, the Rump ordered the arrest of the leaders and they were imprisoned in the Tower of London. In response, the Levellers sought to exploit discontent among the regiments over arrears of pay and the prospect of service in Ireland, by calling for the restoration of the Agitators and the General Council. Not only were their demands ignored by the army leaders, but in April the Baptist churches, hitherto their most reliable allies, publicly disassociated themselves from the movement as a result of the campaign.

In the same month, a minor mutiny over pay by troopers of Colonel Whalley's regiment in London led to the execution of one, Robert Lockyer, and a large demonstration at his funeral. May produced a brief mutiny at Salisbury among some of the men due for embarkation for Ireland and a more serious outbreak at Oxford led by William Thompson, who called on other regiments in the area to join him in rebellion. At the same time, the prisoners in the Tower were putting the finishing touches to a third Agreement of the People, reverting to its most radical elements now that there was no virtue in compromise with the Grandees. On 14 May, Cromwell and Fairfax caught up with the body of the

KEY DATES: THE FAILURE OF THE LEVELLERS

1648

14 December: Army/Leveller talks broke up.

1649

January–March: Pamphlets published attacking Cromwell and Ireton.

February: Leveller leaders arrested.

March: Leveller petitions drawn up in the Army.

April: Death and funeral of Robert Lockyer; Baptist churches reject Leveller aims.

May: Army mutinies and suppression of mutineers at Burford.

mutineers at Burford and, taking them by surprise during the night, captured over three hundred, leaving the rest to disperse without horses or weapons. It is a measure of the Grandees' victory that only three mutineers were shot in a token reprisal. By the time the new Agreement saw the light of day, the movement that had created it was broken.

The Leveller impact

As in 1647, the ease with which Leveller influence was curtailed revealed their limitations, although they retained the power to frighten many in authority. In October 1649, Lilburne was tried for treason, but acquitted amid popular celebration. He was exiled on the orders of the Rump and rearrested on his return despite his promises of good behaviour. From 1654 he was imprisoned, 'for the peace of the Commonwealth', in Jersey where he seems to have found some personal fulfilment through conversion to the Quaker faith. The harsh treatment that he undoubtedly received is a testament to his talent as well as his continued defiance, but the Leveller threat ceased to be significant by the end of 1649. The fact was that the Levellers had no real support or organisation outside London and always relied heavily on pamphlets and a literate readership to spread their ideas. The renewal of censorship by the Rump, while never completely successful, did much to curtail their impact, and the imprisonment of the leaders destroyed the developing party organisation. After 1649 there were demands for radical reforms from within the army and a radical threat to the existing hierarchy was posed by new religious groups such as the Ranters, Diggers and Quakers, but overt political radicalism had effectively ceased. Its legacy was to some degree taken up by the Quakers, with whom a number of leading radicals found a spiritual home.

Coll. John Lilborne.

Between 1638 and his death in 1657, ▶ John Lilburne endured several lengthy spells of imprisonment as a result of his determination to challenge injustice and his refusal to learn the art of compromise. Described as 'combative, indomitable and self-dramatising', he seems to have found peace in his last years as a Quaker. Lilburne left an enduring political legacy that inspired later democratic movements in the nineteenth and twentieth centuries.

The Royalist threat, 1649–51

While the Second Civil War of 1648 had effectively destroyed any military threat posed by the Royalists in England, the execution of the King and his courage in the act of martyrdom had done much to restore his reputation and the image of the monarchy. This was enhanced with the publication of *Eikon Basilike*, containing the martyr King's supposed last thoughts. His son, Prince Charles, had escaped to France, and already claimed that, in God's eyes, he had succeeded to the throne at the moment of his father's death. To make this a reality, however, he would need to build on the support that existed in the more outlying regions of the three kingdoms, in Ireland and Scotland, where the Royalist armies were still active and effective. For the Commonwealth the first task in consolidating its power was to extend that power across Britain.

The military campaign in Ireland, 1649

The Irish rebellion, which had continued since 1641, was not, in itself, a threat to stability in England. However, the news of Charles's execution had united Irish Anglicans and Catholics and enhanced the possibility of invasion by Charles II with foreign help. While the commander of Parliament's forces in Ireland, Michael Jones, had done much to contain the threat, there were Royalist garrisons in many major towns and abundant opportunities for foreign troops to land in the numerous ports along the Irish coast. The defeat of the Levellers allowed Cromwell to lead troops from the New Model Army to Ireland in July, under pressure to achieve a rapid pacification because of the gathering threat from Scotland. This may partly explain the brutality with which his army stormed Drogheda, to the north of Dublin, and slaughtered the garrison for its refusal to surrender. Inevitably, some civilians died in the process. This was followed by a similar attack on Wexford.

Cromwell's treatment of the garrisons at Drogheda and Wexford has become part of the political mythology of Anglo-Irish relations, used over three centuries by Royalists and Anglicans to discredit extreme Protestant views and by Irish nationalists to illustrate English brutality. With the advent of a more analytical and evidence-based approach to history in the twentieth century these claims have been challenged. While Cromwell's behaviour was undoubtedly and uncharacteristically harsh, it was well within the rules of war used at the time, in which a garrison that had refused to surrender was at the mercy of the victors if it was subsequently taken by storm. Civilian casualties may well have occurred in the heat of battle or because of the anti-Catholic attitudes of the rank and file, but recent research by Irish historians using local records has suggested that the later accounts of the massacre of civilians were exaggerated, if not invented. Numbers of civilian casualties were low and may be accounted for by those who had taken up arms in support of the garrison, along with a number of Catholic priests, attacked by English soldiers who blamed them for the rebellion and atrocities carried out by the Irish in 1641. While Cromwell's exultant report of the battles to the Speaker in parliament has been interpreted as implying both cruelty and prejudice, it has also been suggested that his tone arose from relief at dealing with a difficult and dangerous mission where many English armies had disintegrated, and that his greatest crime in Ireland was to be so effective.

The military campaign in Scotland

By the spring of 1650 Cromwell was able to return to Britain to counter the Scottish threat, leaving others to complete the pacification of Ireland, a process that involved the seizure of land and consequent famine for the population. In August, after Fairfax had resigned as Lord General, he was promoted and dispatched by the Rump to Scotland in order to counter the threat of invasion from the north. Although the Scottish Covenanters and nobility had divided over the Engagement with Charles I in 1648, they still possessed a formidable army under the leadership of David Leslie, which they now placed at the disposal of Charles II. Cromwell faced a difficult task, since Leslie had established a strong defensive barrier south of Edinburgh. Initially he hoped to rally support from the Presbyterians and come to an agreement through negotiation, but the leaders of the Kirk were deeply hostile to the Independents and Baptists with whom the army was associated and whom they regarded as responsible for the spread of radical ideas. After months of frustration the English army was trapped in Dunbar, deprived of supplies, weakened by disease and staring defeat in the face.

The reversal of this situation was therefore a major triumph for Cromwell. A combination of impatience on the part of the Scots and a daring (and desperate) counter-assault by Cromwell led to his stunning victory at Dunbar on 3 September 1650, evidence for him of God's approval and blessing of the new order. The Royalist threat, however, was not yet extinguished. Charles turned to the west of Scotland and raised new forces for an attack on England itself. By building up a new force and entering England from the north-west, there was every prospect of raising support as he marched south. It is a reflection of the war-weariness in the formerly Royalist areas through which he passed that his hopes proved unfounded. Cromwell moved to cut him off and with greatly superior numbers destroyed the Royalist army at Worcester on 3 September 1651, the anniversary of Dunbar. With this 'crowning mercy' as he described it in dispatches, he had secured the new regime for the foreseeable future.

The survival of Royalism

While Royalist armies could be dealt with, Royalist sentiment was another matter. If the political revolution of 1649 was to succeed in establishing a successful alternative to the Stuart monarchy, it would have to rely on more than military strength. The army could keep the regime in place, but it could not generate positive support. It was also a political liability. Eight years of war, high taxes and the dislocation of trade had been followed by bad harvests in 1649. The economy was in desperate straits, distress was widespread and the army cost money. In addition, the army was associated with radical groups and ideas that appeared to threaten stability at every level. While it was not impossible to win support, it would clearly take time and would require successful alternatives to be put in place, offering stability as well as reform. This combination, however, would prove difficult to find.

While the older 'Puritan' radicals such as the Baptists and Independents accepted the authority of the Bible as a restraint on individual freedom, a newer generation of radicals had refused to accept even that. The argument that God spoke to the individual spirit directly had been interpreted to suggest that the voice of God within the individual was the supreme authority in religion. The execution of a reigning monarch suggested that anything was possible and while millenarian groups confidently awaited Christ's return to rule in person, others argued that He had already returned in the human heart and mind to justify complete individual freedom. The expression of this freedom varied. The Ranters repudiated conventional morality, declaring that since God made all things, all that was natural was part of God and sin existed only in the mind. The Diggers claimed communal use of the land, since the earth was made by God for all humanity to share. Whatever its form, this spirit was a direct threat to the existing hierarchy and to all semblance of the social stability on which the political nation relied for its authority.

KEY DATES: THE REVOLUTION AND ITS ENEMIES, 1649–51

1649

May: Leveller mutineers defeated at Burford.

August: Cromwell in Ireland.

September–October: Drogheda and Wexford captured and defenders massacred, other towns quickly surrendered.

1650

May: Cromwell returned to England.

August: Cromwell sent north after resignation of Fairfax, to confront Scots and Charles II.

3 September: Scots defeated at Dunbar; Charles II raised a second army from the western highlands and invaded England.

1651

3 September: Battle of Worcester – Charles heavily defeated by Cromwell.

The failure of the Commonwealth

To what extent was the failure of the Commonwealth inevitable?

The piecemeal process by which the Commonwealth was established was accompanied by the gradual return of MPs who had stayed away during the King's trial, but felt able to conform to the new order. By the spring of 1649 the number of MPs reached about 150, and the successes of the army and the gradual defeat of Royalist hopes encouraged more to make peace with the new regime. This also had the effect of increasing the more cautious and conservative elements of the Rump, at the expense of radical influence. This was probably less important, however, than the fact that little thought had been given to the nature of the government that should emerge from the revolution. The army had acted in defence of its interests against a conservative attempt to restore the powers of the monarchy and a coercive national Church. It was clear, therefore, that some kind of religious toleration would have to be established and that there was an expectation of 'godly reformation' in government and society – but beyond this, little was defined.

Conflicting visions, 1649–52

The MPs who were expected to carry out this godly reformation found themselves beset by conflicting pressures. On the one hand the army, the radicals and other idealists demanded wholesale reform. The Council of Officers favoured reform and refurbishment of the Church alongside a significant measure of religious freedom, simplification of the laws and greater social justice, such as an end to imprisonment for debt. The Baptist churches favoured the end of a national Church and the reliance of all ministers on voluntary contributions. The Independents favoured the retention of a reformed national Church with the payment of ministers by some means other than tithes. The more radical sects demanded complete religious freedom. Individual reformers like the scientist, Samuel Hartlib, and the Independent minister, Hugh Peter, proposed schemes for reform in education and medicine, the provision of work for the poor and guaranteed agricultural prices. Against a background of economic distress, these measures were appealing but were financially impossible.

On the other hand, most MPs were well aware of the need for control and the restoration of authority if confidence was to be restored across the political nation, especially among the governing elite in the localities. Complaints of social unrest, the behaviour of radicals and the breakdown of parish administration led to county petitions demanding the restoration of order and the established Church. In addition, there were real obstacles in the way of reform. Law reform, for example, was a difficult and complex subject, which required careful consideration if the cure was not to be worse than the disease. The Rump was responsible for both the planning and debating of necessary legislation, and also the daily maintenance of government – a huge workload that parliaments had never previously undertaken. To add to the burdens, the army leaders also wanted to see progress made in constitutional reforms, to lay the foundations for a permanent new structure.

The growth of hostility

There is, therefore, something to be said on behalf of the MPs who took on these burdens in the aftermath of the King's execution. Their task was undeniably difficult and complex. Nevertheless, a summary of the measures that they took reveals the conservative and authoritarian character of the regime and explains its general unpopularity as well as the growing dissatisfaction of the army. Although the statutes compelling attendance at

> **Blasphemy and adultery**
>
> *Blasphemy* means an insult to God, while *adultery* was interpreted as sexual immorality. Both laws were used to prosecute those whose behaviour offended the moral conventions of the time. Religious enthusiasm could lead to eccentric attitudes and a tendency to equate nakedness with purity led to actions and gestures that less enthusiastic souls found plainly shocking. Some early Quakers, for example, paraded naked through village streets carrying braziers of hot coals to symbolise the fires of hell. These laws allowed such actions to be punished without regard for the intentions and motives that lay behind them.

church were repealed, providing a measure of religious freedom, the Blasphemy and Adultery Acts of 1650 increased repression and launched an attack on the more radical sects. Measures were taken to improve the supply of good preaching ministers, especially in Wales, which was regarded as a 'dark corner' of the land, but no steps were taken to replace tithes or find a less oppressive means of supporting the ministry.

Measures of economic regulation, especially the Navigation Acts, were passed to encourage the development of trade. A successful war against the Dutch helped to build up the navy and encouraged expansion of overseas trade. In the long run these measures laid the foundations of economic growth, but at the time they seemed merely to be furthering the interests of the merchants who were establishing an ever-growing influence in Parliament. This appearance of self-interest increased with time. The Hales Commission was established to consider law reform in 1651, under pressure from the army after Worcester, but its report was set aside in February 1653. Whether or not the numerous lawyers in Parliament engineered this inaction, it suited their interests.

The dissolution of the Rump, 1653

Progress with electoral reform and new constitutional measures was also remarkably slow, nudged on only by the frequent prompting of the army and Cromwell. After Dunbar, Sir Henry Vane suggested a plan for 'recruiting' new members, which would protect the seats of existing MPs and simply add new members for those which were vacant. After Worcester the House focused on arrangements to include members for Scotland and Ireland, and on the war with the Dutch, which was not entirely popular among the more consciously 'Protestant' members, such as Cromwell himself. As the prospects of reform dwindled, so the irritation of the army rose. The Rump's attitude indicated a willingness to cling to power, and the growing hostility with which MPs reacted to army pressure suggested that its views would have less and less influence. By the end of 1652 the Council of Officers was pressing General Cromwell to take action.

What finally goaded Cromwell into action is not entirely clear. On 20 April 1653 he entered the House of Commons with a military escort, delivered a tirade of criticism at the astonished members and ordered them to leave. He later justified his action by claiming that they were planning to maintain themselves in power indefinitely, but there is evidence that they were at last preparing a bill for dissolution. It has been suggested that they were reviving Vane's idea for 'recruiting', but this seems unlikely. The best explanation seems to lie in a combination of the Rump's growing hostility to the army and the character of Cromwell.

The role of Cromwell

Throughout 1652 Cromwell had tried to restrain the more radical sections of the army and maintain unity with the Rump to protect the common cause, but by early 1653 this had become increasingly difficult. As so often, however, Cromwell was reluctant to act until he was sure of God's will – he sought guidance from providence. Just as, in December 1648, he had hesitated until Pride's Purge provided the sign that God wished the King to be removed, he now waited for some providential event to show him the way forward. The

▲ 'The Dissolution of the Rump'. This contemporary engraving illustrates the general approval with which the dissolution of the Rump was greeted. The owl wearing glasses is intended to represent the blinkered and short-sighted stupidity of its members. Cromwell was probably speaking the truth when he later claimed that 'not a dog barked' at its removal.

sign seems to have come in April, when the Rump finally considered a bill for its own dissolution. Cromwell knew that new elections on the existing franchise would produce a large number of conservative MPs. He therefore wanted some measures for electoral reform to be built in and a Council of State that included both MPs and army officers to be appointed to govern in the interval and to supervise new elections. In April, however, he discovered that MPs planned to rush ahead with a bill that made no changes to the system and to appoint a committee of Rumpers to supervise elections and vet new MPs. There could be no clearer indication that the army would be allowed no part in proceedings and that the new Parliament would be even more hostile to reform than this one.

This explains the haste and anger with which he acted in April 1653. Having been forced to act, Cromwell was faced with the problem of finding a replacement that would serve the cause of reform and find some justification for its own power. As the Lord General, he was virtually the only senior official who could make any claim to legal power, and even that was doubtful. As the head of the army, God's chosen instrument, he no doubt felt morally justified in making such decisions, but the problem was to find an adequate alternative to the Rump. Not surprisingly, he turned to his officers for advice and found two possibilities. Colonel John Lambert suggested a small executive council, an army Council of State, which would take over the King's functions alongside new parliaments. From the Fifth Monarchist Colonel Thomas Harrison came the suggestion of an Assembly of Saints, called to plan a government fit to welcome the returning Christ! Cromwell chose the latter, although in a rather more practical form.

Millenarianism – The belief that the Second Coming of Christ was imminent. The Book of Revelation at the end of the New Testament foretold Christ's second coming, and many radicals believed that the English civil war was sent to prepare the nation for this event.

Fifth Monarchists: millenarianism in action

The Fifth Monarchists believed in an extreme form of the more widespread **millenarian** idea that the world was dominated by a great struggle between God and the devil, the forces of good and evil. It would end with the final triumph of good and the return of Christ to rule on earth in person for a thousand years – the millenium. Many of these ideas were based on the biblical Book of Revelations, a mystical and often obscure description of visions and dreams, and there was considerable variation in the way they were interpreted. Some argued that there were four great earthly monarchies, which would be followed by the fifth monarchy, the rule of Christ. The fourth monarchy was brought to an end with the execution of Charles I and Christ's return was therefore imminent. The Fifth Monarchists argued that it was the duty of the 'saints' to tear down earthly government and prepare the way for Christ's return. Others took a less extreme view, arguing that God would act in His own way, while some even argued that the Kingdom of Christ would only ever exist in human hearts and minds.

The Godly Experiment, 1653

The key to understanding the contradictions of the Interregnum is to understand the contradictions of the man who now dominated it, Oliver Cromwell. The profile of Cromwell on page 150 analyses the events that shaped his character, and it is the complexity of this character that has fascinated biographers and led to conflicting interpretations and judgements. On the one hand, Cromwell was a conservative member of the gentry, concerned with maintaining social order, upholding the existing social hierarchy and protecting the interests of his class. He was never an original thinker in terms of political organisation and relied on associates to provide the theoretical understanding behind the constitutional changes that he endorsed. In his own words, he was not 'wedded and glued' to particular forms of government, but was willing to consider any practical alternatives.

This explains why Cromwell was so hated by men like Lilburne and by the republicans who supported the Rump. He listened to their plans, sometimes tried them out, and was able to abandon them when they proved unworkable, leaving their authors feeling they had been used and betrayed. His own preference was for a 'government with something of the monarchical in it'. Like most gentlemen of his time, Cromwell believed that England was a 'mixed' monarchy, in which king, lords and commons all had some powers within the rule of law, and were able to act as a check on one another against any abuse of power. This preference had been strengthened by the problems arising from government by a single authority, such as the Rump, and would reappear in the establishment of the Protectorate at the end of 1653.

In the spring of 1653, however, the other side of Cromwell's character came to the fore. If his political thinking was conventional, his religious convictions were those of a radical. It is difficult to define his views in relation to the various sects of the time, but he was probably closest to the Independents, who supported the idea of a national Church with limited toleration for voluntary groups whose views were neither too outrageous nor dangerous to others. This

Cromwell's military advisers

Until 1651 Cromwell's closest associate and political adviser had been his son-in-law, Henry Ireton. The gap left by Ireton's death in that year was increasingly filled by the able Yorkshireman, John Lambert, whose family held substantial estates in the Craven area. Lambert was a republican by political conviction, influenced by the example of ancient Greece and Rome rather than religious views, and he was one of the few leading officers in the New Model who did not have strong Puritan convictions.

broadly describes the kind of Church that he sought to create as Lord Protector. What is clear is that he was deeply committed to the work of godly reformation and to the right of the godly to search for truth without unnecessary restraints. His whole career demonstrates his belief in providence and his desire to serve God and to act to further God's will. His notorious periods of hesitation arose from his desire to interpret the signs and understand God's will before acting. Once convinced, he acted with energy and determination. He did not share the extreme millenarian convictions of a man like Harrison and had no intention of allowing the 'Saints' to tear down government. However, he was prepared to consider the possibility that the civil wars and execution of the King might indicate that the struggle for godly reformation was approaching its climax. In such circumstances, an assembly drawn from the godly part of the nation might be able to contribute to the work. The result was the calling, in July 1653, of the Parliament of Saints.

The Parliament of Saints

The army council had requested advice from local dignitaries before selecting those who were to attend, and, as historian Derek Hirst has pointed out, over one-third of the members were men of sufficient status to have been elected to any Parliament and over two-thirds had been JPs for more than three years. Many were moderate and cautious reformers rather than fiery enthusiasts. However, they were often from the minor gentry rather than the greater families, some had links with the more flamboyant radical groups and about a dozen out of the total of 144 were Fifth Monarchists, determined to destroy man-made government and the national Church in order to usher in the rule of saints and the return of King Jesus.

These conflicting influences soon became apparent. To Cromwell's irritation, the Assembly began by declaring itself to be a Parliament, with all parliamentary privileges. This did not promise well for an assembly whose task was to create a new constitution. Nevertheless, the members soon warmed to their task and in the five months of its existence, they passed over 30 acts, many of them eminently sensible and moderate. A new Council of State was established, with a good mix of members to represent both moderate and enthusiastic opinion. The work of the Hale Commission on law reform was taken up, producing some reform of the laws on debt, a civil marriage act and a plan to abolish the notoriously slow and expensive Court of Chancery. Progress was made in uniting Scotland and Ireland with England and Wales and in modifying lay control of Church livings. Here, however, the assembly began to tread on dangerous ground, since an attack on advowsons and tithes (see Chapter 2, page 21) was seen by many as an attack on property itself. This strengthened the unease of the moderate members, who were concerned by the growing clamour of the Fifth Monarchists for the introduction of biblical laws and by the changes that were taking place in local government. The summer of 1653 saw a series of purges in the commissions of the peace (JPs) that removed members of the gentry and replaced them with yeomen and shopkeepers. When the radicals succeeded on 10 December in pushing through a vote against tithes, the moderates decided to act before social order was seriously undermined. On 12 December they met early in the absence of the radicals and voted to dissolve themselves, handing power back to Cromwell.

Source A From Cromwell's speech at the opening of the Parliament of Saints.

I confess I never looked to see such a day as this ... when Christ should be so owned as He is, at this day, and in this work ... I say you are called with a high call. And why should we be afraid to say or think, that this may be the day to usher in the things that God has promised ... Indeed I do think something is at the door; we are at the threshold.

Oliver Cromwell (1599–1658)

Cromwell was born in Huntingdon, Cambridgeshire. The grandson of a baronet, he was of the minor gentry, brought up in a generally Puritan environment. After attending Sidney Sussex college in Cambridge he returned to Huntingdon on the death of his father and, after quarrelling with the town corporation, was forced to move to nearby St Ives and work as a yeoman farmer. This may have been the period that he later described as God 'bringing him low' to teach him humility on the road to salvation. Whatever the reason, Cromwell seems to have come close to a nervous breakdown at this point, from which he emerged with the unshakeable belief that he had been restored to health in order to serve God. The visible sign of his recovery was that he inherited from an uncle the position of Steward to the Cathedral of Ely. He moved to the town and lived in moderate comfort there until, in 1640, he became MP for Cambridge. This was a relatively prestigious position for a member of the minor gentry, but Cromwell was probably well known in the area. He had publicly defended the right of fen dwellers to be compensated for fen drainage schemes, which deprived them of customary sources of food and income, and he also had an extensive family network that included cousins such as John Hampden.

As an MP, Cromwell was closely associated with the opposition to Charles, but he was very much a backbencher. What brought him to prominence was the outbreak of war. He always excelled when there was action to be taken and in June 1642 he left London to secure Cambridge Castle for Parliament. He then raised a cavalry regiment for the Eastern Association army and, according to the diarist, Thomas May, played a major part in pressurising the gentry of the eastern counties to declare for Parliament. His energy and commitment led him to command the cavalry under the Earl of Manchester. With no military experience before middle age, he proved astonishingly effective, mainly because of his character and common sense. His famous willingness to promote men on merit and his preference for a 'plain russet-coated captain' over the pretensions of the gentry were based on practical considerations and a concern for what would work best.

Much of his success came from the men that he recruited and the discipline that he was able to instil and his religious views played a part in both. While the idea that he created an army of saints has been shown to be too simplistic, there is little doubt that he encouraged recruitment of men who shared his Puritan outlook and that he used their commitment to the cause to develop a disciplined force both on and off the battlefield. Unlike the dashing Prince Rupert, he taught his cavalry to regroup after a successful charge and return to the battlefield. This discipline proved crucial in the Parliamentarian victory at Marston Moor and would be transferred into the New Model Army formed in the following year.

Despite his reputation as a religious radical, there is little evidence to suggest that Cromwell deliberately sought to challenge authority. He believed in godly reformation and sought to build a national Church and State that would support and enhance such work. The depth of his convictions is reflected in his lifelong habit of 'waiting on the Lord' when faced with difficult decisions. His providential beliefs led him to expect and await a sign from God to indicate how he should proceed in order to best serve God's purpose. Many Calvinists shared such views – what was exceptional about Cromwell was the speed and energy with which he acted once he believed he knew what God required of him. What made him unusual among men of his background and station was his belief that an individual should be free to seek God in his own way, provided he was no danger to others, and that God revealed Himself through such individuals, regardless of education or social rank. Hence he protected separatists and challenged those in authority in order to enhance the search for truth, which he believed to be the main purpose of religion. In many ways unusually humane, he regarded the excesses and eccentricities of religious enthusiasts as misguided rather than wicked.

The turning point in Cromwell's political career came with the army mutiny of 1647, when he allied himself with the soldiers in order to influence the political settlement. Although Fairfax remained as Lord General until 1650, it was Cromwell who was the army's political leader. Throughout 1647 he sought to create a compromise that would restore the King, protect Parliament and secure a measure of religious toleration. The Heads of the Proposals would have created a flexible settlement and even included some Leveller demands for social and legal reforms. Thereafter, through changing circumstances and by different strategies, Cromwell continued to pursue these aims. In order to achieve this he allied in turn with republicans, millenarians, army officers, lawyers and constitutional monarchists. An outstanding military leader, a political pragmatist and a religious zealot who distrusted dogmatic authority and disliked persecution, he spent the remaining years of his life trying to establish a compromise and reconcile aims that were probably irreconcilable except in his own mind.

▲ Oliver Cromwell (1599–1658)

There is no doubt about Cromwell's disappointment regarding the Parliament of Saints, but he was pragmatic enough to recognise failure and to realise that it arose from the same issue that had destroyed the Rump Parliament – the difficulty of balancing the desire for reform with the need for stability. Where the Rump had proceeded too slowly, the radicals of the nominated assembly had moved too fast. He therefore turned to the alternative suggested by Lambert, of an executive council to rule with the help of parliaments. The Rump and Parliament of Saints had demonstrated the problems caused by a single central authority which chose to ignore other opinions. Cromwell and Lambert now sought to restore the principle of mixed government in the hope of achieving a blend of reform and stability. On 16 December 1653 the Commonwealth was ended when Cromwell was appointed Lord Protector, to rule with the help of a Council of State and parliaments elected every three years on a reformed franchise.

KEY DATES: FAILURE OF THE COMMONWEALTH

1652 Council of Officers petitions for reform and Cromwell wrote to the Council of State in support of their case; bill for 'recruiting' rather than holding new elections considered.

1653 Report of the Hales Commission on legal reform ignored by the Rump; bill for new elections considered, without any reform of the franchise.

April: Cromwell dissolves the Rump.

July: Nominated Assembly met and declared itself to be a Parliament; work begun on legal reform, but divisions appear over purges of JPs and plans for changes in the Church.

12 December: Moderates voted for dissolution of the Assembly and formally handed power to Cromwell.

16 December: Cromwell declared to be Lord Protector under the Instrument of Government.

NOTE-MAKING

To develop your own view of Cromwell, use the material in the box (on page 150) to compile a list of the claims made about his character, and as you continue working through this chapter and making linear notes, try to highlight examples that support or challenge them. You could add to your notes by using additional books cited in the Further research at the end of this book (page 253), as well as carrying out your own research online. When you complete your notes to the point of Cromwell's death in 1658, you will be able to review the material and use it to write an assessment of Cromwell as Lord Protector and the extent to which his character and aims shaped the outcome of events.

NOTE-MAKING

As you work through this section you will need to continue your linear notes, using the headings and sub-headings to provide a clear structure. In addition, you will be collecting evidence regarding Cromwell's character. A further aspect of the situation that you need to consider is the extent to which Cromwell's rule has been deemed 'successful' by historians, and as part of that, what constituted 'success'? You should therefore begin by defining what you consider to have been Cromwell's aims (some indications are set out below) and as you work through what follows, make a list of examples that illustrate success and failure.

2 The Protectorate and its problems, 1654–58

The return to government by a single person, and the adjustments made thereafter, has encouraged some historians to see the Protectorate as an essentially conservative regime leading inexorably back to monarchy. While this is understandable, there is considerable evidence to suggest that Cromwell, at least, did not view it in this light. He continued to dress in plain clothes and to pursue a simple personal lifestyle. He adopted some of the trappings of royalty by restoring the palace of Whitehall and some of its treasures, and signing his documents 'Oliver P' in mimicry of traditional royal signatures. This, however, seems to have been intended to encourage outward respect for the regime, especially among foreign visitors and ambassadors, and to utilise the best elements of institutions with which contemporaries were familiar.

The first Protectorate, 1654–57

To what extent did the new government offer stability?

Cromwell's aims were, in his own words, the 'healing and settling' of the nation. While he employed civilian advisers and sought to bring the established gentry back into local government, he also listened to the advice of soldiers like John Lambert and pursued his own vision of reform. In creating space for conservatives and monarchists, he was seeking to broaden the base of support and provide stability. For him the Protectorate represented a new approach to the business of providing balanced government, and to his key purpose of establishing reform while also maintaining an acceptable level of authority and stability. His difficulty lay in the fact that for many of his contemporaries, these aims were essentially incompatible. In addition, while he and Lambert might not see the Protectorate as a stepping-stone to monarchy, there were others who might try to make it just that.

The Instrument of Government, 1653

England's first written constitution was also Britain's first formal constitution, since Scotland and Ireland were to be included. It provided for a single person to rule as executive, with powers that were limited and defined. Parliaments of 460 MPs were to be elected every three years. Voters were required to own £200 of personal property. This maintained a property qualification but removed the need to own land. Seats were distributed on the basis of taxation, and parliaments were to sit for a minimum of five months. Royalists were to be excluded from the first four parliaments. They had control of legislation, although the Protector could issue ordinances when Parliament was not in session and he could veto (forbid) attempts to change the constitution itself. There was to be a state Church, but with freedom of worship for all except Catholics and Prelatists (supporters of bishops). As a constitution, the Instrument had obvious weaknesses, notably the failure to provide for future amendment or for adjudication in case of disputes. Nevertheless, in the words of Derek Hirst, it: *'did wrestle with the central problems of the over-mighty prince and an over-mighty Parliament, and given mutual tolerance and adequate funding, it might have worked'.*

The progress of reform: law and finance

The months before the calling of the first Protectorate Parliament offered the best opportunity for reform. Cromwell quickly appointed Matthew Hale, author of the report on law reform, as a judge and followed this up with a Chancery Ordinance that simplified procedures and reduced fees. Unfortunately, the Council of State felt that it was necessary to entrust reform to the senior lawyers and judges, who ensured that any changes were both cautious and slow. The common law judges introduced some further regulation in December 1654, but thereafter little was done. Similarly, attempts to open up economic opportunities by reducing the power of merchant associations and borough corporations received little support. The Council included too many traditionalists and vested interests to make significant change in this area, so that old methods of organisation persisted. In 1657 the new trade of framework knitting, in which woollen cloth was produced using a weaving frame, was placed under the control of a guild of master craftsmen, in the traditional way. Similarly the monopoly licence by which control of trade with India had been granted to the East India Company was restored in return for a loan to the government.

This also points to a further obstacle in the way of reform measures – the government's serious financial problems. The Rump had confiscated lands from the Church and the monarchy, but this had been swallowed up by the costs of the army and the Dutch War. Although Cromwell quickly brought the war to an end, he embarked in 1655 on a war with Spain. There were a number of reasons for this. Lacking the money to pay off the fleet used against the Dutch, he hoped to use it against Spain in the West Indies, and make the war pay for itself by seizing Spanish treasure ships and colonies. It also encouraged closer relations with Spain's enemy, France, depriving Charles II of possible French aid. Religious considerations played a part in his calculations – Spain had always been a more actively Catholic power than France. In the event, however, sending his *Western Design* to capture *Hispaniola* proved a costly failure, and the seizure of Jamaica was little consolation. While Cromwell's foreign policy brought a measure of prestige, his financial problems continued to hamper the work of reform.

Religion and the Church

Cromwell's first priority, however, was religious reform. Although the upheavals of war had led to some ministers being ejected or voluntarily leaving their parishes, many had simply continued to carry out their duties according to their own preferences. The result was a wide variation of services and ceremonies, supported by voluntary associations such as the Presbyterian group headed by Richard Baxter in Worcestershire. In addition, a growing number of Independents took on duties within the Church, while continuing to lead voluntary groups outside it.

Management of the Church

Cromwell's approach was to encourage such efforts and allow variation within a framework of acceptable doctrine. In March, a Committee of Triers was established with responsibility for examining the qualities and beliefs of the parish clergy, confirming the livings of those who were acceptable, and appointing new ministers to vacant parishes. The committee sought ministers who were educated and capable of preaching, and who accepted the fundamentals of Christianity; neither their personal beliefs about salvation nor their preferences for particular ceremonies were considered. In August, the government added a Committee of Ejectors whose function was to remove

Cromwell's civilian advisers

Cromwell's civilian advisers were disliked by the army, with some good reason. Sir Charles Wolseley was among the moderate MPs who engineered the downfall of the Parliament of Saints, while Sir Antony Ashley Cooper had fought for the King in 1642. Lord Broghill held an Irish peerage and was the brother of Robert Boyle, the Oxford scientist. They sought to reduce army influence but, despite army suspicions, they were not a coherent group. In 1656–57 when Parliament debated the possibility of offering Cromwell the crown, Cooper was one of the republicans excluded from Parliament, while Broghill was a key supporter of the scheme. Essentially, they, like Cromwell himself, were pragmatists, whose main purpose was to restore moderate, civilian government.

the inadequate and the scandalous, but again, the decision was based on their quality as ministers rather than on their denominational preferences.

What Cromwell sought to establish was a broad, flexible and tolerant Church, which would contribute to the godly reformation through education and upholding moral standards. At the same time, as a believer in the search for truth, he allowed freedom to those who wished to meet in voluntary gatherings outside the establishment, provided that their doctrines were neither blasphemous nor dangerous. The dangerous category included both Catholics and Arminians, while the blasphemy laws curtailed the activities of some of the wilder sects. Nevertheless, the system allowed for a broad spectrum of belief, and even those who stood beyond it were often tolerated in practice, provided they were discreet. Both Catholics and the Anglican groups who continued to use the Prayer Book were often able to worship undisturbed.

The case for toleration

Cromwell's personal sympathy with those who followed their conscience was revealed in his attitude to the Quaker, James Nayler, in 1656. When Nayler re-enacted Christ's entry into Jerusalem at the gates of Bristol and was accused of blasphemy, some MPs called for the death sentence. As Parliament debated Nayler's fate, Cromwell intervened to argue that he was foolish rather than wicked, and to challenge Parliament's right to inflict punishment on anyone. His intervention may have saved Nayler's life, but he was unable to prevent Parliament's order being carried out that Nayler should be flogged, bored through the tongue as a blasphemer, and committed to prison.

The Nayler case illustrates the problem that undermined Cromwell's efforts in this area – how to reconcile freedom with order, and how to calm the fears of the conservatives who saw the collapse of social discipline all around them. Within the established Church, ministers were faced with the problem of enforcing parish order and standards of behaviour on a populace who had the freedom to ignore them. Their only sanction was to exclude the sinful from communion, which had little effect on those who chose not to attend. Faced with widespread ignorance among a people who lived short, brutal lives, the educational schemes of government and individuals alike failed for lack of money and resources. The new University of Durham, an attempt to enlighten the 'dark' regions of the north, was a short-lived exception. Despite heroic efforts by individual ministers, the reformation of the ungodly could make little progress without both financial support and legal compulsion.

Meanwhile, the radical sects exercised their right to worship outside the Church. For conservatives this was, in itself, a threat to order and hierarchy. Many voluntary groups acted with discipline and moderation. The 1650s saw the Baptist and Congregationalist Churches take shape, establishing national and regional associations and issuing formal statements of doctrine. Alongside this, however, the activities of the more eccentric sects reinforced the fears of those in authority. By 1654 there was little sign of Ranter activity and the Diggers had long been dispersed, but they had been replaced by a new and more dynamic threat, the Quakers. Their eccentric manners and challenge to authority, their attacks on clerical privilege and social injustice, and above all their success in attracting converts seemed to threaten further revolution. While Cromwell might take pride in his godly reformation, the majority of the population, and especially the gentry in the localities, saw it as seriously undermining authority in Church and State.

'Dark' regions

The 'dark' regions of the north of England were a matter of concern, because they were badly served by the Church. In Yorkshire and the Pennine region, across to Lancaster, Cumberland and Westmorland, the hilly nature of the country meant that the population was thinly scattered and that parishes were therefore very large and often poor. Educational provision was also thin and it was difficult to attract graduates as either ministers or teachers. The problem was highlighted by the strength of the Quakers in the area; the many chapels of rest situated in outlying villages provided meeting places for separate congregations and migrant preachers.

The Quaker movement

Although they were part of a much wider development of separatist groups and the resulting desire for religious toleration, the impact of the Quakers in this period was such that their emergence requires some explanation here. The Quaker movement was founded in the north between 1650 and 1652 when George Fox began a series of journeys through Yorkshire, Lancashire and Cumbria to preach the doctrine of salvation through the inner light planted by God in every human. He found fertile ground for his message in the groups of 'seekers' already established in the area and the movement quickly took shape. By 1654 they were ready to launch a great 'mission to the south'. Some 60 First Publishers of Truth, including the charismatic Fox and James Nayler, set out to convert the world to an understanding of the light within, the voice of God in the human heart, which was the only authority needed in religion. Nicknamed Quakers because of their ecstatic trembling and passionate celebration of God's mercy, they entered churches and harangued ministers for their greed in taking payment for preaching and refused to acknowledge their 'betters' by removing hats and addressing them as 'sir'. Not only did they demand the abolition of tithes and complete religious toleration, they condemned the wealthy and powerful to their faces, for their oppressions and lack of concern for the poor.

Most worrying for those in authority, the Quakers' message held a wide popular appeal and their mission was spectacularly successful. It was by no means unusual for their preachers to draw large crowds and to publicly 'convert' tens and even hundreds of people at a time. It is not surprising that anxious justices complained of this new plague from the north, devouring the land like locusts!

By 1656, when Nayler's theatrics at Bristol brought such fears to a head, Fox was beginning to establish a national framework for the movement, now called the Society of Friends. By 1660 there were probably 60,000 Quakers in England, linked by their travelling preachers and by annual meetings of representatives from all parts of the country. After the Restoration this embryonic organisation was shattered by the onslaught of persecution, and many of the First Publishers died in prison. Fox, however, survived to create a new and more lasting system of local and regional meetings, which became the basis of a worldwide Church.

Failure of the Instrument of Government

Cromwell's hopes of 'healing and settling' therefore proved no more successful than the regimes that he had replaced. In August 1654 a Parliament was called, as required by the Instrument of Government, to ratify the new constitution. Instead, MPs attacked the very authority by which they had been summoned and set out to alter the constitution. Initially, republican MPs such as Haselrig and Thomas Scot, who had been members of the Rump and had never forgiven Cromwell for its dissolution, led the attack. Skilled in parliamentary tactics, they were able to hold up business and deny the government both ratification of the Instrument and financial support. In September, Cromwell responded by excluding MPs who refused to sign a 'recognition' of the constitution and about a hundred republicans withdrew. The remainder, however, turned their attention to the radicals and the army who protected them. They voted against a new tax assessment and for the reduction of the army to 30,000 men. By January 1655, it was clear that Cromwell would get no help from this assembly and he dissolved it as soon as the Instrument allowed.

Threats to security

The first year of the Protectorate therefore revealed that the Instrument of Government had not addressed the continuing problem of a fundamental division between civilian/conservative supporters and the army/radical interest, which had undermined the Rump and Parliament of Saints. In 1655 this threatened to destroy the regime. The winter of 1654–55 saw unrest in the army from Fifth Monarchists and republicans, followed in the spring by a Royalist uprising in Wiltshire, led by John Penruddock. The rising generated little support and was easily contained, but it did raise concern about security and highlight the dangers of division. More seriously, the failure of Parliament to ratify the Instrument threatened the legal and constitutional basis of the regime. Throughout the spring and early summer the government's right to collect taxes was challenged in the courts, driving Cromwell to replace five judges who were likely to find against him. In May the case of George Cony, a merchant who had refused to pay customs duties, provoked Cromwell to imprison not only Cony, but also his entire legal counsel without trial.

Cromwell's treatment of George Cony and his lawyers reflects the growing dangers faced by the regime. Cony was a religious radical and his legal counsel had Royalist links. It was not unusual for the enemies of the regime to co-operate in this way – a number of plots against Cromwell were organised by Royalist agents with ex-Levellers such as Miles Sindercombe, who attempted to assassinate Cromwell in early 1657. Cromwell's reaction to the Cony case also explains why the regime survived the crisis. Whatever his concern for legality, Cromwell had no intention of surrendering control. In the summer of 1655 he reduced the Monthly Assessment (tax), cut the soldiers' pay and brought army numbers down to 40,000 men. At the same time, to maintain security, he divided the country into 11 districts and established a new local militia in each, to be raised and controlled by a Major-General, selected by the regime from the army officers, who would also supervise local government. Their work would be financed by a Decimation Tax – a 10 per cent levy on Royalist estates. In the words of Derek Hirst:

'The ensuing rule of the Major-Generals combined police work and tax-gathering with moral reform in a way that shaped the legend of the Cromwellian years as the triumph of blue-nosed puritanism.'

Rule of the Major-Generals

As Hirst suggests, the rule of the Major-Generals was portrayed by Royalist propaganda (and some historians) as a military dictatorship manned by social inferiors and killjoys. Like most generalisations, this claim contains some truth. Their methods of control could be somewhat arbitrary. In the West Country, Major-General Desborough took bonds for good behaviour from over 5,000 suspected dissidents. Many borough corporations were forcibly purged of suspected 'Royalists' and in Hythe, Kent, Major-General Kelsey surrounded the Town Hall with troops in order to ensure that his orders were carried out. In Lancashire Major-General Worsley was particularly active in the suppression of alehouses, closing 215 in one part of the county, while he shut almost 200 in the city of Chester. The regime was deeply unpopular with the gentry, who resented their loss of control over local government and the restrictions imposed on them.

Nevertheless, the picture is more varied and complex than their complaints would suggest. The social origins of the Major-Generals differed greatly. Worsley was of obscure origins, but Goffe was the son of a clergyman, Haynes was a member of the gentry and Whalley was a cousin of Cromwell. It is undoubtedly true that they were generally not of the greater gentry, but neither were they as obscure and unfit as their enemies suggested. Many provided careful and conscientious administration. The records show a marked increase in both the levying and expenditure of the poor rate and the provision of almshouses. It is certainly possible that some of the resentment felt by the ruling elite arose from the fact that they were paying more for the benefit of the poor. Complaints about the suppression of traditional sports such as cock fighting and horse racing tend to exaggerate the extent to which the killjoy element was in control. The main reason for banning such activities was to prevent them being used as a cover for political action. In addition, there was great variation in the energy and efficiency demonstrated by the new regime. In the north west, where there was a relatively isolated Puritan community surrounded by conservatives, they supported Worsley and enabled him to be particularly effective. In Hampshire and Sussex, William Goffe had little impact.

Despite this, it is clear that the experiment of the Major-Generals was widely resented. The strongest evidence of this came in 1656, when the government's financial needs led to elections for a new Parliament. Local communities proved united against military control and radical influence. In Kent, Major-General Kelsey could not gain one of the 11 seats available, and Baptist candidates were threatened with lynching in Middlesex. Their efforts were further undermined by Cromwell himself, who seemed to disapprove of interfering in elections. He was, however, quite willing to prevent hostile MPs from taking their seats and used the Instrument's requirement for MPs to be of godly character in order to exclude about a hundred republicans and Royalists. The result was a pragmatic assembly, willing to get on with business, while deeply hostile to army and radical influence, which seemed to be embodied in the Instrument on which the regime rested. After three months of dealing with private bills and business, this House of Commons acted to remove it by formally offering the crown to Oliver Cromwell!

'King' Oliver?

Why was the offer of the Crown to Cromwell made and rejected?

This was not the first time that a King Oliver had been suggested as a solution to the country's problems, although it was the first time that the suggestion had been made in Parliament. It was a logical response to the desires of the ruling class for a return to monarchy and civilian government. As king, Cromwell would retain control of the armed forces, but he would operate within a recognised framework of law and custom acceptable to the nation as a whole. A King did not have to mean a Stuart. There were many who remained suspicious of the character and Catholic associations of Charles and his sons, while others feared that a second Charles might wish to punish those who had opposed the first. The rule of the Major-Generals had sharpened fears of military dictatorship, while the James Nayler incident highlighted the dangers of radical beliefs. If Cromwell's position could be given constitutional validity, it might yet offer a real prospect of stable government and lasting reconciliation.

Moreover, Cromwell's own actions in the autumn and winter of 1656–57 raised the possibility that he might accept the Crown. He was well aware of how arbitrary some of his government's actions had been, and if these could not be justified as furthering God's purpose, they could not be continued. In December, when Desborough proposed that Parliament should approve the Decimation Tax and confirm the position of the Major-Generals, Cromwell

KEY DATES: THE FIRST PROTECTORATE, 1654–57

1654 Cromwell forced to purge Fifth Monarchist officers after failure of Parliament of Saints.

1654–55 Secret meetings between ex-Levellers and Royalist agents.

1655 Penruddock's rising in Wiltshire.

1657

January: Plot by Leveller, Miles Sindercombe, to assassinate Cromwell discovered.

April: Fifth Monarchist rising in London.

failed to support him and the tax was voted down. This refusal to defend the Major-Generals might well indicate that Cromwell had lost faith in the army as the instrument of God. It was also clear that Cromwell was disturbed by the arbitrary treatment of James Nayler and his own inability to restrain Parliament. Kingship, with the return of a second chamber in the House of Lords and a clearer definition of his own powers of intervention, might well prevent such incidents in future.

The Humble Petition and Advice, 1657

The trigger to action came in January 1657 when the discovery of a plot to assassinate Cromwell led by the Leveller, Miles Sindercombe, highlighted the lack of any accepted successor. By emphasising Cromwell's mortality, the plot raised the question of what would happen when he died. The Instrument of Government made no effective provision and the possibility of conflict between different factions of the army or renewed civil war between the army and Royalist forces was very real. A monarchy would solve the problem, since Cromwell had two healthy sons. On 23 February 1657, the London Alderman, Sir Christopher Packe, introduced a motion in Parliament to the effect that Cromwell be offered the Crown, with a restored House of Lords consisting of his nominees to sit alongside the Commons. To the fury of republicans and army officers, the proposal was debated for some weeks and finally offered to the Protector in March 1657, as the Humble Petition and Advice.

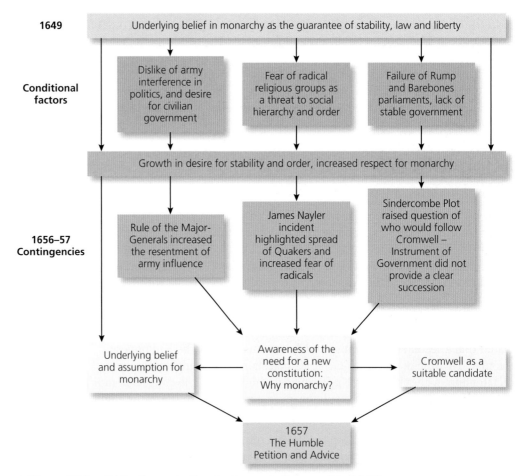

▲ **Figure 2** Why did Parliament offer the Crown to Cromwell in 1657?

The new proposals would have established an effective constitutional monarchy, with a two-chamber Parliament, clear limits on royal power, the great officers of state approved by Parliament and a reduction of the army as well as new restrictions on religious toleration. While some Royalists were enthusiastic, believing this to be a first step towards a Stuart restoration, others were dismayed. In the words of Clarendon, in exile with Charles Stuart:

'The more sober persons of the King's party ... believed that ... much of that affection that appeared under the notion of allegiance to the King was more directed to the monarchy than to the person, and if Cromwell were once made King, and so the government ran again in the old channel ... he would receive abundant reparation of strength by the access of those who preferred monarchy, and which probably would reconcile most men of estates to an absolute acquiescence.'

All that was required was for Cromwell to accept. Instead, he agonised. On 7 March he had received a petition, signed by 100 army officers, opposing the notion of restoring the monarchy. He pointed out to them that a settlement was needed, that arbitrary proceedings must come to an end. Privately, he consulted his closest associates and sought to persuade them that the plan offered the best solution to their problems, but was clearly disturbed by their continued opposition. Finally, in April 1657, he rejected the title of 'King', but accepted a revised Petition in May, in which the title was changed to that of 'Lord Protector for life', with the right to nominate his successor. He was crowned with many of the trappings of royalty in June 1657.

◄ 'The Emblem of England's Distraction', 1658. Although this engraving relates to the later years of Cromwell's rule, it reveals the basis of his power and the image that he sought to present.

> **1** What does the engraving suggest about:
> **a)** the sources of Cromwell's power?
> **b)** the aims of his government?
> **c)** the justification of his rule?
> **2** Is Cromwell depicted here as a King or as a Protector?

Like most compromises, the second Protectorate satisfied few of those involved. Many of the officers remained suspicious of the new regime and John Lambert resigned from the Council of State. The new House of Lords was established, with many of Cromwell's supporters transferred to it, and the excluded republicans were allowed to take their seats in the Commons. Since they had lost neither their hostility to the regime nor their skill in using parliamentary procedures to delay business, the second session of Parliament ended in chaos and frustration for the Protector. In February 1658, he finally dissolved it, but it is likely that financial pressures would have forced him to call another had he lived.

Ironically, the summer of 1658 saw a number of loyal addresses sent from the counties to the Protector. It was widely rumoured that a new Parliament would repeat the offer and that this time Cromwell might accept. The opportunity never arose, for by September 1658, Cromwell was dead, worn out by time (he was 59 years old) and effort. He died on 3 September, the anniversary of his victories at Dunbar and Worcester. In the last week of his life he nominated his elder son, Richard, to succeed him. Although Richard, a country squire of moderate Presbyterian views, was greeted with some enthusiasm by the ruling elite, his lack of political experience and inability to control the army led to his resignation in May 1659. With his demise, the regime turned full circle as the Rump of 1649 returned to power and proclaimed the restoration of the Commonwealth.

Interpretations: assessing Cromwell's effectiveness as a ruler

Source B From *The Stuart Age: England 1603–1714* by Barry Coward, (Longman), 1997, p.200.

Hindsight is sometimes a blessing for historians, but it can also be a curse. The knowledge that the Protectorate was short-lived and that the monarchy was restored in 1660 has caused some historians to give too much emphasis to opposition to the republic, leading to assumptions that Cromwell's rule was a 'failure'. This is a misleading interpretation of the Protectorate between 1653 and 1658. England in the 1650s was not a country seething with growing hostility to Cromwell. Was, then, Oliver Cromwell's rule a success? If, by success is meant the full realisation of Cromwell's own ambitions and enthusiastic support in the country, then the answer is a definite 'no'. If, however, the Protectorate's success is judged by the extent to which it was accepted by England's traditional ruling elites, a different answer can be given. When Oliver Cromwell died in September 1658, not only was there no sign of any demand for the restoration of the Stuarts, the Protectorate had succeeded in becoming accepted by many as a regime that promised stability and security.

ACTIVITY

Sources B–D offer different views of Cromwell's effectiveness as a ruler and the extent to which his character and judgements contributed to the failure of the Protectorate.

1 In what ways do the sources agree and disagree about Cromwell's achievements as Lord Protector?

2 Do they all use the same criteria to judge success and failure?

3 How far do they agree about Cromwell's character?

Source C From 'The Stuarts' by John Morrill in *The Oxford Illustrated History of Britain* by K. O. Morgan, ed. (Oxford University Press), 1993, pp.328–29.

If Cromwell had settled for acquiescence and a minimum level of political acceptance, he could have established a secure and lasting regime. But he yearned for commitment and zeal, for a nation more responsive to the things of God, more willing to obey His commands. This religious radicalism went along with a social conservatism. By executing Charles I, Cromwell cut himself off from justifications of political authority rooted in the past; by acknowledging that a free vote of those who held the franchise would restore the king, that is, by refusing to base his authority on consent, Cromwell cut himself off from arguments of the present. His self-justification lay in the future, in the belief that he was fulfilling God's Will. A unique blend of country gentleman and professional soldier, of religious radical and social conservative ... of charismatic personal presence and insufferable self-righteousness, he was at once the only source of stability and the ultimate source of instability in the regimes that he ran. If he could have settled for settlement he could have established a prudent republic; if he had not had a fire in his belly to change the world, he would never have risen from sheep farmer to be head of state.

Source D From *People, Power and Politics: Was there a Mid-Seventeenth century Revolution?* by Robert Ellis, (Stanley Thornes), 1992, pp.152–53.

Although Cromwell's rule was not an unqualified success, the problems he faced were enormous, and it is doubtful if anyone else could have coped with them as well as he did. By any standards except his own, Cromwell's achievements were remarkable. Although he did not succeed in attracting wide support for the Protectorate, few opposed it openly, mainly because it provided peace, prosperity and a higher level of prestige in Europe than England had enjoyed for many centuries. He failed to provide the country with a system of government stable enough to survive without him, but during his life he was able to prevent the conflicting aims of parliament, the army and the religious sects from tearing the Protectorate apart. He was not a deep political thinker, and major constitutional changes were the work of Ireton, Lambert and Broghill among others, rather than Cromwell. However, it was his pragmatic political skills and his unique ability to command support from both military and civilian quarters that made these changes work. In religion his demands for liberty of conscience were ahead of their time, and, while the religious, social and legal reforms he sought to achieve ultimately came to nothing, they display a deep concern for the spiritual and physical well-being of others.

WORKING TOGETHER

1 When you have completed your response to the questions in the activity on page 160, compare your conclusions with a partner and construct a joint response to the question: 'How far do the interpretations summarised in Sources B–D conflict?'

2 Using the material from the sources and your own notes and interpretations, write a brief response to the question:

How far was Cromwell a political asset to the regimes that he led in the years 1654–58?

The failure of the Protectorate, 1658–59

Why did the failure of the Protectorate lead to the return of the monarchy?

Richard Cromwell was born in 1626 and served in the Parliamentarian army during the Civil War. He sat as an MP in both parliaments of the Protectorate, but held no office until 1657, when he became a member of the Council of State and of the new House of Lords. While he was able and intelligent, and undeserving of the Royalist nickname of 'Tumbledown Dick', there is no doubt that his experience of government was as limited as his ambition. He tried to do his duty, but he had little desire for power. Richard's failure to maintain his own position and the security of the Protectorate has been variously attributed to:

- his own weakness and inexperience
- the inability of the surviving Grandees, Fleetwood and Desborough, to control the junior officers
- the propaganda of the old republican MPs
- the seriousness of the problems that he inherited from his father.

Whatever the causes, the outcome was a collapse into anarchy that brought about the restoration of the Stuarts in 1660.

Failure and collapse

Richard was proclaimed as Protector in September 1658. In October he appointed Fleetwood as Army General, but retained the position of Commander-in-Chief for himself. This may well have been resented by the leading officers, enabling republican MPs like Haselrig to play on army fears and stir opposition. In January, when parliament assembled, Richard's authority was accepted and MPs showed a willingness to vote supplies, but also began to discuss the reduction of the army and its replacement by a local militia. Encouraged by the republicans, the junior officers demanded a restoration of the Army Council in order to discuss grievances. In April 1659, Richard agreed to this, only to be faced with a petition to dissolve Parliament and a declaration from Fleetwood that he could not guarantee the army's loyalty if Richard refused. Fearful of further civil war, Richard dissolved Parliament and on 7 May the army agreed to recall the Rump. Richard retired with a pension and payment of his debts, although he was to endure exile and poverty after 1660, returning in 1680 to live in relative obscurity until 1712.

Richard's failure highlights once more the fatal weakness of all the regimes of the Interregnum – the need to serve two political masters. The propertied classes throughout the country craved stability and order, while the army demanded religious freedom and some measure of reform. No ruler could survive for long without the support of both, but what pleased one would inevitably alienate the other. In Richard's case, the very qualities that enabled him to win popularity in the country and work well with Parliament reinforced the fears of a suspicious army and drove it into opposition. A stronger or more politically determined character might have resisted their pressure, and Richard's resignation does highlight the importance of Oliver Cromwell as an individual. His religious convictions and army links made him uniquely able to seek a wider basis of support without entirely losing the confidence of the officers. From time to time he faced conspiracy or resistance from particular factions, such as Harrison and the millenarians, but for the most part the essential bonds of comradeship and shared dangers, built up over two civil wars and years of struggle, held firm.

Anarchy and order: the return of the Rump, 1659–60

The actions of the army and republicans in 1659 reveal how politically bankrupt the revolutionaries had become. Having forced Richard to resign, the army officers could think of nothing better than to restore the Rump. This was not surprising, since the republican MPs and ex-Rumpers like Haselrig had played a significant part in stirring up army fears against Richard. What is more remarkable is that, having been restored to power by the military, the Rump should so quickly turn on their allies and demonstrate how little they had learned. Determined to assert the superiority of civilian authority, they began to purge the army of moderates whom Cromwell had encouraged, and to promote republicans. A reorganisation of the army was planned, with the establishment of a local militia to complement the professionals. Meanwhile, a similar purge of moderates in local government and the appointment of radicals and even Quakers to office raised fears in the country and led to calls for a free Parliament. In August rebellion broke out in Cheshire, led by the Presbyterian Parliamentarian, Sir George Booth. While this demonstrated the fragmentation of Parliament's ex-supporters, it also briefly united the Rump and army while the rebellion was suppressed. Thereafter, however, the Rump pressed ahead with its plans, and when the army protested and petitioned for reforms in October, voted to dismiss nine leading officers including both Fleetwood and Desborough. In effect, it had signed its own death warrant.

On 13 October the Parliament buildings were once more surrounded by troopers and the Rump was denied entry. A Committee of Safety was established by the Council of Officers to maintain some form of government while alternatives were considered. Quite simply, there were none. While the country slipped into political anarchy and rumours of a Quaker rising spread, Haselrig appealed for support, and General George Monck, commander of the army in Scotland, declared his support for the Rump and civilian government. As he gathered his troops and crossed the river Tweed into England, the Committee of Safety authorised Lambert to raise a force in Yorkshire to resist him. Army morale, however, had at last broken. Forced into open military dictatorship, demoralised by successive failures and devoid of ideas, Lambert's men simply melted away as Monck approached. The providential beliefs that had drawn political justification from military success now destroyed confidence in their cause and ensured military failure.

As Monck continued south at the invitation of the Rump, now restored once more, he was inundated with petitions from the county associations for a free Parliament and the return of monarchy. For the first time, a genuine groundswell of enthusiasm for the Stuarts had begun and would shape the events of the ensuing months. Although it was Monck who controlled the restoration of monarchy and the final collapse of revolution, it was the pressure from a population desperate for stability that ensured that restoration would be both rapid and without prior conditions. In the final analysis, the revolution of 1649 and the 'good old cause' that inspired it had collapsed under the weight of its own failures.

KEY DATES: THE FAILURE OF THE PROTECTORATE, 1658–59

1658

September: Richard proclaimed Protector; Fleetwood given leadership of the army in October.

1659

January: Richard accepted by Parliament, but discussions for the reduction of the army increase unrest among junior officers.

January–April: Army unrest increased by intervention of Rump MPs, leading to restoration of the Army Council and dissolution of Parliament.

May: Resignation of Richard Cromwell; Army leaders restored the Rump; Rump purged army and local government of supporters of the Protectorate.

July–August: Booth's rising in Cheshire temporarily united Rump and army and was easily suppressed.

September: Army petitioned for reform.

October: Rump rebuked Petitioners and voted to dismiss nine leading officers.

13 October: Army stopped Rump meeting; army set up Committee of Safety.

22 October: Monck declared for Rump.

December: Rump restored again.

The Restoration of the Stuarts, 1659–60

Why was the monarchy restored in 1660 without pre-conditions?

'I am engaged ... to assert the liberty and authority of Parliament, to see my country freed from that intolerable slavery of a sword government.'

General George Monck, 1660.

The collapse of army morale removed the last barrier in the way of a restoration, but did nothing to determine the terms on which it would take place. The groundswell of support for monarchy may have convinced Monck that it was the only solution and that it must take place quickly, but this did not preclude some attempt to negotiate terms that would establish some of the constitutional changes for which the wars had been fought. The fact that Charles II returned with no specific commitments to fulfil was the work of two men – Monck himself, and Edward Hyde, soon to be Lord Clarendon. If Monck retained any loyalty to the restored Rump when he arrived in London, its members quickly destroyed it by ordering him to suppress demonstrations against them and by querying the validity of his commission from Cromwell. He responded in February 1660 by recalling the members who had been excluded in 1648, on condition that they voted to dissolve this Long Parliament and call free elections.

Given the public mood, there was no doubt that the elections would produce a majority in favour of a Stuart restoration – the remaining question was, on what terms? When Parliament assembled in April 1660, Monck presented them with a declaration, issued by Charles Stuart from the Dutch port of Breda (where he had moved on Monck's advice). The Declaration of Breda promised harmony and reconciliation, no punishment for actions during the war and Interregnum except against those who had signed the King's death warrant, and declared that a settlement of outstanding issues would be worked out in partnership with Parliament.

The result was that on 5 May, Parliament voted that government was by King, Lords and Commons, and on 25 May, Charles landed at Dover to a tumultuous welcome. Significantly, he claimed that he was taking up his throne 'in the twelfth year of his reign'. Whatever MPs might intend, Divine Right monarchy had returned.

Declaration of Breda

The declaration, drawn up by Hyde on Monck's advice, was an immensely skilful document. Since it promised all that Parliament could have asked, it made preconditions for the Restoration impossible. At the same time, however, it made no specific commitments to which the King would have to adhere. Carefully planned to remove suspicion of the Stuarts, as well as its promised co-operation, it sought to distance Charles from the Catholic associations that had caused his father such difficulty. For this reason it was issued from Breda in Protestant Holland, rather than from Catholic France where Charles had been living until Monck advised him to move.

KEY DATES: THE RESTORATION OF THE STUARTS, 1659–60

1659

October: Army replaced the Rump with a Committee of Safety: Monck declared his support for the Rump.

November: Lambert failed in an attempt to raise forces.

December: Anti-army riots began in London; Monck moved his army to the border with England: the Navy declared for the Rump.

26 December: Fleetwood recalled the Rump.

1660

1 January: Monck's army marched into England and arrived in February; his journey south marked by demonstrations and petitions in favour of free elections.

9–11 February: Monck ordered to take action against anti-Rump demonstrations in London.

21 February: Excluded members returned to Parliament.

March: Lambert imprisoned in the Tower of London; the Long Parliament dissolved itself.

25 April: New Parliament assembled and was known as the Convention Parliament because it was not called by a King.

1 May: Declaration of Breda presented to Parliament.

5 May: Parliament voted government to be by King, Lords and Commons.

25 May: Charles II landed at Dover.

◄ The entry of King Charles II of England into London on 29 May 1660. Coloured engraving after a contemporary Dutch engraving.

Chapter summary

- The execution of Charles I in 1649 was not even considered until late in 1648. It was therefore hastily organised with little time to plan for a replacement.
- The slow and piecemeal establishment of the Commonwealth in the midst of war across Britain demonstrates the lack of support for the regime and the lack of unity even among its supporters. The Levellers and their allies were quickly dealt with, but hostility within the political nation, especially from the ruling elites, was a more serious problem. As late as 1651 there were still debates about the form that government should take, with some MPs and army officers still expressing a preference for government with 'something of the monarchical' in it.
- However, the lack of support for Charles Stuart's attempted invasion in 1651, and his defeat at Worcester, ensured the regime's survival. At the same time, its dependence on an army that was an economic burden and a source of radical influence posed further problems.
- Ultimately it was the internal divisions about the nature and extent of reform, especially in religion, that undermined the rule of the Rump and led to its dissolution by Cromwell in 1653.
- The same problems brought about the collapse of the Nominated Assembly in December 1653 and the establishment of the Protectorate.
- Despite the loyalty of the army and some success in foreign policy, Cromwell's government faced further hostility from several quarters. While his management of the Church was reasonably effective in practical terms, it did little to reassure conservatives about social controls and fear of radicalism. To these problems were now added the deep hostility of ex-Rumpers and republicans, who objected to the influence of the army.
- Their influence in parliaments and the difficulty of widening support among the elites increased financial problems and forced Cromwell to take measures for greater security. The rule of the Major-Generals increased fear of military dictatorship.
- This led moderates in parliament to attempt the restoration of monarchy, with Cromwell as King. The purpose of the plan was to give the regime a legal basis while securing constitutional limits to the power of the monarch and constitutional rights for parliaments.
- Although resistance within the army and his own religious convictions led Cromwell to reject the Crown, the plan did not entirely disappear. The benefits of government by a single person in partnership with parliaments were widely accepted, and it is likely that further moves towards a restoration would have been made had Cromwell not died in September 1658.
- His death, and the inability of his son to retain the loyalty of the army, led to the return of the Rump, a descent into chaos and in the last resort, the restoration of Divine Right monarchy in the person of Charles Stuart. Despite the lack of guarantees for his future conduct, he returned in May 1660 amid widespread public rejoicing.

Working on essay technique

Remember the skills that you built up in Chapters 2–5 on essay writing. The main headings were:

- *Focus and structure* Be sure what the question is on and plan what the paragraphs should be about. Think about the concepts involved – is the essay about causes, changes or the significance of events?
- *Focused introduction to the essay* Be sure that the introductory sentence relates directly to the focus of the question and that each paragraph highlights the structure of the answer.
- *How to use detail* Make sure that you show detailed knowledge – but only as part of an explanation being made in relation to the question. No knowledge should be 'free-standing'.

- *Explanatory analysis* Think of the wording of an answer in order to strengthen the explanation.
- *Argument and counter-argument* Think of how arguments can be juxtaposed as part of a balancing act in order to give contrasting views.
- *Resolution* Think how best to 'resolve' contradictory arguments. These can be about different causal factors, or about the extent and balance of change and continuity.
- *Relative significance and evaluation* Think how best to reach a judgement when trying to assess the relative importance of various factors, and possibly their inter-relationship. If the essay is about change, what changes were most significant?

ACTIVITY

Consider the following practice question:

'To what extent was the monarchy of 1640 restored in 1660?'

1 At the top of a large sheet of paper write out the question.
2 On the left-hand side jot down the main topic areas (in this case, rights, powers and the means of exercising them) that you might cover in an answer.
3 On the right-hand side transform these ideas into a basic plan for an answer. In outline:
a) What powers had the monarchy lost or parliament gained?
b) Are 'powers' always formal and defined?
c) Do attitudes and beliefs come into it? In the light of that, were there any ways in which the monarchy was stronger or better in 1660?
4 Then look at the list of essay writing skills above. See how they can fit into your plan. Some, such as an introduction, will be there automatically. Consider the following:
a) Introduction – is it simple or could it be complex? Does it do more than introduce? Does it highlight the structure of the answer? In this case, the 'monarchy of 1640' is key to the

answer – does the phrase need to be defined? If so, is the introduction a good place to do it? A really good introduction can give you a sense of exactly where your essay is going.
b) Where can you add specific details to your plan so that you show a range of knowledge?
c) Does your plan successfully feature analysis and evaluation? Are you sure it will not lead to a narrative or descriptive approach? Are there clear sections in which you can explain features and evaluate their significance in relation to the question?
d) Can you balance arguments and counter-arguments?
e) Can you reach a judgement which 'resolves' any conflicting arguments, and enables you to assess 'To what extent'?
5 Can you add precise details and/or quotations into this structure to provide evidence to support your arguments?
6 Has your answer shown an awareness of different interpretations?
7 Now write your own answer to the essay.

Working on interpretation skills: extended reading

In earlier chapters of the book you were given the opportunity to develop skills in answering Interpretations questions. It is probably a good idea to re-read the advice given earlier in the book at the end of Chapter 3 before you complete the activity on page 170.

The return of the monarchy in 1660 was an important turning point in the development in government in Britain and creates a need to assess the changes that had taken place as a result of crisis, war and revolution in 1640–60. In judging the significance of events, it is clear that 1660 marked a reversal of the developments that had taken place in matters of political authority, religion and the distribution of power. For that reason the extent of this reversal and the significance of developments cannot be assessed at this point. The terms of the Restoration and how they would be applied in practice were not clear when the King returned, and most historians have chosen to study the events that followed before drawing conclusions about how far the events of 1640–60 had affected the nature of the monarchy, parliaments and the Church. Nevertheless, there are areas of society and government where changes had taken place that were not reversed, or where new techniques and methods developed in the conditions of war and republican government that would help to shape the new institutions that were emerging. It is these matters that are the subject of the interpretation that follows.

How far did the events of 1640–60 enhance the powers of Parliament at the expense of the Crown?

Dr Stephen K. Roberts traces the changing political landscape between 1640 and 1660.

Although parliament assembled in November 1640 at the invitation of Charles I, its members came together intent on a remedial programme covering religion, trade and relations with Scotland and Ireland. Nearly 20 years later, the survivors of that same parliament re-assembled to vote their own dissolution, and to accede to the inauguration of a restored monarchy. Despite this act of self-destruction, the political landscape had been reconfigured. In 1660, it was only by the consent of parliament that Charles II was invited back to the throne. 5 10

The key to parliamentary supremacy lay in taxation. Before 1640, the King had struggled with a series of expedients to raise money, but the real wealth of the country lay in the hands of the gentry and merchants who crowded the benches of the House of Commons. Initially, MPs tried to help the Crown by improvements to the main direct tax on the propertied classes, but soon, relations with the King collapsed. Once civil war had erupted, the Commons proved adept at extending direct taxes and devising new and effective fiscal devices to fund the parliamentary armies. None was more controversial or more effective than the excise tax on commodities. The City of London, staunchly loyal to Parliament, proved crucial to the continuing flow of revenue. By comparison, the royalists' efforts at tax-raising, coordinated in the field or from provincial Oxford, were feeble. After the execution of the King in 1649, and through the constitutional changes of commonwealth and protectorate, the powerless monarchy was in exile, excluded from influencing state development 15 20 25 back at home. Meanwhile in London, the seat of government, successive parliamentary regimes inherited the financial machinery established in 1642–43 under the supervision of John Pym. The result was that the restored monarchy of 1660 was completely dependent on parliamentary taxation for its survival.

A similar process took place in religious affairs. Parliament initially embarked on a limited campaign to reverse Archbishop Laud's ecclesiastical policies of ceremonialism and effective management of church property and revenues. But it soon broadened into something bigger. Not only were bishops soon excluded from the House of Lords, but over time bishops and deans and chapters of cathedrals were completely abolished. In the all-consuming search for funds to pay its army, Parliament confiscated and sold Church lands. During the 1650s, successive governments tried with significant support from Parliament to re-build a state church along broadly Presbyterian lines, which meant a less centralised organisational structure. While the Restoration brought back the episcopal governance of the Church of England, neither the Presbyterian-dominated Convention Parliament nor the Cavalier Parliament elected in 1661 were willing to leave the government of the Church entirely to the King and the Bishops.

In 1640, the poor prospects for the economy were a major concern for the parliament-men of the House of Commons. Not only merchants, but also landowners and lawyers felt the effects of a trade collapse that impacted even more heavily on the mass of the populace. It was thus inevitable that stimulating trade remained a prominent aim of Parliaments through the 1640s and 1650s. The purest distillation of Parliament's promotion of business interests was the 'Navigation Act' of 1651, which stipulated that imports from English colonies must be transported in English ships, and which heralded a decade of colonial expansion and a build-up of naval power. The restored Stuart monarchy therefore inherited policies which have been described with pardonable exaggeration as mercantilist, and was content to re-enact legislation of its republican predecessors. Samuel Pepys, a naval civil servant of the monarchy in the 1660s, could only admire the expansion of the fleet under Cromwell and his supportive Parliaments.

The incompetence of Charles I's government had brought three kingdoms to the point of constitutional breakdown by 1640. The English Parliaments that met in April and November that year were anxious for amicable settlement with Scotland, and were on course to secure one, based on their shared religious outlook; but the revolt of the Irish against their Protestant rulers in 1641 led to a parliamentarian war, with extensive Scots input, against the Catholic interests in Ireland which lasted until the suppression secured by Cromwell's campaign in 1649. Scots support for the future Charles II after his father's execution led to another parliamentary victory over the Scots Covenanters and a forced union of England and Scotland in 1651, imposed by the Parliament in London. After 1660, Charles II either failed to address these achievements or could not be troubled to. The parliamentary policies of the 1640s and '50s led in effect to an enduring 'Protestant Ascendancy' in Ireland, while the Scots, deprived of their union with England, were given nothing to replace it, and became mere dependents of the English Crown. In relations between the kingdoms, as in other fields, it had been Parliament that had made the running.

Dr Stephen K. Roberts is an Editor at The History of Parliament, London.

ACTIVITY

Comprehension

1 What four aspects of government and administration does the essay (pages 168–69) address? For each aspect, write a brief summary of the ways in which the role and influence of parliaments developed between 1640 and 1660.

2 In what ways did these developments reduce the power that could be exercised by a monarch?

Evidence

3 Find and record Roberts' evidence that in all four 'fields', 'it had been Parliament that had made the running' (line 77).

Interpretation

4 To what extent does Roberts suggest that these changes arose from practical necessities in a period of war and conflict, rather than a deliberate attempt to limit the power of the monarchy?

Evaluation

5 Using your own knowledge, write a paragraph explaining how far you agree with Roberts' interpretation of the impact of events in 1640–60 on:

a) The relationship between King and Parliament in England.

b) The relationship between the British kingdoms.

Although the essay here is focused on the years 1640–60, it makes reference to developments both before and after the Restoration in considering the implications of what happened in those years. This is because in order to fully assess the significance of the events described here, it is necessary to look at their longer-term impact and consequences. The historian writing this essay is aware of that, but does not develop the assessment in detail because that is not the focus here. To do this for yourself, keep a record of your conclusions. When you have completed your study of the chapters that follow, revisit them and use your knowledge of how the monarchy developed after 1660 to assess:

● How far these developments affected King and Parliament in 1660–89.

● How far they strengthened the monarchy in the years of co-operation that followed in 1689–1702.

Restoration and intrigue, 1660–78

7

This chapter covers the period from the Restoration of Charles II in 1660 to the moment just before the political crisis that began with the Popish Plot in 1678. The Acts of Parliament known as the 'Restoration Settlement' were mostly passed *after* Charles II returned to England, as King and Parliament sought to pick up the threads of legal process that had been severed by the English Revolution. The chapter focuses on a number of areas:

- the Restoration Settlement, 1660–64
- the fall of the Earl of Clarendon in 1667
- religious divisions and conflicts
- King Charles II and his ministers
- the emergence of Court and Country 'parties' in the 1670s.

These areas also relate to the key questions associated with the extent of change to the monarchy, the extent to which power was shared, and the effects of religious disputes throughout the period.

The main question focused on in this chapter is:

How successfully did Charles II govern Britain in the first 18 years of his rule?

CHAPTER OVERVIEW

Some very famous events took place in these years, especially the Great Plague of 1665 and the Fire of London of 1666. Memorable as these were, other developments in this period were of far greater significance to the long-term development of constitutional monarchy in England. Once the 'honeymoon period' of the King's return faded, problems that remained unsettled by the Restoration returned to haunt both Crown and Parliament.

This chapter begins with an analysis of the Restoration Settlement – the series of parliamentary Acts passed between 1660 and 1664 that attempted to sort out the many issues left unresolved at the time of the King's Restoration. These included constitutional, religious, military and financial problems, the settlement of property, and the punishment of the regicides responsible for Charles I's execution. The chapter then moves on to consider the reasons for the downfall of the Earl of Clarendon, Charles II's chief minister from 1660, who was forced to flee into exile in 1667. The focus then shifts to the religious settlement known as the 'Clarendon Code': the English Revolution had witnessed the growth of religious radicalism, which the Clarendon Code sought to suppress, but with what success? After 1667 the chapter examines Charles II as King, his Court and reputation, before looking at his ministers – the Cabal and the Earl of Danby – during a decade that saw political intrigue, a dangerous foreign policy and the re-emergence of political divisions within Parliament.

1 The Restoration Settlement

In the 1650s Cromwell had aimed at 'healing and settling' the nation after the traumas of the civil wars. With the King restored to the throne, he and Parliament now faced the same task. Charles had promised to permit Parliament to make all the key decisions, so what followed was a series of parliamentary Acts aimed at addressing the key issues – the constitution, religion, property, finance and amnesty.

The constitutional settlement

What was 'restored' during the Restoration?

The most important issue to be resolved at the Restoration was this: to which precise moment in recent history was the monarchy being restored? Charles II's reign was held to have begun the moment his father's head was severed from his body on 30 January 1649. Thus, on all official documents, 1649 was referred to as the first year of Charles II's reign. Lawful parliamentary legislation, however, was held to have ended when Charles I no longer signed Acts into law – in other words, when Parliament began passing Ordinances at the beginning of the First Civil War, claiming the right to issue laws without royal approval. The last parliamentary Act given the royal seal of approval was the Act of February 1642, excluding bishops from the House of Lords, and the first Ordinance passed by Parliament was the Militia Ordinance of March 1642. Therefore, all the legislation passed between March 1642 and the Restoration in 1660 was deemed illegal, null and void, supported by an Act of Praeminure that threatened life imprisonment and forfeiture of land and goods for anyone who suggested Parliament had the right to legislate without the King. The Militia Act of May 1661 placed the armed forces back into the King's hands, who also kept the power to appoint his ministers of state. An Act of 1662 against 'tumultuous petitioning' sought to put an end to popular participation in political decisions.

The monarchy that was restored in 1660 was therefore very different from that of the Personal Rule of the 1630s. By agreeing to the legislation of 1641, Charles I had already made concessions that imposed important limits on the monarchy's power. Chief among these was the Triennial Act, whereby the King agreed to call a new Parliament (with new elections) every three years. Out of sensitivity to Charles II's honour, a new Triennial Act passed in 1664 removed the safeguards that provided automatically for the issuing of new parliamentary writs should the King fail to do so himself. All the Acts of 1641 that constrained the monarch's power in order to end the Personal Rule remained in force – Ship Money, Forest Fines, Distraint of Knighthood, the prerogative courts of Star Chamber and High Commission, the Council of the North – and none of them would ever return. Even before Charles II's return from exile, the Convention Parliament had passed an Act for the Confirmation of Judicial Proceedings, confirming the legality of the work of magistrates and judges since the outbreak of the civil wars. This was necessary in order to maintain continuity of the law courts dealing with, for example, the common law and criminal cases.

The Navigation Acts of 1650 and 1651 were also adopted by the Convention Parliament, as was the Act of 1656 abolishing purveyance and wardship, feudal tenures that had long been unpopular with Parliament.

Despite these changes, the monarchy was restored in 1660 almost unconditionally. Attempts to restrict Charles II's prerogative powers by explicitly confirming parliamentary privileges and the fundamental laws of Magna Carta failed in the House of Lords. None of the terms that Parliament had tried to impose on Charles I, from the Nineteen Propositions of 1642 to the Newport negotiations of 1648, were incorporated in the constitutional settlement of 1660.

Settlement of the kingdom

Most historians have argued that the Restoration failed to settle the issues that divided the kingdom in the 1640s. Barry Coward argued that,

'*the political history of the period 1660–67 is characterised by escalating political instability and by growing conflict between Charles II and Parliament*'.

Source A provides another view.

Before considering these arguments more closely, we need to familiarise ourselves with the various Acts that, between them, tried to return the nation to stability and order. Inevitably, this legislation reflected the vengeful attitude of the Cavalier Parliament.

Source A From *Restoration: Charles II and his Kingdoms* by Tim Harris, (Penguin), 2006, p.6.

It cannot be denied that the Restoration regime faced serious difficulties. Indeed, by the late 1670s these had grown so severe that many contemporaries – including the King himself – genuinely came to fear the possibility of renewed civil war. Healing the divisions that had caused the outbreak of civil war in 1642, and which in turn had been exacerbated by the political experiences of the 1640s and '50s, proved no easy task, and political tensions soon began to reappear.

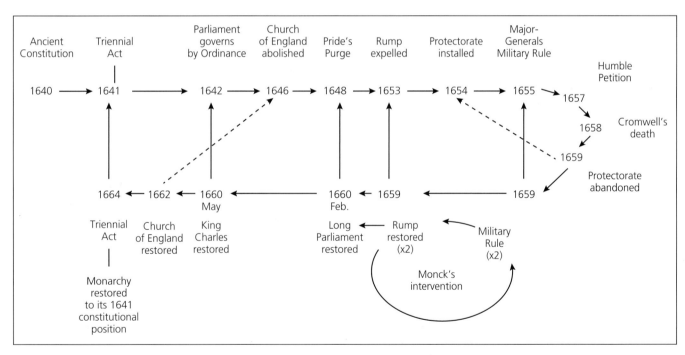

▲ **Figure 1** Restoration road: the way back to monarchy involved revisiting, and undoing, each of the constitutional crises of the revolution, in reverse order.

Cavalier Parliament

The so-called 'Cavalier Parliament' sat from its election in 1660 until its dissolution in 1679, a total of 20 parliamentary sessions, with only one year – 1672 – in which Parliament did not sit. It gets its name from the large number of Royalist MPs elected, a consequence of the reaction against the events and radicalism of the civil war period at the time of the Restoration. The Cavalier Parliament in its early stages witnessed a peculiar 'role reversal', with Parliament imposing an intolerant High Anglicanism while the King attempted to ensure a degree of religious toleration, at least for Presbyterians. In its later stages the Parliament began to divide into Country and Court 'parties', partly as a result of growing national suspicions about the King's policies, and partly as a result of Danby's efforts to create a Court 'party' in the House of Commons.

The religious settlement: the Church of England restored

- Church lands sold during the civil wars restored without compensation.
- Episcopal government of the Church restored – bishops returned to their dioceses.
- Book of Common Prayer restored, with additional sections on Charles the Martyr and references to the wickedness of rebellion.
- Act of Uniformity (1662): all clergy to swear to use the Anglican liturgy. All clergy not ordained by a bishop to surrender their benefices. Some 2000 clergy (one-fifth of the Church) forced to resign.

The Church of England was therefore restored in a form that might have pleased Archbishop Laud, had he been alive to see it. Charles II and the Earl of Clarendon tried to ensure that Presbyterians had a role in the new Church. For example, some prominent non-Anglicans such as Richard Baxter were appointed royal chaplains. Following the Worcester House Conference, a meeting between the King and leading Presbyterians, Charles proposed a settlement in which Presbyterian councils limited the powers of bishops, with committees of both Anglicans and Presbyterians ruling on doctrinal issues. The Cavalier Parliament, however, rejected these proposals.

The religious settlement: the Clarendon Code

Between 1661 and 1665 the Cavalier Parliament passed a series of Acts designed to restore the religious monopoly of the Anglican Church. The Corporation Act was particularly important in this respect, excluding members of religious sects from public office. Members of town corporations had to take Holy Communion according to the rites of the Church of England, renounce the Solemn League and Covenant and swear loyalty to the King. Other Acts imposed press censorship, imposed penalties for attending non-Anglican services and prevented Dissenter clergymen from coming into contact with schools and congregations, in order to limit their influence. Together, these Acts became known as the Clarendon Code.

In the Declaration of Breda (see Chapter 6, page 164) Charles Stuart had made a vague promise that there would be 'liberty to tender consciences'. It is unlikely that he meant by this toleration of the many radical sects that had developed since the 1640s. The Declaration was aimed at the Presbyterians, those conservative-minded allies of the Scots who had been excluded from Parliament by Pride's Purge of December 1649, who had also opposed Cromwell's Protectorate and whose support Charles needed to regain the throne in 1660. Understandably, however, the Declaration raised the hopes of radicals and moderates alike that the new King would adopt a policy of broad toleration, though the Presbyterians were as keen as the Anglicans that religious radicalism should be suppressed. In the event, even the Presbyterians' hopes were dashed by the religious settlement enacted by the Cavalier Parliament, which was punitive and intolerant.

The settlement of property

- Royal and Church land sold by Parliament to be reinstated without compensation.
- Royalists whose estates had been sequestered and sold by Parliament were able to get them back through the courts.
- Royalists who had sold land to pay Decimation Taxes or fines or to raise forces for the King had little chance of receiving compensation.

Property taken from the Church of England or the Crown and sold was restored without compensation to its new owners. People unwise enough to have purchased this property lost their investment. This did little harm to Royalists, however, who were unlikely to have purchased ecclesiastical or royal land. The situation of Royalists whose land had been removed by Parliament was more complicated. The greatest difficulty was faced by those who had remained inveterate enemies of the Interregnum regimes. Thus the land settlement of the Restoration appeared to punish the most loyal and to reward those who had compromised their beliefs to reach an accommodation with Cromwell's government.

The financial settlement

- Parliament estimated that the Crown needed a fixed income of £1.2 million per year.
- The King was granted Tonnage and Poundage for life, worth approximately £800,000 per year.
- Feudal tenures such as purveyance, wardship and forced loans were abolished.
- Dunkirk was sold to the King of France for £400,000.
- Hearth tax was introduced (1662).
- Parliament expected the King to raise a further £100,000 per year from Crown lands.

In retrospect, it is clear that the monarchy was genuinely impoverished in the first half of the seventeenth century. During one year of Cromwell's Protectorate, for example, his government received more parliamentary income than Charles I received during his entire reign. Would Parliament strengthen the Crown after the Restoration by giving Charles II a more adequate income?

The financial settlement left the Crown with a deficit of £120,000 a year short of the estimated costs of government in times of peace. Members of Parliament – even Cavalier ones – had little conception of the real costs of government and lived under the illusion that it could be had on the cheap. Furthermore, it was necessary to keep the King short of money to force him to listen to Parliament. If there is one factor that stands out in the growth of constitutional monarchy in the later seventeenth century, it is this continued reliance of the Crown on Parliamentary income.

General amnesty for participation in the civil wars

- The Act of Indemnity and Oblivion (1660) took up Charles's offer of a 'free and general pardon' for his opponents in the civil wars.
- All acts of hostility between the King and his enemies between 1637 and 1660 were to be erased from the public memory.
- Parliament excluded the regicides from this amnesty – those men who had either signed Charles I's death warrant or were closely associated with his trial and execution. Approximately ten regicides were hanged, drawn and quartered.

History rewritten

- 29 May – Restoration Day – declared a public holiday, celebrated into the nineteenth century by people who pinned sprigs of oak leaves to their jackets.
- Names of some of the Commonwealth's ships changed, e.g. the *Naseby* became the *Royal Charles*.
- Providence, which for many years seemed to favour Cromwell, now seemed to favour the monarchy and the forces of reaction.

Nonconformists and Dissenters

These are terms used to describe those who felt unable to attend Church regularly, or to take Anglican Communion, and preferred to worship in separate, often private meetings. The terms covered a number of denominational groups, but not Catholics, who also refused to attend Church.

The defeat of Millenarianism

You will have seen in Chapter 6, page 148, that millenarianism was a powerful force among the religious radicals in the 1650s. The Fifth Monarchy Men, for example, believed that England was living out the fulfilment of the Bible's prophecies. It was not only 'radicals' who believed this: Cromwell himself, in establishing the Nominated Assembly in 1653, met the new parliament in tears that the prophecy was about to be fulfilled. The trial and execution of King Charles I had likewise excited much millenarian sentiment.

At the time of the Restoration there was bound to be resistance to the return of monarchy from individuals and groups motivated by millenarian beliefs. The most famous incident was Venner's Rising of January 1661. This was a small uprising of perhaps 150 men, quickly suppressed, but it served to confirm the widespread belief that religious nonconformists, if tolerated, would inevitably lead to political sedition. There is plentiful evidence of a widespread public reaction against millenarian sentiments before and during the Restoration.

The Restoration Settlement of 1660–64 has been attacked for its failure to settle the most important political and religious issues of the time. For example, the financial settlement between Crown and Parliament has been condemned as unworkable; the reactionary religious settlement has been condemned as vindictive; the land settlement has been criticised for its unfairness towards the most loyal Royalists; and the constitutional settlement has been slated for the continuing tension between Crown and Parliament in Charles II's reign. These failures have been ascribed to such factors as the disunity between the MPs of the Convention Parliament, the vindictive unity of the Cavalier Parliament and the fear of Quakerism that had played an important part in the Restoration process.

It may be that the term 'Restoration settlement' is misconceived. The nation's priority in the early 1660s was to restore the monarchy and put an end to political disorder. The English Revolution appeared to confirm Charles I's opinion (and that of the Earl of Manchester, as voiced in the debates leading to the Self-Denying Ordinance) that there was no alternative to monarchy. The Presbyterians were bitterly disappointed to find themselves excluded by the narrowly High Church Anglicanism of the Restoration, but they themselves had fought Cromwell tooth and nail to persecute other Protestant minorities. Religious nonconformity was too closely associated with sedition for broad toleration to have worked, and arguably the Church restored in the 1660s was essentially the Elizabethan Church the Puritans of the early seventeenth century had claimed to be defending against innovations in religion. Rather than seeing this as an attempt to 'settle' the kingdom for all time, it might be more accurate to regard the Restoration as a choice made by the political nation brought on by despair at the instability of the 1650s.

It is also necessary to view the Restoration in a broader perspective. Looking back, it could be argued that the process of Restoration began as early as 1649 when, in the wake of the King's execution, Cromwell and the grandees of the army turned on the Levellers to reassure the gentry that the Revolution was political rather than social. By 1657 Cromwell was 'King in all but name', after Parliament had offered him the Crown. Looking forward, the settlement of 1689 also left the Crown deliberately short of funds, a step towards constitutional monarchy which has not been condemned as a 'failure' by historians. Looking at the Restoration in a broad span of time – essential for a breadth study – and in a wider context, we may conclude that the 'settlement' of 1660–64 was an unavoidable stage in an evolutionary process in which violent revolutionary change was rejected. However, in making up your own mind about the supposed 'failure' of the Restoration, you will need to take into account the history of most of the later seventeenth century, as the evidence for failure is to be found in subsequent events.

KEY DATES: THE RESTORATION SETTLEMENT

1660

October: Worcester House Conference on religion.

1661

January: Bodies of Cromwell, Bradshaw and Ireton exhumed and hanged.

May: First session of Cavalier Parliament; Militia Act; Corporation Act; Act against tumultuous petitioning; Act condemning Parliament's former claim to legislate without royal approval.

November: Quaker Act; press censorship imposed.

1662

April: Prayer Book accepted by parliament.

May: Act of Uniformity; Hearth Tax.

December: Declaration of Indulgence.

1663

April: Declaration of Indulgence withdrawn.

1664

November: Triennial Act; Conventicle Act.

NOTE-MAKING

1 In your notes, create a balance sheet for the Restoration settlement, consisting of two columns. One column should be headed 'Evidence for failure', the other column 'Evidence against failure'. Enter onto this sheet any evidence you can find so far that will help you to evaluate the Restoration settlement.

2 Complete this balance sheet as you work through Chapters 7 and 8.

3 When you have reached the end of Chapter 8, complete your balance sheet and answer the following A-level practice question:

'The Restoration settlement failed to settle any of the political and religious issues that had divided the kingdom in the 1640s and 1650s.' Assess the validity of this view.

This is an essay that will help you to practise your essay-writing skills. To answer this type of question you will need to go back as far as the causes of the Civil War and consider the issues that had divided the nation in the 1640s and 1650s (see Chapters 4, 5 and 6). Then you need to consider whether the Restoration settlement actually resolved these causes of conflict. This type of essay will be easiest to write if you consider it issue by issue (religion, finance, constitutional problems, etc.) rather than trying to look at it chronologically. More guidance on this question will be provided on page 220.

2 The Earl of Clarendon, 1660–67

Clarendon was a loyal servant of both Charles I and Charles II, a man of great experience whose moderation reassured those fearful of vengeful royalism.

The fall of the Earl of Clarendon

Why did the Earl of Clarendon fall from power in 1667?

Although the 'Clarendon Code' bears his name, Clarendon himself only came to support an intolerant religious settlement once it became clear that it could not be avoided. For the first seven years of Charles II's rule, Clarendon acted as his principal adviser, but in 1667 he was forced into exile. The factors that led to Clarendon's downfall are described below.

The second Anglo-Dutch War, 1664–67

In 1664 there was a growing consensus between the King, Parliament and the Court for war with the Dutch. The young bloods surrounding the King were anxious to make their mark. Warfare was an accepted aspect of kingship and a king was expected to show his mettle by vigorously defending his kingdom's honour and rights. By 1664 Charles II felt secure enough on his throne to risk conflict and he may even have felt that a war with the Dutch would strengthen domestic loyalty to the Crown.

It is ironic that the main cause of Clarendon's downfall was a war that he had tried to prevent. Clarendon was conscious of the Crown's financial weakness and did not agree with other members of the Privy Council that there were sufficient reasons to go to war. However, Charles was won over by the advice of James, Duke of York, Thomas Clifford and others. Commercial rivalries dating back to the early seventeenth century were being exacerbated by the possibilities opening up to trade with the Far East. In early 1664 the House of Commons, encouraged by the East India Company, endorsed the idea of war with the Dutch.

Edward Hyde, Earl of Clarendon (1609–74)

▲ Edward Hyde pictured in the 1660s. Does this image suggest that Hyde is powerful and wealthy?

Edward Hyde was MP for Saltash, Devon, in the Short and Long Parliaments. At first he supported Parliament's attempts to put an end to Charles I's Personal Rule, but in the autumn of 1641 he came to support the King against John Pym's demands for limits on royal prerogatives. When civil war broke out in 1642 he became a moderate Royalist who continued to work for reconciliation between King and Parliament. However, the suicide of his friend Falkland in 1643 weakened his influence with the King, who was inclined to listen to Cavaliers like the Catholic George Digby, who demanded nothing short of military victory. When the Royalists lost the war in 1646 he went into exile. After Charles I's execution in 1649 Clarendon served as Charles Stuart's adviser-in-exile, for which he was later rewarded with his title. At the Restoration in 1660 he became Lord High Chancellor of England, serving as the King's chief minister for seven years until his political downfall in 1667.

Clarendon wrote the first full history of the English Revolution, *The History of the Rebellion and Civil Wars in England*, at the request of Charles I, though it was not published until 1702. In his history, Clarendon was at times critical of Charles I's decisions, a fact which gave his opinions more credibility.

The military narrative

The war seemed to go well at first, with a great English victory in the Battle of Lowestoft in June 1665, but soon Parliament became critical of the conduct of the war. In August 1665 English ships bungled an attack on a Dutch merchant fleet in the neutral port of Bergen. In early 1666 France and Denmark allied with the Dutch against the English; the appearance of a large French fleet in the Channel prompted the English commanders, Prince Rupert and the Duke of Albemarle, to divide their forces. In the Four Days' Battle with the Dutch in June 1666, 10 English ships were sunk with the loss of 4,250 men, including two admirals. Parliament blamed government corruption and poor administration in the navy for these losses.

It was unfortunate for Clarendon that the Dutch War coincided with two great disasters, the Great Plague of 1665 and the Fire of London of 1666. The Plague was serious enough, with some 70,000 deaths in 1665, but although there was minimal loss of life, the Fire of London was a disaster. Over five days in September the heart of the City of London was destroyed, including St Paul's Cathedral, 89 churches and over 13,000 houses. Speculation that the fire was started by the Dutch contributed to criticism of the management of the war, but the fire led to a decline in the Crown's revenue that prompted parliamentary enquiries into maladministration in the navy board.

The Dutch raid on the Medway

Early in 1667 Charles II began peace negotiations, and in anticipation of their successful outcome, the nation dropped its guard. The most recent parliamentary grant was diverted from the war to pay off an earlier deficit; some ships' crews were paid off and shore defences and naval dockyards were neglected. Then in June 1667, the Dutch Admiral de Ruyter launched a daring raid up the Medway to attack the royal dockyards at Chatham. Charles's ministers could only watch helplessly as the Dutch fleet captured the shore batteries that were intended to protect the naval base, burned numerous ships and towed away the *Royal Charles*, the English flagship. Parliament turned on Clarendon, giving his enemies at court – Buckingham, Arlington and Sir William Coventry – an opportunity to get rid of him. Clarendon managed to end the war with the hastily negotiated Treaty of Breda, in which England acquired New York and New Jersey. But other circumstances, too, conspired to bring about Clarendon's downfall.

Other factors leading to Clarendon's downfall

By 1667, Charles II was growing tired of Clarendon, who disapproved of the King's mistresses (a stark contrast with Charles I's behaviour) and whom he held responsible for the growth of opposition in Parliament and at Court. A number of issues came together by 1667 to weaken Clarendon's position before the Dutch War finally sealed his fate.

- Clarendon's failure to manage Parliament effectively. The growth of opposition may have been inevitable, but as Charles's chief minister, Clarendon was held responsible.
- Clarendon's personality seemed arrogant and self-righteous, the 'older, wiser' figure trying to guide a King who was himself growing older and more confident. These characteristics also alienated the Privy Council, with the result that Clarendon was already losing his grip by 1665, as his failure to prevent the Dutch War illustrated.
- Jealousy of Clarendon's position: though not as bad as the Duke of Buckingham in the 1620s, Clarendon's hold on power was blocking the advancement of ambitious younger courtiers more in sympathy with the King's youth and behaviour.

> ### KEY DATES: THE SECOND ANGLO-DUTCH WAR
>
> **1665**
>
> **February:** Second Anglo-Dutch War began; Parliament granted £2.5 million for the war.
>
> **October:** Parliament granted a further £1.25 million.
>
> **1666** France and Denmark joined the war against England.
>
> **September:** Fire of London; House of Commons attacked corruption of naval officials; Parliament granted a further £1.8 million.
>
> **1667**
>
> **January:** Supply Bill – public accounts to be examined by parliamentary committee.
>
> **May:** Spanish Netherlands overrun by French forces.
>
> **June:** Dutch raid in the Medway.
>
> **July:** Treaty of Breda.
>
> **October:** Clarendon fled to France to avoid impeachment by Parliament.

● Nepotism: Clarendon's daughter Anne Hyde married James, Duke of York, the heir to the throne. This laid him open to accusations of self-aggrandisement: the heir to the throne would normally be expected to marry foreign royalty.

● Charles II's marriage to the Portuguese Catherine of Braganza. The King treated his wife with the utmost respect and kindness, but it was common knowledge at court that he found her boring. The fact that they were childless reflected badly on Clarendon, who had negotiated the marriage.

When it came, Clarendon's downfall was swift and brutal. Under pressure from the King he resigned in August 1667, but his rivals wanted to see him impeached on a charge of treason, which could carry the death penalty. Perhaps remembering the fate of the Earl of Strafford in 1641, the House of Lords refused to imprison him in the Tower, whereupon his enemies tried to create a special court of Lords for his prosecution. What sealed Clarendon's fate was Charles II's refusal to intervene on his behalf. Thus, after 26 years of loyal service to the Crown, Clarendon voluntarily went into exile in France, where he died five years later.

What should we make of Charles II's abandonment of Clarendon? It was Clarendon himself who, when writing about the early years of Charles I's reign, voiced the opinion that the King should have allowed Buckingham's impeachment in 1626 to proceed. Perhaps we should credit Charles II with not making one of his father's mistakes. However, Charles II's treatment of a faithful servant was a foretaste of things to come, and most historians view his treatment of Clarendon as shabby and unprincipled.

3 The Restoration Court

As the monarchy returned to England, so life returned to the Court and Whitehall Palace in London, which became Charles II's favourite residence. King Charles I had tried to make the court and the palace a model of dignified behaviour, an austere and formal setting for a king who ruled by divine right. By contrast, Charles II's court is associated with the King's **hedonistic lifestyle** and his mistresses, his love of theatre and his daily walks in St James's Park. One other difference was particularly important: whereas Charles I had totally inadequate security around the palace in times of popular tumults, Charles II had a guard of approximately 8,000 men.

Hedonistic lifestyle – A life lived in the selfish pursuit of pleasure.

Charles II as King

Did Charles II's character contribute to the political and religious problems of his reign?

Popular folklore sees the Restoration as a period of thankful reaction to the sanctimonious religious piety of the Interregnum. Having studied the Interregnum, you probably realise that this popular view of Cromwell and his government is mostly false. The image of Cromwell as a kill joy who banished Christmas does a disservice to his greatness of heart and to the pragmatism and achievements of the Interregnum regimes. It is also likely that the popular image of the Restoration is based on a few famous incidents and personalities, rather than a sea-change in public behaviour. Nevertheless, the return of the King marked something of a watershed in the atmosphere of the times, as Sources B–D illustrate:

Source B From *A Gambling Man: Charles II and the Restoration* by Jenny Uglow, (Faber & Faber), 2009, p.272.

In July 1663, Buckhurst and Sedley, with the Lincolnshire squire Sir Thomas Ogle, staggered into the Cock Inn in Bow Street, near Covent Garden. 'Being all inflam'd with strong liquours', they went out on to the balcony. Sedley then stripped naked, gave a jovial pantomime ... and preached a mock sermon which conflated priest, quack and pimp ... As an encore he pissed on the crowd in the street. A minor riot began as angry townsfolk battered the locked doors and hurled stones and empty wine bottles through the windows. In court next day, Sedley was bound over to good behaviour on a bond of £500, which he tried hard to get reduced ... In the end he borrowed the money for the fine from Charles himself – a gesture of royal amusement, instead of chastisement, which was quickly noted by hostile observers.

Much of our knowledge of day-to-day life under Charles II comes from the *Diary of Samuel Pepys*, in which he recorded, among many other things, evidence of the aristocracy's sexual behaviour (Source C).

Source C From *The Diary of Samuel Pepys*, entry for 9 June 1667.

In comes my Lord Berkeley, who is going down to Harwich also to look after the militia there; and there is also the Duke of Monmouth, and with him a great many young Hectors, the Lord Chesterfield, my Lord Mandeville, and others: but to little purpose, I fear, but to debauch the country-women thereabouts.

The Restoration's image as an era of hedonistic sexual counter-revolution is perpetuated today in films such as Laurence Dunmore's *The Libertine* (2004), in which Johnny Depp portrayed the infamous John Wilmot, Earl of Rochester, of whom Pepys wrote that it was 'to the King's everlasting shame to have so idle a rogue his companion'. A recent biography of Rochester describes how he criticised Charles's behaviour (Source D).

Source D From *Blazing Star: the Life and Times of John Wilmot, Earl of Rochester* by Alexander Larman, (Head of Zeus), 2014.

Seeing his country worn down by war and poverty, Rochester mocked 'the easiest King and best-bred man alive' as someone who was occupied with 'starving his people' and 'hazarding his crown' in the pursuit of carnal desires. He dismissed the royal mistresses who manipulated Charles, most notably the vile-tempered and covetous Barbara Villiers, Countess of Castlemaine ...

Charles II's mistresses are a well-known aspect of his reign, three of whom are particularly significant. Barbara Villiers, Duchess of Castlemaine, cousin of the second Duke of the Cabal and whose grandfather was half-brother to the first Duke of Buckingham, was the King's longest-serving companion, a woman sometimes blamed for excessive political influence at court. Nell Gwyn was an actress whom the King mentioned on his death-bed in 1685, imploring his brother James:

'Let not poor Nelly starve'.

Finding her carriage surrounded by an anti-Catholic mob during the Exclusion Crisis, Gwyn leaned from the coach and called out,

'Pray good people be civil; I am the Protestant whore'.

The Catholic mistress was the French Louise de Keroualle, Duchess of Portsmouth, deliberately planted as a spy at Charles's court by Louis XIV.

The court of Charles II was centred in Whitehall, an old rambling Tudor palace through the middle of which ran the road from Westminster to the Strand. Relatively little is known of the precise structure and plan of this palace, which burned in the 1690s with the loss of many priceless works of art, including the great Holbein painting of the family of Sir Thomas More. The only surviving part today is the 1620s Banqueting House designed by Inigo Jones, from which Charles's father was led to his execution. Glimpses of the palace in Charles's time can be seen from contemporary paintings such as that which is reproduced here, showing the Banqueting House on the left, the staircase to the Privy Gallery on the right, beyond which can be seen the Holbein Gate. Today you would be standing in Horse Guards Parade, and indeed a troop of musketeers can be seen drilling in the middle distance. In the foreground the King is taking his daily constitutional, exercising his spaniels, walking towards St James's Park, where he often indulged in games of Pall Mall.

If you ride today on the London Eye and look directly across the Thames, you are looking down on the site of the old palace of Whitehall, roughly everything between Parliament Square and Nelson's Column. The royal apartments were close to the river. The bedrooms of Charles's mistresses were played like a game of musical chairs; in the early 1660s the Duchess of Castlemaine's rooms were above the Holbein Gate overlooking King Street (modern Whitehall), connected to the King's bedchamber by a direct corridor that ran past the Council Chamber. The Queen's bedchamber was beyond, so Charles was located conveniently between his Queen and his mistress. As the King's relationships ebbed and flowed, so the mistresses' bedchambers were located more or less closely to the centre of power, the King's Privy Chamber.

It is only possible in this short space to give an impression of the way that historians have interpreted Charles II's style of kingship. In the following sources, we see two contrasting views of the King, the first generous, the second more critical.

▲ 'Whitehall Palace from St. James's Park' c.1675.

Source E From *The Stuart Age: England 1603–1714,* by Barry Coward, (Longman), 2003, p.291.

The tittle-tattle related by that arch-gossipmonger Pepys is too often used to argue that Charles' pursuit of women was the root cause of his neglect of state affairs ... Moreover, criticisms of Charles' undoubted cynicism and unprincipled behaviour are often also moral rather than political judgements. His cynical treatment of his friends and enemies alike, his double-dealing, and resort to short-term political expediency were just the amoral qualities required by Machiavelli in a successful ruler.

Source F From *Charles II, King of England, Scotland and Ireland* by Ronald Hutton, (Oxford University Press), 1991, p.454.

His classic way of ruling, especially in foreign affairs, was to have different lines of policy running at once, conceived with different groups of advisers and often mutually contradictory. For all his [careful] attendance of the Privy Council, he loved to hatch schemes in private discussions with one or a few confidants, and to inform the whole government of them later, if at all. Likewise, he would assure ministers to their faces of his affection and support and then allow them to be criticized, or dismiss them, in their absence. Instead of dominating and leading, he preferred to ensure his supremacy by setting Counsellor against Counsellor and mistress against mistress. Such practices provoked confusion, demoralization, and distrust, among his servants, in Parliament, and in foreign states. They also multiplied the occasions upon which, while conceiving himself to be a puppet-master, he was manipulated by his advisers.

The survival of the monarchy through the civil war and republican period was seen as the work of providence, a quality that hitherto had seemed to belong to Cromwell and the army. Likewise, Charles's own survival and exile, and particularly his escape after the Battle of Worcester, were seen as providential events. Charles had numerous stories to tell of the many close calls endured during his escape to France, such as the occasion when his horse dropped a shoe that had to be replaced. On examining the other horseshoes, the farrier commented that his horse had last been shod at Worcester, a heavy hint that he knew that Charles was a Royalist fugitive. The association of the King's restoration with divine providence appeared in the new Book of Common Prayer, as Source G illustrates.

Source G From the 1662 Book of Common Prayer, 'King Charles the Martyr'.

Blessed God, just and powerful, who didst permit thy dear Servant, our dread Sovereign King Charles the First, to be (as upon this day) given up to the violent outrages of wicked men, to be despitefully used, and at last murdered by them: Though we cannot reflect upon so foul an act, but with horror and astonishment; yet we do most gratefully commemorate the glories of thy grace, which then shined forth in thine Anointed ... And albeit thou didst suffer them to proceed to such an height of violence, as to kill him, and to take possession of his Throne; yet didst thou in great mercy preserve his Son, whose right it was, and at length by a wonderful providence bring him back, and set him thereon, to restore thy true Religion, and to settle peace amongst us ...

Charles II was a complex character, a man of undoubted bravery whose courage during the civil wars won him the admiration of friend and foe alike. His escape following the Battle of Worcester was the stuff of romantic fiction and it showed that he had 'brass', which endeared him to many ordinary people and was essential in a man of quality. During the Great Fire of London

Machiavelli – A late fifteenth-century Italian political philosopher who broke with tradition by arguing, in his most famous work *The Prince*, written in the sixteenth century, that expediency was more important to a ruler than moral, principled behaviour. In other words, a ruler should think mainly about self-interest, and do the things that must be done, rather than worry about the rights and wrongs of his or her actions.

he took personal command of the efforts to halt the spreading of the flames. Charles was by all accounts a very likeable character, someone who enjoyed life to the full. Unlike his father, Charles II was pragmatic enough to realise that a king needed to be flexible in both politics and religion, though he could also be resolute.

It was his flexibility, however, that brought him in for some criticism. Charles II was quite prepared to sacrifice others, like Clarendon, in the interests of expediency. When he was crowned King of Scotland in 1650, he swore an oath of loyalty to the Covenant and denounced his parents. Ministers and mistresses were discarded once he was finished with them, and he was even prepared to allow others to take the blame for decisions that had been his own. We shall see in Chapter 8 how he allowed the Earl of Danby to shoulder the responsibility for negotiating subsidies from Louis XIV when this was clearly the King's own policy. Some people see him as unprincipled and unscrupulous. His over-riding objective, however, was to retain his throne in a nation that had recently shown all too clearly how easily order could slide into chaos. Both his father before him, and his brother after him, lost their thrones, yet Charles ruled for 25 years. What made the difference was that they – Charles I and James II – were men of high principle, inflexible in their beliefs and calculating in their politics. By contrast, Charles II was blessed with a sort of open and bemused cynicism that suited the times he lived in. He was sustained in power by the memory of the civil wars, but he was also aware of the Crown's weaknesses, and did what was necessary to limit their impact.

4 The emergence of Court and Country 'parties', 1667–78

The origin of England's two-party system is complex. Parliament assembled in the old chapel in the palace of Westminster. Because it was a chapel, the seating was arranged down either side of the central aisle, encouraging an 'adversarial' form of debating – 'us' and 'them', the 'ins' and the 'outs'. However, the formation of parties did not begin until the late 1660s when opposition to the Court formed around a 'Country' viewpoint.

Foreign policy, religion and parliament

Why did Parliament grow increasingly suspicious of the King's policies?

During the decade following Clarendon's downfall, there developed a complex and dangerous interaction between foreign policy, religious policy and the Crown's relations with Parliament. This period witnessed two ministries, that of the Cabal followed by that of the Earl of Danby; several attempts by the King to extend greater religious toleration to both Protestants and Catholics; and a secretive and potentially dangerous foreign policy centred on the power of the King of France. As time progressed there emerged a growing rift between Court and Country that would eventually develop into the Tory and Whig parties. Towards the end of the decade Danby was treading a difficult political path, attempting to persuade the King to adopt policies more in tune with the feelings of the Country, but determined also to maintain his hold on power. All this while the growing danger of France was reawakening anti-Catholic feeling in England, building towards the great crisis of the reign that broke in 1678.

The Cabal

Between 1667 and 1674 Charles relied on a group of five advisers known collectively as the Cabal. Clarendon was not replaced by a chief minister: instead, Charles played the members of the Cabal off against each other, picking and choosing policies to suit himself. The Cabal thus had no co-ordinated policy and little in common, apart from the fact that none of them were High Church Anglicans. The word 'Cabal' was an acronym of their names:

- **C** – Sir Thomas **Clifford**: Treasurer of the Household and a Catholic sympathiser, supporting a pro-French and anti-Dutch foreign policy.
- **A** – Anthony **Ashley** Cooper, First Earl of Shaftesbury and Chancellor of the Exchequer: a former Royalist who had switched sides in 1644 and became a member of the Council of State in 1653. He had been part of the delegation sent to The Hague in 1660 to invite Charles Stuart to return to England.
- **B** – George Villiers, Duke of **Buckingham**. Son of Charles I's favourite, Buckingham had fought for Charles Stuart at Worcester in 1651 and gone into exile with him, but returned to England in 1657 where he married Mary Fairfax, daughter of Parliament's 1640s' Lord General. Imprisoned until 1660, he was appointed to the Privy Council, where he became one of Clarendon's chief opponents.
- **A** – Henry Bennet, Earl of **Arlington**: Another opponent of Clarendon, Arlington was a Catholic who advised Charles in exile. He worked closely with the other Catholic in the Cabal, Clifford.
- **L** – John Maitland, Duke of **Lauderdale**: a Presbyterian Scot who had once supported the Covenant but then supported the Engagement (and the King) during the Second Civil War in 1648. Captured at Worcester and imprisoned until 1660. Secretary of State for Scotland after the Restoration.

The men Charles chose as his closest advisers therefore had interesting and diverse experience, some changing sides during the civil wars, others sharing Charles's exile or suffering imprisonment in the 1650s. Charles believed this collection of former parliamentarians and Royalists, Presbyterians and Catholics gave him the flexibility he needed. There were certainly rivalries within the Cabal, especially between Buckingham and Arlington. It is difficult, therefore, to discern any consistency of policy under the Cabal, but there were two linked developments – a pro-French foreign policy and attempts to develop greater toleration for Dissenters and Catholics. This lack of consistency may have created uncertainty in Parliament and contributed to the growing suspicion that the King was pursuing his own, secret, agenda.

The Secret Treaty of Dover, 1670

In the mid-seventeenth century France replaced Spain as the greatest power in Europe, a consequence of Spanish decline and long-term French reconstruction after the disastrous civil wars of the sixteenth century. After 1661, when Louis XIV began his personal rule, his policies and reforms began to unlock the potential of the French economy and population (France had a population of approximately 20 million compared to England's 4.5 million). This turned France into a great military power.

Charles II was inclined to favour a pro-French policy for several reasons. Part of his time in exile had been spent at the French court. His French mother, Henrietta Maria, was the aunt of Louis XIV. His favourite sister, 'Minette', was married to the Duke of Orleans, the French King's brother. The splendour of the French court, based at the new royal palace of Versailles, was the envy of Europe. French culture, language, music, art, philosophy and literature set the tone of the age.

Louis XIV's foreign policy

In the course of the 1670s, Charles's pro-French leanings put him increasingly at odds with a nation that was becoming progressively more anti-Catholic. The main reason for this was Louis XIV's expansionist foreign policy, revealed in the period covered by this chapter in two wars:

● The War of Devolution, 1667–68
● The Dutch War, 1672–78

To understand the Secret Treaty of Dover it is necessary to know something about these wars. In the War of Devolution, Louis was pursuing a dynastic claim to territories in the Spanish Netherlands that he claimed were the rightful inheritance of his wife, Maria Theresa. Louis XIV's military successes were so alarming that Charles II and the Dutch ended the second Anglo-Dutch War in January 1668 and formed a Triple Alliance with Sweden.

The Secret Treaty

In response to the Triple Alliance, Louis XIV began negotiations with Charles II in order to isolate the Dutch. In May 1670, Charles and Louis concluded the Secret Treaty of Dover, a treaty that was to have momentous consequences for the rest of Charles's reign. England and France agreed to attack the Dutch. Assuming the war was successful, both countries would receive parts of the Dutch Republic, the rest being governed by Charles II's nephew, William of Orange. This much of the Treaty became public knowledge in February 1672. What remained secret, however, was that Charles II promised to declare himself a Catholic when it was possible to do so, and Louis agreed to pay Charles £225,000 per year.

The Secret Treaty of Dover was extremely dangerous for Charles. The purpose of the French King's money was to provide Charles with a secret source of income, making him less reliant on parliamentary subsidies and therefore changing the constitutional relationship between Crown and Parliament. Like Ship Money in the 1630s, Louis XIV's pension might make it possible for the King of England to rule arbitrarily. Charles's promise to announce his conversion to Catholicism was potentially even more dangerous, for although it was not yet illegal for the King to be Catholic, nothing had greater potential to provoke open rebellion. Worse still, Louis XIV could now blackmail Charles with the threat of making the treaty public, endangering the independence of English foreign policy.

No one can give a definitive answer to the question why Charles II signed the Secret Treaty of Dover. To Charles it may have seemed sensible to align himself with the most powerful kingdom in Europe. Domestically, the consequences of the treaty were hugely important. In the course of the 1670s parliament became suspicious that there was more to the public treaty than it had been told, and the Third Dutch War of 1672 to 1674 raised an important question: in whose interests, England's or the Crown's, did the monarchy govern? During the Exclusion Crisis, in 1678, the former English ambassador to France, Ralph Montague, revealed to Parliament that Charles had been negotiating a secret subsidy treaty with Louis XIV, confirming what Parliament already suspected was true, though it never learned all the details of the Secret Treaty of Dover.

In March 1672, in alliance with France, Charles II declared war on the Dutch. At first the war went well for France, with the capture of many towns forcing the Dutch to abandon their first lines of defence. England's war effort was less successful, with a series of inconclusive naval battles. The war had important consequences: it provoked the first major continental coalition against Louis

XIV, including the Dutch, the Emperor Leopold and the Elector of Brandenburg. In the United Provinces the war led to a change of government: Johan De Witt and his brother Cornelius were assassinated, bringing to power William of Orange as Stadtholder. In England the war was unpopular as enmity towards the Dutch was replaced by fear of the strength of Catholic France. Parliament refused to vote the money needed to continue the war, forcing Charles to make peace by the Treaty of Westminster in February 1674.

In that same year, the Earl of Danby finally replaced the Cabal as Charles's main adviser. Danby pursued a pro-Dutch policy: in November 1677 he negotiated a marriage between James Duke of York's eldest daughter, Mary, and William of Orange, the new Stadtholder of Holland. In December 1677 he negotiated an Anglo-Dutch treaty in which England agreed to force Louis XIV to make peace with Holland, if necessary by force. Parliament voted to raise an army of 30,000 men and £1 million for this purpose.

In August 1677 Ralph Montagu, the English Ambassador to Paris, negotiated a new secret arrangement with Louis: if England remained at peace with France and Charles kept parliament prorogued, Louis would grant Charles 2 million livres. Danby knew of this negotiation but was in an impossible position, having to please the King while trying to serve what he saw as Charles's best interests. A further secret treaty was negotiated in May 1678: Charles agreed to disband the new army of 30,000 men and keep parliament prorogued in return for even more French money. He then antagonised Louis by taking the money and keeping the army voted for him by parliament. By this stage neither the Dutch nor Louis trusted Charles, and in July 1678 they negotiated an end to the Dutch War with the Treaty of Nijmegen. Parliament was now deeply divided between Court and Country factions, the Court defending Charles's prerogative rights over foreign policy while the Country was deeply suspicious of the King's motives. In this volatile situation, it would not take much to push the kingdom into a serious political and constitutional crisis.

Treatment of Dissenters and Catholics

Alongside the uncertainties of Charles's foreign policy was doubt over his attitude towards religion and the laws governing religion put in place by the Cavalier Parliament. Before 1672, Charles seems to have supported a policy of broad toleration. We have already seen how, at the Restoration, Charles and Clarendon tried unsuccessfully to reach a Church settlement in which Presbyterians would work alongside Anglican bishops. In the early years of his reign Charles seems to have tried to use his authority as king to soften the impact of the Clarendon Code. In 1668, the Conventicle Act expired and was not renewed, giving non-conformists the opportunity to meet together in larger numbers. His efforts at intervention reached their zenith in 1672 when, on 15 March, he issued a second Declaration of Indulgence in England, claiming a dispensing power over the penal laws against both non-conformists and Catholics. Coinciding with the French alliance against the Dutch, this raised suspicions of Charles's Catholic sympathies, with his declared support for Protestant non-conformists being widely seen as a smokescreen for suspending the penal laws against Catholics.

Predictably, Parliament reacted to these efforts by defending the law and denying that the King's dispensing power was so broad. In 1669, Parliament refused to grant the King a £300,000 subsidy in response to the lapsing of the Conventicle Act. In 1672, Parliament attacked the Declaration of Indulgence as unconstitutional, forcing Charles to withdraw the Declaration and issue instead a Test Act.

Stadtholder – The United Provinces (the Dutch Republic, or Holland) was normally governed by elected representatives of the Dutch states, but the office of Stadtholder could, in times of crisis, be given to the House (family) of Orange, to take emergency measures for the safety of the republic.

Prorogued – Parliament could be dissolved, in which case elections had to be held before a new parliament could assemble. Alternatively, the King could prorogue the existing parliament, leading to a pause between sessions. The Triennial Act envisaged continuous parliamentary sessions, so a lengthy prorogation could be construed as a violation of the law.

Test Act – An Act imposing an Oath of Supremacy and an Oath of Allegiance on all office holders. These men had to provide evidence that they had recently taken Holy Communion in the Church of England and make a declaration against the Catholic doctrine of transubstantiation (the belief that the bread and wine taken in Communion were miraculously transformed into the body and blood of Christ). The purpose of the Act was to exclude Catholics from office.

Dispensing power

This term describes the power of the King to dispense with the normal operation of the law. The principle was enshrined in the Court of Chancery, the central court of equity, distinct from the courts of common law, and based on the idea that the system of justice should not, in itself, get in the way of justice. Chancery represented the 'conscience of the King', the power of the monarch to see that justice was done regardless of the strict letter of the law. The King's dispensing power was sometimes compared with the Judgement of Solomon in the Old Testament, as applied to individual cases. However, Charles II's attempts to apply this principle to religious toleration by issuing Declarations of Indulgence raised the possibility that the King might set aside altogether legislation duly passed by Parliament and accepted by the Crown. There was no precedent for the application of this principle to statutes of which the King did not approve.

The revelation that James, Duke of York, was a Catholic

Playing on English fears of Catholicism, the Dutch began a propaganda war aimed at driving a wedge between the King's policy and public opinion. The most effective pamphlet was published in 1673 and widely distributed in England; Peter du Moulin's *England's Appeal from the Private Cabal at Whitehall to the Great Council of the Nation* drove home the message that 'France, Popery and Absolutism' were all part of the enemy's grand design. At Easter 1673, James, Duke of York, who had privately converted to Catholicism in 1668, refused to take Communion according to the Anglican rites. Then in June, because of the Test Act, James and Clifford resigned their offices as Lord High Admiral and Lord High Treasurer, confirming James's conversion. As Charles had produced no legitimate heir, the nation faced the prospect of a Catholic succession.

▲ Part of a letter sent by Charles II to the English Ambassador at the Hague, January 1672. The letter reveals Charles's preparations for war with the Dutch in league with France: 'I would have you use your skill so to amuse them that they may not finally despair of me, and thereby give me time to make myself more ready and leave them more remiss in their preparations.'

Dutch propaganda therefore fell on fertile ground and the suspicion was clearly growing that Charles was in the pay of Louis XIV. These revelations and suspicions led to a noticeable change in Charles's relations with Parliament, which in late 1673 and early 1674 drew up a list of complaints and draft legislation similar to that drawn up by the Long Parliament before the civil war:

- A new Test Act was proposed to exclude Catholics from both Houses of Parliament.
- In the event of a Catholic succession, the King's children were to be educated by Protestants.
- Parliament drafted legislation to limit the prerogative powers of a future Catholic monarch.
- The French alliance was criticised.
- The Cabal came under attack – Buckingham and Lauderdale were to be excluded from the Privy Council and Arlington was to be impeached.

In the light of these developments, Anthony Ashley Cooper, the Earl of Shaftesbury, abandoned the Cabal. Convinced that the Dutch propaganda was essentially true and that the King did have a secret Catholic agenda, he urged Charles to divorce Catherine of Braganza and remarry in order to produce an heir. As Shaftesbury moved into opposition, Charles dismissed him from the Privy Council and from his office as Lord Chancellor.

KEY DATES: RELIGION, DISSENT AND FINANCE

1671

September: Crown resumed direct administration of customs duties.

1672

January: Stop of the Exchequer (see page 190).

1673

February: Parliament granted the Crown £1,126,000; Declaration of Indulgence; Bill for Relief of Protestant Dissenters.

March: Declaration of Indulgence withdrawn; Test Act.

April: James, Duke of York, refused to take Holy Communion with the Anglican sacraments.

June: James, Duke of York and Clifford resigned their commissions; Danby became Lord Treasurer.

September: James, Duke of York married Mary of Modena; Shaftesbury dismissed from office of Lord Chancellor.

1674

January: New Test Act proposed; proposals to limit power of any future Catholic monarch; Parliament attacked remaining members of the Cabal.

1675

April: Test Bill introduced into the House of Lords.

October: Parliament granted only £300,000 and added an appropriation clause to the supply bill.

1677

February: Shaftesbury, Buckingham, Salisbury and Wharton imprisoned by Parliament for claiming that it had been dissolved; appropriation clause on supply bill defeated; Danby supported limits on power of any future Catholic monarch.

1678

January: Country MPs increasingly distrustful of the Court.

Danby, Parliament and royal finances

After the disintegration of the Cabal in 1674, Thomas Osborne, Earl of Danby, acted as Charles's chief minister. Danby's aims were to:

- remain in power
- restore order to royal finances
- restore good relations between Crown and Parliament by returning to 'Cavalier' policies
- support a High Anglican policy of support for the Clarendon Code and the Church of England
- persuade Charles II to follow a pro-Dutch foreign policy.

Although he was only in power for four years, Danby oversaw certain changes that facilitated more professional management of the state. In 1672 Charles had been forced to introduce a Stop of the Exchequer, suspending for one year the repayment of the capital of loans to government creditors. The Stop made it more difficult to find credit. Danby therefore inherited a difficult task, but he was fortunate to come to power at a time when public finances were actually improving. This was due to a combination of factors, some economic and some directly related to the growing competence and structure of state administration.

By the 1670s the volume of European trade was expanding, increasing the value of customs revenue. The Navigation Acts had had the desired effect, and more trade was being routed through English ports, in English ships. Then in 1671 the Crown ended the practice, begun in James I's reign, of farming out the collection of customs to private entrepreneurs when the Exchequer took over direct administration of customs and excise, cutting out the middle men and ensuring the Crown received a proportion of this income that more accurately reflected the growing volume of trade. In 1670–71 the Crown's ordinary revenue totalled £840,170; by 1678–79 it reached £1,063,723. Danby's achievement was undercut by Charles's extravagance, so when he left the treasury in 1679 the royal debt was actually £750,000 higher than it was in 1674, but beneath the debt was a more professional structure.

Court and Country

During the 1670s political opinion became increasingly divided between Court and Country, a process that developed into the Tory and Whig political parties. 'Country' sentiment was the first to appear and to make its presence felt in Parliament. This had happened before, in the 1630s, when Country sentiment saw the Court as Catholic, exclusive, corrupt and un-English. In 1642, this had had important consequences when the King failed to find support among many of the country gentry. Now, in the 1670s, a similar process was happening. Country opinion believed that Charles II's court was out of touch with the ideals and sentiments of most of the nation. In particular, Charles's known preference for pro-French policies were deeply unpopular, because they ran counter to the anti-Catholic prejudices of the majority of the population. The problem did not stop there: Charles's Declarations of Indulgence, and his known preference for toleration of both Catholics and Dissenters, provoked Anglican opposition in a country which felt it had only just survived the religious radicalism of the civil war period. The influence of the Catholic members of the Cabal (Clifford and Arlington), the presence at Court of Henrietta Maria (until 1665), the authoritarianism of the Duke of York and the influence of the Queen, all gave the impression that the Court remained essentially unreformed. Undoubtedly most people wanted Charles II to get behind the Cavalier Parliament, persecute religious radicals and defend the kingdom from France and its Catholicising aims.

By 1673 the emergence of a Country party in Parliament was having a significant impact on politics. 'France, Popery and Absolutism' became a common and effective criticism of royal policy. Consequently the parliamentary sessions of late 1673 and early 1674 were dominated by demands for a new Test Act to exclude Catholics from Parliament, attacks on royal ministers and demands that the King's children should be educated by Protestants. One historian has questioned the existence of any sort of organised party 'machine' in the 1670s, but even he concedes that Country MPs were co-ordinating their attacks on the King's government:

Source H From *The Stuart Age: England 1603–1714* by Barry Coward, (Longman), 2003, p.312.

Although the evidence is slight, there are brief glimpses of MPs in the early 1670s meeting to coordinate tactics before and during parliamentary sessions. Inevitably those who did this were usually critical of the court, echoing the Crown's critics before 1640, accusing it of corruption and extravagance at the expense of impoverished gentry and of harbouring conspiracies to introduce absolutism ... By 1674 there was a hard core of such 'opposition' MPs, including Sir William Coventry, Lord Cavendish, William Russell, Sir Thomas Meres, and William Sacheverell; in addition, from the summer of 1673 there was a strong political issue – James's Catholicism – round which opposition groups could coalesce. To that extent by 1673–4 a 'country party' had emerged.

The fall of the Cabal and the rise of Danby as Charles's chief minister has raised the possibility that a 'Court party' formed in response to 'Country' opposition. Danby's management of Parliament was certainly aimed at countering and reassuring country sentiment. Perhaps for the first time since James I's reign, the Crown had a minister who understood MPs' motives and concerns. His purpose was to build a core of MPs who could be relied upon to support the Crown – in effect, a Court party. He did this through patronage, a mixture of bribes and offices and by entertaining individuals through his own personal largesse. Inevitably his efforts provoked a reaction that further helped to form a Country opposition to Court policies. However, it would be wrong to think of these groupings as political parties in any modern sense: modern parties are characterised by rigid party discipline, party 'whips', party manifestoes and close party involvement in the selection of candidates for elections, none of which pertained to these seventeenth-century groupings and Danby himself was not a prime minister.

Conscious of the Country opposition to the Court, Danby pursued 'Cavalier' policies aimed at winning more popular support. The most important aspect of this was his support for the High Anglican Church settlement and for the Clarendon Code. From 1674 onwards Charles II virtually gave up his earlier support for a policy of broad toleration and fell in with Parliament's preferred policy of persecution of Dissenters. Danby was unsuccessful, however, in his attempts to persuade Charles to adopt an anti-French foreign policy, possibly because Charles knew that Louis could expose the Secret Treaty of Dover if pushed too hard.

The consequences of this growing rift between 'Court' and 'Country' are difficult to pin down with any certainty, and perhaps historians have been guilty of falling into the classic historical trap of reading history backwards – knowing that the Tory and Whig parties emerged during the Exclusion Crisis after 1678, they have looked back at the earlier part of the decade and seen the prototypes of these associations in Court and Country sentiment. Nevertheless, the speed with which the Whigs and Tories identified their positions at the end of the decade does suggest that they were building on prepared ground. It also suggests that Charles II managed to squander the unity and goodwill of the Restoration by pursuing policies associated in many people's minds with absolutism, Catholicism, corruption and intrigue.

Chapter summary

- Charles II was restored to the monarchy in 1660 with no conditions. However, all the legislation of the Long Parliament approved by Charles I remained in force, though the Triennial Act of 1641 was replaced with a new Triennial Act that had no fail-safe clause should the King refuse to call a new Parliament within three years.
- The Cavalier Parliament witnessed a Royalist reaction against the events and attitudes of the English Revolution. It also witnessed a peculiar reversal of roles as Parliament imposed an intolerant religious settlement while the King attempted, at least half-heartedly, to honour his promise of consideration for 'tender consciences' made in the Declaration of Breda.
- For the first seven years of his reign, Charles relied on advice from his father's ageing courtier, the moderate Royalist Edward Hyde, Earl of Clarendon. By 1667 Clarendon's enemies were looking for an opportunity to get rid of him and this was provided by the second Anglo-Dutch War.
- The court of Charles II was very different from that of his austere father. Things were much more relaxed after the rule of the Puritans, but Charles's mistresses and the antics around Court were disapproved of by many people.
- Charles II's reign coincided with the rise to power of Louis XIV in France, whose aggressive foreign policy raised fears of a new Catholic power dominating Europe. Charles's policy towards Louis was ambivalent, but by signing the Secret Treaty of Dover in 1670 he limited his freedom of action and placed his monarchy in jeopardy.
- Following Clarendon's downfall, Charles took advice first from a group of five known as the Cabal, followed from 1674 by the Earl of Danby.
- Charles's treatment of his ministers was controversial. He has a reputation for abandoning his closest advisers when they became inconvenient, but it may have been sound practice to distance himself from unpopular policies.
- In the course of his reign Parliament began to divide into Court and Country 'parties', especially under Danby, who deliberately created a 'Court' faction in order to manage Parliament more effectively.
- By 1678, anti-Catholic fears were reaching fever pitch, partly as a result of growing concerns over the succession, as Charles's brother James, Duke of York, was Catholic.

Working on essay technique

Think back to the advice from Chapters 2–5 and the summary provided at the end of Chapter 6 (see page 166).

Here is a practice question covering the period 1649–1678, involving breadth issues over a roughly 30-year period.

'The events from 1649 to 1678 prove that neither the Head of State nor Parliament could govern effectively without the assistance of the other.' Assess the validity of this view.

The Head of State in this case refers to the person or persons who were taking the executive decisions – usually the King, but from 1653 to 1659 the Lord Protector. So, you could begin the essay by addressing two issues:

1 Why has this question been asked? The question has been posed because this period was very important to the development of a constitutional monarchy – i.e. a monarchy constrained by Parliament. Did the experiences of the Interregnum and Charles II's reign demonstrate that the Head of State and Parliament had to work together to govern effectively?
2 What needs to be done to answer this question? The best way to approach this is by a sequential analysis – examine in chronological order the periods that illustrate best the problems of the executive/legislative relationship, analysing them as you go.

There were periods when either Parliament or the Head of State tried to rule independently – think of the Commonwealth or the rule of Cromwell's Major-Generals or the events of 1659. These reflected echoes of the Personal Rule of Charles I. But think also of Cromwell and Charles II's relations with Parliament. What were the problems they experienced – finance, religion, foreign policy? And do these years show that England could only be governed effectively if the Head of State's power was constrained by Parliament, and vice versa?

You might also wish to give special consideration to the only written constitution England has ever had – the Instrument of Government. General Lambert and the army grandees who wrote the Instrument were attempting to achieve the right balance between executive and legislative authority. But as you know, the contradictions of the Interregnum regimes undermined the ability of the Instrument and its successor (the Humble Petition and Advice) to achieve long-term political stability. So the Restoration represents a return to the 'ancient constitution' of the King in Parliament, but with some significant changes. You would also need to evaluate Charles II's relations with the Cavalier Parliament and explain why that relationship became more difficult during the 1670s.

Working on interpretation skills

Differences in interpretation can arise for many different reasons. Historians may have focused their research on different aspects of the same event, or set the event in a broader or narrower context.

The Restoration is an event poised in time between the Interregnum and the great political crises of the Popish Plot, the Exclusion Crisis and the Glorious Revolution. It marks a unique moment when the English people looked back to the instability and radicalism of the English Revolution and sought

to create a more stable and legal regime. Not surprisingly, historians have mixed views about how successful they were.

The sources on page 194 are all taken from relatively recent histories of the Restoration and the reign of Charles II. In each case, the author is reaching conclusions about the totality of the Restoration settlement – the reign of Charles II until the mid-1670s. Read them carefully before answering the questions that follow.

Extract A

Charles II reclaimed his crown without condition, but it was a different crown from the one that had tumbled into the basket in 1649. Parliament, Church and King were now inextricably tied together. By withstanding attacks from monarch and army, Parliament had made good its claim to be the representative of the people, even if the concept of representation and the definition of the people remained elusive. If it had ever been an event, Parliament was now an institution. By enduring assaults upon its structure and doctrine, the Episcopal Church proved an essential part of the spiritual life of the nation. Its place as the mean between extremes of papists and Puritans gave Anglicanism, as it would soon be called, the essential identity it had lacked. By surviving overthrow and exile, the monarch laid claim to the hearts of the people. Though it retained its trappings of divinity ... monarchy was revealed as a system of government rather than the reign of a king. It was a system of government that the English people had self-consciously chosen when they had a choice: a system best able to provide security, stability and prosperity.

From *A Monarchy Transformed* by Mark Kishlansky, (Penguin), 1996, p.225.

Extract C

Arguably, though, the most important cause of instability after 1660 continued to be religion. The intolerant Church established in the early 1660s did not reflect the aspirations of all the people in the country by any means. The different hopes for the future of the Church among Protestants continued after 1660 and in some respects they were intensified by what had happened during the 1640s and 1650s. The politically-dangerous associations of godly Protestant ideas that had been cemented during the English Revolution weakened but did not eradicate support for Protestant groups that were not included within the restored Church in the early 1660s. During the Restoration period different attitudes towards the toleration of Dissent became apparent and were reflected in the emerging Whig-Tory political divisions of later Stuart England ... Moreover, what also ensured that religion was at least as powerful in shaping the history of later Stuart England as it had been in dictating events before 1660 was that fear of popery continued to be powerful and strong.

From *The Stuart Age: England 1603-1714*, third edition by Barry Coward, (Longman), 2003, p.283.

Extract B

In a different sense, a balance had been achieved in the monarch's constitutional position by 1664 ... In England he had failed to gain a standing army, but the reorganized militia had proved capable of dealing with discontent. He had been thwarted in his attempts to dispense Catholics and Dissenters from penal legislation, but for the time being he wished that Dissenters be persecuted in any case. The revenue was still inadequate, but was improving naturally. He had received some snubs and humiliations from the Commons, but retained the power to prevent their bills from passing and regained that of choosing when a new Parliament was called without reference to the system appointed by the defunct Triennial Act. He had failed so far to produce an heir, but, while his brother survived the dynasty was safe ... As long as the Crown rule successfully ... it would remain strong. Its immediate future appeared to be a steady and peaceful growth in security, achieved principally at the expense of religious and political nonconformity.

From *Charles II, King of England, Scotland and Ireland* by Ronald Hutton, (OUP), 1991, p.212.

ACTIVITY

1 According to Extract A, how had the constitutional role of Parliament, Church and monarchy been strengthened by the civil wars and Interregnum?

2 Read Extract B. According to Hutton, in what ways was the monarchy in 1660 stronger than the monarchy before the civil war era?

3 According to Extract C, England after 1660 was troubled by political instability caused by the survival of religious dissent. Yet Extract A says that the Church had been strengthened by the experience of the civil wars. How would you explain the difference between these two assessments?

4 All three of the extracts mention the ongoing hatred of Catholicism in England after 1660. How do you account for the deeply-rooted loathing of the Catholic Church in the Stuart period?

5 Now complete the following practice question:

Using your understanding of the historical context from 1640 to 1664, assess how convincing the arguments in Extracts A–C are in relation to how successfully the Restoration settled the constitutional problems England had faced since the beginning of the Long Parliament.

Crisis and revolution, 1678–89

8

This chapter covers a period of just 11 years, from the Popish Plot that began in 1678 to the Glorious Revolution of 1688–89 and the political settlement that followed. It deals with the following areas:

- the Popish Plot and the Exclusion Crisis, 1678–81
- the growth of authoritarian rule under Charles II
- the 'Glorious Revolution' of 1688
- the revolution settlement of 1688–89.

The chapter focuses on two main questions:

Why did Parliament fail in its attempts to exclude James, Duke of York, from the line of succession?

Why did James II lose his throne to William of Orange in 1688?

These two questions between them pose a problem. If James held onto the succession during the Exclusion Crisis, then why did he lose the throne so quickly after his succession?

In order to explain this problem you will need to evaluate James II's use of power once he became king in order to understand how he threw away the advantages he enjoyed at the time of his succession, and succeeded only in uniting Whig, Tory and Anglican opinion against him. This chapter therefore deals with the following key breadth questions: 'To what extent and why was power more widely shared during this period' and 'How effective was opposition?'

CHAPTER OVERVIEW

This chapter begins with the Popish Plot. It explains why a series of fabrications invented by two down-and-out fantasists led to national hysteria that the kingdom was about to be subverted by a Catholic plot to murder the King and take over the realm. Central to this is the question of why so many English Protestants equated Catholicism with tyranny and arbitrary government, and how the popular fear played into the hands of politicians intent on preventing the succession of the King's Catholic brother, James, Duke of York.

The chapter then examines the growth of authoritarian government from 1681 to 1687, including the succession of James II and the failure of Monmouth's rebellion. By 1686 it looked as if James II's reign was secure, but James's policies provoked resistance among both Whigs and Tories and within the Anglican Church. The chapter then explains how events in England became bound up in the larger issue of the European balance of power as William of Orange invaded England with a Dutch army and replaced James II as king. The chapter closes with the 'Glorious Revolution', its constitutional settlement in England, and the consolidation of the revolution in Scotland and Ireland.

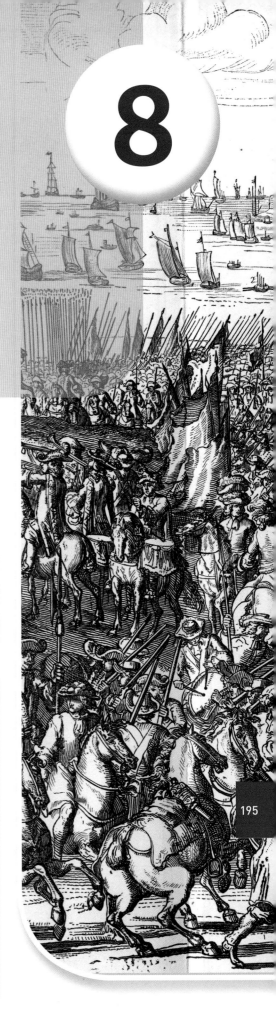

195

1 The Exclusion Crisis, 1679–81

The Exclusion Crisis refers to the attempts by the Whigs in Parliament, led by the Earl of Shaftesbury, to exclude James, Duke of York, from the succession to the throne. This was a novel idea in English politics: never before had Parliament claimed the authority to interfere with the line of succession as defined by primogeniture. Charles II defended this ancient law and his brother's right to the throne, although he was prepared to work with Parliament to establish limits to his brother's authority. Throughout the crisis he steadfastly refused to acknowledge the Duke of Monmouth as his legitimate son – Monmouth being Protestant, he saw himself as an obvious alternative to his Catholic uncle James (see later in this chapter for details of Monmouth's career). The Exclusion Crisis was played out against the backdrop of the Popish Plot, an extraordinary episode in seventeenth-century history in which an anti-Catholic 'witch hunt' became focused on the alleged traitorous intent of the heir to the throne.

The Popish Plot

Why did allegations of a Popish Plot lead to an anti-Catholic 'witch hunt'?

The Popish Plot was a fantasy cooked up by two unstable and desperate characters, Titus Oates and Israel Tonge. Oates was a failure at everything in life. In 1677, he briefly converted to the Catholic faith and spent a little time in Jesuit colleges in Spain and France. Returning to London, and now disenchanted with Catholicism, Oates was ready to use his 'insider knowledge' of the Jesuits to make his wild accusations. Israel Tonge was a man whose mind was unhinged by religion. In 1666, his church living was destroyed in the Great Fire. Like many others, Tonge believed the Fire of London was lit by Jesuit incendiaries. When the two men met they quickly concocted a tale of Jesuit intrigue. As with all conspiracy tales, the absence of factual evidence merely confirmed the conspiratorial nature of the threat. All they needed was someone who would listen to their story.

The Popish Plot grows

Tonge and Oates claimed to have stumbled upon a plot similar to the Gunpowder Plot of 1605. According to their story, the Pope had hired assassins to shoot, stab and poison King Charles before raising a Catholic insurrection throughout the three kingdoms. Tonge approached Charles II through a mutual acquaintance, Christopher Kirby, a chemist with connections in the Royal Society, who handed the King a letter outlining these allegations. Charles then interviewed both Kirby and Tonge, who elaborated on the story. Implicated in the plot was the Queen's physician, Sir George Wakeman, and Thomas Bedingfield, the Duke of York's Jesuit confessor. Fearful that their lies were about to be discovered, Oates forged incriminating letters which he sent to Bedingfield in the hopes that they would be intercepted by Danby's spies. On receipt of the letters, Bedingfield took them to the Duke of York, who was anxious to expose Oates's and Tonge's lies.

In the meantime, Oates had implicated Edward Coleman, the Duke of York's secretary, who had indeed been in correspondence with Louis XIV's confessor, La Chaise. In this correspondence, Coleman had fantasised about converting England back to the Catholic faith. His correspondence was like pouring fuel on the fire, and Coleman was arrested. Already Oates had been interviewed by the King, the Privy Council and the Committee of Foreign Affairs. The Popish

Primogeniture – The ancient law that established the order of succession within the royal family. The oldest legitimate male heir was the monarch's successor. In the absence of a male heir, the crown passed to the oldest female. In the seventeenth century there was no law prohibiting the succession of a Catholic.

Jesuit Order – The Society of Jesus, founded by Ignatius Loyola in 1534, was a Catholic religious order dedicated to the papacy and defining itself in complete submission to the Pope's authority. Jesuit priests were among the most educated and dedicated in the Catholic world, frequently undertaking dangerous missions to inhospitable territories, but in England their reputation as the vanguard of the Counter-reformation ensured that they instilled fear and loathing wherever they were mentioned.

Plot was coming perilously close to implicating James, Duke of York, in a plan to assassinate his own brother. James's conversion to Catholicism was a matter of public record, and with both his confessor and his secretary implicated in treason, his position was precarious.

The murder of Sir Edmund Godfrey

All that was needed was some unforeseen incident to elevate the Popish Plot from a round of private accusations to a full-blown crisis. It came with the murder of Sir Edmund Godfrey, a Middlesex magistrate whose body was found stabbed with his own sword just outside London. Oates had sworn a deposition before Godfrey attesting to the truth of his accusations, so Godfrey was presumed to know the full details of the plot. His murder was therefore interpreted as an attempt to hide the identities of the conspirators and it unleashed an explosion of popular anti-Catholic hysteria unlike anything seen since the Civil War. Godfrey was immediately elevated to the status of a Protestant martyr. His funeral procession brought tens of thousands of Londoners onto the streets. Finding himself a sudden celebrity, Titus Oates gave testimony before the House of Commons to MPs hungry for lurid details.

The Popish Plot now began to reap its grim harvest of victims. Three men – Green, Berry and Hill – confessed under torture to Godfrey's murder and were hanged. As the accusations grew bolder, leading Catholic peers were incriminated, including the Duke of Norfolk and the Earls of Berkshire and Arundel, Lord Belasyse and Pickering. The most notable victim of the plot was the Catholic Lord Strafford, a long-standing Royalist who had shown nothing but loyalty to the King. Strafford refused to save his life by confessing his fault and was sent to the block. In the next two years a further thirty-five men were executed for treason. In the provinces many Catholics were persecuted.

Context of anti-Catholicism in seventeenth-century England

It was one thing to have allegations of a Catholic plot made by a couple of ne'er-do-wells, but why did their false allegations ignite a full-scale political and religious crisis? To understand why this happened, we need to grasp the context into which the allegations fell, a context created not only by short-term events but also by the long-term history of religious strife in the British Isles.

Conflict over Catholic influence at Court

This had been a recurring theme ever since the succession of Charles I in 1625. The presence of Queen Henrietta Maria in Whitehall had been a major concern because of her presumed influence on royal policies. Protestant propaganda portrayed Henrietta Maria as the power behind the throne, urging her husband to introduce Arminian practices in the Anglican Church. During the 1630s she antagonised Protestant opinion by holding a weekly Catholic procession to mass in London, presided over by the priests she kept at Court. She was blamed for the attempt to arrest the Five Members in January 1642 and for trying to arrange for French troops to support the Royalist cause in the Civil War. At the Restoration, Henrietta Maria returned to England as the Queen Mother and resided in Whitehall until 1665. It was well known that she urged her son to adopt pro-Catholic policies.

The conversion of James, Duke of York, to Catholicism, followed by his public refusal to take the Anglican sacraments in 1673 brought Catholic influence at Court to the forefront of political discourse. Charles II's childless marriage to the Catholic Catherine of Braganza had already resurrected fears of Catholic influence at Court, as did the influence of Clifford and Arlington in the Cabal (page 185) and the King's relationship with his French mistress, Louise de Keroualle. As in the 1630s, the rift between Court and Country was largely the result of the growing suspicion in the provinces that the Court had been infiltrated by foreign Catholic influences, the purpose of which could be none other than the subjection of England to Rome.

Why were English Protestants so afraid of Catholicism?

Fear of Catholicism in England had deep roots, dating back to the reign of Mary I and the publication of John Foxe's *Acts and Monuments* (more commonly known as the *Book of Martyrs*) which contained the stories of people who had died for the Protestant faith. By the 1670s layer upon layer of murders, plots, massacres and atrocities had accrued within the Protestant collective consciousness, some European, some distinctively English, including the following:

● Queen Mary had burned nearly 300 Protestants in the 1550s.
● In 1570 the Pope excommunicated Queen Elizabeth, meaning that any Catholic who assassinated Elizabeth would be pardoned for all their sins. This, in the minds of many Protestants, turned all English Catholics into potential traitors.
● The Gunpowder Plot of 1605 came close to assassinating not only King James I but the entire House of Lords and Commons. In the 1670s, 5 November was celebrated as an annual holiday of deliverance from tyranny.
● The Irish Rebellion of 1641 was blamed for England's descent into civil war in 1642.

The core of the problem was the equation of Catholic religion with political absolutism. Just as the papacy admitted no spiritual limits to the Pope's authority, so Catholic monarchs were assumed to accept no legal constraints to their political power. In the seventeenth century a number of continental political tracts expressed support for the divine right of kings and the growing authoritarianism of monarchy. The Catholic view of power was that authority radiated downwards from anointed magistrates, whose word was law. This contrasted with English common law, Magna Carta, parliamentary privilege, *Habeas Corpus* and an independent judiciary, all of which owed their origin to the *law of the land* and to centuries of negotiation in which magistrates had themselves accepted limits to their power. The clash between the two cultures played a major part in causing the civil wars and by 1678 the political nation believed its liberties were once again under threat, this time from the prospect of the succession of a Catholic king.

> **Magna Carta** – The Great Charter of liberties dating from 1215.

KEY DATES: THE POPISH PLOT

1678

August: Allegations by Titus Oates and Israel Tonge of a Popish Plot.

October: Parliament condemns the Popish Plot; Charles II agrees to a new Test Act; murder of Sir Edmund Godfrey; anti-Catholic hysteria.

November: Edward Coleman, Duke of York's secretary, and three others executed.

The Exclusion Crisis

Why did Parliament fail in its attempts to exclude James, Duke of York, from the throne?

Between 1678 and 1681 four different parliaments – the Cavalier Parliament, and then three so-called 'Exclusion' parliaments – tried to either limit the power of James, Duke of York, if and when he became king, or to exclude him from the throne altogether. This confrontation between King and Parliament was the culmination of the Popish Plot, but also of 18 years of Charles II's reign, in which a rift had opened up between Court and Country factions. At first it looked as if the nation might be heading down a similar route to that which had led to civil war in 1642, but for various reasons Charles II managed to avert such a catastrophe. This section of the chapter describes what happened and then offers various explanations for the failure of Exclusion.

The end of the Cavalier Parliament

By the end of October 1678 the Popish Plot was having a direct impact on politics. As rumours circulated of a new 'Gunpowder conspiracy', a Bill was introduced to exclude all Catholics from Parliament and the King issued a proclamation banishing all Catholics within 20 miles of London. In early November, against a background of Pope-burning processions in celebration of the failure of the Gunpowder Plot, the Earl of Shaftesbury first took aim at the Duke of York by suggesting that he should be removed from the presence of the King and that he should no longer attend the Privy Council. A new Test Act was proposed to require Catholics to take the oaths of allegiance and supremacy

WORKING TOGETHER

1 Work in pairs or a group to complete your own copy of the spider diagram with details from the text and your wider reading.

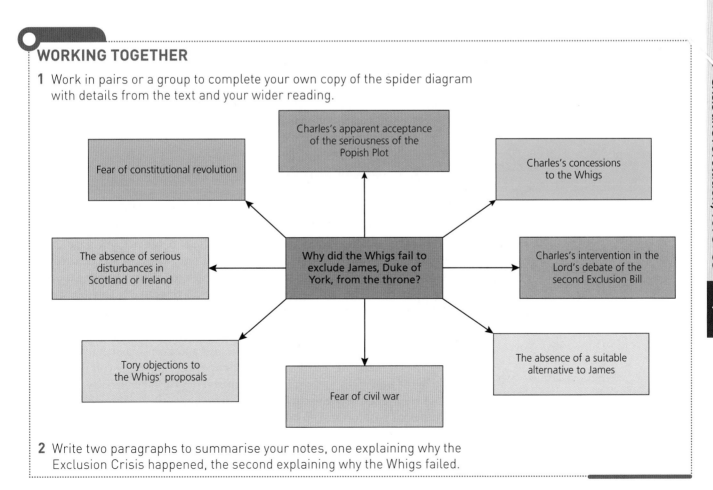

Fear of constitutional revolution

Charles's apparent acceptance of the seriousness of the Popish Plot

Charles's concessions to the Whigs

The absence of serious disturbances in Scotland or Ireland

Why did the Whigs fail to exclude James, Duke of York, from the throne?

Charles's intervention in the Lord's debate of the second Exclusion Bill

Tory objections to the Whigs' proposals

Fear of civil war

The absence of a suitable alternative to James

2 Write two paragraphs to summarise your notes, one explaining why the Exclusion Crisis happened, the second explaining why the Whigs failed.

and to make a new anti-Catholic declaration or be banned from Court. However, under pressure from the Lords and Charles II, the Duke of York was exempted from the Act's provisions – for the time being.

During November the Cavalier Parliament drew up a Bill to limit the powers of any future Catholic monarch. The provisions sounded like a return to the Long Parliament of 1641: the army was to be placed under parliamentary control; Parliament was to exercise control over the chief ministerial appointments and over the Church; and in the event of the King's (Charles II's) death, Parliament was to continue in existence rather than follow the traditional route of a dissolution. This Bill was vetoed by the King on 30 November, but soon the Popish Plot threatened to engulf the King himself. In December 1678, Ralph Montague, a former English ambassador to Paris, revealed that Danby had been negotiating a secret subsidy treaty with Louis XIV. Danby was impeached by the House of Commons, though the House of Lords refused to imprison him while awaiting trial (perhaps mindful of the fate of the Earl of Strafford in 1641 (see page 66). If Danby were to be put on trial, the Secret Treaty of Dover would surely be exposed and the King's position would be in jeopardy. On 24 January 1679 Charles II dissolved the Cavalier Parliament and announced new elections.

The Exclusion Parliaments, 1679–81

In the course of the next three parliaments, in 1679, 1680 and 1681, the Whigs tried to pass an Act that would exclude James, Duke of York, from the line of succession. Charles II and the Tories tried to counter this by proposing not to exclude but to limit James's authority if and when he succeeded to the throne. During the exclusion debates the Whigs and Tories finally crystallised into discernible political parties. In each case, when parliament came too close to passing an Exclusion Bill, the King dissolved parliament.

The first Exclusion Parliament assembled in March 1679 and only lasted until May. It soon became clear that the elections had returned a House of Commons that was determined to exclude the Duke of York. The Exclusion Bill was introduced on 11 May and received its second reading on 21 May. In retaliation, Charles II prorogued and then dissolved the Parliament. Shaftesbury resigned from the Privy Council and moved into open opposition as a petitioning campaign demanded the recall of Parliament.

The second Exclusion Parliament assembled in October 1680 and sat until it was dissolved in January 1681. On 4 November a new Exclusion Bill was introduced and quickly passed in the House of Commons. This new Bill treated James, Duke of York, as if he was dead, calling for the succession to pass to his daughter Mary and her Protestant husband, William of Orange. After passing the Commons the Bill was sent to the House of Lords, where it was debated in the presence of Charles II, who stood with his back to the fire listening to the Lords' arguments. The Lords rejected the Bill by 63 votes to 30. The following January Parliament was first prorogued and then dissolved.

The third Exclusion Parliament met in Oxford in March 1681, in the great hall at Christ Church College, where both Commons and Lords passed an Exclusion Bill. Charles II then called Parliament's bluff by appearing in the full theatrical regalia of the monarchy and dramatically dissolving Parliament. This was a direct challenge to the Whigs, who could either accept the weakness of their constitutional position and go home, or challenge the King's right to dissolve Parliament and risk civil war. The point was not lost on MPs that Charles had chosen to take this decision in the college that had served as his father's headquarters during the First Civil War.

The failure of Exclusion

Much has already been made of the shifting balance of power between the Crown and Parliament in the seventeenth century, but it is worth remembering that this was still an age of personal monarchy, when the King not only reigned but also ruled. To what extent, therefore, was Charles II responsible for Parliament's ultimate failure to exclude his brother from the line of succession?

Charles II's actions during the crisis

Throughout the Popish Plot and the Exclusion Crisis, it could be argued that Charles played his hand very skilfully. During the worst days of the Popish Plot he realised that to dismiss Oates's allegations would be dangerous, and he went along with the investigations as would a king who was genuinely troubled by the threat of assassination. For example, he attended the funeral of Sir Edmund Godfrey, banished Catholics from London, instructed Danby to investigate the affair and permitted the execution of men like Lord Strafford whom he must have realised were innocent. One could blame Charles for failing to defend his loyal servants – Danby included – but to do so in the circumstances would have been to invite direct criticism of the monarchy. And indeed he did, when the stakes were high enough, defending James, Duke of York until the Whigs began to suspect that the King himself was the problem.

Other reasons why Exclusion failed

Beside Charles's own actions, however, there were other reasons why the Whigs in Parliament ultimately failed to secure the exclusion they were hoping for. Perhaps the most important problem for the exclusionists was the absence of a suitable candidate to replace James. The Duke of Monmouth was Charles's eldest son and a Protestant, but he was illegitimate and Charles refused to recognise him as his legitimate son and heir. To place him on the throne would be in breach of the law of succession. The most obvious choice was Mary, James's Protestant daughter, but she was married to William of Orange, who would undoubtedly drag Britain into the continental struggle against Louis XIV. In the face of these problems the Whigs were unable to answer the Tories' objections and besides, many Whigs, too, were uneasy at the thought of making such a revolutionary change.

If we compare the crisis of 1678–81 with that of 1637–42 another difference also stands out: the relative silence of Scotland and Ireland. In the early 1640s the instability of the three kingdoms had a knock-on effect that destabilised England and dragged all three kingdoms into civil war. In 1681, however, neither Scotland nor Ireland was unstable enough to provoke an English crisis. If England descended into civil war, everyone knew it would be England's fault, and Parliament was not prepared to run that risk in the face of Charles's refusal to countenance exclusion. It should also be obvious that the Whigs were outmanoeuvred by the King: had Parliament accepted his various proposals to limit James's powers, they would be as guilty as John Pym of encroaching on the royal prerogative. It was all or nothing – in the end, the kingdom chose nothing.

KEY DATES: THE EXCLUSION CRISIS

1678

November: Cavalier Parliament attempts to limit the prerogative powers of any future Catholic monarch.

December: Ralph Montague's revelations of Danby's secret negotiations with Louis XIV; Danby impeached.

1679

January: Cavalier Parliament dissolved.

March: First Exclusion Parliament; impeachment of Danby; *Habeas Corpus* Amendment Act; discussion of impeachment of James, Duke of York; Exclusion Bill read twice in House of Commons.

April: Coleman's correspondence with Rome made public; Shaftesbury appointed to the Privy Council.

June: Scottish Covenanters' rebellion defeated at Bothwell Bridge.

November: Pope-burning demonstrations.

1680

October: Second Exclusion Parliament; Exclusion Bill passed by the Commons.

November: Exclusion Bill defeated by the Lords following Charles II's personal intervention; Pope-burning demonstrations.

1681

March: Third Exclusion Parliament met at Oxford; Exclusion Bill passed both Commons and Lords; Charles II dissolved Parliament.

July: Shaftesbury imprisoned on a charge of treason.

November: Shaftesbury acquitted.

2 The growth of Authoritarian Rule, 1681–85

This section examines the final years of Charles II's reign, a period that saw a growing trend towards royal authoritarian rule. In the aftermath of the Exclusion Crisis Charles II set out to strengthen royal power throughout the kingdom. The failure of the exclusionists had left the monarchy in a strong position and the King intended to take advantage of this opportunity to shore up the institutions of royal authority. When Charles II died in 1685, James succeeded smoothly to the throne, easily brushing aside the rebellion of the Duke of Monmouth. This in turn was followed by the 'Bloody Assize' of Lord Chief Justice Jeffries in the West Country, an episode that suggested that authoritarian government was set to turn towards royal absolutism.

What was absolutism? Most seventeenth-century Englishmen would have called it 'arbitrary power', a government run by the personal will and opinion of the king. In essence, absolutism was a system of government in which no other institution could challenge the monarch's authority, where the king ruled and his subjects were expected to obey. The best and closest example of an absolute monarchy was Louis XIV's France: there, in order to make laws, the king had only to register royal edicts with the Parlement of Paris. If the Parlement refused to register a new edict, the king could hold a *lit de justice* and force the Parlement's compliance. Other European states were taking their cue from France as 'miniature Versailles' sprang up in Germany and Vienna, reflecting a continental trend towards absolute monarchies underwritten by a Church preaching the Divine Right of Kings.

Parliament had faced this threat before, in the 1630s. Charles I probably was not attempting to make England an absolutist state, but he did believe the kingdom needed reform and that the institution of monarchy needed to be strengthened. In the 1680s the same threat seemed to be reappearing. As long as Charles II was king there was little opposition to the growth of authoritarian government, but with the accession of a Catholic king the threat of absolutism quickly seemed to become real.

The growth of authoritarian government, 1681–85

Why did James II succeed smoothly to the throne in 1685?

In 1663, Parliament replaced the Triennial Act of 1641 with a new Triennial Act based on trust. By the provisions of the new Act, writs for new elections would not be sent out to the county sheriffs automatically if the king failed to do it. It was implicit, however, that Parliament would be held at least once every three years – and, of course, Charles II had signed the Act. But from the dissolution of the Oxford Parliament until his death four years later, Charles II did not recall Parliament. How did he get away with it?

An exhausted opposition

Probably the most important answer to this question is that without parliament in session, there was no one to enforce the Act. Only the King could call parliament. If he refused to do so, who had the authority to force his hand? At critical times in the past, the King had been forced to recall parliament in order to gain financial subsidies. But England was not at war, Charles had reduced his

NOTE-MAKING

Complete your own copy of the table below by adding factual detail within each section.

How did the following factors strengthen the Crown after 1681?	
Quo warranto writs	The exhaustion of the Whigs
Charles II's persecution of dissenters	The Rye House Plot

expenditure and was in receipt of secret funds from Louis XIV, Scotland and Ireland were quiet and there was no urgent need for parliamentary subsidies. Since the early 1670s the Crown had been collecting customs duties directly; this was followed by the hearth tax and the excise tax in 1683, further evidence of the growing sophistication of the state. As trade expanded, the revenues from these taxes increased to the point where ordinary revenue reached £1,370,750 by 1685, exceeding the £1.2 million of the Restoration settlement.

We have also seen that Shaftesbury and the Whigs had been outmanoeuvred during the Exclusion Crisis. Faced with the choice of acceptance of defeat or rebellion, MPs had chosen the only alternative open to them and had gone home quietly. The Tories were able to discredit the Whigs by referring to them as Republicans, with all the horrible connotations of 1649 and the Interregnum. The point was emphasised when the King ordered a declaration to be read from all church pulpits recalling the disaster of the civil war. By 1685 the Whigs were in disarray: Shaftesbury had gone into exile in Holland, where he died in 1682. In that same year James, Duke of York, returned home from France to a tumultuous welcome, having retreated abroad during the worst of the crisis. In short, the opposition had given it their best shot and had failed.

◀ An image of James II produced after the Glorious Revolution. The images around the portrait refer to his Catholicism and his flight from England during the Revolution.

Provincial government strengthened

What did the 'growth of authoritarian government' mean in practice? We have seen how, in the 1670s, Danby had systematically gone about the task of creating a Court party in Parliament – a significantly more sophisticated managerial style of government. Charles II continued this trend by systematically strengthening the authority of the Crown in the provinces. This was a far more effective policy than that which his father had overseen in 1631 when he issued the *Book of Orders* for local magistrates.

To purge political opposition from the boroughs, *quo warranto* (literally 'by what warrant?' – in other words, show us your legal right) writs were issued requiring them to prove the legality of their royal charters. These were often found to be faulty, in which case new charters were issued granting the King the power to veto the appointment of civic officers. The most important of these *quo warranto* actions was for the City of London itself, a campaign that took nearly three years but which resulted in a royal victory. Henceforth the lord mayor, sheriffs and other major office-holders needed the King's approval to take office. Once London lost its case, many boroughs voluntarily surrendered their charters. Between 1681 and 1685, 51 new charters were issued, with another 47 in the first three months of James II's reign. The result of this campaign against municipal independence was to entrench the Tories in municipal government and had the additional benefit of helping to ensure the return of Tories in future parliamentary elections.

Persecution of Dissenters

The campaign to strengthen royal authority also took other forms. Charles II finally abandoned his attempts to promote religious toleration and gave his full support to the persecution of both Catholic and Protestant dissenters. By harnessing the power of the Church to the authority of the monarchy, the King was at last winning the propaganda campaign for public opinion. Loyal addresses to the King received thousands of signatures. The judiciary, too, was mobilised to crush Whig opposition. In the seventeenth century the defendants in criminal trials struggled to prove their innocence. A number of leading Whigs were executed, including Algernon Sidney and William Lord Russell in 1683 for their involvement in the Rye House Plot. Shaftesbury himself was arrested on a charge of treason in 1681 and imprisoned in the Tower, but survived because he was acquitted by a grand jury chosen by Whig sheriffs. As we saw above, he died in exile in 1682.

Charles II died aged 58 in 1685, attended by his physician, Dr Scarborough, who probably bled him to death in an attempt to balance the humours of his body. For ten years he had fought to ensure that the Crown passed to the lawful heir, his Catholic brother. His efforts were vindicated: the monarchy that James inherited appeared stronger and more secure than at any time since the Restoration.

Succession of James II

When James, Duke of York, succeeded to the throne in February 1685 there was virtually no opposition. The new king made it clear that he intended to govern 'in a parliamentary way' and that he would respect the Anglican Church settlement as established by law. His first parliament, which assembled in May 1685, was dominated by Tories and Anglicans. This was hardly surprising:

Rye House Plot

A plot attributed to the Whigs to assassinate Charles II on his way to the Newmarket races. A number of prominent Whigs were found guilty of treason and executed.

Balance the humours – Physicians believed the body consisted of four elements, which they called humours. If these were not 'balanced' illness was the result. When a person ran a temperature it was believed this was due to too much blood, so the patient was 'bled', either by the application of leeches or by opening the veins in the foot or arm.

the failure of the Whigs in the Exclusion Crisis had left the Tories with a clear advantage and the *quo warranto* campaign of the early 1680s had had the intended effect of depriving many Whigs of their borough constituencies. The 1685 election was itself carefully managed to produce a parliament that reflected the Tory landed interest.

Like most seventeenth-century parliaments, it called for the enforcement of the penal laws against Catholics and declared its support for the Established Church of England. However, Parliament clearly had no intention of contesting James's right to rule and showed that it hoped for a harmonious relationship by proceeding to supply the King with more than adequate revenue from customs duties. The only sign of serious trouble came from two ill-considered and poorly co-ordinated rebellions, one in Scotland led by the Duke of Argyll, the other in the West Country led by the Duke of Monmouth.

Monmouth's Rebellion

In June 1685 Monmouth landed at Lyme Regis in Dorset with a pitifully small force. His intention was to march through the West Country gathering a local following large enough to trigger a more general rebellion. The rebellion, however, failed to gather much support, and soon the King's army was closing in on Monmouth's force near Weston Zoyland, on the Somerset Levels. Monmouth decided on a surprise attack, but the element of surprise in the Battle of Sedgemoor was lost when his troops attempted to cross the water-filled ditch, and in the ensuing fight his forces were easily defeated. Monmouth himself was taken prisoner and beheaded.

Why did Monmouth's rebellion not raise more general support? At the time of the rebellion James II had no Catholic heir, only the Protestant Mary, so the prospect of a Catholic successor seemed remote – better to wait on events than run unnecessary risks. Furthermore, the political nation was not ready for this kind of confrontation, feared republicanism and sought to dissociate itself from armed insurrection. The City of London remained quiet throughout the uprising and in any event, both Parliament and civic corporations in the provinces were dominated by propertied men who abhorred any assault on legitimate inheritance.

The 'Bloody Assize' of Lord Chief Justice Jeffries

The failure of Monmouth's rebellion was followed by a particularly unpleasant persecution in the West Country led by Lord Chief Justice Jeffries. In village after village hundreds of people were condemned on minimal evidence and hanged, or hanged, drawn and quartered. At Norton St Philip, for example, a number of men were hanged in the courtyard of The George Inn before being cut down, still living, to have their bodies dismembered. The victims of Jeffries' vengeance were mostly low-born men and women, boys and girls, old and young, people of no particular standing who posed little threat. In order to convict people who were not caught 'red-handed' at Sedgemoor, the authorities held out the prospect of pardon to those who confessed, who were then summarily executed for treason. As well as the executions, hundreds of prisoners were transported to **indentured servitude**

> **Indentured servitude** – A system by which convicts transported to the West Indies were forced to work on plantations for a specified period. To all intents and purposes the indentured servants were slaves, except that they might look forward to eventual release.

> **Whig historians** – Historians working in a nineteenth-century tradition that saw the rise of representative government as the product of a heroic conflict between Parliament and the Crown.

in the West Indies. The 'Bloody Assizes' became part of the martyrology of the Glorious Revolution – after the event. **Whig historians** in particular produced the West Country trials as evidence of the absolutism of James II's reign. It may be seen as another aspect of the trend towards authoritarian rule dating from 1681.

KEY DATES: THE GROWTH OF AUTHORITARIAN RULE, 1681–85

1681

March: Oxford Parliament dissolved.

July: Shaftesbury arrested on a charge of treason.

November: Shaftesbury acquitted.

1682

November: Shaftesbury fled to Holland and died in exile.

1683 Rye House Plot.

1684 Charles II refuses to summon a new parliament; Danby released from imprisonment; James, Duke of York, restored to the Privy Council.

1685

February: Death of Charles II, accession of James II.

May: First session of James's first parliament.

July: Argyll's rebellion defeated in Scotland; Monmouth's rebellion defeated at Battle of Sedgemoor; 'Bloody Assizes' of Judge Jeffries.

The Duke of Monmouth

▲ 'The Duke of Monmouth's Interview with James II', by John Pettie, 1882. This painting depicts the Duke of Monmouth begging for his life at the feet of James II. Painted in 1882, it is a typically Victorian romanticised image. The meeting portrayed probably never happened, but the picture serves to illustrate the total defeat of Monmouth's rebellion against James II in the summer of 1685.

James Scott, Duke of Monmouth, was the illegitimate son of Charles II and Lucy Walter. Lucy Walter claimed to be Charles's wife, which, if true, would have made Monmouth the heir to the throne. At the Restoration, Monmouth came to London and became one of the King's favourites at Court. Two developments turned a favoured illegitimate son into a dangerous political adversary – Charles's failure to have children with Catherine of Braganza, and James, Duke of York's conversion to Catholicism. During the Exclusion Crisis the Earl of Shaftesbury and the Whigs promoted Monmouth as a possible heir to the throne in place of the Duke of York. During and after the Exclusion Crisis Monmouth took to touring remote parts of England with the obvious intention of promoting himself for the succession. Then in 1685 he landed in Dorset hoping to raise a general rebellion against James II.

3 The Glorious Revolution

Before the King would be overthrown, Whigs and Tories, Anglicans and Dissenters had to unite in a common cause. James II's extraordinary achievement was that he accomplished this. Within three years of ascending the throne, his policies so alarmed the political nation that many members of these disparate groups felt themselves threatened by a common danger.

The reign of James II, 1685–88

Was King James II a Catholic tyrant or a misunderstood, moderate ruler who believed in religious toleration?

There are really only two ways of looking at James II, whose character and policies have divided historians as much as they divided contemporaries. For example, Whig historians like McCauley and Trevelyan saw James as an authoritarian figure who would have subjected Britain to Catholic absolutism if he had been able to. Much more recently, Steve Pincus has argued that James was a king in search of what Pincus calls 'Catholic modernity', a modernised state in which Catholics and Dissenters were both tolerated under a king powerful enough to protect them from their enemies. Either he was an absolutist monarch by nature, determined that royal prerogative should always get its way, or he was a moderate ruler, the misunderstood victim of Protestant bigotry. Modern historians have tried to provide a more balanced, nuanced picture of James and his policies, but in the end it always seems to come down to this choice.

For a long time after 1688, James II was seen as a tyrant. The Whigs dominated English historiography from the eighteenth century to the early twentieth century. They focused on the growth of representative government, believing that the British constitution had achieved the best possible balance between parliament and a limited monarchy. They saw both of the great political crises of the seventeenth century in this light – the English Revolution and the Glorious Revolution were both seen as victories for the people's representatives over a Stuart dynasty that threatened the nation's liberties. The Glorious Revolution, in particular, was seen as the foundation stone of liberty. For this to be so, James II had to be the villain of the piece.

Modern historians have tended to reject the Whig assertion that James II was an absolutist monarch. They have argued that James was not attempting to reinstate the Catholic faith in England; that he intended to work with Parliament; that he respected *Magna Carta* and the liberties of the subject. These revisionists have argued that the King was a moderate, an authoritarian, certainly, but one with limited aims. There is, however, no escaping the fact that much of the political nation – men and women who had acquiesced in Monmouth's failure – was prepared to ditch him for a Dutch Protestant alternative when the opportunity arose. If James really was a moderate, interested only in achieving freedom of worship for Catholics and Dissenters alike, then the only way out of this conundrum is to argue that he was politically naive. In reaching your own opinion about James II, you will need to consider this question: was James II an absolutist ruler in the making?

Interpretations of King James II

James II is a controversial figure in history, for many reasons. His actions led to his downfall – most historians are agreed on this point. Most people believe that James II was arrogant, over-confident and rather unpleasant. His famous 'nosebleed' at Salisbury (see later in this chapter) may have cost him his throne.

However, his aims and intentions as king have been hotly debated. The issue that has caused most discussion is whether James II intended to forcibly convert England back to Catholicism – and with it, the issue of his absolutist principles of divine right monarchy. The two issues were clearly linked in the minds of contemporaries.

Source A From *1688: The First Modern Revolution* by Steve Pincus, (Yale), 2009, p.178.

James II, the evidence suggests, was committed to a thoroughgoing project of Catholic modernisation. He went a long way toward transforming the English state into a centralized, efficient, and bureaucratic machine. James made certain that both the English army and navy had the most modern equipment and learned the most up-to-date techniques. And like many modernizing regimes, James extended the tendrils of the state much wider and deeper into society than any of his predecessors. Like Louis XIV across the Channel, James's modernization programme had a religious dimension. He shared the disdain of French Catholics for Protestantism. Although it was politically impossible for James, in an overwhelmingly Protestant country, to suppress the established religion, James did everything he could to promote re-Catholicization.

Source B From *The Glorious Revolution 1688: Britain's Fight for Liberty* by Edward Vallance, (Little, Brown Book Group), 2006, p.80.

Most historians now accept that James did not, in fact, hope to convert England back to Catholicism by force. Although he became a very committed Catholic follower, his conversion had been a lengthy process … When James spoke of wishing to see Catholicism 'established' he meant that he wanted to see Catholics afforded the same political and religious freedoms as members of the Church of England, rather than to see Roman Catholicism immediately replace Anglicanism as the national church … The King's readiness to brutally repress his rebellious subjects [following Monmouth's rebellion] betrayed a deeply authoritarian streak in his character that sat paradoxically with his genuine commitment to toleration. Contemporaries noted that in the last years of Charles II's reign it had been James who had urged him to exert himself more forcefully, telling him that 'monarchie must be either more absolute or quite abolished'.

Another major issue concerning the Glorious Revolution is whether it was a revolution at all. It might be more accurate to borrow a modern phrase and refer to the events of 1688 as 'regime change', one in which popular revolution played little part. James II was overthrown by a Dutch invasion, not by a great national uprising.

ACTIVITY

1 The line below represents the two extremes in the debate. Decide where on the line the views of each historian in Source A and B should be placed. Mark the source letters in the relevant position on your own copy of the line.

> James II was an absolutist monarch who was intent on re-Catholicising England.
>
> James II was a reforming monarch who believed in religious toleration for Catholics and for Protestants.

2 Why is it so difficult to be certain of James II's intentions?

The Anglican Revolt

In so far as James II was toppled by an English rebellion, it began with a revolt by the Anglican Church. The King made no secret of the fact that he wanted the Test Acts and the Corporation Act to be repealed. In the wake of Monmouth's defeat he felt strong enough to push this agenda, but the second session of the 1685 Parliament made clear its opposition to this and was prorogued after only two weeks. When Halifax objected to the idea of challenging this legislation from Charles II's reign, he was dismissed from the Privy Council. James also began 'closeting' members of the Court, holding one-to-one interviews to try to pressurise individuals to convert, but with little success.

What did James II actually want? It has been claimed by recent historians that he was interested only in gaining religious toleration for Catholics, and that to achieve this he was prepared to extend toleration to Dissenters as well. It is difficult to believe that a seventeenth-century Catholic king was genuinely prepared to offer religious toleration to Dissenters. What is undeniable is that James was determined to open up positions of power in the State, in local government, in the army and in the universities to Catholics, whether the law permitted it or not. When Parliament did not co-operate with this policy, the King claimed authority to use his dispensing power to exempt individuals from the parliamentary statutes banning Catholics and Dissenters from office. In June 1686, he found support from the judiciary in the case of *Godden vs. Hales*.

In March 1686 the King found himself in a confrontation with the Bishop of London, Henry Compton, over James's Directions to Preachers to desist from preaching about provocative issues of doctrine. When a London minister, John Sharp, disobeyed this instruction, the King ordered Compton to discipline him. Compton refused and was suspended by a Court of Ecclesiastical Commission established expressly for this purpose in July 1686.

James had already aroused suspicion by refusing to stand down the army after the defeat of Monmouth, raising fears that the army might be used against his political opponents. These fears were exacerbated when the King began changing the composition of the army's commanders, dismissing Protestant officers and replacing them with Catholics. This was followed by a campaign to force Magdalen College, Oxford, to accept a Catholic president in contravention of the university's statutes.

The Dissenters

Faced with the revolt of the Anglican Church, in 1687 James II changed tactics: he would seek support from the Dissenters. A new Declaration of Indulgence suspended the Test and Corporation Acts and the penal laws, promising toleration for both Catholics and Protestant Nonconformists. Some Dissenters were impressed, as one religious tract from Axminster which marvelled at how,

'a popish prince was instrumental for easing the burdens of many that did truly fear the Lord'.

Halifax was concerned enough to publish his *Letter to a Dissenter* in which he observed that:

'Quakers, from being declared by the Papists not to be Christians, are now made favourites and taken into their particular protection'.

He went on to warn that this was merely the tactics of divide and rule – once Catholicism had been restored, the Quakers and all Dissenters would be

Godden vs. Hales

Sir Edward Hales was an MP who served as one of the Lords of the Admiralty in the 1680s. In 1685 he became a Catholic and thus subject to the Test Act requiring him to take the oath of supremacy, an oath of allegiance, take Anglican Communion and declare against the Catholic doctrine of transubstantiation. Hales instructed his own servant, Arthur Godden, to bring a legal action against him in order to prepare a case that could go before the Court of King's Bench with a view to confirming the King's dispensing power. Hales was convicted and the case went to the higher court. Here, by a majority of eleven to one, the court found in Hales' favour. The whole affair was concocted deliberately by the Crown to strengthen the King's dispensing power in individual cases.

suppressed. In April 1687, James's first parliament was dissolved and the King prepared to summon a new parliament packed with Dissenters. This parliament was never held, because the Glorious Revolution occurred before it could be summoned.

The turning point

What tipped the scales was the King's reinvigorated campaign to intimidate the local magistrates. As part of a systematic campaign to turn the electoral system to his advantage, James II ordered that all JPs should be asked three questions to see how they would react to the proposed repeal of the Test and Corporation Acts. A renewed *quo warranto* campaign then gave the King the chance to dismiss those magistrates whose replies indicated their opposition to this plan, and new JPs were commissioned in their place who would support the repeal of these Acts. As evidence of James's moderation, it has been claimed that by 1686 less than a quarter of JPs and deputy-lieutenants were Catholics. Yet no historian has ever suggested that, in the reigns of James I or Charles I, it would have been acceptable for 25 per cent of local magistrates to be Catholic.

In April 1688, James II issued a second Declaration of Indulgence and ordered the clergy to read it from the pulpit. Archbishop Sancroft and six other bishops refused to publish the Declaration on the grounds that the dispensing power had been declared illegal by Parliament, and throughout the country Anglican clergy refused to read it out to their congregations. Accused of seditious libel, the seven bishops (including Sancroft) were unexpectedly acquitted by the jury on 30 June, an indication of the strength of popular feeling that the liberties of the Church were being undermined.

If one thing could create a common cause between Anglicans and Dissenters, it was fear of Catholicism. On 10 June 1688, the Queen, Mary of Modena, gave birth to a son. The prospect of a secure Catholic dynasty also meant that, for a brief moment, the Tories and Whigs had something in common. On 30 June, seven Protestants – the Earls of Shrewsbury, Danby and Devonshire, Bishop Compton of London, Lord Lumley, Edward Russell and Henry Sidney, a group that included both Whigs and Tories – wrote to William of Orange offering their support if he brought an army to England to confront James.

Contrasts and comparisons

The crisis that led to the intervention of William of Orange and the Glorious Revolution was a unique event in English history, but in it one can find certain similarities with previous seventeenth-century crises and problems. In a broad perspective, James II had lost the trust of the Protestant nation just as his father had done. Ultimately it did not matter whether James II intended to impose a Catholic tyranny or not. Had the Protestants not resisted his policies, they might have found themselves, a few years later, unable to resist a Catholic absolutist regime. Put another way, James may not have intended to impose such a regime, but had he intended to, this is how he would have gone about it. Similar concerns had driven the Puritans into opposition to Charles's Personal Rule in the 1630s.

There are also more detailed incidents that bear comparison: for example, the building of a predominantly Catholic army in Ireland in the 1630s and in the 1680s raised fears that it could intervene in English affairs. James's suspension of Archbishop Sancroft in 1686 for refusing to discipline John Sharpe was similar to Charles I's suspension of Archbishop Abbot in 1626 for refusing to license Robert Sibthorpe's sermon supporting the Forced Loan. Constitutionally, James II's claim to a dispensing power was similar to Charles I's insistence on royal prerogative. In 1686 James tried to win the

LOOK AGAIN
Turn back to Chapter 3 and think about the reasons why Charles I's religious policies during the Personal Rule provoked opposition.

support of William of Orange and Mary for his projected repeal of the Test and Corporation Acts, and had he succeeded this would have undermined their status as potential alternative monarchs. In 1642, Charles I did something similar by taking his brother-in-law Frederick, Elector Palatine, into the Commons chamber with him during the Attempt on the Five Members, a move that discredited Frederick in the eyes of Parliament.

The Dutch invasion

The last successful foreign invasion of England was not in 1066. In 1688, a vast Dutch fleet, four times the size of the Spanish Armada of 1588, conveyed an army of between 15,000 and 21,000 Dutch soldiers safely from the United Provinces to Torbay, where they landed without opposition. The English knew they were coming: James had assembled an army of at least 25,000 men outside London, with some 15,000 others manning fortresses and ports, and the Royal Navy was fully prepared to intercept the Dutch fleet at sea. James had even installed an enormous weathervane on the roof at Whitehall to indicate when the Dutch fleet might sail. But setting sail in October, the 'Protestant wind' that drove the Dutch along the south coast towards Torbay also kept the English fleet bottled up at Chatham and the Thames. The first troops came ashore on 5 November, an auspicious date for Protestants.

When they landed, the Dutch were bemused at their enthusiastic reception, as the following account from a recent history of the Glorious Revolution illustrates:

Source C From *The Glorious Revolution 1688 – Britain's Fight for Liberty* by Edward Vallance, (Little, Brown Book Group), 2006, p.126.

While, over several days, the whole invasion force was gradually landed, William's secretary and childhood tutor, Sir Constantijn Huygens, used his spare time to record the unusual habits of the local people. He was particularly struck by the fact that Englishwomen seemed to be habitual pipe smokers: 'At one spot,' Huygens recorded in his journal, 'there were five women saluting (the Prince), each with a pipe of tobacco in her mouth, as we very often saw, smoking quite shamelessly, even young children of 13 or 14. We enjoyed studying the way these island people lived, and how addicted to tobacco they all were, men, women, even children.' Huygens couldn't stop laughing when his hostess, 'young and pretty', breastfed her baby while she smoked a pipe, which she handed to the child when he stopped sucking. The astonished Dutch politician recorded that the baby 'took it and put it in his mouth and tried hard to smoke'.

The international context of William's invasion

William of Orange's motive in 'descending' on England was primarily diplomatic. For several years he had been trying to build a European coalition of nations with which to confront Louis XIV's military aggression. At first, circumstances had counted against him, but in 1685 Louis XIV revoked the Edict of Nantes. Suddenly there were thousands of Huguenot refugees in the United Provinces (and in England), bringing with them tales of persecution that stirred public opinion against France. In 1686, William constructed the League of Augsburg, joined by the Holy Roman Emperor in 1687 after his forces defeated the Turks at the Battle of Mohacs. But England, with its powerful navy and formidable financial resources, was still neutral. William's motive was mainly to gain England's support in the struggle against France.

> Source C suggests that the Dutch were not treated as an invading enemy army when they landed at Torbay. Similarly, the image of the invasion shows the landing proceeding smoothly with no visible opposition. Do you think that these sources are merely Dutch propaganda to give the impression that the English welcomed William's arrival, or do you think they can be trusted to give an objective account?

The flight of James II

The success of William's invasion was due to a number of factors. Skilful diplomacy had minimised the risk that Louis XIV would attack the United Provinces during the invasion and had provided for a defence of the Dutch borders in that event. The logistical preparations for the assembly of the fleet and the invading army had been thorough, a fact that was ultimately impossible to conceal from James's envoys. The Dutch also launched a propaganda campaign to undermine loyalty to James II, focused on the unfounded rumour that James's new-born son was illegitimate. William issued a declaration to this effect on 10 October in which he also claimed that James's autocratic and pro-Catholic government of Ireland was his intended model for England's subjugation. The army that William brought to England was small but consisted of the United Provinces' best troops, veteran battalions with years of experience. Unlike Monmouth three years earlier, William was not relying on a popular uprising, although in places throughout England uprisings occurred. The largest was a northern rebellion, led by Lord Delamere and the Earl of Devonshire, that succeeded in capturing York, Scarborough and Hull, but elsewhere corporations, towns and individuals also declared for William. In London and Norwich anti-Catholic rioting suggested that William's arrival had created a 'now or never' moment.

▲ A Dutch engraving of William of Orange's army landing at Brixham, 5 November 1688. How might this image be useful as Dutch propaganda?

England's failure to rally behind its legitimate king against the invader was at least as important a reason for William's success as his careful preparations. In this respect the invasion crisis revealed the same systemic problems in mobilising military force that had been revealed by the Bishops' Wars in the 1630s. When James II realised that William was about to invade, he frantically made concessions to win back the support from Tory Anglicans that he had alienated through his policies, but it was too late to undo the damage he had inflicted on his own natural supporters. Similarly, his campaign of intimidation of chartered towns in order to 'pack' the next parliament now backfired as officials responsible for raising the county militias refused to co-operate. The army itself was demoralised and riddled with officers ready to defect to William.

James's first instinct was to fight, and with that in mind he and his army moved to intercept William's army in Wiltshire. At Salisbury, however, he decided not to fight. The first army units sent to locate William's army defected to the Dutch, and in heavy snowfall James decided to fall back on London, at which point his second-in-command, John Churchill, went over to William. He also suffered a prolonged nosebleed at Salisbury that may have sapped his resolve. As William's army moved slowly and steadily on London, James II decided to flee to France, but was captured and brought back to London. Neither William nor the Whigs or Tories wanted to see another King of England put on trial, and James was allowed to slip away into exile.

KEY DATES: THE GLORIOUS REVOLUTION, 1685–88

1686

March: James II issued Directions to Preachers to suppress anti-Catholic sermons.

May: Bishop Compton of London refused to suspend John Sharp for disobeying the Directions to Preachers.

June: *Godden vs. Hales* case: judges ruled in favour of James II's dispensing power.

September: Bishop Compton of London suspended by the new Court of Ecclesiastical Commission.

1687

April: James II tried to force Magdalen College, Oxford, to appoint a Catholic president; James's first Declaration of Indulgence.

Summer: Halifax published his *Letter to a Dissenter* warning the Dissenters not to ally with the King.

October: JPs ordered to answer three questions to assess their reactions to the idea of repealing the Test and Corporation Acts.

1688 William of Orange decided to invade England.

April: James's second Declaration of Indulgence; Archbishop Sancroft and six other bishops refused to publish the Declaration.

June: Birth of James, the son of James II and Mary of Modena; Archbishop Sancroft and six bishops acquitted; seven Whigs and Tories invited William of Orange to invade England.

November: William of Orange landed at Torbay; provincial risings broke out in his support; James II retreated to London from Wiltshire.

December: James II fled to France.

NOTE-MAKING

As you work through this section of the chapter, make notes on how radical or conservative the revolution settlement was by making your own copy of the table below.

Radical?	Aspects of the Revolution Settlement of 1689	Conservative?
	William and Mary's joint sovereignty	
	The succession	
	The Bill of Rights	
	Religion	
	Finance	

Regency – A period when someone other than the rightful monarch rules the country on their behalf. The regent is usually a close relative of the monarch – a parent, sibling or child.

Consort – A consort is the spouse of the ruling monarch, whether male or female. In this case, William refused to be merely the husband of Queen Mary – he insisted on joint sovereignty with himself acting as king in his own right.

4 The Revolution Settlement

The Dutch invasion and the flight of James II placed the Tories in a dilemma. They had been as keen as the Whigs to defend the Anglican Church and the law against James's policies, but they remained committed to the constitutional principles of Divine Right and lawful succession. In the circumstances, however, William of Orange was the only possible guarantor of public order and arrangements for continuity of government had to be made. Towards the end of December an assembly of 60 peers of the realm asked William to arrange for elections to a new parliament and to run the country until a constitutional settlement could be made. The Convention Parliament duly assembled on 22 January 1689 and began the process of hammering out a settlement.

The constitutional dilemma

How radical was the revolution settlement of 1689?

The most important problem faced by the Convention was the succession. The MPs faced several options, none without its problems. They could declare James II incapacitated and establish a **regency**, but James clearly was not incapacitated, nor was it obvious whether the regent should be William or Mary. Assuming that James II had lost the throne, who was to be his replacement? Mary was his legitimate heir, but William had taken the key decisions and made it clear that he would not agree to act merely as the Queen's **consort**. The issue divided Whig and Tory opinion along constitutional lines (see Figure 1 below).

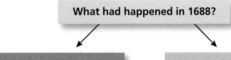

What had happened in 1688?

The Whig View

The Whigs believed in 'contract theory', which was the idea that a king ruled under conditions established by a social contract. As with any business contract, if the king violated the conditions under which he ruled, the people (i.e. parliament) had the right to depose him and install a new sovereign. The Whigs therefore believed that James II could be declared lawfully overthrown.

The Tory View

The Tories believed in Divine Right and lawful succession by primogeniture. If James II was not to be reinstated with restrictions on his power, a formula had to be found that would enable Tories to accept William and/or Mary with a clear conscience. In no circumstances would they accept the idea that King James II had been deposed or overthrown.

▲ **Figure 1** The Whig and Tory views of the events of 1688.

The revolution settlement

Like 1660, 1689 was an opportunity to reconsider the political and religious settlement of the kingdom. What decisions were taken in the immediate aftermath of William's successful invasion?

The settlement of the Glorious Revolution stopped short of a major expansion of liberties for the subject in several important respects. Critically, full religious toleration for Dissenters was not achieved; James II had lost his throne because Anglicans were opposed to the suspension or repeal of the Test and Corporation Acts, and were not prepared to see their victory lost in the settlement that followed. Like the parliamentarians of 1642, the 'revolutionaries' of 1688–89 were reluctant revolutionaries, conservative in their outlook, who believed they were fighting to preserve the ancient liberties of the subject against the innovations of a reforming regime. Those who called themselves 'True Whigs' felt betrayed by the settlement because they had failed to establish a right of rebellion – they believed the King had broken a 'social contract' that existed between the Crown and the people, who therefore had the legal right to remove him – or to extend liberty into new areas of public life. The settlement was essentially conservative, not radical, and may in some ways have represented a missed opportunity to resolve persistent problems. Nevertheless, the change of regime that occurred in 1688–89 paved the way for war with France, since William's main motive in 1688 was to bring England into the grand alliance he was building on the continent. The war that followed had a significant impact on the economic, financial and political life of the country.

> **Transubstantiation** – The doctrine whereby the wine and bread taken in communion were believed to be transformed miraculously into the blood and body of Christ.

The succession

- Parliament declared that James II had abdicated by fleeing from the country, thereby leaving the throne 'vacant'.
- The throne was offered to William and Mary as joint sovereigns.
- If Mary predeceased William (as happened), William would continue to rule alone until his death, after which either his legitimate heir would succeed or, if there were no children, Mary's sister Anne would become queen.

The Bill of Rights

The Declaration of Rights was presented by Parliament to William and Mary in March 1689, before they were crowned. The Bill of Rights restated the Declaration in the form of a parliamentary statute in December 1689. It attacked James II for attempting to subvert the Protestant religion and the fundamental laws, and decreed that:
- maintaining a standing army in peacetime was illegal
- raising tax money without parliamentary approval was illegal
- the king's use of the suspending power was illegal
- the king's use of the dispensing power 'as it hath been exercised of late' was illegal
- parliaments must be held on a regular basis
- parliamentary elections must be 'free'
- freedom of speech in Parliament was to be respected
- no excessive bail or fines were to be imposed
- no cruel and unusual punishments were to be imposed.

Finance

The financial settlement of the Crown came in two steps:
1 The Convention Parliament, 1689:
  - Existing arrangements for collecting ordinary revenue to continue until 24 June 1689.
  - Ordinary expenditure estimated at £1.2 million, as in 1660.
  - Extraordinary revenue to be voted by Parliament for war as and when required.
2 The Parliament of 1690:
  - Excise duties voted for life.
  - Customs duties voted for four years.

In effect, the financial arrangements ensured that the Crown depended on Parliament for subsidies.

Religion

- Toleration Act: freedom of worship permitted to any Protestant who took the oath of supremacy and allegiance and denounced the Catholic doctrine of transubstantiation.
- Parliament rejected a settlement of comprehension in which all public offices would be open to all Protestants. William had made a speech on 16 March in which he proposed that the Test and Corporation Acts should be effectively repealed for Protestants. This led to an Anglican reaction condemning the proposal, which effectively put a stop on any moves towards a more comprehensive Church settlement.

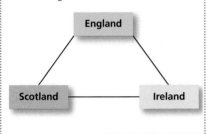

The consolidation of the revolution in Ireland and Scotland

How easily was resistance to the Glorious Revolution overcome in the three kingdoms?

In England the revolution was consolidated by the 1689 settlement and was carried out with remarkably little bloodshed. The same cannot be said of the kingdoms of Ireland and Scotland. In each case, James's religious policies had created a political situation in need of resolution. However, because Scotland was predominantly Protestant while Ireland was mainly Catholic, the revolution of 1688 was received differently. In both kingdoms there was bloodshed, and in Ireland in particular the events of 1688–90 became the foundation of the Protestant Irish identity and thus the historical foundation on which Ireland's subsequent troubles were built.

Consolidation of the revolution in Scotland

To understand the impact of the 'Glorious Revolution' in Scotland, it is necessary to know something about how Scotland had been affected by the reign of James II. During his short reign, James had managed to antagonise Presbyterian sentiment by his assault on conventicles – unofficial outdoor Presbyterian services. Alongside this, James had made it clear that he regarded law making in Scotland as the creation of the King's absolute prerogative, with the Scottish parliament playing a very secondary role.

As with Monmouth's rebellion, the defeat of Argyll's rebellion in Scotland was followed by bloody repression, and was used as an excuse to promote Catholics into military and administrative roles. The Protestant reaction was swift and uncompromising: preachers flatly refused to obey the King's directive against anti-Catholic sermons and riots broke out in some towns. James intensely disliked Scottish Presbyterians; not only could he remember the role of the Covenanters in the Civil War, but he blamed Presbyterianism for expelling Mary Queen of Scots (his great-grandmother) from Scotland. In 1687, he issued an Edict of Toleration that suspended all penal laws against Roman Catholics, offered freedom of worship *in private* to Presbyterians and permitted Quakers, whom he regarded as harmless eccentrics, to worship in public, insisting that Presbyterians who wished to avail themselves of his generous offer had to take an oath of non-resistance confirming the King's absolute power. James's government appeared to confirm the association between Catholicism and royal absolutism in the minds of Protestants in Scotland.

The 'Glorious Revolution' in Scotland

The Glorious Revolution therefore came as a welcome relief to Protestant public sentiment north of the border, especially when James was forced to withdraw his army in Scotland to try to deal with William's invasion. At first the revolution in Scotland was relatively bloodless, consisting of Pope-burning processions and attacks on Catholic chapels. Early in 1689, William was persuaded to summon a Scottish Convention to decide the political settlement in the north. The Convention offered the Scottish crown to William and Mary and stated that James had 'forfaulted' his throne in Scotland by attempting to convert the 'legal limited monarchy' there into 'an arbitrary despotic power'. In July, the Convention abolished prelacy (bishops) in the Scottish kirk. A year later, in 1690, Presbyterian ministers who had lost their livings as a result of the 1662 Act of Uniformity were restored. Scottish Presbyterianism was taking the opportunity to reassert itself following the revolution, which, to them, was indeed 'glorious' in being providential. There is no way that the Scots by themselves could have brought about this change in fortunes.

Not everyone in Scotland, however, welcomed the revolution. The Highlands and islands remained mostly Catholic and the Jacobites were a powerful force both there and in parts of the Lowlands. In July 1689, a Jacobite rising defeated William III's forces at the Battle of Killiecrankie, using a Highland charge to get in among the English musketeers before they could reload or deploy bayonets. In August, however, the Jacobites were defeated at the Battle of Dunkeld and by September they were in disarray. Fort William was established as a military base from which to keep a military presence in the Highlands and the conflict was officially ended by the Treaty of Achallader in June 1691. The terms were generous: the clans agreed to take the oath of allegiance to William in exchange for a full indemnity and the payment of £12,000 to cover the costs of the war.

The Glencoe massacre

Unfortunately for the MacDonald clan, William III's Secretary of State for Scotland, Sir John Dalrymple, took an opportunity provided by the peace to eradicate some of the Catholic Highland clans. In January 1692, he ordered the destruction of the Catholic clans in and around the mountain pass at Glencoe, an area from which escape could be easily blocked. In February the government's forces attacked the MacDonalds in a snowstorm, killing 45 people in cold blood, most of whom were women and children.

Consolidation of the revolution in Ireland

As in Scotland, James II's policy in Ireland was to press for the promotion of Catholics in both the army and administration. He hoped to emancipate the Catholics in Ireland and create an Irish parliament that would be compliant and submissive to royal policy. In Ireland's case, however, Catholics were in the majority. Between 1685 and 1688 the Earl of Tyrconnel was entrusted with the task of purging the Irish army of Ulster Presbyterians and returning property from the Church of Ireland to the Catholic Church. Not only were Protestant officers removed from their commands, but Protestant rank-and-file soldiers were replaced with Catholics.

The revolution of 1688 threatened to unravel all Tyrconnel's work, prompting him to send an embassy to France (where James was now residing) to persuade him to come to Ireland and take up the reins of monarchy himself. James's plan was to use Ireland as a springboard for a recovery of England and Scotland. Louis XIV realised that a Jacobite revolution in Ireland could force William to divert some of his forces there. He encouraged James to claim his Irish throne with the help of a small French force.

The siege of Londonderry and the Battle of the Boyne

James landed in Ireland in March 1689 as Jacobite forces laid siege to Londonderry (Derry), the focal point of the Protestant plantations. Many Protestants had fled to Derry for refuge and now found themselves in a desperate siege. Meanwhile, on 22 June, the Irish Parliament was threatening the death penalty for all those Protestants who had declared for William of Orange. James's policy of religious toleration was quickly unravelling. The civil

Jacobites – Those who remained loyal to James II and his line after the Glorious Revolution.

Highland charge – A disorganised but effective rushing attack made by Highland clansmen, in which they aimed to close the distance with more heavily armed forces in order to fight hand-to-hand, thereby negating their enemies' superior firepower.

war that broke out in Ireland after the Glorious Revolution was turning into the set-piece confrontation between Protestants and Catholics that would define Irish politics for generations.

Needless to say, the plight of the Protestants in Ireland excited the sympathies of the English, just as it had done during the Irish Rebellion of 1641. On 28 July a relief force from England lifted the siege of Derry. In June 1690, William himself arrived in Ireland to take command of his forces. Speed was of the essence – he needed to return to England to take control of the new war with France, so he was looking for a decisive confrontation with James and his army. James obliged him by ignoring the advice of his French counsellors and advancing to meet William. The two armies clashed at the Boyne River on 1 July 1690 and the result was a decisive victory for William of Orange.

The Battle of the Boyne did not put an immediate end to the war in Ireland, but after the Boyne there was no prospect of a Jacobite victory. James himself returned to France, where he died in exile. The Jacobite cause continued to threaten Queen Anne and the **Hanoverians**, however, until the defeat of the Scottish clans at Culloden in 1745.

> **Hanoverians** – King George I and his descendants, to whom the monarchy passed by the Act of Settlement following the death of Queen Anne in 1714.

▲ Many Protestants in Northern Ireland still look to the events of 1688–90 as the birth of their national identity. This image is one of many such paintings displaying the religious and political loyalties of Ulster Protestants.

Chapter summary

- The Popish Plot unleashed a period of anti-Catholic hysteria that not even King Charles himself could safely resist.
- The Exclusion Crisis occurred when the Whigs in Parliament, led by the Earl of Shaftesbury, sought to take advantage of the Popish Plot for their own political ends. Specifically, they tried to use the anti-Catholic hysteria to pass an Act of Parliament that would exclude James, Duke of York, from the throne. The exclusionists failed, however, and the crisis effectively ended with the dissolution of the Oxford Parliament in 1681.
- Charles II's final years were dominated by a more authoritarian style of government. The Crown conducted a campaign of political reorganisation that undermined the political basis of the Whigs. When the King failed to call a new parliament within the legal term, there was no outcry.
- The succession of James II took place smoothly on the death of Charles II. Parliament was dominated by Tories and Anglicans and voted revenue for the new king.
- The only opposition to James's succession came from the rebellions of Argyll in Scotland and Monmouth in the West Country. Both rebellions failed and were followed by brutal repression.
- James II then threw away his advantage by alienating the Anglican Church and the Tory Party. By promoting Catholics in violation of the Test Acts and the Corporation Act, he challenged the rule of law and provoked opposition from powerful elements in both Church and state. The last straw was the birth of a son and heir by Mary of Modena, James's wife, which threatened a Catholic succession.
- William of Orange invaded England with a large army on the invitation of seven members of the House of Lords. Landing in Torbay, his army marched towards London, gathering support as it went. Faced with the prospect of civil war, James II fled the country and the Crown was offered to William and Mary.
- Tories and Whigs interpreted the events of 1688 differently. Whigs believed that James had been overthrown in a 'Glorious Revolution' and that Parliament had offered the Crown to William and Mary. Tories believed that James had left the throne vacant by his flight and that Mary (and William) was the lawful heir.
- The constitutional settlement of 1689 was essentially conservative in nature and was not based on Whig principles. Nevertheless, the Glorious Revolution strengthened the Whigs' position because by offering the Crown to William and Mary, parliamentary sovereignty was strengthened.
- The Glorious Revolution led to a fundamental realignment of England's foreign policy in favour of the United Provinces and against France.

Working on essay technique

Return to the activity on page 177. You should now have created a balance sheet of failures and successes of the Restoration settlement of 1660–64, with evidence drawn from across the whole period from 1660 to 1689. Looking back over the reigns of Charles II and James II, how successful do you think the Restoration settlement was? In planning your answer to the practice question below, you need to think about issues such as:

● the constitution, including the issue of the succession and the dispensing power claimed by the Crown

● royal finance
● the religious settlement, including the Clarendon Code and the treatment of Dissenters.

'The Restoration settlement failed to settle any of the political and religious issues that had divided the kingdom in the 1640s and 1650s.' Assess the validity of this view.

Working on interpretation skills

Because the Glorious Revolution did not result in a civil war, it has tended to get less attention than the English Revolution of the 1640s. However, in terms of its lasting significance for English history, the events of 1688 are far more important than those of 1642. The English Revolution ended in a constitutional dead end, with Oliver Cromwell's government unable to reach a stable constitutional arrangement that could survive the Lord Protector's death. By contrast, the Glorious Revolution resolved many of the constitutional and religious tensions dating from the Stuart succession of 1603, and in particular two things: It ensured that Parliament was now a permanent feature of political life, and because the Crown was now vested in an unambiguously Protestant royal family, it enabled Crown and Parliament to work more harmoniously together. The national interest and the interests of the Crown were no longer working at cross-purposes.

The extracts on page 221 are all taken from relatively recent histories of the reign of James II and the Glorious Revolution. In each case, the author is reaching conclusions about the significance of the events of 1688–89. Read them carefully before answering the following question.

Using your understanding of the historical context from 1625 to 1689, assess how convincing the arguments in these three extracts are in relation to the long-term significance of the Glorious Revolution.

Extract A

The Revolution of 1688–89 was not a self-contained event lasting only a few months. To understand it in such narrow chronological terms is to miss the radical significance of the revolution. Instead, it is best to understand the revolution as a process set in motion in the wide-ranging crisis of the 1620s, which unleashed an opposition movement deploying modernizing polemical [deliberately controversial] strategies and coming to an end only when the Whig prime minister Sir Robert Walpole chose to consolidate his power by guaranteeing that revolutionary change would go no farther. Walpole's decision in the 1720s and 1730s to appeal to moderate Tories by rolling back the land tax and by refusing to extend civil rights to Dissenters marked the end of the Whig revolution. Revolutionary rumblings had begun with debates over foreign policy, the nature of the English Church, and the role of state finance in the tumultuous decade of the 1620s. By the end of the revolutionary century, English state, society, culture, and religion had been transformed. England had diverged from the Continental pattern on every dimension.

From *1688: The First Modern Revolution* by Steve Pincus, (Yale), 2009, p.483.

Extract B

The most important effect of the Glorious Revolution was that it brought to the English throne a man whose prime aims were centred, not in England, but in Europe. William III was first and foremost a European, interested in establishing the peace of the continent by maintaining a balance of power between the two major European dynasties, the Habsburgs and the Bourbons. Since Louis XIV's France was the major threat to European peace William was committed to curbing French power. Therefore, a major effect on England of William's accession was to force a radical realignment in her foreign policy away from the puppet-like dependence on France of Charles II and the isolationist pose adopted by James II. William dragged England into Europe against France, and in the process transformed his new kingdom into a major world power. The resulting pro-Habsburg, anti-Bourbon direction of British foreign policy was to last until the mid-eighteenth century; Britain's status as a great power endured even longer, until the mid-twentieth century.

From *The Stuart Age: England 1603–1714* by Barry Coward, (Longman), 2003, p.365.

Extract C

Contemporaries called this a revolution and there remains significant evidence to support this view. The English people were deeply involved in the changes brought about during the Revolution. It was ordinary people, not the gentry, who first flocked to William's cause in the west of the country. Secondly, if the Revolution did not represent the advent of parliamentary 'democracy' it certainly enshrined parliamentary government. Parliament became an integral, permanent institution at the heart of government. Thirdly, the change of monarchs ushered in cultural, as well as political, change. Many contemporaries spoke as much of a Williamite 'reformation' as 'revolution': 1688 was seen as an opportunity to return divine blessings upon the nation in terms of its salvation from popery, through a thorough reformation of public morals and manners.

From *The Glorious Revolution* by Edward Vallance, (Abacus), 2006, p.307.

9

Revolution and War, 1689–1702

This chapter covers the period from the Glorious Revolution to the death of King William III in 1702. The chapter focuses on a number of areas:

- government under William and Mary, including the changing influence of Crown and Parliament and the reasons for the development of limited monarchy
- religious changes, including the growth of greater religious toleration and the position of the Anglican Church
- the Whigs and Tories and the importance of political parties and ministers
- the condition of Britain and its monarchy by 1702.

All of the key breadth questions are covered in this chapter, in particular:

- How far did the monarchy change?
- Why and with what results were there disputes over religion?
- How important were ideas and ideology?

The following question forms the main overall focus of the chapter:

To what extent did Britain develop into a 'constitutional monarchy' in the final years of the seventeenth century?

CHAPTER OVERVIEW

This chapter begins with the nature of government under William and Mary and the impact of the French wars on the relationship between the Crown and Parliament. It examines the financial revolution of the 1690s that laid the basis for the expansion of British military power on land and sea. It also explores the concept of 'limited monarchy' and how Parliament came to exert more control over the monarchy, and the importance of ministerial government. The chapter then focuses on religious changes, in particular the growth of limited religious toleration in this period. Linked to religious changes is the further development of the Whig and Tory parties and how this affected politics. There is then a brief summary of the main historiographical arguments concerning the post-1689 period. The chapter concludes with a review of the state of Britain in 1702, including the Act of Settlement, the balance of power between the Crown and Parliament and the condition of the Church of England, including the transition from a 'confessional' state, in which everyone must share the same religious beliefs and practices, to a 'secular' state.

1 Government under William and Mary

During the joint reign of William and Mary two important and permanent changes occurred. They happened simultaneously and were closely linked to each other: England found a way to achieve sustained military power through the development of an effective system of administration and taxation, one that was more successful at discovering the wealth of individuals and institutions. In so doing, the process led to a 'constitutional monarchy' in which the power of the Crown was more effectively kept within limits by Parliament. Although the King remained powerful, never again would the kingdom be threatened with arbitrary government.

NOTE-MAKING

Make your own copy of Figure 1 and add more detailed notes to each part to show how each issue contributed to the development of 'limited monarchy' in England. To find out about the Act of Settlement of 1701 you will need to look at page 241 of this chapter.

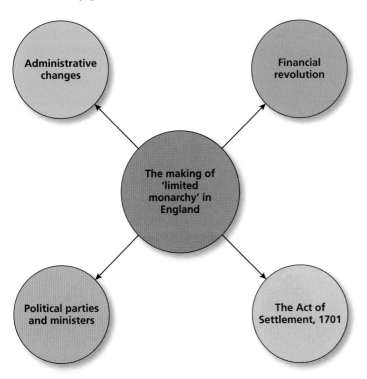

▲ Figure 1 Issues contributing to the development of 'limited monarchy'.

The development of a limited monarchy

How did the English State develop between 1689 and 1702?

For a long time historians argued that the 'Glorious Revolution' of 1688–89 was the event that was responsible for the development of 'limited monarchy' in England. They viewed the Bill of Rights, for example, as a document that placed limits on the monarchy's power, and they emphasised the role of Parliament in making these constitutional changes. In recent years, however, the focus has shifted towards the war with France that followed the revolution. William's purpose in invading England in 1688 had been to attach Britain to the anti-French coalition he was building on the continent. Once he was King, his attention remained focused on the continental war and in order to win this he had to agree to changes in British government that placed further limits on the monarchy's power. These changes involved two important developments:

1 A new Triennial Act not only required Parliament to sit at least once in every three years, but forced the King to call a new parliamentary election every

three years. This forced the King to work more closely with Parliament and also encouraged the development of the Whig and Tory parties as they competed regularly for seats in the House of Commons.

2 The State itself evolved a more efficient bureaucracy, what we would call today a 'civil service'. New taxes were levied by Parliament, which also supervised more closely the way this money was spent by the Crown.

The financial revolution

The phrase that historians use to describe this new stage in the evolution of British government is the 'military-fiscal state'. To understand what this means, we need to go back briefly to understand how government finance worked earlier in the century.

The old system

Before the Civil War, the King's 'ordinary' revenue from Crown lands and feudal dues was sometimes supplemented with 'extraordinary' revenue in the form of parliamentary subsidies. Because parliament was an occasional event, these subsidies were an occasional tax. When parliament raised a subsidy, it turned to the records of previous subsidies (the subsidy rolls) to find out how much the counties and leading individuals had contributed. To raise the new subsidy, counties were allocated a certain target and it was the responsibility of the county sheriffs to meet their targets by taxing individuals. The system was not based on any rational assessment of wealth or income, but simply on precedent and tradition and on the discretion of the sheriff to adjust his demands in the light of local circumstances. The Ship Money taxes of the

▲ The official coronation medal of William and Mary, 1689. The obverse shows William and Mary ruling as joint sovereigns, a unique event in English history. The reverse of the coin shows James II falling from his chariot, struck by Jupiter's (William III's) lightning. Why did Parliament make William and Mary joint sovereigns over Great Britain?

1630s had been an attempt to introduce a more regular and 'fair' source of income (regular because it was collected annually and 'fair' because it was less discretionary and all counties had to pay it), but it was short-lived and was not based on any rational evaluation of an individual's wealth.

During the Civil War, Parliament had put in place the essential elements of a more effective system. The excise taxes on beer and salt were unpopular but they were taxes on purchases rather than wealth. Far more effective were the monthly assessments raised by county committees comprised of people appointed by Parliament rather than local magistrates, who enquired more closely into the wealth of individuals and were less likely to let their friends off the hook. This financial revolution helped Parliament to win the war, but in the long run it was unsustainable because it was seen as a threat to the very 'traditional liberties' for which Parliament was fighting. Not surprisingly, the system was dismantled at the Restoration. For the next 30 years Parliament attempted to check the power of the Crown by 'capping' its estimate of what the King needed to £1.2 million per annum. The Crown never received this sort of income until the 1680s and the figure was always an underestimate of what the Crown actually needed.

Taxation and the national debt

As we saw in Chapter 8, a number of important developments in the 1670s and 1680s were already leading towards more efficient administration and income. From 1670, the Crown had replaced the system of **farming out the customs** with the collection of customs duties by paid royal officials. During the 1680s this enabled the Crown to benefit directly from the expansion of trade, giving Charles II a healthy surplus provided he remained at peace. The expansion of the Royal Navy, combined with a number of naval defeats requiring boards of enquiry, had also led to closer parliamentary scrutiny of royal accounts. Impressive as these changes were, they were inadequate for William III's task of defeating Louis XIV.

The enormous cost of achieving this is reflected in the available statistics of royal expenditure. It has been estimated that between 1689 and 1697 the costs of warfare averaged £5.5 million per annum, rising to £7 million per annum between 1702 and 1713. To find this money, the Crown had to accept much greater parliamentary scrutiny of royal accounts. In 1690, William agreed to the Public Accounts Act, which established a Public Accounts Commission to examine government income and expenditure. Such public accountability opened the way for a new approach to royal expenses and much greater access to national resources through taxation. During the 1690s the Excise Tax was extended to cover a wider range of commodities, alongside a series of money making schemes that included a state lottery. Another important innovation was the Land Tax, introduced in 1692, levying four shillings in the pound (20p) on income from land. This became a regular tax, voted annually by parliament, though not always levied at such a high rate. By 1710, the Crown was in receipt of over £5 million a year from taxation, of which over 30 per cent came from the Land Tax.

The most important change of the 1690s was a revolutionary new approach to government borrowing. Monarchs had always borrowed money, in anticipation of revenue, from private creditors such as the merchant companies of London. Since they were not always able to repay their loans on time, this could lead to embarrassing refusals of further credit and paralysis of government such as that suffered by Charles I in 1640. In 1672, Charles II was forced to suspend repayments in the Stop of the Exchequer (a temporary halt to the repayment of loans) and was only rescued by Parliament after promising to withdraw

Farming out the customs – For most of the seventeenth century the Crown leased the authority to collect customs revenue to businessmen for a fixed sum. These 'farmers of the customs' were then able to keep as profit any figure over and above the amount they had paid to the King.

The Nine Years War, 1688–97

William III's aim in the Nine Years' War was to force the French to give up the territories won in the previous wars, restoring the French frontier to that of 1659. The League of Augsburg, which he helped to construct, was a formidable coalition which, with the addition of Britain, became known as the Grand Alliance. Faced with this range of enemies, Louis XIV was forced to fight a defensive war that took the form of Allied sieges of French frontier cities. At sea, the French won a victory off Beachy Head in 1690 that gave them temporary control of the English Channel and opened the prospect of a French invasion of England, but the danger passed with an Anglo-Dutch victory at La Hogue in 1692.

The war ended in 1697 with the Peace of Ryswick. The war had not achieved William's full aim of restoring the frontiers of 1659, but the tide had turned in the European struggle against France, made possible by William's invasion of England in 1688 and the development in England of more sophisticated links between government, administration and finance. Louis XIV recognised William III as the legitimate King of England, an important step in gaining international recognition of the 1688 revolution.

Ships-of-the-line – The largest warships of the time.

the Declaration of Indulgence (Charles's attempt to suspend the Test and Corporation Acts). In both cases Parliament had used financial weakness as a means of forcing an untrustworthy King to accept parliamentary demands.

With William III the nation gained the first indisputably Protestant king since James I, easing relations between Crown and Parliament and creating a new level of trust between them. In 1693, William was permitted to raise a loan of £1 million by the Million Loan Act, which guaranteed repayments out of parliamentary taxation. Then in 1694, the government created the Bank of England. In return for a further loan of £1.2 million, the creditors were permitted to set up the bank to provide banking services and to arrange future government borrowing. The debt was to be underwritten by Parliament, so it was no longer a royal debt, but the responsibility of the nation – a National Debt – covered and managed by future tax receipts. To complete the transition from personal to government finance, the Civil List was introduced in 1698 to provide for the monarch's personal and household expenses as a separate item, clearly distinguishable from the costs of government. The system of personal gifts and courtier administration that had undermined attempts at financial reform and encouraged corruption in the reign of James I had finally been reformed and replaced.

Military expansion

The reforms outlined above made possible an extraordinary expansion of British military power. With common goals, King and Parliament were much more prepared to take each other into their confidence, unlocking the kingdom's wealth and turning Britain into a nation capable, with its continental allies, of defeating Louis XIV. After 1688 the combined English and Dutch fleets outnumbered the French and from 1700 the Royal Navy alone significantly outgunned the French fleet. The army too experienced a significant increase, from 10,000 in 1689 to 76,000 in 1697. The effectiveness of this 'financial revolution' is revealed in the growth of the English navy, which went from 46 ships-of-the-line in 1650 to 122 by 1705.

The Glorious Revolution and the war that followed cleared the way for a resolution of many of the political problems that had beset the kingdom since the Stuart succession in 1603. In the 1690s England laid the foundations of sustainable military power which, in the eighteenth century, was able to challenge and defeat France in European and colonial conflicts. The catalyst of this transformation was warfare. Ironically, it was also England's small population and weakness compared to its continental rivals that forced it to modernise in ways that made it significantly different from the other great powers.

The impact of administrative changes

The reforms of the 1690s introduced a new era of constitutional government, a parliamentary monarchy in which Parliament was a regular and necessary part of the administration. The Triennial Act of 1694 specified that new elections had to be held every three years, preventing any perpetual parliaments such as the Long Parliament (1640–53) or the Cavalier Parliament (1660–78). It was the administration of finance, however, that effectively deprived the monarch of the power to dissolve Parliament as and when he wished. Arguably, therefore, it was not so much the Glorious Revolution, but the Nine Years War, that was the key cause of the development of limited monarchy in England – a monarchy limited by Parliament. The war shaped the new constitutional arrangements and ensured that William accepted them.

On the other hand, the new structures that were put in place also reflected major changes in the attitudes of Parliament and the willingness and ability of MPs to take on new responsibilities. Earlier in the seventeenth century Parliament had used finance as a political weapon to restrict the powers of the monarch. In the 1690s, however, the Bill of Rights, the Public Accounts Commission and the confidence of Whig MPs that William shared at least their basic aims, created a sense of trust and co-operation in a common enterprise. These changes would surely not have occurred had James II remained on the throne. Furthermore, Parliament had gained considerable experience of government during the Civil War and Interregnum. The war with France in the 1690s provided the motive for co-operation and dictated the strategies required, but Parliament was able to draw on a fund of experience gained in earlier conflicts.

The importance of political parties and ministers

The need to work closely with Parliament also affected the monarch's freedom of choice regarding advisers and policies. In theory the King was still free to choose his ministers and to decide on peace, war and foreign policy without restriction. In practice, however, William found that he needed advisers who could manage Parliament and ensure political support, especially in the House of Commons.

This also encouraged the development of a cabinet of ministers to carry out these tasks, so-called because they met in a private room in Whitehall. In the 1690s the need to manage parliaments on a regular basis, combined with the King's frequent absence from the country while conducting the war with France, led to the selection of a small group of parliamentary advisers to carry out the tasks of government on his behalf. The death of Queen Mary in 1694 made this cabinet even more essential, because with the King still preoccupied with the war, he needed someone else to help manage the new parliamentary system.

The management of Parliament in turn encouraged the growth of political party organisation, both during and after elections. We will see later how religious differences widened the divisions between Whigs and Tories, but with parliamentary elections required every three years it was inevitable that these parties began to develop more coherent party positions on a range of issues, and in turn this forced them to create a political machine in the counties and boroughs to raise money, support candidates and enforce greater party discipline. The frequency of elections also encouraged the development of what has been called 'the rage of party', a period of bitter politics that divided the political nation. William's successor, Queen Anne, relied on particular 'managers' to plan government strategy and ensure parliamentary majorities on her behalf, though the position of prime minister did not develop until the 1720s.

KEY DATES: THE DEVELOPMENT OF LIMITED MONARCH

1690

March: Grant of excise duties to the Crown for life and customs receipts for four years.

October: Parliamentary grants totalling £4.6 million.

December: Public Accounts Act.

1692

November: Land Tax introduced; Parliament approved war expenditure in excess of £4 million.

1693 Million Loan Act.

1694

April: Bank of England established.

November: Triennial Act.

1698 Civil List established.

During the English Civil War and the Interregnum, Parliament had to govern the country without a king. It therefore gained administrative experience that was not normally part of its responsibility – for example, by creating county committees to oversee the collection of the excise and assessment taxes.

Prime minister – During the reign of George I, the King, who was unable to speak English, relied on Robert Walpole to manage his government. Walpole was England's first prime minister.

The political life of the English nation therefore changed rapidly and decisively between 1688 and 1702. The change of regime brought about by the invasion of William of Orange in 1688 drew Britain into the larger conflict taking place in continental Europe. In fact, in a negative way, British politics had been dominated by the European conflicts since the Secret Treaty of Dover in 1670, because the political nation felt that the Crown was supporting the wrong side. The Glorious Revolution resolved that conflict of interests, but immediately created another: to play an effective part in this conflict, the Crown had to share power with Parliament to such an extent that the nation emerged with a 'limited', or 'constitutional' monarchy. But this was not simply the product of the Glorious Revolution: arguably the growth of government administration and parliamentary supervision of royal expenditure from the 1670s was just as important as the constitutional adjustments made between 1688 and 1702. And as Source A shows, the Glorious Revolution certainly did not meet with universal approval.

Source A From *The Command of the Ocean* by N. A. M. Rodger, (Penguin/Allen Lane), 2004, p.140.

By April 1689, when they were crowned, the 'Glorious Revolution' had already fallen apart. The English, obsessed by their fear of Catholicism, had imagined that nothing but love of the Church of England could have persuaded William III to risk his life and the Dutch Republic to spend over seven million guilders. Now they began to realise that their new king, though a Calvinist rather than a Catholic, was an ally of Catholic princes such as the Holy Roman Emperor, Leopold I, with reasons of state to be as tolerant in matters of religion as James II had been. It also began to dawn on them that he meant to involve them in an overseas war of ruinous expense.

Interpretations

What was the significance of the 'financial revolution' of the 1690s?

What was the historical significance of the last decade of the seventeenth century? The following sources are taken from historians, all of whom have considered the significance of the 'financial revolution' of the 1690s, though possibly from different angles. Read them carefully before answering the questions that follow.

Source B From 'The Rise of the Fiscal State' in *A Companion to Stuart Britain* by Michael J. Braddick, edited by Barry Coward (Blackwell), 2003, p.69.

The structure of English national finances underwent a profound transformation during the seventeenth century, and the new structure was markedly more productive than the old. Before 1640 the Crown struggled to meet the increasing demands for expenditure, particularly military expenditure, using an increasingly complex set of financial arrangements. This elaborate structure collapsed in the political crisis of the 1640s, but the demands for mobilization for the subsequent wars led to the creation of new forms of revenue which were of lasting significance. Before the Civil War perhaps three-quarters of revenues were not under the control of parliament ... After the Civil War non-parliamentary revenues provided only about 10 per cent of total income, and by the 1690s that figure had dwindled to around 3 per cent ... The result was a vastly increased capacity for fiscal-military mobilization. By the 1690s England was a significant European power.

Source C From *Elusive Settlement* by Barry Williams, (Nelson), 1984, p.206.

It is arguable that the most significant aspect of this Revolution [the Glorious Revolution of 1688] was the immediate reversal of England's foreign policy, and that everything else stemmed from this. William certainly intended it, but most Englishmen, though vaguely anticipating a re-alignment, never expected nor wanted the full military commitment and prolonged war which William's plans in the end entailed. Reality was abrupt and harsh. William as King, and therefore Commander-in-Chief of England's armed forces, pointed out the unpalatable truth: if Englishmen wished to preserve the Protestant succession, then they had to fight for it and pay for it. Reluctantly, over a period of several years, a significant portion of the tax-paying nation came to recognise that war was imperative to preserve their country from a French invasion and the restoration of James II as a French puppet. William's task remained very difficult, though, for there existed a tiresome remnant of independent country gentlemen whose county horizons and uninformed prejudices on national and particularly foreign policy matters mirrored those of their predecessors, [who had caused so much trouble for] Pym and Cromwell.

Source D From *England's Apprenticeship* by Charles Wilson, (Longman), 1984, p.224. This extract discusses the financial 'revolution' of the 1690s.

This structure of public finance was only possible because it was accompanied by a fiscal system that was, by contemporary standards, remarkably well devised and administered. Taxation was drawn from two main sources: direct taxation of the propertied classes, indirect taxation of trade, manufactures and consumption (through customs and excise duties). Thus all classes of society contributed. All grumbled and cursed – but all paid. The burden was therefore spread between propertied and non-propertied, producers and consumers. It did not fall so heavily on industry (as it did in Holland) that production costs, wages especially, were raised to levels that priced its products out of the market. It did not fall (as it did in France) on the non-privileged classes so as to create deep and permanent grievances. For all its faults, the system provided a steady flow of revenue without destroying the economic and social conditions within which trade, industry and agriculture could expand. Many eighteenth-century writers were to believe that this was the greatest single achievement made possible by the English constitutional settlement worked out between 1660 and 1702.

ACTIVITY

1 According to Sources B,C and D, what was the nature of the financial transformation that England went through in the seventeenth century, and why was it so important?
2 In Source D, Charles Wilson compares England's tax system favourably to those of France and the United Provinces. In what ways was England's system superior to theirs?
3 In the context of your knowledge of both the 1640s and the 1690s, why was the 'financial revolution' of the 1690s more effective, and less unpopular, than that of the 1640s?

2 Religious changes

It is commonly believed – wrongly – that the Glorious Revolution ushered in an age of religious toleration where people of different Protestant faiths could worship freely, without interference from the state. Perhaps more than any other single issue, the position of the Anglican Church and the treatment of non-conformists divided the Whig and Tory parties and drove their political disputes in Parliament. This section of the chapter will examine the extent to which greater toleration came about as a result of the events of 1688–1702. In Section 4 it will then expand the discussion to consider the possibility that the most important development by 1702 was not religious toleration, but the secularisation of society as a whole.

NOTE-MAKING

The sliding scale below represents a range of religious attitudes, from the intolerant Church of England created by the 'Clarendon Code' in the 1660s at one extreme, to the idea of complete religious toleration on the other. In other words, on the left side there is no toleration of Protestant Nonconformists or Catholics; on the right side both Nonconformists and Catholics are tolerated, including the repeal of the Test Acts that prevented these religious minorities from holding public office.

Make you own copy of this sliding scale and on it indicate how far you think religious toleration had been established in Britain by 1702. Justify your decision by writing one paragraph summarising your reasons.

'Clarendon Code' Test and Corporation Acts enforced	Religious toleration Test and Corporation Acts repealed

The Anglican Church and religious nonconformity

How far did religious toleration develop by 1702?

We saw in Chapter 8 that the religious settlement of 1689 stopped short of establishing full religious toleration. Two bills had been placed before Parliament in 1689, a Comprehension Bill that would have made the Anglican Church more 'comprehensive' and able to accommodate Dissenters through a more flexible order of service, and a Toleration Bill to offer freedom of worship for all Protestants. In the event the Church of England closed ranks against comprehension, causing the bill to fail, and although the Toleration Act was passed, the Test Act and the Corporation Act remained in force, so Dissenters still could not hold public office. Many historians see the revolution settlement of 1689 as another missed opportunity to create a genuinely more tolerant society.

William III attempted to prepare for a comprehensive settlement by reassuring Anglicans of his support while arranging for detailed proposals for comprehension to be put before Convocation, but when Convocation met it rejected any moves towards making life easier for Dissenters. Now that the 'Catholic threat' had receded, the Church of England had rediscovered its old opposition to dissent.

The Toleration Act of 1689 granted freedom of worship to all Protestants who took the oath of supremacy and allegiance and made a declaration condemning transubstantiation to ensure that they were not Catholics. However, most Dissenters were disappointed by the Act. In practice many Dissenters were still subject to various penalties. Dissenter meeting houses had to leave their doors open during services to allay fears of dangerous practices. Furthermore, the Unitarians – those who denied the doctrine of the Holy Trinity – were still outlawed. To quell the growing threat of religious strife, William III adjourned Convocation at the end of 1689. It did not meet again until 1701.

Anglicans and Dissenters in the reign of William and Mary

Throughout the 1690s, Anglicans and Tories became more and more concerned about the state of the Church. Their fear was that non-conformity had found political allies, and that henceforth it would be impossible to preserve the religious monopoly and political power of the Church of England. In the early 1700s the High Anglicans developed a new rallying cry, 'the Church in danger', to frighten conservative opinion. About the same time, memoirs from the civil war era were published, such as Clarendon's *History of the Great Rebellion and Civil Wars in England* and Edmund Ludlow's *Memoirs*. This renewal of interest in the civil war era reflected both the frustrations of the non-conformists and the fears of the Anglicans. It was evident that the revolution 'settlement' of 1689 had failed to settle the religious issue.

The national religious debate also generated a number of new publications concerning the place of religion in society. In 1695 John Locke, the author of *Two Treatises on Civil Government*, published *The Reasonableness of Christianity* in which he argued that reason, rather than divine revelation through the sacred text of the Bible, was the chief origin of the Christian faith. A year later John Toland published his more radical *Christianity Not Mysterious*, in which he denied the truth of any beliefs not based on logic, and accused the ministry of complicating simple ideas with specialised 'scholastic jargon', rather like the legal profession. The Anglicans also had their spokesmen: in 1696 Francis Atterbury published *A Letter to a Convocation Man*, in which he demanded that the King recall Convocation to enable the Church to debate the growing crisis.

This sense of crisis had been made greater by the death of Queen Mary in 1694, at just 32 years of age. Her funeral was a great state occasion, dignified by funereal anthems composed by Henry Purcell that reflected the sense of national loss and constitutional crisis. It reopened the political wounds between Whigs and Tories over the succession and William's right to rule: while Mary had lived, Tories could more easily accept William as a joint sovereign, linked to the state by the legitimacy of his wife's claim. Tories also feared that the Glorious Revolution had opened the floodgates to non-conformity. If the monopoly of the Church of England had been broken, what was to stop the proliferation of radical sects like

Deists – A group that believed in the existence of God on purely rational grounds. By definition, they denied the importance of inspired religion or a sacred text such as the Bible.

Occasional conformity – The practice developed by some Protestant Dissenters of attending Church a few times a year and taking Communion occasionally. This allowed them to avoid the restrictions of the Test and Corporation Acts and to hold public office. It infuriated the High Anglicans because Dissenters seemed to have found a way of getting around the law, and because those who retained office by this method often used it to protect other Dissenters from persecution.

those which had flourished during the civil wars? Already a new sect, the Deists, was arguing that the existence of God was itself subject to reason. Was atheism to be tolerated too? A new front in this cultural war opened over the practice of occasional conformity, by which the Tory Anglicans feared that Dissenters were evading the spirit, if not the letter, of the law. As soon as William III died, the Tories demanded that an Occasional Conformity Bill outlawing the practice should be placed before Parliament.

In the final years of William III's reign, therefore, militant Anglicanism reappeared as a powerful political force allied with the Tory party. In 1697, a Blasphemy Act tried, and failed, to suppress the open discussion of ideas. In 1701, William called a new Convocation of the Church and immediately it unleashed a torrent of criticism of Archbishop Tenison's liberal stress on the importance of reason and his rejection of religious 'enthusiasm'. The Anglican counter-attack on nonconformity coincided with the growth of the 'cult' of King Charles the Martyr, as Tories attempted to associate dissent with the republican excesses of the Civil War and Interregnum. Dissent was here to stay, although as yet it was not given the equal social or legal standing as the Church of England.

It went without saying, of course, that Catholics were still persecuted. The Anglican Church had turned on James II in 1687 because it feared his toleration of Catholics was aimed at returning England to the Catholic faith. This fear of Catholicism had deep roots and it was not until nearly another century had passed (and the 'secularisation' of British society had developed much further) that moves began to free Catholics from the penal laws banning mass and preventing Catholics from holding public office. In 1702, Catholics were still prevented from holding any public office and it was still illegal for Catholics to attend mass. A range of oaths and requirements prevented them from getting around these penal laws – for example, they had to accept Holy Communion according to the rites of the Church of England and specifically deny the Catholic doctrine of transubstantiation – the miracle by which, according to Catholic belief, the bread and wine are changed into the body and blood of Christ.

KEY DATES: THE CHURCH OF ENGLAND AND RELIGIOUS NONCONFORMITY

1689

January: Toleration Act.

December: Convocation adjourned – did not meet again until 1701.

1694

December: Death of Queen Mary.

1695 John Locke's *The Reasonableness of Christianity* published.

1696 Francis Atterbury's *A Letter to a Convocation Man* published; John Toland's *Christianity Not Mysterious* published.

1701

February: Convocation met for the first time since 1689.

1702

March: Death of William III and succession of Queen Anne.

October: Tory demands for an Occasional Conformity Bill.

3 Party politics in the reign of William and Mary

'The period between the Revolution of 1688–89 and the peaceful accession of George I [in 1714] was dominated by the legacy and consequences of the Revolution … One was a deepening and transformation of the role of party in politics. The period is often characterised as one of "the rage of party". Fired by the dramatic events of the Revolution and its impact on the political values and religious views of the people … fanned by the necessity, under the 1694 Triennial Act, of contesting elections every three years, the partisan competition in the House of Commons and in individual constituencies became more vigorous than at any time before.'

From the History of Parliament website: www.historyofparliamentonline.org

The purpose of this section is to explore the issues that divided Whigs and Tories.

The Whigs and the Tories

What were the issues dividing the Whig and Tory parties at the end of the seventeenth century?

In the course of the last three chapters we have been tracing the development of England's first political parties. Before examining the issues that divided these parties in the 1690s and early 1700s, we need to briefly remind ourselves where they came from and some of the issues that led to their formation.

In the early seventeenth century there were no political parties. 'Parties' were equated with 'factions', which were assumed to be divisive and harmful to the kingdom. Politics in the reign of James I, for example, was focused more around the Court and the King's favourites than around Parliament. This was bound to be the case in the immediate post-Elizabethan age of personal monarchy and occasional parliaments. The Court was the source of patronage and while factions did coalesce around individuals (or against individuals, as in the case of the Duke of Buckingham), the very idea of forming a semi-permanent group of MPs to oppose royal policies would have been seen almost as a form of treason. Even during the civil wars when Parliament was divided between Presbyterians and Independents, the majority of MPs remained unaligned. There was never anything remotely like a party organisation.

In the reign of Charles II, a 'Country' party began to form in response to the widespread belief that the Court was pro-Catholic and pro-French. Faced with mounting opposition to the King's government, Danby deliberately created a 'Court' faction in the 1670s in order to expedite royal business in Parliament. This was not yet a political party, more a common core of support for the Court that could be relied upon to vote the Crown's way. However, during the Exclusion Crisis the Country and Court factions quickly evolved into the Whig and Tory parties over the issue of the succession, with the Earl of Shaftesbury acting, in effect, as the Whig's first national leader. By 1681, the Whigs were identifiable by their opposition to a Catholic succession, the Tories by their insistence that social order depended on the observance of legal and political rights, starting with the Duke of York's right to succeed. From 1681 to 1688 the Tories were in the ascendant as the Crown manipulated local politics through its *quo warranto* proceedings to build Tory support in the boroughs.

LOOK AGAIN

Look back to Chapter 7 (pages 190–92) to remind yourself of what the 'Country' party was and why it came into existence.

The Glorious Revolution restored the confidence of the Whig party and gave it the Protestant king it had been seeking. Many Tories, too, agreed to the overthrow of James II, but were only able to reconcile themselves to it by arguing that the King had abdicated by abandoning his kingdom. Thus the Whigs and the Tories developed diametrically opposed explanations of what had happened in 1688, with the Tories insisting that James had abdicated while the Whigs argued that he had been lawfully overthrown because he had violated the social contract that existed between a king and his people. To the Tories the idea that the people had the 'right' to depose a monarch was dangerous and unacceptable. The rift between these party positions widened over the religious settlement and the position of Dissenters.

Divisions in the political nation

The Nine Years War had a major impact on party politics. The financial costs of the war, combined with concern about maladministration and corruption, helped to forge a realignment of political parties in which country Whigs and Tories gradually worked together to curb the financial excesses of the Crown. To begin with, both parties supported the war effort and accepted its inevitable costs: James II's invasion of Ireland in 1690 forced William to confront him there, where James was defeated at the Battle of the Boyne, but the war brought home the threat of invasion. Similarly, the French victory at the Battle of Beachy Head demonstrated the possibility of another foreign invasion, temporarily helping to smooth relations between Whigs and Tories in Parliament. The two parties co-operated during William's first parliament (1690–94) to pass the financial legislation described in Section 1. The war, however, also led to much closer parliamentary scrutiny of wartime spending: Parliament developed the habit of calling royal officials to account for public expenditure, and began the practice of appropriating grants of money for specific uses. These 'innovations' worried Tories because they saw in them an attack on royal prerogatives.

By about 1693, therefore, relations between the Whigs and the Tories were getting steadily worse, and William III was increasingly disillusioned over the nature of English politics. His chief ministers were the Earls of Nottingham and Danby, who had survived the failure of the Exclusion Crisis and found their way back into government. Needing the support of a more capable parliamentary manager, he turned to the Earl of Sunderland. On his advice, William promoted Whigs to a number of prominent government positions.

The Whig 'Junto'

From 1695 to 1701 parliamentary politics was dominated by a group of Whig politicians known collectively as the 'Junto' – Sir John Somers, Philip Lord Wharton, Charles Montague (Lord Halifax), Admiral Edward Russell and Sir John Trenchard. Their power and influence derived from their ability to gain parliamentary supplies for the war with France. Their chief aim seems to have been the desire to control royal patronage and control of government offices. With the Whigs in the ascendant, the Tories began to define themselves as united in opposition to the direction of Whig policy. As the diagram on page 235 shows, four key issues now divided Whig and Tory opinion. Perhaps chief among these was Tory opposition to the strategy of a continental war, requiring large armies and high taxation, linked to the growing suspicion that England's wealth was being hijacked by the Dutch to fight a foreign war. Like Parliament in 1618–24, the Tories preferred a 'blue water strategy' focusing on naval power and attacks on French commerce. As with James I and his Scottish advisers, there was also resentment at William's Dutch connections and the influence of Dutch advisers at Court.

A strange reversal of roles therefore seems to have taken place in Whig and Tory attitudes since the revolution of 1688. By the mid-1690s it was the Whigs who were defending royal prerogative through their close association with the Court, while the Tories became associated with the old 'country' suspicion of the government and its centralising tendencies. In 1696, in an effort to undermine the Bank of England, a group of Tory businessmen created a 'Land Bank' to offer credit without funding a national debt, but the project failed to attract much support. As the Whigs tried to dissociate themselves from their radical past, the political alliance between the Tories and the 'old Whigs' of the 1680s grew closer. However, the Whigs were strengthened by the revelation of a plot to assassinate William III, which they exploited to flush out William's opponents with an oath of loyalty that was refused by some 19 Tory peers and 90 MPs. In 1696 an 'association oath' was employed to purge Tory doubters from local offices, filling the vacancies with Whig 'placemen'.

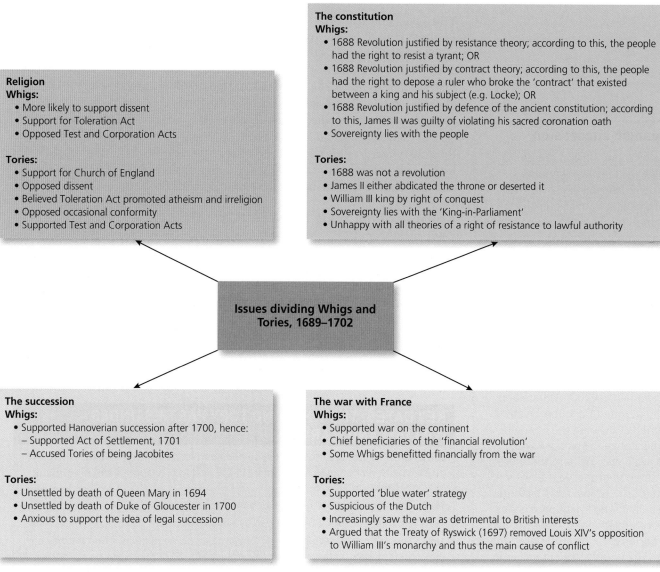

Religion
Whigs:
- More likely to support dissent
- Support for Toleration Act
- Opposed Test and Corporation Acts

Tories:
- Support for Church of England
- Opposed dissent
- Believed Toleration Act promoted atheism and irreligion
- Opposed occasional conformity
- Supported Test and Corporation Acts

The constitution
Whigs:
- 1688 Revolution justified by resistance theory; according to this, the people had the right to resist a tyrant; OR
- 1688 Revolution justified by contract theory; according to this, the people had the right to depose a ruler who broke the 'contract' that existed between a king and his subject (e.g. Locke); OR
- 1688 Revolution justified by defence of the ancient constitution; according to this, James II was guilty of violating his sacred coronation oath
- Sovereignty lies with the people

Tories:
- 1688 was not a revolution
- James II either abdicated the throne or deserted it
- William III king by right of conquest
- Sovereignty lies with the 'King-in-Parliament'
- Unhappy with all theories of a right of resistance to lawful authority

Issues dividing Whigs and Tories, 1689–1702

The succession
Whigs:
- Supported Hanoverian succession after 1700, hence:
  – Supported Act of Settlement, 1701
  – Accused Tories of being Jacobites

Tories:
- Unsettled by death of Queen Mary in 1694
- Unsettled by death of Duke of Gloucester in 1700
- Anxious to support the idea of legal succession

The war with France
Whigs:
- Supported war on the continent
- Chief beneficiaries of the 'financial revolution'
- Some Whigs benefitted financially from the war

Tories:
- Supported 'blue water' strategy
- Suspicious of the Dutch
- Increasingly saw the war as detrimental to British interests
- Argued that the Treaty of Ryswick (1697) removed Louis XIV's opposition to William III's monarchy and thus the main cause of conflict

▲ **Figure 2** Issues dividing the Whigs and Tories, 1689–1702.

The political issues dividing the Whig and Tory parties are rather complicated, dating back to the Exclusion Crisis of 1678–81 and encompassing the Glorious Revolution, the Revolution settlement and the Nine Years War. To help you to consolidate your understanding of these issues, try the following exercise:

1 Work in pairs. One person takes the role of a Whig, the other of a Tory. The date is 1696, one year before the Nine Years War ended.
2 Each person writes a paragraph explaining why he or she has decided to support their chosen party. Swap paragraphs.
3 Now prepare a speech to be delivered in Parliament attacking the other side's attitudes and policies.
4 Use your speech in a class debate on the following motion: 'This House would make an immediate peace treaty with France.'

When the Nine Years War ended in 1697, the Tories saw their chance. Like the Presbyterians of the late 1640s, they sought to return power to the traditional rulers in the provinces – the JPs and landowning gentry who resented high taxation and centralised government 'meddling' in local affairs. The discovery that William III intended to maintain a large standing army despite the coming of peace led to a short-lived alliance between Tories and some Whigs which some historians have called a 'new Country party'; a spontaneous reaction against high taxation and foreign alliances. William's reason for wishing to keep the army intact was his fear that the issue of the Spanish succession would soon lead to another war with Louis XIV, a fear that was realised in 1700 with the death of Charles II of Spain and the outbreak of war in 1702.

Collapse of the Whig 'Junto'

Between 1697 and 1701 the Whig 'Junto' collapsed in the face of the public reaction against the war, its financial costs and the expansion of government it had brought about. In 1701, the Duke of Gloucester died, forcing the succession issue to the fore and leading to the Act of Settlement. During the final year of William's reign the distinctions between Whigs and Tories broke down to a remarkable degree as the nation united in opposition to war, high taxation and centralisation. However, new controversies emerged over religion, the succession and the renewal of the war against Louis XIV's France. These were the issues that were to continue to split the Whig and Tory parties until the Treaty of Utrecht (1713) and the death of Queen Anne in 1714.

Spanish succession

Both William III and Louis XIV tried to prevent another large European war over the succession to the Spanish monarchy. An international crisis was brewing because Charles II of Spain had no children and was likely to leave Spain and its empire to Louis XIV's grandson, Philip, Duke of Anjou. If this was allowed to happen it would have created a hugely powerful Bourbon monarchy in Western Europe and would have upset the balance of power. In 1698, and again in 1700, William and Louis signed Partition Treaties aimed at dividing the Spanish inheritance in such a way as to avoid war. William therefore wanted to preserve the army after 1697 to make his diplomacy credible. The Partition Treaties were undermined, however, by a series of untimely deaths, and in 1702 Louis XIV went to war in support of Philip V's claim to the Spanish throne. The war that followed – the War of the Spanish Succession (1702–14) – was even larger and more expensive than the Nine Years War.

KEY DATES: THE WHIG AND TORY PARTIES UNDER WILLIAM AND MARY

1689 Parliament voted that the throne had been left 'vacant'; Parliament offered the throne to William and Mary; Toleration Act; Bill of Rights; Grand Alliance against France formed.

1692 Tories demanded a 'blue water strategy'.

1693 Triennial and Place Bills vetoed by William III.

1694 Formation of the Whig 'Junto'; Tory attacks on Whig finance and the war on the continent; death of Queen Mary; Triennial Act.

1695 Tory Land Bank failed.

1696 c.90 Tory MPs refuse to swear an oath of loyalty to William III.

1697 Treaty of Ryswick; parliamentary attacks on William's standing army.

1700 Death of the Duke of Gloucester.

1701 Act of Settlement.

1702 Death of William III, succession of Queen Anne.

4 The condition of Britain and its monarchy by 1702

In this closing section of the book we will consider the condition of Britain and its monarchy in fairly broad terms and in particular two issues – secularisation and constitutional monarchy. Each one of these has been the subject of intense historical debate, and although it is not possible in this space to consider these in full, some indication of the nature of the arguments will be provided.

A survey of the state of Britain in 1702 is meaningless unless it is used to draw conclusions about the historical processes that were shaping Britain in the seventeenth century. Describing Britain at the beginning of the eighteenth century without placing this in the context of continuity and change would be a sterile and ultimately useless exercise; in the broad context of British history, we need to know where Britain was coming from, and where it was going to, in order to appreciate where it was. What follows is therefore an attempt to indicate why the study of the seventeenth century is vital to an understanding of how modern Britain came into existence.

The secularisation of the state

To what extent had Britain become a 'secular state' by 1702?

Given the political arguments surrounding religious toleration in the 1690s, it may come as a surprise to discover that one of the principal debates about the seventeenth century is whether the 1600s witnessed the growth of a more secular state. If one compares the role of religion in society in 1702 with the role it played in 1603, the process of secularisation seems clear. On the other hand, the Tories' defence of High Church Anglicanism against both dissent and Catholicism in the 1690s should warn us that religious intolerance was not a spent force.

In 1603 England was a 'confessional' state, one in which uniformity of worship was seen as essential to the survival of the community. Monarchy and uniformity of belief were seen as the twin pillars of strength and social order, with religion binding society together – to paraphrase one modern philosopher, religion gave sanctity to marriage, underpinned all oaths and promises and upheld the sacrifices needed both in peace and war. Early seventeenth-century politics was riven by arguments over matters of worship and theology, but nearly everyone shared the assumption that uniformity of worship was essential to the survival of the community. By 1702, however, this assumption was being challenged in an increasingly secular society. On the other hand, recent historians have challenged this assumption of change by arguing that there was more continuity in the importance of religion than has been hitherto admitted.

The argument for change and secularisation

In the early eighteenth century religious 'enthusiasm' became a term of abuse – the state had acquired new forms of social binding that were not dependant on divine commands. The religious conflicts of the civil war era had left the people of Britain wary of causes that were expressed in purely religious terms. By 1702 a number of developments had occurred that meant that the confessional state of 1603 was giving way to secularisation and the growing separation of Church and state.

Long-term influences

Some of these influences were very long term, dating back to the Renaissance and Reformation of the fifteenth and sixteenth centuries. England was deeply affected by the major cultural and religious changes taking place in Europe from the fifteenth century onwards. The Renaissance (literally 'rebirth') started as the spread of a renewed interest in ancient Greek and Roman literature, revealing a world and a belief system that predated Christianity, and the somewhat surprising revelation that this pre-Christian civilisation had a sense of morality that owed nothing to Mosaic Law. The Renaissance also had a direct impact on biblical scholarship, encouraging translations of the Bible into the vernacular modern European languages. The Catholic Church tried and failed to prevent vernacular translations from undermining its control of the divinely inspired text, but Protestantism inevitably downgraded the role of the Church in the process of salvation. Protestants emphasised the individual's relationship with God through the text of the Bible, so literacy became a Christian duty.

Medium-term influences – the survival of dissent

You have already seen in Section 2 how the English Civil War led to an explosion of radical ideas and separatist movements. Religious radicalism became one of the key issues dividing Presbyterians from Independents, the Presbyterians seeing religious toleration as a threat to the cohesion of the state. The appearance of separatist groups – Quakers, Seekers, Anabaptists, Diggers and Ranters – frightened both Presbyterians and Anglicans, who united briefly in 1660 in their determination to restore the social order that they equated with a national Church. As we have seen, the Presbyterians were then shocked to discover that the High Anglicans had no intention of sharing control of the Church with Presbyterians.

As we saw in Chapter 7, the Clarendon Code was an attempt to destroy non-conformity and restore the confessional state. How, then, did dissent survive the Restoration? By defining the Anglican Church so narrowly as to exclude Presbyterians, the Royalists of the 1660s swelled the numbers of potential Dissenters and excluded many whose views were known to be moderate. Had they established a broadly comprehensive Church at the Restoration, they would have had the support of the Presbyterians in driving the others to the margins of religious life.

Help also came from within the Church itself, in the form of the Latitudinarian Party, made up of men who emphasised the Church's breadth and capacity to embrace a variety of views. As the heirs of the Great Tew Circle (see page 239) they were concerned above all to establish religious peace, emphasising forgiveness and brotherhood. Some drew on scientific principles, arguing that belief must be supported by reason and that which could not be demonstrated through rational argument was not sufficient cause for persecution. The Latitudinarians emphasised the virtues of tolerance and dismissed persecution as unworkable. Moreover, it was shared to a certain extent by Charles II himself.

Short-term influences

Charles II's role in the survival of dissent is in some ways contradictory. On the one hand, his Declaration of Indulgence in 1672–73 provided a vital breathing space and allowed Dissenters to organise effectively. He was, however, probably motivated by the desire to ease the conditions of Catholics. In the aftermath of the Exclusion Crisis, in 1682–85, Charles was responsible for the revival of

Mosaic Law – The Ten Commandments.

LOOK AGAIN

Go back to Chapter 7, page 174, to remind yourself why the Presbyterians felt betrayed by the Restoration religious settlement.

harsh persecution. The most likely explanation is that Charles II was above all a politician who had few religious convictions. In that sense, he embodied the interests and values of a more secular society.

What finally drove the Anglican authorities into alliance with dissent was fear of Catholicism. When James II challenged the power of the Church on behalf of Catholics, Anglicans and Dissenters closed ranks against him. In return for their loyalty to the Protestant cause, the Dissenters expected and obtained a degree of religious toleration. The Toleration Act of 1689 did not mean the end of religion as a political issue, but it did signify the end of the 'confessional state'.

The argument for continuity

Against this argument for change and secularisation, close examination of the political debates of the 1690s and early 1700s has suggested that religion continued to lie at the heart of politics. Two historians in particular need to be singled out for their emphasis on continuity rather than change. Jonathan Scott has emphasised 'the unity of the seventeenth-century experience', arguing that party politics merely took old religious disputes and 'institutionalised' them by turning them into party political issues (*England's Troubles: Seventeenth-Century English Political Instability in European Context* by J. Scott, (CUP), 2000). Similarly, Jonathan Clark has recently argued that the political debates between Whigs and Tories was a form of 'confessional politics' in which religion played a dominant role, similar to that experienced in the reigns of Charles I, the English republic of the 1650s, Charles II and James II (*English Society 1660–1832* (2nd edn.) by J. Clark, (CUP), 2000).

Even if one accepts that the eighteenth century *as a whole* was a more secular period, it could also be argued that this was not achieved until political stability was restored under Walpole in the 1720s. Historians of Northern Ireland might also argue that in this corner of the United Kingdom, at any rate, where images of the Battle of the Boyne still adorn the ends of some Protestant houses and the Orangemen continue their annual victory parades through Catholic districts, confessional politics has never been replaced by a truly secular vision of society.

Ideas and ideology – the 'scientific revolution'

If there is one thing that differentiates the modern world from that of the seventeenth century, it is science. In the modern world, we expect scientific explanations for the things we see around us. In school we learn how to conduct experiments and to reach conclusions based on the results. We take it for granted, for example, that the weather, disease, the night sky, the motion of objects and the evolution of species have rational explanations. It is worthwhile asking, therefore, whether Britain was a more 'scientific' nation in 1702 than it was in 1603.

In 1605, Sir Francis Bacon published his essay, 'The Advancement of Learning', in which he encouraged scholars to subject all aspects of society to rational examination. This was applied not only to the natural world, but also to society and religion. In the 1630s Lucius Carey, Lord Falkland, opened his house at Great Tew in Oxfordshire to a small circle of friends, who met regularly to engage in intellectual debates. The Great Tew Circle emphasised the importance of rational logic and the need for intellectual freedom in religious and social debate. Tragically, Falkland committed suicide during the Civil War, but his intellectual circle reflected a growing spirit of rational theology that also influenced the Parliamentarians. In 1641, Robert Greville, Lord Brooke, a leading figure in the Puritan opposition, published a plea for religious toleration entitled *A Discourse Opening the Nature of that Episcopacy which is Exercised in England*. Brooke argued that religion was first and foremost a search for 'truth', by which he meant a more accurate knowledge of God. Freedom to pursue this search should be extended to all. Brooke declared:

'The ways of God's Spirit are free and not tied to a university man or to any man, to any bishop, or magistrate or church. The light shines where it will among men, no matter how humble or ignorant, moves them to utterance, to inquiry and discussion, to ceaseless search for more light, until truth in its entirety shall become known to all, and men have once more become one with God.'

The same spirit of freedom to pursue religious truth is evident in the prayer meetings of the New Model Army and in Cromwell's frequent references to liberty of conscience. Only through the free transfer of beliefs and ideas could people test those beliefs and come towards a greater understanding of God's purposes. As Lord Protector, Cromwell argued for a national Church that would lead by example rather than by force. Cromwell believed that in due course the free search for religious truth would bring the nation together in understanding and faith.

In 1660, the foundation of the Royal Society marked an important step in the separation of scientific from religious rationalism. The Society grew out of a small circle of scholars in Wadham College, Oxford, that began meeting around 1650 to conduct scientific experiments. John Wilkins, the Warden of Wadham College from 1648, was a Cromwellian who had been promoted following a purge of Royalists from the city after the Civil War. It was Wilkins who first gathered around him an extraordinarily diverse group of former parliamentarians and Royalists united by their common interest in mathematics, astronomy and scientific inventions. Under the patronage of Charles II, Wilkins' group was expanded and granted a royal charter. Early members of the Royal Society included men such as Robert Hooke, Robert Boyle and Sir Isaac Newton, names which form the bedrock of modern mathematics and physics. For example, Sir Isaac Newton discovered gravity, split sunlight with a prism and published his famous *Philosophiae Naturalis Principia Mathematica* (*Mathematical Principles of Natural Philosophy*) in 1687. This was a generation that was excited at the prospect of *natural* philosophy.

There is still considerable debate among historians about the nature and extent of the seventeenth-century 'scientific revolution' and the part played in it by the Royal Society. In particular, one needs to be wary of attributing to these seventeenth-century scientists modern attitudes towards science and religion. Many of the early scientists were motivated by a desire to gain a better understanding of God, or to put scientific discoveries to use in biblical study. For example, John Woodward employed Newton's theory of gravity to try to explain how the biblical Deluge (Noah's flood) worked in practice. The flood, he argued, resulted from a miraculous intervention by God to *suspend* the law of gravity, leading the Earth to fly out into chaos. God then *re-imposed* gravitational force, at which point the Earth's matter came back together according to the specific densities of its materials, resulting in the bedding planes visible in sedimentary strata. It would be wrong to dismiss such theories out of hand because we now know them to be incorrect. What was important was the gradual realisation that God worked through natural causes and the development of scientific methods in which theories could be tested by observation of the natural world. However, it is worth noting that in 1702 the primary subject taught at Oxford and Cambridge universities was still theology.

Constitutional monarchy

To what extent had Britain developed a 'constitutional monarchy' by 1702?

One of the hallmarks of the British constitution is that it is 'unwritten'. Unlike the United States or France, for example, which have written constitutions dating from their respective revolutions, the British constitution is not a single written document. The only written constitution Britain ever did have – the Instrument of Government (1654), later modified by the Humble Petition and Advice (1657) – was short lived. Britain's constitution consists of many things: parliamentary statutes, common law, custom and tradition, precedent and 'time immemorial'. It changes with use over time and is something that is not fixed in a fundamental law. By 1702 these changes had resulted in a monarchy that was held in check by Parliament, one which was also constrained by the law of the land. It is therefore correct to assert that Britain had a 'constitutional monarchy', but it was not one that owed its existence or its powers to a 'constitution' as such.

The Act of Settlement, 1701

One of the most important changes to the constitutional monarchy occurred in 1701, when Parliament passed the Act of Settlement. This Act determined how the line of succession would follow the death of William III. For Parliament to pass such an Act was itself evidence of the changing relationship between Parliament and the Crown: it is impossible to imagine Parliament in 1600 passing an Act telling Elizabeth I that James VI of Scotland would be her successor!

Princess Anne was the younger daughter of James II by his first wife, Anne Hyde, who was the daughter of the Earl of Clarendon. The Duke of Gloucester was Anne's sole surviving child. His death in 1700 forced Parliament to pass an Act of Settlement to make future arrangements for the succession. Already the Bill of Rights (1689) stated that no Catholic was to inherit the throne; nor could the King marry a Catholic. The Act of Settlement now made the following provisions: that in the event of the death without issue of William and Anne (his successor) and any surviving children they might have, the throne was to pass to the descendants of James I's daughter Elizabeth and her husband, Frederick, Elector Palatine, i.e. Sophia, the Electress of Hanover, and her heirs. This is exactly what happened: when Queen Anne died in 1714 the Crown passed to George Ludwig, Elector of Hanover, who was the grandson of Elizabeth of Bohemia.

Ideas and ideology – the development of political theory

In 1603 the dominant political theory in Western Europe, including England, was the Divine Right of Kings. Monarchs derived their authority directly from God, so defiance of royal authority was a form of blasphemy. In England the Reformation under Henry VIII reinforced the concept of royal supremacy by placing the king on level terms with the Pope.

The revolutionaries of 1649 tried hard to justify the execution of Charles I. They called him a tyrant, accused him of breaking his coronation oath and produced examples of Old Testament kings who were overthrown with God's approval. Years later, when Cromwell was trying to justify the trial and execution of the King, he quoted the New Testament (Acts 26, verse 26), saying that:

'[T]his thing was not done in a corner'.

NOTE-MAKING

To help you to form your own opinion on whether or not Britain had become a more secular society by 1702, complete the following simple table:

Arguments in favour of secularisation	Arguments against secularisation

To make sure that you understand what this means, use the internet to look up what a 'secular society' is. Write your own definition and discuss it with your class. Do you think that Britain today is a secular society? How does it differ from countries that are not essentially secular in nature?

LOOK AGAIN

To remind yourself who Elizabeth of Bohemia was, return to Chapter 2, page 29, and read about the outbreak of the Thirty Years War in Germany.

A Theory for Revolution

'Men being … by nature all free, equal and independent, no one can be … subjected to the political power of another without his own consent, which is done by agreeing with other men to join and unite their comfortable, safe and peaceable living … [agreeing that power] is to be exercised by such alone as shall be appointed to it amongst them; and by such rules as the community, or those authorised by them to that purpose, shall agree on … And so, whoever has the legislative or supreme power of any commonwealth is bound to govern by established standing laws, made known to the people, and not by arbitrary decrees … And all this is to be directed to no other end but the peace, safety and public good of the people.'

Two Treatises on Civil Government by John Locke (1690)

Their arguments looked back towards the medieval and biblical past. They did not break new ground.

In 1689, a year after the Glorious Revolution, John Locke published his *Two Treatises on Civil Government* (see text box) in which he argued that a social contract existed between a king and his subjects. As with a legal contract between two businessmen, if the king failed to keep his side of the bargain the people were released from their obligation to obey his commands. This 'social contract' had nothing to do with religion: it was based on philosophical principles, especially the idea of *utility* or usefulness. Locke was hugely influential in forming the modern world. In 1776, the American, Thomas Jefferson, used Locke's ideas to justify the American Revolution. His ideas were taken up by Thomas Paine to justify the French Revolution of 1789, which in turn inspired many of the revolutions of the nineteenth century. But John Locke was not the first person to put forward the idea of a social contract.

The first Englishman to do this was Thomas Hobbes, a philosopher from Malmesbury in Wiltshire, who fled to Europe when the English Civil War broke out. Hobbes did not believe in the Divine Right of Kings. He argued that civil war was the greatest evil that could befall a nation. It was therefore every subject's duty to obey the king, even if they thought he was a tyrant. The people had formed a social contract, surrendering their freedom to the king for their own self-preservation. In other words, people should obey the king not because it was *right*, but because it *made sense*. By placing political philosophy onto a rational basis, Hobbes and Locke were taking a major step away from the 'confessional state' and its reliance on divine laws.

In 1603, the monarch was the sovereign ruler of the kingdom, constrained by the law, by *Magna Carta*, by the coronation oath and by parliamentary privileges, but enjoying royal prerogatives that ensured that he directed both domestic and foreign policy. In 1702 the king owed his crown to Parliament, which had determined the succession by parliamentary statutes. Nevertheless, the King of England in 1702 still wielded enormous power, choosing his ministers, controlling foreign policy, distributing patronage and making alliances. The monarch was still the Supreme Governor of the Church of England and in spite of a degree of toleration for Dissenters, the Church still controlled a vast swathe of family law and acted, through the parish, as another arm of central government.

It could be argued that the Crown in 1702 was considerably more powerful than in 1603, but the Crown referred to here is the King-in-Parliament, a king working together with triennial parliaments to deliver a foreign policy that enjoyed broad national support. By 1702, the king's prerogatives were constrained in all sorts of practical ways, particularly through the oversight of investigative committees, the earmarking of funds for particular policies and the whole range of financial changes referred to earlier as the 'financial revolution' of the 1690s. The 'rage of party' was the price the kingdom had to pay for this oversight of royal policies.

It would be difficult to over-emphasise the broader historical significance of these developments. Britain's limited monarchy was unusual in Europe, where the dominant trend was towards royal absolutism. European history would soon show that a monarchy dominated by the will and power of one individual (e.g. the King of France) was less dynamic and successful than one in which the king and the nation's representatives were forced to confer and negotiate over policy, a policy that then was more likely to enjoy broad political and economic support.

Chapter summary

- The period 1689–97 was dominated by the Nine Years War with France. This war was increasingly unpopular, as 'Country' and, increasingly, Tory opinion believed England's interests had been 'hijacked' by the Dutch.
- The war was William III's main concern. Although he was determined to preserve the Crown's powers intact, William found that he had to make some concessions in order to gain Parliament's support for the war, including a new Triennial Act.
- In the early 1690s the Whigs oversaw a financial revolution that increased the Crown's regular income from approximately £1 million to approximately £5 million per annum.
- The financial revolution was accompanied by a dramatic increase in the supervision Parliament exercised over royal expenditure. This placed greater limits on the monarch's power and contributed significantly to the creation of a 'limited' monarchy.
- The financial revolution also made possible a dramatic increase in British military power, both on land and at sea. The growth of the army, however, was unpopular with 'Country' opinion that saw it as a potential threat to English liberties.
- From 1695 until 1701, politics were dominated by the Whig 'Junto' which enjoyed a dominant position in the House of Lords and occasional dominance in the House of Commons.
- During the 1690s the Whig and Tory parties argued about four main issues – the succession, the war, the constitution and religion.
- Because of the Glorious Revolution of 1688–89, the death of Queen Mary in 1694 and the death of the Duke of Gloucester in 1700, Parliament passed legislation determining the succession. By 1702, the King could not be a Catholic, could not marry a Catholic, and the Crown would pass to the Hanoverian descendants of James I's daughter, Elizabeth, on Queen Anne's death. This happened in 1714.
- Religious toleration became a major political issue following the Toleration Act, as Tories tried to defend the religious monopoly of the Church of England against Dissenters.
- By William's death in 1702, Britain was embarking on another major war with France, one that would see major British victories but lead to further animosity between the Whig and Tory parties.

▼ **Figure 3** This diagram represents the development of the secular state.

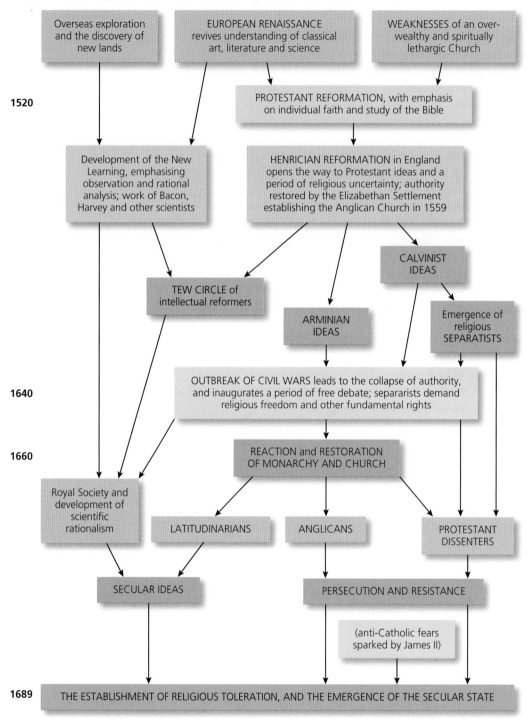

Working on essay technique

In previous chapters, you have built up skills in planning and writing essays. In particular in the second part of this book you should have become more confident in producing essays that reach high levels in the AQA essay mark scheme.

Here is another example of an A-level practice question:

'Warfare was the catalyst that drove the development of the English state in the seventeenth century.' Assess the validity of this statement for the period 1649–1702.

This question is about the constitutional and administrative changes that occurred in the period from James I's war with Spain in 1624 to the outbreak of the War of the Spanish Succession in 1702. In your answer you could consider the constitutional balance between Crown and Parliament; the growing sophistication of English administration; and the way that parliamentary taxation came to replace the Crown's 'ordinary' income as the main source of government revenue. The question has been deliberately framed to make you consider the seventeenth century as a whole.

Working on interpretation skills: extended reading

Changes in British society, including beliefs and attitudes 1603–1702

Dr Andrew Hopper considers the state of Britain at the end of the reign of the Stuarts.

During the seventeenth century Stuart Britain transformed from being a sparsely populated, largely agrarian society of limited consequence in Europe, to a more powerful, urbanised and commercial fiscal-military state. During this period, despite plague, disease and warfare, the population of England and Wales grew from about four to five million. As farming methods improved and more land was cultivated, famine became far less frequent. Plague disappeared after 1665. Literacy rates improved, grammar schools were established and the mental horizons of even the poor were widened as they learned to use the law to protect their interests. Towns expanded and some became multi-cultural communities, taking in immigrants from Protestant northern Europe. More of the population participated in their own government as unpaid parish officeholders such as churchwarden, constable and overseer of the poor.

Popular political awareness increased with the outbreak of civil war in Scotland in 1639 and England in 1642, when both King and Parliament appealed for the people's support. Committed royalists and parliamentarians began as activist minorities, but both came to recognise that allegiance was to be negotiated, not commanded. Influenced by state oaths and declarations, sermons from church pulpits, a revolution in cheap pamphlet literature, gossip, rumour, tavern songs and alehouse banter, people learned to take sides and change them as necessity or conscience dictated.

The civil wars that followed were in no sense a 'civil' or gentlemanly conflict in which shared values guaranteed that all prisoners and non-combatants would be spared from violence. Up to 3 per cent of the population were lost in England and Wales – a higher proportion than in the First World War, with 6 per cent lost in Scotland and possibly 20 per cent in Ireland. The wars' material impacts were felt many years later as national, county, town and parish governments struggled to provide pensions and relief for maimed soldiers, war widows and orphaned children. Thousands lost their homes as suburbs were demolished during sieges or fired in reprisals by the enemy. The housing stock took decades to recover, but the psychological scars lasted for centuries.

This conflict drove much further change. It produced Britain's first professional, state-financed standing army: the New Model Army. Driven by godly zeal, this force developed a revolutionary politics that overturned divine monarchy, trying and executing Charles I in public. It then projected English rule over Scotland and Ireland through military conquest and occupation, developing the fiscal-military state in the process that underpinned British imperial successes in subsequent centuries. After 1660, King and Parliament remained nervous that the military might again intrude into their affairs. Therefore the sovereign remained as its head, in name only, with regiments dispersed overseas and the navy relied upon instead for the nation's defence.

Since the 1640s, the English have proved very reluctant to rebel. For propertied gentlemen, godly, reforming zeal became tainted with rebellious politics, and after 1660, increasingly associated with vulgar plebeians. The wars' aftermath also spawned party conflict as the Restoration stifled political issues rather than resolving them. Abusive labels such as 'Whig' and 'Tory' emerged from Scotland and Ireland during the 1640s and were regularly used by the 1680s to smear political opponents. The idea of divine monarchy was again overturned in 1688 when the Roman Catholic monarch, James II, was hounded from the throne. Consequently, beliefs that monarchy and government were contractual and rested upon the consent of the governed gained ground.

In matters of religious belief, the seventeenth century had begun with state-backed churches in England, Scotland and Wales assuming a theoretical monopoly, with Church courts to compel obedience and attendance at worship. This situation was transformed by the experience of civil war as both the Church of England and 'puritan' coalition fractured and numerous sects and denominations emerged such as Presbyterians, Congregationalists, Baptists, Fifth Monarchists and Quakers. Although the Restored Monarchy tried to restore a more narrowly defined Church of England, nonconformity had grown too large to eradicate through persecution. Local communities had to learn to accept religious plurality. Yet far from growing more religiously tolerant as the seventeenth century progressed, the state only allowed a grudging, partial 'toleration' of Protestant Dissenters by Act of Parliament in 1689, while popular anti-Catholicism remained virulent and Roman Catholic worship illegal. From the 1660s onwards prosecutions for witchcraft plummeted, not because of advances in 'rational' thinking and the supposed 'Scientific revolution', but because the legal system required stronger standards of proof, making prosecutions riskier and convictions more difficult to achieve.

In conclusion, Stuart Britain emerged from its century of troubles as a more politically stable, militarily secure and economically powerful entity. England was better connected with alliances to European states, respectful of English naval might and maritime expansion. The British had grown into a more confident, commercial and urbanised people, accustomed to participating in their own government. The degree of change from the impoverished and isolated Britain of 1603 is striking and perhaps explains why the seventeenth century remains the most heavily-studied period of British history beyond the recent past.

45
50
55
60
65
70
75
80

Dr Andrew Hopper is Senior Lecturer in English Local History at the University of Leicester. His main research interest is the interaction between the gentry and the people in forming allegiances, especially during the English civil war. In his own words, 'My work hopes to break down old divisions that distance political from social history, and national from local, hoping to establish stronger integration between the politics of the parish and the politics of the state'. In this essay, he considers the social and political changes of the seventeenth century and how they affected ordinary people.

ACTIVITY

Having read the essay, answer the following questions.

Comprehension

1 Why does Hopper refer to the seventeenth century as England's 'century of troubles' (line 72)?
2 What are the major differences Hopper identifies between the England of 1603 and England at the end of the seventeenth century?
3 To what does he attribute these changes?

Evidence

4 Find and record Hopper's evidence that the English Civil War was 'in no sense a 'civil' or gentlemanly conflict'.

Interpretation

5 What were the long-term consequences of the English Civil War that Hopper identifies in this essay?

Evaluation

6 Using your own knowledge, write a paragraph explaining how far you agree with Hopper's interpretation of English developments as outlined in paragraphs 4 and 5.

Key questions: Britain, 1603–1702

The course that you are now completing on Stuart Britain is one that has focused on breadth issues rather than depth events. In other words, it requires you to investigate the big themes of the seventeenth century, rather than the details of particular events. Now that you are coming to the end of the course, it is time to tease out those big themes and focus your revision on the six key questions of the course.

As mentioned in Key Questions: Britain 1603–49 (page 134), the six key questions include three that are focused mainly on change and development and three that look primarily at cause and effect. We will therefore complete our review of these key questions by grouping them together in the same way as before.

Change, continuity and development

The development of monarchy and government in Stuart Britain can be explained using the three key questions below:

Key Question 1: How far did the monarchy change?

Key Question 2: To what extent and why was power more widely shared during this period?

Key Question 3: How effective was opposition?

As at the end of Part 1, the best way to explore the issues relating to changes and development was to combine the questions by asking:

'How was power exercised, and by whom, at different points in time?'

This time, however, we need to consider not only the period from 1649–1702, but also the seventeenth century as a whole.

Key Question 1: How far did the monarchy change?

Questions to consider, 1649–1702

- After the execution of Charles I, when did the process of restoring the monarchy actually begin? For example, would you begin the process as early as 1652, when Cromwell discussed the advantages of monarchy with Bulstrode Whitelock? Did the role of Lord Protector represent a return to the principles of monarchy, if not the form of it?
- In 1660 the monarchy was restored without any preconditions. Why, then, was the monarchy 'limited' by 1702 and in what sense? In what ways did practical considerations limit monarchical power?

Questions to consider, 1603–1702

- Think about King James I and then King William III. How different was the power of the monarchy in these two reigns? What was the nature of the difference?
- To what extent, if at all, did the English Revolution and the Interregnum contribute to these differences? Was the Civil War and its effects completely undone by the Restoration?

Key Question 2: To what extent and why was power more widely shared during this period?

Questions to consider, 1649–1702

- Why did Parliament fail when it tried to govern the nation by itself during the period of the Republic, 1649–53?
- Consider General Monck's insistence that the Long Parliament be reinstated in 1660. Did the process that led to the Restoration prove that Parliament was an essential part of the constitution?
- There were three different Triennial Acts after 1641. What were the differences between them and how did these reflect the changing political circumstances of the period?
- In what ways did Parliament supervise different government departments and decisions after 1660? How did this supervision, and the growing complexity of government, affect the relationship between Parliament and the Crown?

Questions to consider, 1603–1702

- In what ways, and for what reasons, was Parliament asserting its privileges between 1603 and 1642? Why do we hear less about 'parliamentary privileges' after 1660?
- Compare the absence of political parties in 1603 with the 'rage of party' in the 1690s. What had changed to divide Parliament along party lines by 1702?

Key Question 3: How effective was opposition?

Questions to consider, 1649–1702

- What forms of opposition to authority existed between 1649 and 1660? You might consider:
  - the New Model Army's opposition to the Republic
  - parliamentary opposition to Cromwell from former republicans
  - Cromwell's opposition to the Protectorate Parliaments' opposition to religious radicalism
  - the Levellers' opposition to the Republic and the reasons for it.
- What role did the fear of opposition to all forms of authority play in the Restoration?
- When the Country party developed in the 1670s, it did so largely because of opposition to the Court. What were the issues that brought the Country together? And why did this then result in the formation of a Court party?
- When, and why, did these Country and Court parties evolve into the Whig and Tory parties?

Questions to consider, 1603–1702

- Why did a parliamentary opposition to Charles I's policies develop in the 1620s and 1630s?
- Pro-Spanish vs. anti-Spanish in the 1620s; Country vs. Court in the 1630s; Royalist vs. Parliamentarian in the 1640s; Presbyterian vs. Independent in the 1640s; Court vs. Country in the 1670s; Whig vs. Tory in the 1680s and 1690s. Why was England so divided during the seventeenth century? And how effective was opposition in changing government policies during this century?

WORKING TOGETHER

To help you to consider both the period from 1649–1702 and the century as a whole, from 1603–1702, discuss with others what should go in these boxes before completing your own copy of the table below. You can go back to the work you did at the end of Part 1 (page 134), to complete the boxes for the period 1603–1649.

How far did the monarchy change?	To what extent and why was power more widely shared during this period?	How effective was opposition?
How was power exercised and by whom at different points in time?		
Changes to the monarchy, 1603–49	Power-sharing, 1603–49	Effectiveness of opposition, 1603–49
Changes to the monarchy, 1649–1702	Power-sharing, 1649–1702	Effectiveness of opposition, 1649–1702
Changes to the monarchy, 1603–1702	Power-sharing, 1603–1702	Effectiveness of opposition, 1603–1702

Cause, effect and significance

The remaining Key Questions focus on causation, specifically the causes of change and the relative importance of ideas (including religious belief) and of individuals motivated by these ideas:

Key Question 4: Why, and with what results, were there disputes over religion?

Key Question 5: How important were ideas and ideology?

Key Question 6: How important was the role of key individuals and groups, and how were they affected by developments?

At the root of these questions lies another, broader question:

'How far were the historical changes of the seventeenth century due to beliefs and ideas?' And linked to that is a further important question: **'To what extent did beliefs give way to ideas?'**

This latter question is important because it is really asking whether religious belief began to give way to ideas that were not based on Christianity or any other religion.

As before, we need to consider these questions in two parts, firstly between 1649 and 1702 and then over the century as a whole, from 1603 to 1702. We need to look at the second half of the century separately because you need to be able to distinguish between changes and developments in Part 1 and Part 2.

Key Question 4: Why, and with what results, were there disputes over religion?

Questions to consider, 1649–1702

- To what extent was religious toleration practised between 1649 and 1660? Why did Cromwell's ideas about religion bring him into dispute with his parliaments in the 1650s?
- Why was the Religious Society of Friends (Quakers) singled out for particular criticism in the years immediately before the Restoration? And why were Quakers persecuted in the 1660s?
- How great an impact did religious radicalism and the growth of religious sects during the English Revolution have on religious beliefs and attitudes later in the century? Why did religious Dissent survive the Restoration? To what extent had religious toleration been established by 1702?

Questions to consider, 1603–1702

- What does it mean when we describe England as a 'confessional state' in 1603? To what extent, and for what reasons, had it become a 'secular state' by 1702?
- Why were political disputes expressed in religious terms in the seventeenth century? Were these 'religious disputes' always exclusively about religious beliefs?

Key Question 5: How important were ideas and ideology?

Questions to consider, 1649–1702

- How did political philosophy develop in this period?
- Consider the ideas of Thomas Hobbes and John Locke – what is meant by the phrase 'contract theory', and how did Hobbes and Locke's ideas about a social contract lead them to different conclusions?

Questions to consider, 1603–1702

- In 1603 the King claimed to rule by 'Divine Right'. What did this mean?
- Did the theory of the 'Divine Right of Kings' survive the English Revolution?
- In 1689, and again in 1702, Parliament passed Acts that determined the succession to the monarchy. Does this mean that the 'Divine Right of Kings' was now dead and buried as a political ideology?
- Was there a scientific revolution in the seventeenth century?

Key Question 6: How important was the role of key individuals and groups, and how were they affected by developments?

Questions to consider, 1649–1702

- The English Civil War is famous for the great variety of groups that sprang up in this period. How much impact on events did groups like the Levellers, the Fifth Monarchists or the Diggers have? Did they leave their mark on England's development, or are they merely 'a footnote' in the nation's history?
- On a scale of 1 to 10 (with 1 being not important and 10 being the most important), how important do you think the following individuals were in the developments of the period:
  - Shaftesbury
  - Danby
  - William of Orange?

Questions to consider, 1603–1702

- Do you think that the English Civil War would have happened if Charles I had never been king? This could easily have happened, since the premature death of his older brother, Prince Henry, is what led to Charles's succession. How important do you think Charles I was in seventeenth-century history?
- Was the personality of the monarch as important in 1702 as it was in 1603?

WORKING TOGETHER

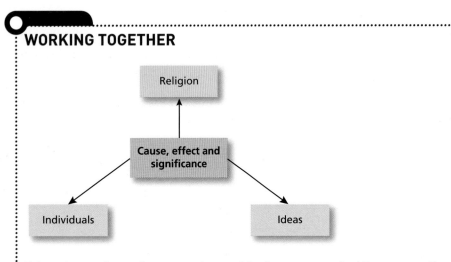

Take a large sheet of paper and copy this diagram onto it. Allow yourself plenty of room on which to add notes. Working with a partner, discuss Key Questions 4, 5 and 6 and make bullet point notes around each of the three questions to summarise your findings.

Further research

There are scores of excellent books on the history of Stuart Britain. It is impossible for most students to consult more than a few of these. However, it is vital that you read some. It is a common complaint of all history examiners that candidates do not read widely enough. The following suggestions are meant to serve as a guide.

Also listed in this section are novels, films and places to visit which are recommendations intended to extend your overall sense of the period.

General books on the Stuarts

Four general histories of the seventeenth century are readily available for students. None of these texts should be read from cover to cover – the best way to use them is to read the relevant chapters as and when they are being studied in class.

Kishlansky, M. (1996) *A Monarchy Transformed: Britain 1603–1714*. London: Penguin.

A very readable account.

Coward, B. (2003) *The Stuart Age: England 1603–1714*. London: Longman.

First published in 1980 but having gone through four editions this has, for many years, been the standard authority on the period.

Wormald, J. (2008) *The Seventeenth Century: 1603–1688* (Short Oxford History of the British Isles). Oxford: Oxford University Press.

This title provides an approachable introduction to most of the period.

Williams, B. (1984) *Elusive Settlement*. London: Nelson Thornes Ltd.

A text that provides a broad analysis of the problems involved in acquiring political stability, with a more thematic approach to the period.

Other useful general works covering all or most of the period include the following:

Hill, C. (1961) *The Century of Revolution, 1603–1714*. London: Routledge.

Offers a broadly social and economic interpretation of the period.

Wilson, C. (1985) *England's Apprenticeship* (2nd edn.). London: Longman.

Provides an economic approach.

Coward, B. (2003) *A Companion to Stuart Britain*. Oxford: Blackwell Publishing.

A most useful collection of essays covering the whole of the seventeenth century.

Books on particular periods
Books on Part 1, 1603–49

Sometimes it is useful to treat James I and Charles I in the same text.

Harris, T. (2014) *Rebellion: Britain's First Stuart Kings, 1567–1642*. Oxford: Oxford University Press.

An important recent contribution to the period.

Seel, G. and Smith, D. (2001) *The Early Stuart Kings, 1603–1642*. London: Routledge.

Also deals with both James I and Charles I.

Houston, S.J. (1995) *James I* (2nd edn.). London: Longman.

James I is covered in this 'Seminar Studies in History' series.

Cust, R. (2005) *Charles I*. London: Pearson Education Ltd.

The best biography of Charles I.

Russell, C. (1990) *The Causes of the English Civil War*. Oxford: Oxford University Press.

The causes of the English Civil War is an enormous subject about which a huge amount has been written. This is a collection of lectures in which Russell outlines his thesis that the civil war was the consequence of instability in three kingdoms.

Hughes, A. (1998) *The Causes of the English Civil War* (2nd edn.). London: Macmillan.

An excellent summary of the state of the historiography at that time.

Morrill, J. (1976) *The Revolt of the Provinces*. London: Longman.

Moving into the Civil War period this title was a ground breaking local study.

Morrill, J. (1993) *The Nature of the English Revolution*. London: Longman.

A fascinating collection of essays.

Hexter, J.H. (1968) *The Reign of King Pym* (3rd edn.). Cambridge, MA: Harvard University Press.

An important study of Pym's parliamentary leadership in the first year of the Civil War.

Roots, I. (1966) *The Great Rebellion 1642–1660* (reprint edition). London: Batsford.

Still one of the most accessible general narratives of the period.

Woolrych, A. (2002) *Britain in Revolution, 1625–1660*. Oxford: Oxford University Press.

An outstanding history of the whole period from Charles I's accession to the Restoration.

Oliver Cromwell has generated more excellent studies than most seventeenth-century individuals.

Morrill, J. (2007) *Oliver Cromwell*. Oxford: Oxford University Press.

In this text, originally an essay in the *New Dictionary of National Biography*, which has been reissued, we learn, among other things, that Cromwell was a descendant of Thomas Cromwell's sixteenth-century adopted family member.

Coward, B. (1991) *Profiles in Power: Cromwell*. London: Longman.

Provides a most useful series of significant moments in Cromwell's career.

Gaunt, P. (1996) *Oliver Cromwell*. Oxford: Blackwell.

Published by the Historical Association, this is an essential study of Cromwell for any Sixth Form student.

Hill, C. (2000) *God's Englishman*. London: Penguin.

Still offers a highly readable narrative and analysis of Cromwell's religious beliefs.

Books on Part 2: 1649–1702

Hutton, R. (1989) *Charles II, King of England, Scotland and Ireland*. Oxford: Oxford University Press.

Probably the best biography on Charles II, Hutton's familiarity with the English Civil Wars and the Interregnum helps him to place Charles in perspective, and he offers a highly critical view of his subject.

Fraser, A. (1979) *King Charles II*. London: Weidenfeld & Nicholson.

A popular biography, very readable, and one where the author clearly relates to the romanticised view of her subject.

Uglow, J. (2009) *A Gambling Man: Charles II and the Restoration*. London: Faber & Faber.

A readable and entertaining account of Charles II's first decade in power, from the Restoration to the turning point of the Secret Treaty of Dover. Highly recommended.

Harris, T. (2006) *Restoration: Charles II and his Kingdoms*. London: Penguin.

A detailed study of the Restoration. In it, Harris focuses not only on the dynamics of English politics but on the relationship between the three kingdoms of England, Scotland and Ireland.

Harris, T. (2007) *Revolution: The Great Crisis of the British Monarchy, 1685–1720*. London: Penguin.

Harris' follow-up work, this goes beyond the AQA specification but is mostly relevant.

The Glorious Revolution and the end of the century have not been studied in as much depth as the civil war period, but they have generated some excellent studies.

Vallance, E. (2007) *The Glorious Revolution*. London: Abacus.

A highly readable account of the causes, course, and aftermath of the revolution.

Dillon, P. (2006) *The Last Revolution*. London: Jonathan Cape.

Provides a vivid narrative.

Films, television dramas and documentaries

Films

The seventeenth century has been poorly served by the makers of feature films.

Cromwell Ken Hughes (dir.), 1970.

This film is riddled with factual inaccuracies but looks good: the choice of an Irish actor (Richard Harris) to play Cromwell was an act of faith, given Cromwell's reputation in Ireland.

To Kill a King Mike Barker (dir.), 2003.

This looks even better and tries to steer a more historically accurate course, but comes unstuck over Cromwell's character.

Television dramas

The same problem of anomalies and oversights has troubled television dramas.

Charles II: The Power and the Passion Joe Wright (dir.), BBC, 2003.

This will help you to visualise the Restoration period, and one would like to believe in Rufus Sewell's portrayal of Charles II.

The Devil's Whore Marc Munden (dir.), 2008.

This has the advantage of John Simm playing the improbably but accurately named Edward Sexby, one of the Leveller negotiators at Putney, but again it comes unstuck with Cromwell, as it must, since the story is told from the viewpoint of the radicals.

Documentaries

There have been some good documentaries over the years, but the best ones are hard to get hold of.

Cromwell: New Model Englishman, Wall to Wall, 2001.

Top of the list, this is a Channel 4 documentary. While having his portrait painted, Cromwell talks about the decisions he took and Charles I's character.

The English Civil War – Cromwell.

Roger Allam plays Cromwell in a drama-documentary that examines Cromwell's life and career.

General English histories by David Starkey and by Simon Schama.

These contain episodes that cover the seventeenth century. They are worth watching because they will contribute to a broad understanding of the period.

Battlefield Britain by Dan and Peter Snow.

This includes *Naseby*, an excellent reconstruction of the 1644 battle. In *Empire of the Seas* Dan Snow looks at the role of the British navy in seventeenth century history, including its political importance.

Places to visit

- The Cromwell Museum in Huntingdon, Cambridgeshire, is housed in Cromwell's old grammar school. Though small, it is well worth a visit for seeing Cromwell's personal effects. Cromwell's house in Ely is a public museum.
- The battlefields of Edgehill, Naseby and Marston Moor are all accessible, as are numerous smaller battle sites.
- Banqueting House in Whitehall is the site of Charles I's execution.
- In Oxford, Christ Church was Charles I's headquarters during the first Civil War, and Christ Church Hall was the venue for both the Oxford Parliament of 1644 and for Charles II's final parliament in 1681.
- Powick Bridge near Worcester has the distinction of being the site of both the first skirmish between the royalist and parliamentarian armies in 1642 and the final battle between Charles Stuart and Cromwell in 1651 – from the latter battle one can still see where a volley of musketry hit the church tower.
- Still in Worcester, the Commandery covers the Civil War period, especially the Battle of Worcester (1651).
- The Civil War Centre, Newark on Trent. Newark was an important fortress standing at the place where the Great North Road crossed the River Trent. A new Civil War museum opened here in 2015, dedicated not only to the siege of Newark but also the entire Civil War.
- The National Armouries Museum in Leeds has excellent displays of Civil War armour and weapons.
- Hampton Court served as Oliver Cromwell's palace for a time.
- The Royal Dockyards at Chatham are worth a visit, to marvel at the audacity of the Dutch in 1667 when they sailed up the Medway and burned the English fleet.
- Boscobel House, an English Heritage property in Shropshire includes two of Charles II's hiding places in the 'Royal Oak' tree, and a priest-hole in the attic.

Glossary of terms

Absolute monarchy A monarchy in which the king is responsible only to God, and thereby has absolute, unchallenged power. His will and decisions alone make the law. Fear of absolutism was increasing at this time, because the French and Spanish monarchies were moving in this direction by destroying the independence and in some cases even the existence of local assemblies and parliaments. Because these were Catholic monarchs and the Catholic Church was also organised in this way, the association of Catholicism, absolutism and tyranny in English minds was deeply entrenched.

Balance the humours Physicians believed the body consisted of four elements, which they called humours. If these were not 'balanced' illness was the result. When a person ran a temperature it was believed this was due to too much blood, so the patient was 'bled', either by the application of leeches or by opening the veins in the foot or arm.

Books of Orders A set of 314 books of instructions to JPs, detailing their duties in the collection of Poor Law rates, treatment of beggars, law enforcement, storage of grain, control of local markets, movement of goods and upkeep of roads and bridges. Under Laud's supervision, the issue of instructions was followed up to ensure that they were carried out.

Boroughs Towns that had been granted a royal charter giving them some particular rights and privileges, for example, the right to hold a market. In some cases they also had the right to send two MPs to parliaments, and the number of these increased significantly in the later sixteenth century.

Catechism The Catechism provided an outline of the key doctrines and creeds of the Anglican Church, as set out in the Prayer Book. It was taught as a set of questions and learned responses, some of which appeared as set prayers in certain services. It therefore supported uniformity of belief, unlike preaching, and was reminiscent of traditional, Catholic practices.

Consort A consort is the spouse of the ruling monarch, whether male or female. In this case, William refused to be merely the husband of Queen Mary – he insisted on joint sovereignty with himself acting as king in his own right.

Covenant A contract or agreement in which the parties bind themselves to carry out certain obligations. The Scottish Covenant was a national treaty in which those who signed it agreed to come together to defend the existing Kirk, if necessary by force of arms, and to remain together until its safety was assured. It was therefore an act of rebellion, which Charles could not ignore.

Deists A group that believed in the existence of God on purely rational grounds. By definition, they denied the importance of inspired religion, or a sacred text such as the Bible.

Enclosures Fences used to designate private land, often taken from land that had previously been for communal use, and hence much resented by the poorer members of the community.

Excise Tax This was placed on home-produced beer and cider, and on a range of imported goods. It was easy to collect and, in principle, no different to customs duties. But it was unprecedented in England, and was highly unpopular.

Farming out the customs For most of the seventeenth century the Crown leased the authority to collect customs revenue to businessmen for a fixed sum. These 'farmers of the customs' were then able to keep as profit any figure over and above the amount they had paid to the King.

Feoffees A group of Puritan trustees who were empowered to raise money and buy up impropriated parishes in order to provide good preaching ministers for them. Established in 1626, they had acquired a little over thirty parishes, and were looking to extend their work to the purchase of advowsons when Laud banned them and took over the parishes that they had bought. Although they shared his objective of improving the quality of the ministry, their preference for Puritans and emphasis on preaching earned them his disapproval. His action offended Puritans on religious grounds, and many others as an attack on property.

Feudal dues Payments made by the nobility and gentry, a relic of the feudal system when they were seen as holding their land as tenants of the King.

Forced loan A relic of feudalism, in which the king had the right to ask his wealthier subjects to lend him money in an emergency. In fact they were rarely paid back, so it was a form of taxation outside parliaments.

Habeas Corpus A Latin phrase, meaning 'to have the body'. A writ of Habeas Corpus issued by a court was the standard way of preventing someone from being held in prison indefinitely, without being properly charged and brought to trial. It was regarded as a vital safeguard for personal liberty against the abuse of power by the monarch or those acting in his name.

Hanoverians King George I and his descendants, to whom the monarchy passed by the Act of Settlement following the death of Queen Anne in 1714.

Hedonistic lifestyle A life lived in the selfish pursuit of pleasure.

Heretic/heresy The name given by the Roman Catholic Church to those who challenged its teachings and the denial of its beliefs. Heretics could be 'excommunicated' (expelled from the Church) or imprisoned. Ultimately, if they refused to give up their views, they were handed over to the civil authorities to be burned alive.

Highland charge A disorganised but effective rushing attack made by Highland clansmen, in which they aimed to close the distance with more heavily armed forces in order to fight hand-to-hand, thereby negating their enemies' superior firepower.

Holy Roman Emperor The head of the Holy Roman Empire, which was established in Germany in the early Middle Ages, bringing 329 small German states together under a single leader. By the late fifteenth century the Austrian family of Habsburg had established a right to be 'elected' to the position, giving them effective control of modern Germany, Austria and much of Central Europe.

Indemnity The protection of ex-soldiers from legal proceedings for any action undertaken as part of the war. For example, troopers who had requisitioned horses as part of their wartime duties might find themselves sued or accused of theft if they did not have the protection of a legal indemnity. Given the range and type of actions that they might well have carried out under orders, this was a serious matter for soldiers of all ranks.

Indentured servitude A system by which convicts transported to the West Indies were forced to work on plantations for a specified period. To all intents and purposes the indentured servants were slaves, except that they might look forward to eventual release.

Impeachment This had been developed by medieval parliaments as a means of bringing royal advisers and members of the nobility to justice. They were called to trial before the House of Lords by a petition from the Commons. The device had been unused since 1459, but was revived in 1621 to impeach the monopolists, Mitchell and Mompesson, and Lord Chancellor Bacon for bribery. Thereafter the Commons began to apply it as a political weapon, against unpopular ministers and advisers.

Impropriation The practice of taking over [impropriating] the collection of tithes (a 10 per cent tax on all households in a parish levied as income for the parish priest). This allowed the impropriator to play a part in choosing the minister. Many parishes had come under the control of the local gentry in this way. Another way of controlling the choice of minister was to buy up the advowson for the parish, which gave the holder the right to nominate a particular minister. Many advowsons were held by the King and the bishops, but a significant number were acquired by the gentry and by borough corporations.

Jacobites Those who remained loyal to James II and his line after the Glorious Revolution.

Jesuit Order The Society of Jesus, founded by Ignatius Loyola in 1534, was a Catholic religious order dedicated to the papacy and defining itself in complete submission to the Pope's authority. Jesuit priests were among the most educated and dedicated in the Catholic world, frequently undertaking dangerous missions to inhospitable territories, but in England their reputation as the vanguard of the Counter-reformation ensured that they instilled fear and loathing wherever they were mentioned.

King-in-Parliament Refers to government by the king, but implies that some of his functions, in particular the making of law, are carried out in Parliament rather than by the king alone. Through Parliament, the king could make statute law, the highest form of law: a statute (Act of Parliament) that had been agreed by both houses and signed by the king took precedence over any earlier law or custom, and could only be changed by another statute.

Kirk The Scottish Kirk was a Presbyterian Church, founded by John Knox in 1560. When Mary, Queen of Scots, returned to Scotland from France in 1560 she found a Protestant Reformation already completed. The result was that the Kirk, run by committees of ministers and elders rather than bishops, was in many ways independent of the monarchy. Worship was based on preaching and improvised prayers, both provided by ministers who had little hesitation in speaking their minds. From the point of view of the Monarch, this independence needed to be curbed, but for many Scots, the Kirk was a symbol of both their religious and cultural identity.

Machiavelli A late fifteenth-century Italian political philosopher who broke with tradition by arguing, in his most famous work The Prince, that expediency was more important to a ruler than moral, principled behaviour. . In other words, a ruler should think mainly about self-interest, and do the things that must be done, rather than worry about the rights and wrongs of his or her actions.

Millenarianism The belief that the Second Coming of Christ was imminent. The Book of Revelation at the end of the New Testament foretold Christ's second coming, and many radicals believed that the English Civil War was sent to prepare the nation for this event.

Millenary petition A list of requests given to James I by Puritans in 1603 when he was travelling to London in order to claim the English throne. It is claimed, but not proven, that this petition had 1000 signatures of Puritan ministers. This carefully worded document expressed Puritan distaste regarding the state of the Anglican Church, and took into consideration James's religious views as well as his liking for a debate.

Mosaic Law The Ten Commandments.

Occasional conformity The practice developed by some Protestant Dissenters of attending Church a few times a year and taking Communion occasionally. This allowed them to avoid the restrictions of the Test and Corporation Acts and to hold public office. It infuriated the High Anglicans because Dissenters seemed to have found a way of getting around the law, and because those who retained office by this method often used it to protect other Dissenters from persecution.

Patronage A system of influence in which a patron, usually rich and/or powerful, uses their position to help individuals in an inferior position in return for their respect or support.

Predestination The belief held by Calvin and his followers that God chooses beforehand those to whom he will grant salvation.

Presbyterianism A system of church organisation in which the individual congregations were governed by a minister with the help of lay Elders (senior members) under the supervision of an elected assembly known as a Synod.

Prime Minister During the reign of George I, the King, who was unable to speak English, relied on Robert Walpole to manage his government. Walpole was England's first Prime Minister.

Primogeniture The ancient law that established the order of succession within the royal family. The oldest legitimate male heir was the monarch's successor. In the absence of a male heir, the crown passed to the oldest female. In the seventeenth century there was no law prohibiting the succession of a Catholic.

Prorogued Parliament could be dissolved, in which case elections had to be held before a new parliament could assemble. Alternatively, the King could prorogue the existing parliament, leading to a pause between sessions. The Triennial Act envisaged continuous parliamentary sessions, so a lengthy prorogation could be construed as a violation of the law.

Providence Providential beliefs were widespread among seventeenth-century Protestants, although they tended to appear in their most extreme forms among radicals. They were based on the belief that God intervened directly in the affairs of men to ensure that the outcome of events conformed with His will. Matters such as the victories of the New Model Army or Charles's refusal to compromise were therefore interpreted as acts of providence – evidence of God's judgement and purpose. Men like Cromwell sought to read these providential signs in order to know God's purpose before deciding what action to take.

Pym's junto The term 'junto' refers to a small, organised group who work together to gain or maintain power.

Recusancy A refusal to attend Anglican services on a regular basis, which had been made compulsory in the reign of Elizabeth. Absentees (usually Catholics) were required to pay a fine. The fines provided a useful source of revenue for the Crown.

Regency A period when someone other than the rightful monarch rules the country on their behalf. The regent is usually a close relative of the monarch – a parent, sibling or child.

Retaining The practice, common among the medieval nobility, of keeping servants and supporters who were trained in military skills. In effect this created a private army which could be used to keep the peace, or to overawe rivals and even rebel against the Crown.

Sacraments Sacred acts or ceremonies. The key point about sacramental religion is that taking part in the ceremony is considered to be a sacred act in itself, regardless of the spirit or level of understanding of the congregation who take part. This gave great power to the church that provided the sacraments, and could encourage mechanical or superstitious acts by the congregation, which reformers found unacceptable.

Sectarians Sectarians or 'sectaries' was the word used to describe the Puritan Separatists. The forms of organisation and worship used in sectarian meetings tended to encourage open discussion between the minister and the other members of the congregation. Within the army, the Frequent absence of any ordained clergy encouraged talented speakers among the soldiers to lead worship and preach in their place. The whole experience of radical religion helped to produce men of the 'middling sort' who were both willing and able to challenge the assumptions of their social superiors.

Self-Denying Ordinance The Self-Denying Ordinance was proposed by a member of the War Party, Zouch Tate, and supported by Cromwell. The military failures of late 1644 led to recriminations among Parliament's generals, revealing their political and religious differences. While Cromwell accused Manchester and Essex of preferring negotiations to victory, Manchester and the Scots accused Cromwell of favouring political and religious radicals. By separating military and political functions, the Ordinance allowed the political and religious divisions to be set aside while a new and more effective army was created.

Ships-of-the-line The largest warships of the time.

Stadtholder The United Provinces (the Dutch Republic, or Holland) was normally governed by elected representatives of the Dutch states, but the office of Stadtholder could, in times of crisis, be given to the House (family) of Orange, to take emergency measures for the safety of the republic.

Test Act An Act imposing an Oath of Supremacy and an Oath of Allegiance on all office holders, who had to provide evidence that they had recently taken Holy Communion in the Church of England and make a declaration against the Catholic doctrine of transubstantiation (the belief that the bread and wine taken in Communion were miraculously transformed into the body and blood of Christ). The purpose of the Act was to exclude Catholics from office.

Transubstantiation The doctrine whereby the wine and bread taken in communion were believed to be transformed miraculously into the blood and body of Christ.

Vote of No Addresses A vote in the House of Commons on 3 January 1648 that no further addresses (i.e. offers to negotiate) be made to the King. This was in response to his perceived betrayal by signing an Engagement with the Scots, but, above all, it reflected the anger and despair felt by most MPs at his consistent refusal to enter genuine negotiations.

Whig historians Historians working in a nineteenth-century tradition that saw the rise of representative government as the product of a heroic conflict between Parliament and the Crown.

Yeomen Independent farmers who usually owned at least some of the land they farmed and were able to achieve a reasonable level of prosperity. They were distinguished from the minor gentry by the fact that they worked their land themselves rather than renting it out.

Index